Theories of Scientific Method

Philosophy and Science

Series Editor: Alexander Bird

This new series in the philosophy of science offers fresh treatments of core topics in the theory and methodology of scientific knowledge and introductions to new areas of the discipline. The series also seeks to cover topics in current science that raise significant foundational issues both for scientific theory and for philosophy more generally.

Published

Philosophy of Biology
Brian Garvey

Theories of Scientific Method
Robert Nola and Howard Sankey

Forthcoming titles include

Empiricism
Stathis Psillos

Models and Theories
Roman Frigg

Philosophy of Chemistry
Robin Hendry

Philosophy of Physics
James Ladyman

Psychiatry and Philosophy of Science
Rachel Cooper

Theories of Scientific Method
An Introduction

Robert Nola and Howard Sankey

McGill-Queen's University Press
Montreal & Kingston • Ithaca

For Alan Musgrave

© Robert Nola & Howard Sankey, 2007

ISBN: 978-0-7735-3344-8 (bound)
ISBN: 978-0-7735-3345-5 (pbk.)

Legal deposit third quarter 2007
Bibliothèque nationale du Québec

Published simultaneously outside North America
by Acumen Publishing Limited

Library and Archives Canada Cataloguing in Publication

Nola, Robert
    Theories of scientific method / Robert Nola and Howard Sankey.

(Philosophy and science ; 2)
Includes bibliographical references and index.
ISBN 978-0-7735-3344-8 (bound)
ISBN 978-0-7735-3345-5 (pbk.)

    1. Science--Methodology--Textbooks. 2. Science--Philosophy--Textbooks.
I. Sankey, Howard II. Title. III. Series: Philosophy and science
(Montréal, Québec) ; 2

Q175.N652 2007   507.2   C2007-903400-4

Designed and typeset by Kate Williams, Swansea.
Printed and bound by Cromwell Press, Trowbridge.

Contents

Abbreviations   ix
Acknowledgements   x
Introduction   1

I The idea of methodology

1 What is this thing called scientific method?   12
1.1 Different methodological practices within the sciences   13
1.2 Methodology and clinical trials   15
1.3 Methodology within the context of discovery and the
     context of justification   19
1.4 Methods for discovery   22
1.5 Heuristics as methodology   26
1.6 Scientific method and the methodology of logic   28

2 Theoretical values in science   32
2.1 Aims of science and scientists   33
2.2 A broad classification of kinds of value   35
2.3 Some virtues of scientific theories   37
2.4 Kuhn on values   45
2.5 Aims and values of science: Popper   49
2.6 Aims and values of science: Duhem   52
2.7 Epistemic and pragmatic values   55

3 Rules and principles of method   57
3.1 Values, rules and principles of method   58
3.2 Some features of principles of method   63
3.3 Methodological principles from the history of science,
     I: Descartes   65

3.4 Methodological principles from the history of science,
     II: Newton   68
3.5 Methodological principles from the history of science,
     III: Duhem   74

4 Metamethodology   80
4.1 A three-tiered relationship between science, methods and
     metamethods   81
4.2 Metamethodology: what is it and is it possible?   83
4.3 *A priori*, empirical and expressivist approaches to
     metamethodology   86
4.4 The metamethodology of reflective equilibrium   91
4.5 The historical turn, methods and metamethods   98

II Inductive and hypothetico-deductive methods

5 Induction in science   106
5.1 Deduction and induction   108
5.2 From induction to probability and confirmation   109
5.3 Enumerative induction   113
5.4 The rule of inference to the best explanation   119
5.5 The problem of grue   130
5.6 Simplicity of equations   134
5.7 Simplicity and curve-fitting   138

6 Some justifications of induction   143
6.1 Attempting a justification of deduction   144
6.2 A sceptical argument against the justification of induction   148
6.3 The inductivist justification of induction   152
6.4 The pragmatic vindication of induction   158
6.5 Externalism and the warrant for induction   163

7 The hypothetico-deductive method   170
7.1 The structure of the H-D method   172
7.2 Refinements of, and problems for, the H-D method   176
7.3 Problems for H-D confirmation   179
7.4 Appendix on some paradoxical results of confirmation theory   181

III Probability and scientific method

8 Probability, Bayesianism and methodology   186
8.1 Principles and theorems of probability   187
8.2 Bayes's theorem in some of its forms   195
8.3 Bayesian confirmation   199
8.4 The H-D method in a Bayesian context   202

8.5 Subjective degree of belief as a probability   204
8.6 Metamethodological justification and the Dutch book theorem   210
8.7 Bayesian conditionalization and pure subjective Bayesianism   216

9 Bayesianism: applications and problems   220
9.1 The problem of priors   221
9.2 Is Bayesianism complete?   227
9.3 New evidence and the problem of old evidence   231
9.4 Kuhnian values and Bayesianism   236
9.5 Bayesianism and inference to the best explanation   240
9.6 Induction and Bayesianism   242
9.7 The Quine–Duhem problem and Bayesianism   245

IV Popper and his rivals

10 Popper, Lakatos and scientific method   252
10.1 Popper's theory of scientific method: critical rationalism   253
10.2 Lakatos's methodology of scientific research programmes   274

11 Kuhn and Feyerabend   285
11.1 Kuhn and methodology   285
11.2 Feyerabend: the methodological anarchist?   298

V Naturalism, pragmatism, realism and methodology

12 Naturalism, pragmatism and method   312
12.1 Quine and naturalized methodology   314
12.2 Laudan's normative naturalism   321
12.3 Rescher's methodological pragmatism   329

13 Scientific realism and methodology   337
13.1 Aspects of scientific realism   337
13.2 The success argument for scientific realism   341
13.3 Realist axiology and the meta-level success argument   347

Epilogue   351
Notes   355
Bibliography   367
Index   375

Abbreviations

AC	affirming the consequent
AIC	Akaike information criterion
BIC	Bayesian information criterion
CEI	counter (enumerative) induction
CS	cognitive system
EI	enumerative induction
GSK	growth in scientific knowledge
H-D	hypothetico-deductive (method)
IBE	inference to the best explanation
IBS	inference to the best systematization
MIR	metamethodological inductive rule
PUN	principle of the uniformity of nature
REM	rapid eye movement
SIS	sufficient isolation of the system
SRP	scientific research programme
STEP	Benson *et al.*, "Study of the Therapeutic Effects of Intercessory Prayer (STEP) in Cardiac Bypass Patients" (2006).

Acknowledgements

We wish to dedicate this book to Alan Musgrave, a good friend, mentor and stimulating critic who might well not agree with some of the things we write in it. We have both profoundly benefited from his very clear-headed and "no nonsense" approach to philosophy.

We have also benefited from comments made by Gürol Irzik, Stathis Psillos and Ruth Weintraub on different parts of this book, and an anonymous reviewer of the whole of an earlier draft; none of these are responsible for anything that finally appears here.

This book grew out of an introduction we both wrote, "A Selective Survey of Theories of Scientific Method", in *After Popper, Kuhn and Feyerabend: Recent Issues in Theories of Scientific Method*, Robert Nola and Howard Sankey (eds), 1–65 (Dordrecht: Kluwer, 2000). It also draws on some of the material in Part II of Robert Nola and Gürol Irzik, *Philosophy, Science, Education and Culture* (Dordrecht: Springer, 2005), especially chapter 9, 251–81. This material does not reappear as such, but has largely been reworked for the purposes of this book. We would like to thank Kluwer and Springer for permission to use this material.

Introduction

This book is a defence of the idea that there is such a thing as scientific method. It is also a defence of the idea that such methods can be justified, warranted or legitimized. There is a large core of people who think there is such a thing as a scientific method that can be justified, although not all agree as to what this might be. But there are also a growing number of people who think that there is no method to be justified. For some, the whole idea is yesteryear's debate, the continuation of which can be summed up as yet more of the proverbial "flogging a dead horse". We beg to differ. There are reasons for the negative view, some of which will emerge as we investigate contemporary views for and against the existence of scientific method. Two sources of negativity come from different, but surprising, directions: first, from some scientists; secondly, from some philosophers alongside an even larger group of historians and sociologists of science and those in cultural studies.

Some scientists on method

The position of many scientists is amusingly characterized by the Nobel prize-winning scientist Peter Medawar, who was himself quite willing to take up the cudgels on behalf of scientific method (largely following Karl Popper). He tells us that scientists (he includes Charles Darwin) are often self-deceived about whether or not they have been following scientific methods; and if they have been following them, they are deceived about what these methods might be. He then adds that scientists:

are not in the habit of thinking about matters of methodological policy. Ask a scientist what he conceives the scientific method to be, and he will adopt an expression that is at once solemn and shifty-eyed: solemn, because he feels he ought to declare an opinion; shifty-eyed, because he is wondering how to conceal the fact that he has no opinion to declare. (Medawar 1984: 80)

Medawar goes on to say that scientists are ready to deplore many of those in other fields for being non-scientific, from politicians to educationalists; but they are not able to state what it is to be scientific.

Perhaps Medawar takes an uncharitable view. One way of challenging his characterization is to say that scientists' understanding of method is tacit, something they just "pick up" in the course of being trained in their science. It is tacit in much the same way as our understanding of how to make logical inferences is tacit (although there is a considerable body of empirical research that shows that this tacit understanding is often quite faulty). But, as Medawar says in response, it ought to be possible to be more explicit about what this tacit understanding of method and logic might be, instead of leaving it as yet another unfathomable mystery. If scientists are not able to do the job of making their understanding more explicit then perhaps the task is to be left to others. Philosophers? Sociologists? Perhaps statisticians might be the best bet?

It is not easy to explain why scientists do not have an explicit understanding of science and its methods. But the fact of a lack of interest by scientists in methodology is something that strikes Medawar forcibly:

> You must admit that this adds up to an extraordinary state of affairs. Science, broadly considered, is incomparably the most successful enterprise human beings have ever engaged upon; yet the methodology that had presumably made it so, when propounded by learned laymen, is not attended to by scientists, and when propounded by scientists is a misrepresentation of what they do. Only a minority of scientists have received instruction in scientific methodology, and those that have done seem to be no better off. (*Ibid.*)

Another Nobel laureate, physicist Richard Feynman, endorsed the last sentiment when he reputedly quipped, "Philosophy of science is about as useful to scientists as ornithology is to birds". One may ask: who benefits? If the birds do not benefit, the ornithologists can benefit, at least as far as their scientific understanding of bird behaviour goes. But the birds, too, might benefit if what the ornithologists uncover assists in their survival. Analogously to the birds, if scientists do not benefit from philosophy of science then at least philosophers and other investigators can benefit themselves and the rest of us, at least in so far as our understanding of the nature of science itself goes. And one can add that scientists might benefit too, not merely in making them more aware of the methodologies they might employ, but also in gaining clarification about the nature of the enterprise in which they are engaged. The Feynman quip is not without a philosopher's *tu quoque*: "most scientists tend to understand little more *about* science than fish about hydrodynamics" (Lakatos 1978: 62 n.2). Just as the principles of hydrodynamics are necessary for the survival of fish, so the principles of method are necessary for science; but fish and scientists equally have no grasp of their respective principles.

Some scientists do try their own hand at being methodologists. When Feynman does, he blandly speaks of "science as a method of finding things out. This method is based on the principle that observation is the judge of whether something is so or not. ... observation is the ultimate and final judge of the truth of an idea" (Feynman 1998: 15). But this is far too narrow and does not get much further than a simple confirmation/refutation account of the method of hypothesis-testing. Importantly, Feynman does not always disparage the attempts of philosophers since they do have some role to play: "most of what philosophers say about science is really on the technical aspects involved in trying to make sure the method works pretty well" (*ibid.*: 20). Feynman's talk of "the method" here concerns, in part, attempts at greater precision both in the context of the meaning of words (which in his view can be overdone) and in the following context: "The more definite a statement, the more interesting it is to test" (*ibid.*: 19). What does this mean? Is it correct? Should this be elevated to a rule of method about how to get interesting tests in science? Here Feynman's talk of "technical aspects" of methodology comes to the fore since, as will be seen, much work has been done on what this claim entails, especially concerning degrees of falsifiability, or testability, of statements and their openness to test.

Even though scientists might think that there is such a thing as scientific method, they are not always sanguine about the attempts of philosophers of science to say much about it. In a chapter entitled "Against Philosophy", Nobel laureate Steven Weinberg asks, "Can philosophy give us any guidance towards a final theory?" (Weinberg 1993: 132). The answer seems to be no. He says of philosophy of science, which includes methodology, that "we should not expect it to provide today's scientists with any useful guidance about how to go about their work or about what they are likely to find" (*ibid.*: 133). The task of philosophers seems to be as useful assistants in the construction of the final theory of everything of which Weinberg and others dream. But if this is their task, then philosophers would have ceased to be philosophers and to have become just like any other active research scientist. If their task is to provide methodological advice about, say, how to construct theories, then they might have no useful advice to give. (There is in fact no general algorithmic, or even non-algorithmic, procedure for doing theory construction: an important negative result amid the more particular cases where there are such procedures; see §1.4.) So, what is left for philosophers to do that might be useful for scientists?

In posing questions in this way, there is an imposition of a particular agenda on philosophy of science that it does not have for itself. This creates unreal expectations in scientists, as the philosopher of science Wesley Salmon (1998b: ch. 26) usefully points out in his critical response to Weinberg. What that different agenda might be is a task for philosophers to make clear to scientists. One agenda is conceptual clarification, which is not an empirical, scientific exercise. Much has been written by philosophers of science about concepts such as scientific confirmation, scientific laws, realism, reduction, emergence, methodology and, importantly, explanation. Salmon takes Weinberg to task for not noting some of the advances that philosophers have made in coming to terms with the complex notion of explanation.

John Passmore (1983) points out that there is a stock Baconian answer to the question, why science? It helps us understand and master nature and ourselves. But he argues that there is no such easy answer to the question, why philosophy of science? Passmore spells out many different ways in which the question can be answered, one of which is conceptual clarification, as just mentioned. Three of Passmore's further agendas for philosophy of science are as follows. It can play a *critical* role with respect to the sciences, for example in examining whether claims of the form "science has shown that …" really do hold, especially in the case where ethical conclusions are alleged to follow from scientific claims. It can also play a *coordinative* role in spelling out the relationship between science and other human endeavours such as religion, art, law, philosophy and even science itself. Finally a *substantive* philosophy of science often plays a role alongside science, but at a highly theoretical level, for example, in theoretical artificial intelligence where issues about the nature of consciousness become paramount. In a broad sense, the various agendas for philosophy of science can help science in telling us, for example, what might count as a final theory of everything, but it might not help in producing that theory (if there is one).

Finally some make much of a remark Albert Einstein made in the context of his views about the interdependence of epistemology (including methodology) and science. He begins by paraphrasing Kant, writing: "Epistemology without contact with science becomes an empty scheme. Science without epistemology is – insofar as it is thinkable at all – primitive and muddled." But because epistemology has become a very systematic discipline, he adds:

> The scientist, however, cannot afford to carry his striving for epistemo-
> logical systematic that far. He accepts gratefully the epistemological
> conceptual analysis; but external conditions, which are set for him by
> experience, do not permit him to let himself be too much restricted
> in the construction of his conceptual world by the adherence to an

epistemological system. He therefore must appear to the systematic epistemologist as a type of unscrupulous opportunist.

(Einstein 1959: 684)

This has been taken to suggest that what philosophers say within epistemology and methodology is too hidebound for those freewheeling practising scientists who are successful in their fields. They might appear to be opportunists but in reality the business of science does not work the way philosophers have prescribed. On the basis of this, philosopher of science Paul Feyerabend proposes a kind of philosophical anarchism (or Dadaism), which proclaims that to follow the simple rules proposed by methodologists would be to cripple science (Feyerabend 1975: 17–22). However, there is another way of taking Einstein's remark. He was quite deeply conscious of the value and use of methodology in science. His opportunism is better understood as a recommendation to scientists to use philosophy as a resource, or a deep well, from which they can draw in the course of pursuing their science. How it might be a resource needs to be spelled out.

Debunkers of methodology?

Mention of Feyerabend brings us to the second direction from which criticism of the idea that there is such a thing as scientific method has arisen: from philosophers, historians and sociologists of science. Feyerabend is famous for claiming that the only principle of method, and indeed scientific rationality, that can be defended at all times and in all circumstances is *"anything goes"* (*ibid.*: 28). This has created the impression that there is nothing to the theory of method at all and that books like this can only be an ornamental gravestone for a dead subject. Although this view has wide currency, it is not shared by Feyerabend, whose position we set out in §11.2. As we shall show, in writings after his widely read 1975 book, Feyerabend realized that the joke he intended in saying "anything goes" had backfired on him; it was not really his view, but the view he attributed to certain people he was criticizing. In these later writings, not so widely read, he tried – unsuccessfully – to backtrack. His position is much more complex, we shall argue, and it supports the idea of a methodology, but not a traditionally accepted view of it.

Thomas Kuhn is another who has been widely thought to have undermined the idea of a scientific method in his 1962 book *The Structure of Scientific Revolutions*. But, as we shall argue in §2.4 and §11.1, this was an early phase of Kuhn's views on method that underwent considerable refinement in subsequent writings. The upshot of his post-*Structure* work is that there is such a thing as scientific method based in his theory of values in science; and, surprisingly, he claims that these values can be tested against the very meaning of the term "science" itself (see §11.1.3). Despite the common view that Kuhn and Feyerabend are debunkers of methodology (grounds for which can be found in some of their writings), this does not reflect their more mature and considered positions.

The idea that there is such a thing as scientific method is challenged by many sociologists of scientific knowledge. Earlier sociologists of scientific knowledge, such as Karl Mannheim writing in the 1930s, did leave some room for the explanation of beliefs in science by appeal to principles of method while much else is to be explained sociologically. However, advocates of what has become known as the "strong programme" in the sociology of scientific knowledge adopted the much stronger position that there is no role for principles of scientific method. All explanation of scientific belief should eschew such principles in favour of explanations by means of social, political and cultural causal factors. One of the advocates of this programme, David Bloor, adapts a remark by Wittgenstein and refers to the strong programme "as one of 'the heirs of the subject which used to be called philosophy'" (1983: 183), understanding philosophy to include methodology with its systems of values, principles and the like. Bloor then reveals "the true identity of these heirs: they belong to the family of activities called the sociology of knowledge" (*ibid.*). Although there are considerable differences between the burgeoning numbers of practitioners of sociology of knowledge, there is one thing they all agree on: the privileged role philosophers have ascribed to methodology is to be debunked and their entire subject is to be replaced by another. Many historians of science also subscribe to this view; their task as historians of science is not one in which methodology is to be privileged in any way. Of course one may ask if their own practice of history is itself to be guided by methodological principles (concerning evidence, hypothesis-testing, etc.) some of which have a role in both science and historiography.

A large number of others have followed in the wake of the sociologists of scientific knowledge, including social constructivists, multiculturalists, students of cultural studies and the large variety of postmodernists of many different stripes, including the French postmodernists criticized by Alan Sokal and Jean Bricmont (1998) and Noretta Koertge (1998). It is not our task here to enter into all these debates, although some of these matters have been addressed elsewhere in a manner consonant with this book's overall approach.[1]

Part of the suspicion of the very idea of scientific method comes from a more pervasive suspicion of science itself that is widespread in society. Given the new perils that threaten the world through nuclear war, growing pollution, climate change and the like, there has grown a general ethos that is anti-science and anti-technology (see Passmore 1978; Holton 1993). From this there arises scepticism about the very methods whereby our scientific knowledge has been generated. Given that these threats to human existence are believed to have arisen solely out of science, it is asked, "What is so great about science and its methods?" The answer has often been "Nothing". In contrast it is alleged that there are "alternative" ways of gaining "knowledge" that are not countenanced in science but are to be found elsewhere in ordinary life, in a number of religions and in various, usually non-Western, cultures. It is alleged that the hegemony of science and its methods has suppressed or subjugated their "knowledges". This is not a theme we address here,[2] but it is a third direction from which the very idea of scientific method has been called into question. These three different directions will suffice to illustrate some of the ways in which the idea of scientific method has been called into question.

Central to a broadly conceived, modernist, Enlightenment viewpoint is that there is such a thing as scientific rationality, however that is to be character-ized. Opponents of this view claim that science and its methods are simply another effusion of our culture on a par with any other cultural activity and with no more legitimacy than any other practice we might indulge in, or game that we might play, within specific cultures. Given this quite broad delineation, the stance of this book is within the Enlightenment critical tradition. It hopes to provide at least the outlines of an account of recent attempts to say some-thing about what scientific method might be. Many have played a role in this enterprise, including some leading scientists, a wide range of twentieth-century statisticians and a large number of philosophers of science, starting with the logical positivists at the beginning of the twentieth century. Despite Medawar's pessimism, there are also some working scientists who have taken their practi-cal experience in science and developed an account of methodology out of it (see Gauch 2003).

The idea that there is no such thing as scientific method, rather than being an important discovery made recently in our postmodern world, is, from a broad historical point of view, nothing but a momentary aberration in the history of thought about methodology. From the very inception of science in the ancient world, particularly ancient Greece, philosophers (who were not to be distin-guished from the scientists of the time) provided not only particular scientific and mathematical theories but also theories about the endeavour of science itself. Although he did not begin such investigations, Aristotle's treatises that go under the collective title *Organon* (literally instrument) contain our first systematic account of a number of issues that fall within the philosophy of science and methodology. Aristotle gives us an account of matters such as the nature of explanation and causation, he sets out theories of deductive inference, particularly syllogistic inference, and he tells us something about induction and the structure of theories. Aristotle did not give us the word "science"; rather, he spoke of knowledge and understanding, but in a context that we would recog-nize as being about science.

The word "science" comes from the Latin *scientia*, "knowledge", a derivative from the verb *scire*, "to know". Alongside the growth of scientific knowledge itself, methodologists have added to our store of theories *about* science. Particularly notable are Francis Bacon's own *New Organon*, Descartes's rules (for a brief account see §3.3) and Newton's rules (§3.4). William Whewell, who coined the word "scientist" on the basis of an analogy between "art" and "artist", produced both a history and a philosophy of science that had an influence on nineteenth-century conceptions of science (including Darwin's science). During the first half of the twentieth century, the influence of logical positivism in science stimulated greatly growth in theories of logic (deductive and inductive) and in theories of method. Some of this important history we shall briefly address, but much we will pass over. Our focus will be largely, but not entirely, on more recent conceptions of method proposed by philosophers; the impetus for this derives largely from general epistemological problems and not immediately from the practical needs of scientists (met more readily by statisticians). Perhaps because of this focus a Feynman or a Weinberg will see this as yet another "ho hum" effort from philosophers.

A brief synopsis of this book

In Chapter 1 we set out a number of different things that "methodology" might mean. In Chapter 2 we consider the view that methodology is, in whole or part, the values or virtues that our theories ought to exemplify. In Chapter 3 we consider the view that theories of scientific method are to be understood as a set of rules or principles to which our theories ought to conform; and we show that this encompasses the idea of methodology as a set of values. Once we have values and principles some natural questions to ask are: what is so great about them? What justification do they have? This sets the scene for the topic of meta-methodology: the attempt that methodologists make to show that our scientific methods are rational (Chapter 4). Part II sets out some principles of inductive method and raises the problem, well known since Hume, about how these may be justified. We also discuss a method commonly thought to rival inductivism, namely, hypothetico-deductivism; despite some differences we argue that they go hand in hand. While the hypothetico-deductive (H-D) method does capture some aspects of science it has some serious shortcomings in providing a theory of confirmation that other theories of method are able to remedy.

Part III is an introduction to probabilistic modes of reasoning, particularly Bayesianism in its several guises. Much current work in methodology takes its cue from this theory of method. It is able to give an account of many of the values and rules of method mentioned in Part I, including inference to the best explanation, confirmation, hypothetico-deductivism, aspects of induction, the values that Kuhn advocates and the like. Although subjective Bayesianism is one of the more widely advocated versions of probabilistic reasoning, some have proposed modifications to overcome some of its perceived problems. These problems and proposed solutions take us to the forefront of much current research in theories of scientific method.

Part IV considers a number of philosophers who have proposed distinctive theories of method such as Popper, Lakatos, Kuhn and Feyerabend. Part V continues this theme by considering philosophers who have proposed "naturalized" theories of method such as Quine, Laudan and Rescher. The book concludes with an account of the role principles of method have in arguing for scientific realism as opposed to various versions of non-realism in science.

I. The idea of methodology

1. What is this thing called scientific method?

What is meant by "method" in the sciences? The English word derives from the ancient Greek *methodos*, which has its roots in the idea of being crafty or cunning. Later for the Greeks it came to mean "the pursuit of knowledge" or "a way of enquiry" (literally "way of pursuit"). For us moderns it has a wider usage. The *Oxford English Dictionary* tells us that a method is a way of doing something in accordance with a plan, or a special procedure; or it is a regular systematic way of either treating a person or attaining a goal. It is also a systematic or orderly arrangement of topics, discourses or ideas. In general one can speak of a method for gutting and filleting fish, baking a cake, wiring a fuse box, surveying a given piece of landscape, conducting a funeral or cracking a safe. Not following the prescribed method usually leads to a botched, or socially unacceptable, outcome. There are also methods for teaching languages, for example, the immersion method; there are methods for teaching the violin to the very young, for example, the Suzuki method; there are methods for learning and playing curling, or a nose flute; and so on. In general there are methods whereby one can not only best teach or learn a given subject, but also present an effective case in a law court, write up a report, conduct an orchestra or a meeting, and so on.

It would be very surprising if one did not find methods in the sciences. As all researchers know, there are methods to use in applying for grants, methods for presenting research results, methods for writing up papers, methods for getting ethics approval, methods for conducting surveys and the like. The activity of science itself is replete with its own methods: methods for initially forming or discovering hypotheses; methods for extracting hypotheses out of data; methods for testing hypotheses once they are formed; different methods for conducting different kinds of experiment; methods for applying theories in different situations; methods for making calculations; and so on.

In this chapter we consider four broad categories of method: methods as practices within the various sciences (§1.1, §1.2), methods of discovery and methods of justification (§1.3, §1.4), and methods as heuristics in theory construction (§1.5). In the final section (§1.6) we consider methodology in relation to logic. All this is a preliminary to setting aside those methodological matters that do not directly impinge on methods for assessing our systems of belief in science; as is common in the philosophy of science, the main focus of this book is on methods for justification.

1.1 Different methodological practices within the sciences

There is a range of different practices in the sciences that are methodological in character; mastering these methods is part of the apprenticeship in each science. Here we mention observational practices, material practices in experimentation and mathematical practices. They are part of the proper use of acquired skills and abilities embodied in our knowing *how to* observe, *how to* experiment and *how to* calculate.

Observing is an intentional activity that requires the observer to pay attention and to notice, and to do so in the right way for particular purposes. Different sciences have different methods that constitute their *observational practices*. Jane Goodall, when new to the community of chimpanzees she was to observe in Gombe National Park, Kenya, had to find ways of observing them without interfering with their activities (Goodall 1986: 51–9, 597–608). Initially her observing activities were too obtrusive; she even engaged with the chimpanzees in limited ways such as feeding them. Eventually she learned to keep a discrete distance sufficient for observation, and to become such a familiar part of their surroundings that chimpanzee life went on as if she were not present. Such methods of unobtrusive observation are paramount in ethology, from bird-watching to whale-watching. More difficult to follow are the methods of unobtrusive observation that anthropologists living in some alien society must apply.

In an observational science such as astronomy, special methods must be employed for observing, and then noting, the position at a time of items in the night sky. But this can give rise to systematic mis-observations, usually involving a time lag, that are to be eliminated if one is to be a methodological observer. The method of elimination involves finding each observer's *personal equation*. The normal method for making observations with optical telescopes is to fix the position of an object by its coincidence with a cross-wire in a telescope viewfinder, and then noting the time of the coincidence. It is said that the effects of a personal equation were first detected by the Astronomer Royal Nevil Maskelyne in 1786 working at Greenwich. His assistant David Kinnebrook made observations of position and time, using a clock beating seconds, which were systematically 0.5 to 0.8 seconds later than his employer's observations. Maskelyne solved the problem by sacking Kinnebrook. But once the phenomenon of different mis-observations for each observer became generally recognized for all observers, different means had to be employed to eliminate or lessen them. These included developing telescopes to be used by multiple observers to research in the experimental psychology of perception to measure each person's extent of mis-observation, that is, their personal equation. This yields a factor to be added to any observational results they make. It is an important part of the methodology of astronomers when using optical telescopes, but not other kinds of telescope where observers are replaced by machines, which might have different kinds of systematic error in recording that have to be determined.

Quite different are the methods that must apply in experimentation if there is to be a successful experimental outcome. These we call the *material practice of experimentation in science*. There is a wide variety of experiments in science that involve methods and methodological procedures; not to follow these commonly leads to an unacceptable or unscientific outcome. For example, there are methodological procedures developed for measuring a quantity, such as Robert Millikan's procedures for measuring the mass/charge ratio of an electron. There are many techniques to be mastered in making this experimental determination, not least of which is how to observe the motion of small drops with a microscope when they move in an electric and gravitational field. Initially Millikan worked with a water-drop technique but the experiment was vastly improved when he changed to oil-drops. This is one sense in which we can talk of an improved method of obtaining more accurate results for the mass/charge ratio. Experimentation also involves methods for making interventions in some process to investigate alternative outcomes in different situations, such as the use of growth hormones to increase or retard metabolism in different organs and tissues. Experimentation is also used to test the outcome predicted by some theory. But sometimes experiments are merely the display of some phenomena, as in the early use of electric discharges in closed, evacuated tubes well before their use as neon lights or television tubes.

Procedures of various sorts can be included under the broad heading of experiments. There are definite methods to follow in all medical procedures, such as inserting a stent into an artery to prevent or rectify any narrowing. For biologists there are methods for the preparation of tissue for viewing under a microscope, the kind of preparation differing according to the kind of microscope to be used. Some optical microscopes require the staining of clear tissue so that it can be seen at all, while electron microscopes require a quite different style of preparation of materials for viewing. For chemists there are methods, say, for preparing solutions with a specific pH value, or determining the pH value of a given solution. Finally, biochemists learn the specific methods involved in performing a polymerase chain reaction for magnifying and then "photocopying" small amounts of DNA. These methods underlie the technique of DNA fingerprinting used in forensic investigations, and these in turn have their own additional elaborate methodologies to avoid contamination, mistaken labelling and the like.

An important part of most science is the application of mathematics in the development of scientific theories. In so far as a theory has been mathematized, there is a host of *mathematical practices* that need to be mastered in the process of understanding and developing the theory, solving puzzles posed within the theory or finding applications of it. As is well known, the method of infinitesimals was applied by Newton in order to develop his mathematical theory of the motion of terrestrial and celestial bodies. The combined work of Newton, Leibniz and others led to our modern theory of differential and integral calculus. This provides methods for finding maxima and minima of functions, the areas under curves and much else. There are also methods in the sense of strategies for proving mathematical results for any mathematized science. We say more on this in §1.6.

1.2 Methodology and clinical trials

A line of the blurb on the back of Lawrence Friedman *et al.'s Fundamentals of Clinical Trials* (1998) reads: "The randomised control clinical trial has become the gold standard scientific method for the evaluation of pharmaceuticals, biological devices, procedures and diagnostic tests". And rightly so, since R. A. Fisher began his reforms of experimental design in the 1920s setting out some of the methods of randomization and statistical inference that ought to be employed. Clinical trials concern the investigation of the effect and value of interventions involving human beings, although the same methods can be extended to non-human domains such as agriculture. The task is to control for just one putative variable deemed to have an effect on an outcome amid many other possible variables – some of which are actually relevant, others mistakenly thought to be relevant, and yet others that are actually relevant but are not even envisaged – and then to see if that variable does affect the outcome. There are definite procedures for doing this detailed in the host of books about the methodology of such trials; they draw on the many years of experience since the beginning of the general use of such trials in the 1930s.

We set out a truncated version of the many procedures laid down in books such as Friedman *et al.* (1998) and Pocock (1983). To illustrate, we consider an experiment to determine whether there are any effects of distant intercessory prayer on the recovery of patients undergoing coronary bypass operations. Patients are known to have a high rate of postoperative complications in the month following their operation, including depression, stress and even death; these are alleged by some to be relieved or prevented by prayer. A study of this is set out in Herbert Benson *et al.*'s "Study of the Therapeutic Effects of Intercessory Prayer (STEP) in Cardiac Bypass Patients" (2006) (STEP). This was a $2.4 million US project supported by the John Templeton Foundation.

The procedural methods of clinical trials involve at least the following.

1. The purpose of the (prospective rather than retrospective) trial needs to be set out with a definite well-formed question to be answered, usually in the form of a hypothesis to be tested, such as: prayer decreases postoperative complications for coronary bypass patients. If two or more questions are to be asked then separate trials ought to be conducted.

2. A written protocol is required. This is an agreement between the investigators, the participants and the scientific community at large that sets out the purpose, design and conduct of the trial and includes at least the following matters:

(a) the background to the study (the final publication will usually include an account of other studies; STEP mentions four previous studies that had conflicting results, with some criticized for lacking sufficient statistical power to reach any conclusion);

(b) the objectives of the experiment;

(c) an outline of the experimental design, which covers such matters as the enrolment of participants, possible risks to them, the kinds of intervention and the randomization methods to be employed, the degree to which the experiment is blind, follow-ups with the participants, the data acquired and their analysis, the termination of the experiment and so on;

(d) the specification of organizational matters, such as the involvement of statisticians, the use of different centres of investigation (STEP was conducted using several hospitals and churches), the funding and its sources, and so on.

As well as the protocol there is also the involvement of human ethics committees and their approval of all the above.

3. Full details of the technical aspects of the design of the experiment (of which more shortly) need to be determined and then the trial needs to be actually carried out.

4. Details of the statistical analysis of the data and an account of what conclusions can be drawn about the hypothesis under test need to be specified.

5. Finally the results are published in a standard form in line with the above.

These five features of trials set out a methodology that is procedural. But within steps 3 and 4 there are different methodological requirements that are logical in character; these lie at the heart of the methodology of clinical trials. We highlight three aspects of this, the first being randomization. This is an extremely important matter resulting from Fisher's reform of trial experiments. It distinguishes between those factors influencing an outcome that experimenters know about and can control for, and those factors whose influence is not known or even not suspected; randomization is intended to minimize or remove the "noise" of any influence that the latter factors might have. One common procedure is randomly to select a group of people for study. These are randomly divided into an experimental group that is given some procedure, medication or treatment and a control group that is not given these but instead some "placebo". Then the outcomes are noted.

In the case of STEP a sufficiently large group of people were already chosen on the basis of some common feature, such as being about to undergo a coronary bypass operation; then they were randomly assigned to a control and an experimental group. STEP is slightly different in that three different groups were randomly chosen. A group of 1802 patients were randomly assigned as follows: group 1 consisted of 597 patients who were told that they *might* receive intercessory prayer and, unbeknown to them, did *not* receive it; group 2 consisted of 604 patients who were told they *might* receive intercessory prayer and, unbeknown to them, actually *did* receive it; and group 3 consisted of 601 patients who were told that they would receive intercessory prayer and *did* receive it. Those delivering intercessory prayer were from three different Christian church groups who were given the names of the people to include in their prayers each day for two weeks beginning from the night before the operation. No controls were imposed on personal prayer, the prayer of relatives and friends, or any content the prayers might have.

The second important methodological matter is whether patients and experimenters are "blind" to (i.e. ignorant of) certain kinds of information about the experiment. This is to eliminate biases that can arise in the subjects being experimented on, the investigators and even those who analyse the data. In an unblinded trial the subjects and the investigators know which intervention which subject has. In single-blinded experiments members of one of these groups, usually the subjects, do not know who is in the control or the experimental group; thus each subject will not know whether they are getting a placebo or the procedure under trial. In double-blinded trials neither subjects nor investigators know. And in triple-blinded experiments the analysers of the data do not know who is in the control or experimental group. Such biases have been revealed through experimentation itself, particularly research on placebo effects. So on good empirical grounds, controls of blinding need to be imposed to eliminate any effects experimenters and subjects can have on one another. The case of STEP exhibits slightly different kinds of blinding; some of the patients knew that they were being prayed for while others were uncertain. But none of the doctors performing the cardiac bypass operations, the hospital nurses and the experimenters or those analysing the data had such knowledge.

The third kind of methodological matter concerns the statistical theory on which the experiment is based, from issues to do with the statistical power of the experiment to issues concerning which hypothesis is best supported by the experimental data collected. One hypothesis established by STEP was that a major postoperative occurrence such as the number of deaths within the month after the operation was not statistically significant across all three groups. The results concerning overall postoperative recovery were as follows. Complications occurred in 51 per cent of group 1 (those who were uncertain of receiving intercessory prayer and did not get it); complications occurred in 52 per cent of group 2 (those who were uncertain of receiving intercessory prayer and did actually get it); and complications occurred in 59 per cent of group 3 (those who were told that they were being prayed for, and were in fact prayed for).

STEP established the following hypothesis: intercessory prayer itself has no effect on a complication-free recovery from cardiac bypass operations, but certainty of receiving prayer is associated with a higher incidence of complications. Naturally there have been responses to these results. One suggestion is that there ought to be further study of the worst-off group, that is, those who knew they had been prayed for; another is that the very expensive experiment has been a waste of time, because it is just that (a waste of time) or because spiritual matters such as prayer cannot be scientifically investigated.

These three methodological matters are different from the procedural methods that govern the entire conduct of any trial; they concern matters such as empirically discovered facts about the ways in which trials can fail to be successful (e.g. matters to do with blinding to control for bias), or logical matters to do with statistical inference and randomization. In the medical sciences and elsewhere lack of proper controls on trials has led to a number of unfortunate conclusions being drawn throughout its history. But also in the general public there is a lack of appreciation of the crucial role that controls play in any such experimentation.

The nature of the controls and the extent of them is not an uncontroversial matter within the statistical theory of trials. One important issue concerns the role of randomization and the setting up of experimental and control groups. Some have argued that while Fisher's advocacy of randomization is a very important matter to consider in experimental trials, it does not follow that, when Fisher randomization is not employed, such trials are always worthless and unscientific. Randomization imposes strong requirements on trials that can in some respects be removed while other methods are imposed. To illustrate, consider the case of breast cancer surgery. The traditional surgical procedure has been a radical mastectomy in which the whole breast and much muscle and other tissues are removed. More recently some surgeons have suggested that less radical mastectomies can be performed in which sufficient breast tissue is removed while ensuring that the remainder is tumour-free. How would one test for whether the new conservative procedure has the same recovery rate from cancer as the older, more radical procedure? The standard methods of randomization with control and experimental groups have been used in this case. However, randomization appears to rule out the comparison of the use of the earlier historical procedure with any later new procedure due to lack of controls; historical patients are not randomly assigned to control and experimental groups. But could a control group be set up in some other manner using historical cases gathered from the records of the older radical procedure that are then compared with very similar cases of a growing group of patients who are subject to the newer less radical procedures?

Some have argued that this can be done and have developed different methods arising from an approach based on Bayes's theorem that enable something like the above suggestion to be employed. Bayesian methods also overcome some undesirable financial and ethical problems arising from randomization. An approach *via* randomization can commonly require that a large number of people be involved in the control and experimental groups, and this can be an expensive matter. In addition pilot studies might suggest that a new form of treatment or procedure will be successful. But if control and experimental groups are to be set up, those in the control group might be denied what is in fact a successful form of treatment. Such was the case when various treatments of AIDS were proposed; those assigned to the control groups left in large numbers in order not to miss out on any benefits that might arise from the new medication under trial. Again a Bayesian approach, in avoiding traditional forms of randomization, can sidestep such ethical and financial problems. It allows experimenters to use incoming information to update on their hypotheses concerning the relative merits of a new procedure when compared with the old, or a new form of medication when compared with either an old form or in the absence of any prior medication at all. The Bayesian approach to clinical trials is not something we can discuss here.[1]

1.3 Methodology within the context of discovery and the context of justification

Philosophers of science draw a distinction between two kinds of method. First, the context of discovery comprises those methods for *finding, inventing, constructing* or *discovering* hypotheses (theories or concepts). Secondly, the context of justification comprises those methods of *justifying, proving, validating, warranting* or *appraising* hypotheses (theories or concepts) once they have been given. Not all philosophers draw this distinction in the same way. Here the context of justification will be taken to be strongly normative in that it aims to tell us that we have the right, correct or best available hypothesis, or that we have some warrant for believing, or for accepting or rejecting, some hypothesis. In contrast the context of discovery sets out methods for arriving at some hypothesis without necessarily telling us that it is right or correct, or the best hypothesis. Most philosophers agree that there are methods within the context of justification. It is methods in this context that will largely be discussed in this book. However, something needs to be said about what methods there might be for invention or discovery.

Philosophers differ over whether there are methods in the context of discovery. Some claim that there are no methods of discovery, and that at best this is a realm only to be investigated, in so far as it can, by psychology or sociology. The human wellsprings of creativity and invention are said to run deep and are not amenable to logical analysis but are open to empirical investigation. This might appear to be so in the case of, say, composers inventing their musical works; and the analogy is carried over to scientists such as Darwin or Einstein inventing their respective theories. In contrast others claim that there are some methods of discovery, the position endorsed here.

But first, some comments on the wide variety of different "objects" of discovery. Consider the case where the verb "to discover" grammatically takes a direct object. If a person, or a group, P discovers X (where X is a particular, e.g. material object or event), then since "to discover" is a success verb, it follows that X exists, or obtains. We cannot discover an X that does not exist. The verb "to discover" can take a "that" clause as its grammatical object; thus Herschel discovered *that there is a planet beyond Saturn* (i.e. Uranus). We can also discover *that X* does not exist, for example, P discovers *that* there is no cold fusion. The range of grammatical "objects" X is quite broad, including objects, events, properties, processes and so on, such as: the discovery of objects such as quasars; the discovery of states of affairs, such as the discovery of the current rate of employment in some society; the discovery of causal agents, such as a cure for AIDS; and so on.

Importantly, one can make discoveries with respect to hypotheses, such as discovering which hypotheses best fits some data, for example, Johannes Kepler's discovery that it is an ellipse that best fits the observations that Tycho Brahe made of the orbit of Mars. The "object" of discovery can also be expressed propositionally, such as *that some particular hypothesis H best fits some given data*. Or the "object" can be the discovery of some evidential support, that is, *that some hypothesis gets strong support by some evidence*, such evidence in turn also being a further object of discovery. Finally, the discovery might be *that some hypothesis is true* (or most probably true), or *that some hypothesis is false* (or probably false). Here we discover that some hypothesis H has certain epistemic properties: those of being true (or false), or being well (or badly) supported by evidence.

These last kinds of "objects" of discovery are often said to be part of the quite different context of justification. While there is some point to this, the claim about exclusivity can be overdone. The very same "object", for example, that some hypothesis *H* is true or best supported by some evidence, can be both an object of discovery and an object of justification. Discovery has a success dimension. But the success claim often needs to be backed by a justification that shows that *H* has the alleged epistemic properties; otherwise the success feature of "discovers" cannot be seen to obtain. Popper is well known for writing a book with the title *The Logic of Scientific Discovery* (in German *Forschung*) and then for writing inside the book: "there is no method of having new ideas, or a logical reconstruction of this process" (Popper 1959: 32); that is, there is no logic of discovery. But the scientific discovery of what? This can make sense only if the above remarks about the different "objects" of discovery and their overlap are kept in mind.

Popper, the arch-methodologist, also surprises when he writes in a preface with the title "On the Non-Existence of Scientific Method": "As a rule I begin my lectures on Scientific Method by telling my students that scientific method does not exist" (Popper 1983: 5). But it transpires that what he means by this are the following three claims:

(1) There is no method of discovering a scientific theory;
(2) There is no method for ascertaining the truth of a scientific hypothesis, that is, no method of verification;
(3) There is no method for ascertaining whether a hypothesis is "probable", or probably true.   (*Ibid.*: 6)

However he goes on to claim that "*the so-called scientific method consists in … criticism*" (*ibid.*: 7). An account of Popper's method of criticism is given in §10.1. But are these three claims correct?

His first point reiterates his long-held view about there being nothing amenable to logical analysis within the context of discovery; at best it might be amenable to empirical investigation. But this must be wrong as statisticians have, since the middle of the nineteenth century, been developing methods for extracting hypotheses out of a given set of data. Within the broad topic of regression analysis can be found the method of least mean squares and methods for curve-fitting. In the next section we shall briefly outline some programmes that have been developed for getting hypotheses out of data.

His second point is correct if "verification" means "actually show to be true". While this is possible for singular, contingent claims within science about ordinary observable matters, it is not possible for claims that are quite general and apply to domains that are either indefinitely or infinitely large. We human beings, collectively or individually, do not have enough time to hunt through such large domains to ascertain truth owing to the number of cases to investigate; nor do we have sufficient access to all of their domains owing to their dispersal throughout all of space and time. Moreover the problem of induction stands in the way of any inference to their truth, and so verification. If we cannot show that a hypothesis is true, then perhaps we can show that it is probably true, as the third point suggests. There has been a long dispute (into which we shall not enter) between Popperians and probability theorists about how we are to understand remarks such as "the probability of hypothesis H on evidence E is r". But in subsequent chapters we shall consider some Bayesian accounts of this that run counter to Popper's claim in (c) and display some of the virtues of a probabilistic approach to scientific method.

1.4 Methods for discovery

If there are methods for discovering hypotheses, then does this mean that there is a "logic" for their discovery? As noted there is a long tradition that says that there is no such thing. Carl Hempel gives three commonly cited reasons why not. The first begins with a naïve inductivist view that there is an infinity of observational facts to gather, such as the changing shapes of clouds, all the features and relations of grains of sand on a beach, and so on. Given this plethora, there is no reason why one should focus on one fact rather than another. To make any advance there must be some relevant sorting procedure. But this leads to a second objection. If the vast numbers of facts are supplemented with only canons of logical inference, then there is still no way we can sort all the facts since logic alone is not enough to put them into any relevant groupings. Hypotheses need to be introduced: "Empirical 'facts' or findings, therefore, can be qualified as logically relevant or irrelevant only in reference to a given hypothesis" (Hempel 1966: 12). But since our problem is to discover hypotheses in the first place we seem to have advanced nowhere.

A third objection is that there is an insurmountable act of conceptual creativity that no mode of inference, deductive or inductive, can overcome:

> Induction rules of the kind here envisaged would therefore have to provide a mechanical routine for constructing, on the basis of the given data, a hypothesis or theory stated in terms of some quite novel concepts, which are nowhere used in the description of the data themselves. Surely no general mechanical rule of procedure can be expected to achieve this.　　　　　　　　　　　　　　　　　　　　　(*Ibid.*: 14)

Hypotheses expressed using concepts such as "electron" or "virus", allegedly transcend any data from which they could ever be routinely inferred. Hempel then goes on to say that the transition from data to hypotheses "requires creative imagination" or making "happy guesses" (*ibid.*: 15) of the sort made in the invention of quantum theory or the theory of relativity. Can a case be made for a "logic of discovery" that applies to simpler laws and hypotheses rather than such grand theories?

Recently some programmable methods have been proposed for discovering hypotheses from data, and even inventing concepts. There are software programs now available, and widely used by scientists, that provide, for any given amount of suitably expressed data, a mathematical function that fits the data to some degree of specified fit. Such programs provide a means of realizing a time-honoured goal in science: that of bringing a vast amount of observational data under some law, or mathematical formula. The classic case of such a procedure in the history of science is Kepler's use of the observations of the positions of the planet Mars made by Brahe. In his *Astronomia Nova* of 1609, Kepler sets out the tortuous path whereby he tried a number of different figures, from circles to various kinds of ovals, eventually arriving at his elliptical law (and his area law as well). Today Kepler's task would be much easier. In fact, using Kepler's data, computer programs have been devised that arrive at Kepler's very laws.

Pat Langley *et al.* (1987) show that the various BACON discovery programs they have devised will, from Kepler's own data, discover his third law of planetary motion:[2] the cube of a planet's (average) distance from the sun, D, is proportional to the square of its period, T, that is, $D^3 \propto T^2$ (*ibid.*: ch. 3). In fact the BACON programs also discover, from the scientists' own data, Boyle's law (for a given mass of gas at a fixed temperature well away from its liquefaction point, the product of pressure and volume is a constant), Galileo's law (distance fallen is proportional to time squared), and an early law of Ohm's linking the current flowing in a wire of given length and the voltage across it.

The list can be impressively extended to other historically discovered laws such as Snell's law of refraction, the ideal gas law, an experimentally based version of the law of universal gravitation and so on. Theory-driven programs have also been devised; they take on board theoretical assumptions from science about the data under investigation in the process of discovering other laws. Yet other programs – such as GLAUBER, STAHL and DALTON – have been developed to deal with the discovery of qualitative rather than quantitative laws such as those listed above. They have been applied, as the names indicate, to uncover qualitative claims within phlogiston theory and Dalton's early theory of the molecular constituents of chemical reactions.

Not only do the programs discover new laws, but they can, in a limited way, introduce new concepts, *pace* Hempel, by introducing them into the laws that they discover. The authors do not claim that their programs currently provide thoroughgoing paradigm shifts replete with large amounts of conceptual change. But it is part of their ongoing programme to show that their approach can be extended to radical cases such as these that will result in the discovery of concepts and laws that are qualitatively different from those used in expressing the data used by their programs. In fact they claim that their basic approach to issues of scientific discovery is one that is continuous with a fairly normal problem-solving process, but one adapted to the particular features of the domain under investigation.

So how is this done in some simple cases, and what of the objections raised by Hempel? Much depends on what one means by a "logic of discovery". In reply to some of his critics Herbert Simon makes it clear that he does not mean by this a formal system of inference, inductive or deductive, guaranteed to find some laws: "I simply mean (and have always meant) a set of normative rules, heuristic in nature, that enhances the success of those who use them (as com-pared with those who don't) in making scientific discoveries" (Simon 1992: 75). Alongside data there is a crucial role for what Simon calls "heuristic rules". These, as will be seen, are not the same as the empirical hypotheses that Hempel supposed would overcome his second objection to a method of discovery. There is an overwhelming plethora of facts to sort and logic alone cannot cope with this task. Here heuristic rules play a crucial role in guiding the discovery of hypotheses.

Do programs such as BACON really replicate the context of discovery of, say, Kepler and his law $D^3 \propto T^2$? On closer examination the matter is not clear-cut (see Gillies 1993: §3.5). Kepler may have worked relatively blind as to the final outcome, but the makers of BACON do not since they have the hindsight of Kepler's discovery. In programming much depends on what one puts into the program. Of course the data is essential; but a prominent role is also played by three heuristic principles that help generate the result of BACON.

The first matter to consider is what variables are to be related to one another. The variables D (average distance from the sun) and T (orbital period) have to be selected from among several that might form some law-like relation concern-ing planetary motion, such as period, distance, average distance, colour bright-ness and so on. Already it had been noted that, on the Copernican model, the more distant planets orbit more slowly; so here is a relevant selection hypothesis concerning planetary distance and period to accompany the data that Kepler might have used to select possible variables (but not Brahe as he was not a strict Copernican).

Next concerns the matter of the functional relation between D and T. How does a law of the form $D^x \propto T^y$ become a point of focus? The heuristic rules employed recommend the following choices:
(a) if the value of a variable is a constant, assume it is always a constant;
(b) if the values of two variables increase together consider their ratio;
(c) if the values of one variable increases as the other decreases, consider their product.

As Langley *et al.* set out in greater detail (1987: 66–7), from the data it is noted that D and T increase together; so by heuristic (b) some kind of ratio is involved. Using data again, heuristic (c) is applied twice to arrive at the ratio D^3/T^2. Finally it is shown that this ratio is a constant by the application of heuristic (a). Thus one arrives at Kepler's third law from data and the crucial help of the three heuristic rules.

The above outline shows that the BACON programs do not involve a random search through endless data with no heuristics to assist. Note that this vindicates Hempel's first objection. But it does not fully vindicate his second objection. True, there is an appeal to a broad empirical fact of an increase in orbital period with distance from the sun. This leads one to focus on a small number of variables to consider, among which are D and T; but it does not take us directly to D and T. But once D and T are selected, then the three heuristic rules are needed to find the right functional relation between them. Why these three heuristic rules rather than some other rules are chosen might well involve some hindsight about the kind of functional relation one is looking for. Whether they are akin to any heuristics that Kepler might have applied is an open question. Importantly the heuristic rules are not the same as empirical hypotheses; but they perform the same function of guiding the processes as do any empirical hypotheses that Hempel suggests could be involved. Hempel is partly correct in his claim that something additional is needed, but not what that something is.

Where does this leave us? Perhaps it is just a debate over the term "logic of discovery". Some have meant by this a formal logic of some sort; in contrast Simon explicitly means that it is a set of heuristic rules. If "heuristics" comprise a "logic", so be it. Given this divergent terminology, aspects of the confrontation between Hempel and Simon are merely a stand-off.

Such programs are designed to find some law that fits given data. But is there any guarantee that the law will fit any *new* data that comes along? There is no guarantee. The program merely finds a law that fits a given data set; it does not, and cannot, show that the law is inductively correct. This is important because it draws quite sharply one aspect of the distinction between the contexts of discovery and justification. BACON is a program of discovery, not a programme for justification. BACON gives no guarantee about normative matters concerning the inductive support, or justification, of the discovered hypothesis. All it does is run a program on data to find a hypothesis that fits the data to a specified degree.

Given the programs' apparent success in replicating aspects of actual historical episodes of discovery, there is some evidence to support the view of Langley *et al.* that there is such a thing as a method, or a "logic", of discovery. A program that regularly finds a particular item, such as a law, can be quite properly said to provide a method for discovery. If this is right, then the claim that there are no methods of discovery cannot be generally true *simpliciter* and needs qualification.

1.5 Heuristics as methodology

It is commonly thought that within each science there are (non-algorithmic) methods, prescriptions or general guidelines for constructing theories or models, and for constructing explanations and/or predictions. Such methods are obviously not part of the material practice of science; nor are they part of methodology in the sense of the context of justification, or the *appraisal* of theories, as Imre Lakatos says to avoid inductivist overtones arising from talk of justification. Here we shall draw on some useful ideas contained in Lakatos (1978: ch. 1 §3): his notion of a *scientific research programme* (SRP) (further discussed in §10.2.1). Lakatos replaces the common idea of a theory, viewed somewhat statically as an axiomatized system, by that of an SRP, which, like any organic thing, grows and then decays over time. Like any temporal item, SRPs have distinct temporal parts for which Lakatos uses the term "theory". An SRP is simply a sequence of distinct theories, growing and decaying over time. What unites all the theories is what Lakatos calls a common *hard core* of theoretical principles and a common *heuristic*. Lakatos's heuristic is different from the rules of heuristic mentioned in the previous section, but both play a role in discovery.

Given the more dynamic view of the structure of a science as an SRP, one task of a methodology of appraisal is to tell us whether each theoretical phase is progressive or degenerating and how a total SRP, comprising all the theoretical phases, is to be appraised. This is a matter discussed further in §10.2.1. A different task for methodology is considered here; this concerns the construction of each theoretical phase of an SRP. Here we can talk of methods of discovery, since the "objects" constructed are the new, different, phases of an SRP. Their construction is governed by what Lakatos calls "heuristic". Our word "heuristic" derives from Greek words such as *heuretikos*, being inventive or ingenious, and *heuresis*, a finding or discovery. The word is commonly used in education where heuristic methods are the ways in which children find things out for themselves (after some appropriate instruction). This can be extended to the case of science; scientists construct for themselves the various phases of an SRP to accord with what will be called the SRP's *heuristic*.

In Lakatos's analysis there are two kinds of heuristic. Negative heuristic is simply the non-specific directive not to allow any of the anomalies that a program faces to refute what Lakatos calls the "hard core" principles of the program. The negative heuristic does not tell us in what ways we should do this; only that we should do it, by whatever means. Using Newton's theory as an illustration, the hard core principles would be his laws of motion. The negative heuristic tells us that we are not to give up on these laws and are directed to find other ways of protecting them when, as is to be expected, they confront difficulties that threaten to overturn them. The negative heuristic is a general directive in support of a value of tenacity; one is not to allow anomalies to overturn the "hard core" laws before they have had a chance to display their efficaciousness in producing a progressive SRP.

Finding ways of protecting the "hard core" is the task of the positive heuristic. More than this, the positive heuristic is the driving force of the program that tells us how to develop the various theoretical phases of the program, particularly its models. Its primary focus is not on saving the program from its anomalies; rather, it is to reveal the power of the heuristic by showing how the phases of the program can be developed successfully even in the face of the surrounding anomalies. Appraising the various phases as correct or not is not part of heuristics as method. The task of positive heuristic is to show how we are to construct, build or discover the various phases in the first place.

Using the example of Newtonian mechanics for illustration, it is possible to express the positive heuristic as a quasi-metaphysical principle: all motion results from the inertial and gravitational interaction of bodies. Expressed as a methodological principle the positive heuristic would direct us as follows: account for all motion as the interaction of inertial and gravitating bodies. The metaphysical principle may be false (as it is in this case since it ignores other kinds of force that produce motion), but when understood not as a proposition but as a heuristic principle it can have much success credited to it. As a principle it is not all that specific, but it does rule out other kinds of heuristic such as an appeal to other physical forces, non-physical or occult forces, or to the action of a deity or an intelligent designer. Nor does it tell us how we are to account for such motions, only that we should account for them in terms of the directive. It is up to scientists to build models of motions that accord with the positive heuristic. But they are not to go outside the prescriptions of the heuristic in doing so. This is a central point, since to ignore the heuristic prescriptions in model-building is tantamount to abandoning one of the central features that individuate one SRP from another.

Note what heuristics can and cannot tell us. It cannot tell us what theoretical phase to construct next; it is not an algorithm for constructing theoretical phases. But what it does tell us, when we have constructed the next phase, is whether or not it is in accordance with the positive heuristic of the program. This leaves the construction of each theoretical phase to the scientist as creative theory builder. But the building must be in accordance with the directives of the positive heuristic.

The construction of each phase can be illustrated once again using the Newtonian SRP. As Lakatos describes the case (1978: 50) there is a sequence of models that were constructed: (i) a fixed point-sun around which orbits a single point-planet; (ii) the sun and planet have a common centre of gravity that is not, as in (i), at the centre of the sun; (iii) all the planets orbit the sun with a common centre of gravity; (iv) the planets and sun are no longer point-like but are bulky bodies; (v) all the bodies perturb one another gravitationally; (vi) the planets spin on their axes, which also wobble; and so on. In each case the construction of the models is in accordance with the directive of the positive heuristic; but it does not contain a recipe telling us what model to construct. There may be sufficient "heuristic power" for the sequence of models to be constructed in accordance with the positive heuristic. The driving force may come largely from the heuristic itself and not from attempts to solve any anomalies confronting the SRP (although it will be involved here as well).

This is one of the many examples that Lakatos uses to illustrate the way in which heuristic is involved in the development of any science. It turns on separating methodology as heuristic from methodology as a means of appraising theories, and as a means of justifying them. The task of (positive) heuristic is to help us discover and build ever-new variants of some SRP that are then open to test by other aspects of method.

1.6 Scientific method and the methodology of logic

Having highlighted different kinds of methodology, such as methodological practices in science, methods for discovery and heuristic methods, we are now in a position to set these aside and focus on the aspect of methodology to be addressed in this book. But it is not all plain sailing to reach this point as there is a further reef to circumnavigate. One is the objection made by some Bayesians, such as John Earman, that there is nothing left for methodology to do that is not accounted for by Bayesianism; so methodology can be left to wither. But ahead are the more navigable waters of Rudolf Carnap's account of the connection between logic and method.

Earman writes, "I agree with Feyerabend that there is no Methodology" (1992: 205), but his reasons have nothing to do with Dadaist epistemology; rather, they arise from "a little Bayesianism and a lot of calm reflection". In his view, if Popper, Lakatos and Kuhn are to be taken as one's models of methodologists then there are several objections to be raised against them. First, what is good in each of these methodologists can be captured within Bayesianism, while the bad stuff that they endorse is not, and should be dropped. As Earman puts it, "All the valid rules of scientific inference must be derived from the probability calculus and the rule of conditionalisation. It follows that there is nothing left for methodologists to do in this area" (*ibid.*: 204).

A second objection turns on the attempt by some methodologists to use their methodology as a demarcation criterion for science: "the methodologists are wasting their time in searching for a demarcation criterion that will draw a bright red line between science and non-science in terms of the methodology of belief formation and validation" (*ibid.*). In Earman's view what does demarcate science is something that has social dimensions, namely, "the professionalized character of its [science's] quest for well founded belief". Some advocates of the idea of scientific method, for example Popper and Lakatos, do endorse the idea that a reasonably bright red demarcation line can be drawn. Popper proposes a demarcation criterion in terms of the logical and epistemological features of falsifiability; Lakatos proposes the criterion of a research programme being progressive in at least one phase of its development. But others who also advocate the idea of a scientific method deny that there is any substantive demarcation line to be drawn of the kind sought by Popper and Lakatos (e.g. Laudan 1996: ch. 11). However, there are still rules of method to be found. Our belief systems will be scientific just when they accord with principles of scientific method; the pseudo-scientific belief systems breaks some rule(s) of method. Perhaps a case can be made for placing Earman in the second camp. There are rules of conditionalization that are part of a Bayesian theory of scientific method or rationality; not to update one's belief in accordance with the rule is to be irrational, and so not scientific.

Earman suggests a final refuge that methodologists might like to carve out for themselves in the domain of the "tactics and strategies of research". But even then he says that "there is nothing left for them to do except repeat, perhaps in disguised form, the advice to choose the action that maximizes expected utility" (1992: 205). In Earman's view the methodologist is a kind of derelict tramp eking out a living around the fringes of science while the Bayesians have usurped their former position and have ensconced themselves at the heart of the scientific enterprise.

In contrast Carnap finds respectable employment for methodologists. In Carnap's view, systems of deductive and inductive logic require roles for both logicians and methodologists of logic (the same person perhaps performing both tasks). Logicians will tell us what the theorems of a system of deductive logic are. The role of methodologists is to provide suggestions or strategies for finding a proof of a theorem, or how to give simpler proofs, or when an indirect proof might be more effective, and the like. Such strategies can be thought of as the heuristics of theorem-proving. They also fall under what we referred to in §1.2 as the methodology of mathematical practices. Although there may be little in the way of the codification of such practices, there are at least rules of thumb that any person applying mathematics in science will pick up and follow.

Within Carnap's inductive logic there is a bigger role for the methodologist. In Carnap's view inductive logicians have a role similar to that of the deductive logicians. Just as the aim of deductive logicians is to tell us whether, given any two propositions P and Q, one is, or is not, a valid deductive consequence of the other, so inductive logicians aim to tell us, for any propositions H and E, what is the *degree of confirmation* of H given E. That is, the task of the inductive logician is to work out the value of the confirmation function, or c-function $c(H, E)$; their task is to find some r such that $c(H, E) = r$, where $0 \leq r \leq 1$. The methodologist takes over from the logician in various ways. As in the case of deductive logic, there is a role for the methodologist in providing strategies for proving theorems in inductive logic. But there is a further role.

One of the methodologist's new tasks will be to determine what kind of experiment will yield evidence E for H. This logicians do not do; they require that evidence already be given. Or where evidence seems to be incompatible with all available hypotheses, methodologists will work on ways of discovering new hypotheses since there is no effective procedure for inventing hypotheses within Carnap's inductive logic. Methodologists have even more to do in Carnap's scheme. In working out the value of $c(H, E) = r$, just how much evidence should we employ: some, or all that is available? What we need to add is the following methodological "requirement of total evidence" (which has no counterpart in deductive logic): "in the application of inductive logic to a given knowledge situation, the total evidence available must be taken as basis for determining the degree of confirmation" (Carnap [1950] 1962: 221). Here methodologists play the role of epistemologists in determining what is the total evidence.

Methodologists also have an important role in establishing rules for the application of inductive logic to practical decision-making. Unlike Earman, who sees this as subsumable under maximization of expected utility, Carnap sees this rule, and five other rules he proposes, as the proper province of methodology outside that of Carnapian inductive logic. In general, for Carnap, methodological rules must be added to his inductive logic if it is to have any application in either scientific or everyday contexts. As such methodology has a much more substantive role to play than merely providing heuristics for theorem-proving.

One of the big differences between Earman and Carnap is that, even though they both assign probability considerations a big role, they have different views of it. When Earman endorses Bayesianism (which is not every day of the week) he is a subjective Bayesian while Carnap is not so, at least in his *The Logical Foundations of Probability* ([1950] 1962). There Carnap distinguishes the tasks just outlined: that of the logician who is to determine for any pair of sentences a c-function such that $c(H, E) = r$, and that of the methodologist who is to determine how the inductive logic is to be applied. However, most are now agreed that Carnap's programme of finding c-functions cannot be completed and has run into a dead end. For the triumphant subjective Bayesians, with an end to the idea of c-functions there is also the end of any role for a Carnapian methodologist.

Perhaps the differences between these theorists turn merely on how one uses the motley term "methodology". Here we shall go further than Carnap and use the term to cover both principles of logic and those principles that pertain exclusively to Carnapian methodology, together with many other principles that characterize other methodologies (see §3.1). Having now distinguished a few of the many different uses of the term "methodology", in Chapters 2 and 3 we consider what contribution values and rules make to different theories of scientific method and the account of scientific rationality they provide.

2. Theoretical values in science

This chapter is concerned with the values, or virtues, that different methodologists have claimed our scientific theories and hypotheses ought to exemplify. Such values and disvalues, or virtues and vices, they argue, enter into our decisions about science, especially those concerning the acceptance or rejection of theories, hypotheses or, indeed, any system of beliefs whatever. A wide range of different kinds of theoretical values (epistemic, pragmatic, etc.) has been proposed that concern matters internal to science in that they are directed on the very content of the theories and hypotheses themselves. These, we can say, are values that are *intrinsic* to science (whether they are also essential to science is a different, much stronger claim). Other values inform choices that are external to science: the *extrinsic* values. Such choices are *about* the utility of various sciences; they are not directly concerned with the content of the science. The dominance of science in our lives attests to the wide range of uses to which science has been put, for better or worse, and the values informing the choices that have been made. Both kinds of values and the choices they lead to are equally important. We discuss extrinsic values briefly in §2.1. Our main concern is with the many different intrinsic, theoretical values that have been proposed, what these values have been taken to mean and how adopting them might be justified. Of the many methodologists who have advocated intrinsic values for science, we restrict our discussion in this chapter to those proposed by W. V. Quine and Joseph Ullian, Kuhn, Popper, Duhem and Bas van Fraassen. Their proposals are characteristic of those made by many other methodologists; different proposals are discussed in other chapters.

2.1 Aims of science and scientists

Human beings commonly engage in activities that are rational in the sense that they have aims (goals or ends) that reflect their values and that they attempt to realize by employing means that are believed to realize those aims. The activities of scientists are no exception; they also have aims that reflect what they value. Thus they might have personal aims they wish to realize through science, such as satisfying their curiosity, obtaining job security and comparatively high level of pay or engaging in an activity that is exciting and challenging. Scientists can also have professional aims such as attracting grants, organizing research teams or editing an influential journal in their field. Finally they might have humanitarian goals to realize through science, such as increasing human powers over nature (e.g. the prediction, control or amelioration of floods and earthquakes), increasing powers over ourselves (such as the illnesses to which we are prone, or means of social control, etc.), or making innovations that increase productivity, employment and wealth through a "knowledge economy". Generally, but not always, scientists who apply science have humanitarian goals in mind. But, as is all too well known, there can be unintended consequences of their choices that can undermine these goals; we mention one of these shortly.

Values are also involved in making decisions about science. Budding scientists will make, on the basis of values they hold, decisions about which research programmes they should join in order to promote the growth of science. They might have a choice between research that holds promise for, say, enhancing the survival of near-extinct species as distinct from research into whale-meat processing; or research that could lead to the reduction in diabetes as distinct from research into cosmetics; or research into the production of stem cell lines that hold out promise for yet unknown kinds of cures. When a research project leads to new scientific results or technological development, values also enter into making decisions about their application and their social utility or disutility. The most famous example of this is the production and use of the atomic bomb. This is one of the more recent decisions that have been made in a long history of the development of the technology of weapons, beginning with spears, bows and arrows, leading more recently to a weapons technology underpinned by science. No less dramatic are values that enter into decisions about, say, the use of *in vitro* fertilization, or decisions that will have to be made in the future about (currently unrealized) stem cell research.

Socially endorsed values and social needs can also be drivers of research and development, as when it was discovered that chlorinated fluorocarbons (CFCs) could be used as refrigerants, thereby leading to the expanded use of refrigerators, air-conditioners and the like in the second half of the twentieth century. However, researchers such as Mario Molina and F. Sherwood Rowland showed that CFCs could deplete the ozone layer above the earth that protects us from harmful ultraviolet light from the sun. And in the mid-1980s this was discovered to be so, with ozone depletion occurring in greater amounts even into the first decade of the twenty-first century. (CFCs can be released into the atmosphere from many sources, such as abandoned refrigerators.) Initially there was much resistance to these discoveries from companies that produced refrigerants.[1] But ultimately a research programme was developed to discover other refrigerants that would not deplete the ozone layer and that were not much more costly to produce than CFCs. In this example, the values of scientists were often quite different from those of the companies in which some of them worked. The aims of scientists and their associated values, the values of the wider community and the values of industry need not all be compatible and can pull in different directions. But it is important to distinguish between the value of having non-ozone-depleting chemical agents in our technological applications of science, and a quite different matter, which is our main concern, namely, what values, if any, are involved in the epistemological task of critically evaluating the truth or evidential support of hypotheses such as CFCs *are the chemical agents causing atmospheric ozone depletion.*

Concerning scientists, we might also ask what intellectual virtues they ought to exemplify. Taking our cue from Aristotle (*Nicomachean Ethics* Book 6) we could consider intellectual virtues such as: having the requisite skills of the science (*technē* or art); having knowledge and understanding of the theoretical foundations of the science (*epistēmē*); having practical intelligence and judgement in using the right means to some end (*phronēsis*); and having wisdom (*sophia*) at least in the sense of knowing the appropriate ends to which knowledge can be used. Such intellectual virtues need not be realized in all scientists, but they can serve as ideals worth achieving. Wisdom, even with much knowledge, is not a virtue easily attained.

If scientists can have aims and exemplify virtues, can the sciences (considered as theories or bodies of belief) also have aims and virtues? In so far as science has something to do with rationality it too could be said to have aims and means for realizing them. So what are these aims? Popper, who poses this question (1972: ch. 5), says that the aim of science is to give *satisfactory explanations* that also display increasing depth of explanation. Independently of how this might be understood, it is a contested aim, especially by those who downplay the explanatory aspects of science in favour of its descriptive aspects. This also raises the question: what is the difference between an aim and a value in science? Although there is no agreed distinction here, we will adopt the view that aims for science are a quite small number of high level, or ultimate, values, or virtues, which have a role in determining what other values we should endorse, or what other virtues our theories ought to exemplify. The connection here is consequentialist or teleological in that the values we adopt are those that are most likely to lead to the realization of the high level, or ultimate, aim (we shall say more in §2.5). In so far as rationality is applicable to science, aims of some sort must be involved. Science is not an aimless activity, although there might be no single overarching aim recognized by all. Certainly there are wide differences in the values endorsed by scientists. Before turning to some examples of theoretical values, consider first a number of different kinds of values.

2.2 A broad classification of kinds of value

Broadly speaking values can be intellectual, cognitive or theoretical. Talk of values is part of the general theory of *axiology* (from the Greek *axia*, meaning value), which includes accounts of aesthetic and moral values as well as the intellectual and cognitive values that people ought to exhibit and the theoretical values that our sciences and belief systems ought to exhibit. The values that our theories ought to exemplify need not be the same as the values exemplified by the common beliefs provided by our cognitive apparatus. For example, both might value truth but our common beliefs need not have the predictive or explanatory power we expect of scientific beliefs. Here we shall be concerned with the features of theories that are generally desirable and on the basis of which we choose to have some engagement with the theory, such as working on it, believing it, accepting it and the like. These desirable features we shall call either *values* or *virtues*. Although there is a difference in other contexts between values and virtues, when these terms are applied to scientific theories there is no significant difference and we shall not draw one. Some theories may lack these desirable features; yet others may exhibit undesirable features, or vices; they are either not valued or positively disvalued.

Hempel talks of *desiderata* for theory choice; but these come to much the same as the values or virtues our theories ought to exemplify:

> scientists widely agree in giving preference to theories exhibiting certain characteristics which have often been referred to in the methodological literature as "marks of a good hypothesis"; I will call them *desiderata* for short. Among them are the following: a theory should yield precise, preferably quantitative predictions; it should be accurate in the sense that testable consequences derivable from it should be in good agreement with the results of experimental tests; it should be consistent both internally and with currently accepted theories in neighbouring fields; it should have broad scope; it should predict phenomena that are novel in the sense of not having been known or taken into account when the theory was formulated; it should be simple; it should be fruitful.
>
> (Hempel 2001: 384–5)

Hempel provides a sample of values that many have found it desirable for our scientific theories to exhibit. The list is quite close to that of Kuhn's which we discuss in §2.4.

Within scientific methodology we will say that a value v is a *theoretical* value just in case v is involved in the assessment we make of a theory (body of belief, etc.), particularly the choices we make in accepting or rejecting a theory, in choosing between alternative theories, and the like. Theoretical values come in two broad varieties: *epistemic* and *pragmatic*. Generically we can say that v is an *epistemic* value just in case the role of v is to make choices between theories on the basis of their epistemic features such as their truth or their justification. This leads to two species of epistemic value. Truth is the prime *alethic* virtue (from the Greek *alētheia*, meaning truth). Others, such as Alvin Goldman (1999), speak of our beliefs possessing *veritistic* value or virtue (from the Latin *veritas*, meaning truth). The evidential justification of theories concerns their *confirmatory* virtues.

In science we often value those theories that are true and are free from error, where the notion of truth concerns some relationship between theory and the world. (The alethic value of truth need not be tied to a correspondence theory of truth.) If we value truth, then we can all too easily get it by believing everything; but this captures not only the truth but also the false. We can avoid the false by not believing anything (except such things as tautologies); but then we miss out on much truth. Instead we ought to value obtaining truth while avoiding error. More strongly we ought to value those theories that maximize truth and minimize error. This leads to the alethic virtue of *verisimilitude*: a measure of the extent to which a theory approaches the truth but falls short of it. As many methodologists point out, we also value not just any old truth, or the many dull truths; rather, we value interesting truth, such as the truths of the general theory of relativity. Certainly this theory tells us much about the structure of the world and has many interesting consequences and applications. In this respect it is more interesting than the seemingly dull truths about the distribution and direction of cracks on a concrete pavement. But depending on context and circumstance these might be interesting truths, of interest to a seismologist or civil engineer. Another oft-praised alethic virtue is the consistency of our theories; this is alethic since consistence is defined in terms of truth and falsity. Confirmatory virtues have to do with the choice between theories on the basis of their degree of support by evidence. There is a wide range of theories concerning the theory–evidence relation (to be discussed in subsequent chapters) that spell out confirmatory values in different ways.

Choice of theory can be made on grounds that do not appeal to epistemic values such as a theory's aesthetic properties, elegance, ease of communication, degree to which it is axiomatizable, extent to which it can be given mathematical expression and the like. More strongly, some reject any involvement of alethic, and more broadly epistemic, values and advocate instead what are commonly called *pragmatic* virtues. In eschewing truth, pragmatic values enter into theory choice in so far as they reflect human concerns with science such as its use or usefulness, its beauty and so on. As well as endorsing some epistemic theoretical virtues, van Fraassen also endorses pragmatic virtues, which "provide reasons for using a theory, or contemplating it, whether or not we think it true, and cannot rationally guide our epistemic attitudes and decisions" (1980: 87). Here pragmatic virtues, stripped of any linkage to alethic virtues, remain important theoretical virtues. Further difference between the kinds of virtues will be discussed later. In what immediately follows some theoretical virtues are sketched, independently of how they might be further classified.

2.3 Some virtues of scientific theories

Values that we might want our theories to exemplify could be quite specific in that they pertain to some particular features of a theory. Thus consider theories that involve quantitative laws or functions. For various purposes we might value functions that are differentiable and/or integrable over those that are not (or integrable only under assumptions that are too strongly ideal); or we might value equations that are computable with ease rather than those that involve much time and computing power or are not computable at all; or we might value those functions that are simple (in some sense) over those that are not; or we might value those functions that are continuous over those that exhibit discontinuities; and so on. In more advanced physics there are other kinds of constraints that can be construed as theory-specific values that ought to be realized. For example, in physics the theory of relativity tells us to value those equations that are invariant with respect to all frames of reference over those that are not; or quantum mechanics tells us to value theories that satisfy certain constraints of symmetry over those that do not; and so on. None of the values mentioned are applicable to non-quantitative theories. So what more general values might there be that are deemed to be widely applicable to all, or most, scientific theories?

Taking our cue from Quine and Ullian (1978: ch. 6), here are five theoretical *virtues* that many others also claim any scientific hypothesis (or theory) ought to exemplify: conservativeness, modesty, simplicity, generality and refutability. Science, they tell us, cannot get by on the basis of observations alone; it needs hypotheses for both explanation and prediction. Any theory that failed to explain anything, or failed to predict anything, would lack virtue, and even exhibit vice. Quine and Ullian do not include explanatory and/or predictive power in their short list of virtues; rather they presuppose it in characterizing the virtues they do list. Here it might be useful to think of explanatory and/or predictive power as quite high-level, ultimate values or virtues; or better, we could think of (degree of) explanatoriness at least as an overriding *aim* for science that sets the scene for other values. We shall adopt the latter view and so follow Duhem and Popper, who think of providing explanations (but not necessarily predictions) as an important, if not the ultimate, aim of science. This aim is quite general and is not tied to any particular theory of explanation. Recent philosophy of science is replete with different models of explanation; which model one adopts need not concern us here but the choice of model can reflect further values. This reveals that looming behind a seemingly simple but general aim such as explanatoriness there may be hidden a large philosophical theory to be spelled out within methodology.

Note also that false hypotheses can exemplify many of the listed virtues but they will lack the virtue of being true. Truth is not a virtue that Quine and Ullian list. It remains unclear whether its absence indicates that they adopt a pragmatic account of the virtues that excludes truth. Let us now turn to the five virtues (values) they list.

Virtue 1: Conservatism. This is a virtue that mainly concerns the dynamics of change in hypotheses in science. Any hypothesis H that we propose can come into conflict with other hypotheses H^* we also hold. If there is no conflict, and H is independent of, or logically consistent with, H^*, then there is no problem. But scientific theories grow and evolve so that later theories often rival earlier accepted theories in the sense that they are at least contraries in that both cannot be true (both might even be false). Why should we wish to resolve contradiction among our beliefs? One reason might be that, according to classical logic, from a contradiction any arbitrary claim follows: the vice of having many arbitrary logical consequences of our hypotheses. This and other considerations have been important drivers leading to the removal of contradictions in theories in philosophy and science from the time of Zeno's paradoxes onwards. In order to spell out the virtue of conservatism we need to highlight a further virtue not found explicitly in the five virtues listed by Quine and Ullian, but made explicit by other methodologists.

Virtue 6: Consistency. For any hypothesis H: (a) H should be internally consistent; (b) H should be externally consistent with other hypotheses H^* we also hold, where H and H^* are part of the same broad system of belief.

Consistency is an alethic virtue. Many, but not all, methodologists will accept 6(a) as a virtue; but some might reject 6(b) as a virtue. Those who advocate dialethic logic would not accept a role for Virtue 6(a) even at the end of science; they argue that we ought to learn to live with contradictions (and deal with alleged vices such as arbitrary consequences in other ways that can involve rejecting classical logic and adopting some form of dialethism). Even the final state of science need not be contradiction free; the best final science might embrace contradiction. So there is a dispute over whether consistency is a genuine virtue and, if it is, how that virtue might be understood (such as whether it is a long-term virtue, or must be realized immediately or not even in the long run).[2]

Other methodologists, such as Lakatos and Feyerabend, claim that they have methodologies that enable us to live with internal and external contradictions. They are important drivers of scientific growth and without them SRPs could stagnate. Inconsistent claims can also be sufficiently isolated and quarantined, and meanwhile the science progresses without necessarily eliminating them. In their view any methodology worth considering ought to encompass the useful role contradictions can have. So not all contradictions are vices. They can be allowed to prevail over long periods of time and perhaps only be eliminated in the long run so that the virtue of consistency need be realized only at the end of science, if there is an end. In fact Feyerabend advocates the virtues of the "principle of proliferation", which tells us to reject Virtue 6(b) and actively seek out and develop theories that are inconsistent with the prevailing point of view (see §11.2.1).

If we grant Virtue 6, what is conservatism? If H and H^* are externally inconsistent theories, how much change in one of H or H^* ought to be permitted to remove the contradiction we regard as a vice? Wholesale change, or only the minimum sufficient to restore consistency? The second alternative assumes that one has a procedure for finding the minimum, but this might not always be available or evident. Conservatism proposes that we make the smallest number of changes to restore consistency. Elsewhere Quine expresses this in rule form as "the maxim of minimum mutilation" (1995: 49). Why should we adopt such a virtue, or rule? If H is our old set of beliefs and new H^* disrupts it through contradiction, then there might be some good methodological grounds for not countenancing H^* in the first place; so no revision is needed. Some might propose, and adopt, the rival value of tenacity, or of not giving up too easily, and cling to H in the hope that the problematic H^* can be dealt with in other ways.

A borderline case is envisaged by William Lycan in which Scientist I, who holds hypothesis H, is confronted with a new theory H^*, proposed by Scientist II, which is inconsistent with H, but both equally exemplify all the other values of evidential support, simplicity, explanatory power, consistency with all known observations and so on. The value of conservatism reigns supreme when Lycan advises: "I say, *keep the original* [H], *without shame, because it was there first*" (1988: 176). In this case the value of conservatism is a fainthearted tiebreaker for Scientist I; if either theory were to win out over the other on just one other value then conservatism goes by the board. The same would apply to Scientist II, who, let us suppose, had not heard of H when they proposed H^*. In adopting conservatism Scientist II will cling to H^* when confronted with H because H^* was there first. It would appear that conservatism in this extreme case cannot do better than the contingencies of history.

Virtue 6 plays its role when H is inconsistent with some new well-established observation we make, or when H comes into conflict with some well-established theories we also accept. H can be renovated by turning it into H^R thereby restoring consistency with the observation or the other well-established theories. Here conservatism becomes a virtue to adopt in the dynamics of choosing theories under the process of revision. But why be conservative in revision rather than liberal in making any of a number of changes to H? Given that H is our prior system of belief, which we used before it was renovated thereby creating H^R, it might appear that it is more *a priori* plausible to hold that few claims in H are at fault than a whole lot of them (although this latter case cannot be ruled out). So a rationale for conservatism in making modifications to H can be based on plausibility considerations. It is more plausible to suppose that a hypothesis H, which has served us well in the past, has few things wrong with it and implausible to suppose that it has much that is wrong with it. So in revising it we should make minimum changes. Pursuing this further takes us to probabilistic theory of method (see Part III). Conservativeness also has some rationale within one or other of the several theories of belief revision that set out in detail what principles apply when making changes in one's beliefs. So once more, behind the seemingly simple virtue of conservatism there may be a more complex theory of method, such as belief-revision theory, to be considered in spelling out what this virtue is and what its rationale is.

Virtue 2: Modesty. Quine and Ullian tell us that hypothesis H is more modest than another H^* when it is logically weaker, that is, when H^* implies H but not conversely. Call this *modesty$_1$*. However, it is not obvious that modesty$_1$ should always be a virtue. Galileo's law of free fall can be derived (under idealizing assumptions about gravitational attraction close to the surface of the earth) from Newton's theory comprising the three laws of motion and the law of universal gravitation. Modesty$_1$ would lead us seriously astray in telling us to choose Galileo's law over Newton's laws.

But there is another sense of modesty, *modesty$_2$*, in which when some state of affairs described by E obtains, then (assuming the same background information and two rival hypotheses) we should adopt the hypothesis that is more likely on the basis of E and not the less likely. That is, we are invited to compare $P(E, H)$ with $P(E, H^*)$. (These are to be read as "the probability of E given H", or "the likelihood of H on E"). If we take E to be some evidence, the virtue modesty$_2$ invites us to choose that hypothesis which makes one of $P(E, H)$ or $P(E, H^*)$ the greater. To illustrate using the example of Quine and Ullian, suppose the evidence E is the following: when a ringing phone is answered the caller apologises for having dialled a wrong number. Which hypothesis explains this best: the caller was careless in dialling (H), or a burglar is checking to see if anyone is at home (H^*)? Both $P(E, H)$ and $P(E, H^*)$ can have non-zero positive numerical values, since making mistakes in dialling and the activities of burglars both do occur with a given frequency. Let us suppose, given what else we know, that H wins the day by conferring a higher probability on E than H^* does. H is then said to be more modest$_2$ than H^*; so we choose the more virtuous H over the less virtuous H^*. As such modesty$_2$ is not unconnected to conservatism. Is modesty$_2$ an acceptable virtue? It could be; but like conservativeness it gets its rationale from a probabilistic theory of method. So whether or not modesty in some sense is a virtue depends on what methodological values are embodied in the use of probabilities, especially likelihoods, and is not independent of them. Otherwise it remains a mystery why we should not value the opposite, immodesty, in hypotheses. Modesty might seem to be an old-fashioned virtue not to be countenanced when proposing quite immodest theories that proclaim much and that might thereby better realize our theoretical ends in the many and risky claims they make.

Virtue 3: Simplicity. Simplicity is a popular theoretical virtue, as a survey of Nobel prize-winning economists confirms (Zellner *et al.* 2001: ch. 17). But it is by no means agreed as to what simplicity is and why it should be prized as opposed to complexity, fecundity or plenitude. It might be agreed that much of science ought to be in conformity with some principle of simplicity. But such a principle need not necessarily specify some effective means for discovering simplicity in science; it might only require that there be simplicity, however it is to be obtained. In this book we mention only three aspects of simplicity. In §5.6 we discuss some criteria for determining when one equation is simpler than another; and in §5.7 we discuss the role simplicity plays in finding the equations that best fit a given set of data. These, broadly speaking, concern syntactic features of the equations (such as number of parameters) as criteria for simplicity. Here we shall discuss simplicity as an ontological doctrine; this concerns principles of parsimony, which, given a number of items in some category, tell us to accept the least number rather than more.

Such principles apply parsimony considerations to a number of different ontological items. They have the general form: all other things being equal, where there are rival theories one of which postulates m items and the other postulates n items and $m < n$, then one ought to choose the theory with the lesser number of items, m. (Here the "ought" is methodological rather than the "ought" of rational belief, although the two are sometimes taken together.) Consider some of the following "items" such as axioms, fundamental principles, *ad hoc* hypotheses, ontological categories and so on. (a) Given a number of ways of axiomatizing a system (such as propositional calculus) we ought to prefer the system that has the least number of axioms. To justify this, an appeal to the truths thereby obtained is unavailing as all the different axiomatizations produce the same body of truths. A justification might be found in an appeal to a principle of elegance or efficiency in that one is able to prove just as many theorems but with fewer axioms. (b) When attempting to set out an empirical science in terms of its fundamental laws one might demand a parsimonious set. For example, there are different ways of presenting classical mechanics some of which employ a principle of least action and others that do not, the former often being taken to provide a more parsimonious set of fundamental laws than the latter. But note that ontological parsimony of this sort might come into conflict with syntactic simplicity in that the smaller set of fundamental laws required by parsimony might contain laws that are, on a syntactic criterion, more complex. (c) Theories often make *ad hoc* assumptions; a principle of parsimony with respect to them would require us to choose the theory with the least number (including zero) of *ad hoc* assumptions.

Principles of ontological parsimony may also apply to unobservable entities or causes. (d) Other things being equal, if theory T_1 postulates more entities (within the categories of, say, objects, properties, relations, etc.) than another theory T_2, then we are to choose T_2 over T_1. This is commonly expressed as a version of Ockham's razor: do not multiply entities beyond necessity. (e) Finally, other things being equal, if theory T_1 postulates more kinds of causes (or causal mechanisms) than another theory T_2 then we are to choose T_2 over T_1 (see Newton's first two rules of reasoning in philosophy concerning causes in §3.4). Such principles of parsimony are not necessarily rivalled by other kinds of more permissive principle that tell us that where the postulation of (say) one kind of entity is not sufficient for whatever purpose, then postulate two different kinds of entity. After all Ockham's razor is consistent with a principle that says that if more entities are in some sense "necessary" then we should postulate them and not be disadvantaged by postulating too few entities. However, the "other things being equal" qualification indicates that parsimony is only weakly mandated and is not an overriding consideration in the context of other values or rules of method.

Why should one adopt such principles of parsimony, and what justification do they have? It is not obvious that they are a guide to the truth (or any other value that simplicity is supposed to realize). Nor are they necessarily true. Suppose that we can order theories according to their degree of ontological parsimony. Also suppose that there are principles of parsimony of different strength. The strongest is that which tells us to accept those theories that are maximally parsimonious in that they postulate the least number of entities; but there are other more relaxed principles that are not maximal and tell us to accept the second least number of entities, or the third least number and so on. Then one can readily imagine possible worlds in which a principle of maximal parsimony is not a guide to the truth but the second (or the third, etc.) in the order of principles of parsimony is a good guide to the truth. In this case no principle of parsimony is necessary; they are all contingent. We can now ask the following. Are we in a world in which the principle of maximal parsimony is the best guide to the truth? Or are we in a world in which some more relaxed principle of parsimony holds, say the fifth in the order of principles of parsimony? And are we in a position to discover which principle of parsimony is correct? A review of the history of science might help here. Suppose we have independent access to the truths about the number of kinds of entity there are in some domain of investigation that principles of parsimony are supposed to deliver. Then we might be in a position to test principles of parsimony and discover whether it is a principle of maximal parsimony, or the second principle in order, or the third, and so on, that delivers these truths. Such a procedure would be an empirical approach to the testing of principles of parsimony. However, such a supposition is implausible since independent access to the requisite truths is not available; moreover, methodological principles of parsimony are frequently involved in determining those very truths.

In the light of this, a *priori* approaches to the justification of a principle of parsimony would be unavailing. Theological claims to the effect that God made a simple world require at least that we have some insight into the mind and purposes of God, something that for some is not possible (we cannot know the mind of God) and for others is a non-starter (God does not exist). The theological approach also supposes the correctness of the ontological claim that the world is simple. Even though many scientists are impressed by what they think is a simple world, it is often hard to see how such a claim might be tested. Perhaps the theological justification could be replaced by a metaphysical justification, or by a justification in terms of rationality; but some of these approaches offer no real justification since they often take parsimony to be a primitive self-evident principle that explains other matters in metaphysics or the theory of rationality.[3]

Virtue 4: Generality. As this virtue runs counter to modesty, how is it to be understood? A more general hypothesis H^* can entail a less general hypothesis H. In having the virtue of generality, H^* is to be chosen over H; but in being less modest than H, H^* lacks virtue and is not to be chosen. The virtues of modesty and generality are not co-realizable in that they make different recommendations about choosing between H and H^* (a point Quine and Ullian recognize). The problem is a general one for methodologies based on values (and also rules) and can be put in the following way. In expressing our values we say the following of rival hypotheses:

- other things being equal with respect to all other values, choose the simplest hypothesis;
- other things being equal with respect to all other values, choose the most conservative hypothesis;
- other things being equal with respect to all other values, choose the hypothesis with the greatest explanatory power;
- and so on, for each value.

Such claims are unproblematic only when the antecedent *ceteris paribus* clause holds and where there is some measure whereby we can determine which is the most simple, most conservative or most explanatory. But often these assumptions do not hold, and the various values are in competition with one another as to which we should adopt, or different weightings are assigned to each. This raises the possibility that two or more virtues may not all be realizable at the same time in the same theory; some trade-off between virtues has to be made. But how is the trade-off to be made in a principled methodological way since there appears to be no higher court of appeal to yet more values? Is there a genuine incommensurability between the different choices that values can endorse, and so a version of relativism about theory choice in science threatens? We shall return to this in §2.4 when discussing Kuhn's model of theory choice in terms of weighted values; but do not have high hopes of getting an answer that fends off the threat of relativism.

Generality can be better understood in another way: H^* can have more instances than H and so is more virtuous. This can be illustrated in the case of repeated experiments. No two experiments are ever exactly the same: they will occur at different times and places; some of the quantities examined will have different magnitudes in different experiments conducted in different places and times; and so on. A hypothesis can have these different experimental outcomes as instances of it. The more such instances some hypothesis H^* has, the greater will be its generality; the fewer such instances hypothesis H has the less will be its generality. So understood, on the basis of the virtue of generality, H^* is to be preferred over H. Modesty is not a virtue here.

The virtue of generality can be illustrated in another way. Suppose that there is a set O of experimental observations that are relevant to the domain of two hypotheses H and H^*, and that we require both hypotheses to entail the observations in O. Suppose that the set O of observations divides into two subsets, O_1 and O_2. Suppose further that hypothesis H^* captures all the observations in both subsets; in contrast H entails only the observations of one subset, O_1, and entails none of the observations in the other subset, O_2. Suppose finally that none of the observations in subset O_2 refute H; nevertheless they are relevant to the domain of H. Given all the above, H is too narrow in not entailing any of the observations of O_2 that are relevant to its domain. Although H is not refuted by members of O_2, it can still be rejected in favour of H^* because of its narrowness; it suffers from the vice of lack of generality in capturing only what is in O_1 and nothing in O_2. In this case the more modest hypothesis is overridden by the more general one.

Virtue 5: Refutability. This virtue is close to Popper's virtue of falsifiability, and is expressed as follows: "some imaginable event, recognizable if it occurs, must suffice to refute the hypothesis. Otherwise the hypothesis predicts nothing, is confirmed by nothing, and confers upon us no earthly good beyond perhaps peace of mind" (Quine & Ullian 1978: 79). Clearly this virtue must be realized if the overriding *aim* of explanatoriness is to be realized; that is, there is some actual, known event that the hypothesis explains. Failure to explain or predict, or more generally entail, anything we know about is certainly a lack of virtue in a hypothesis. But the vice of irrefutability draws attention to a different defect in our hypotheses. A hypothesis (when applied in some situation) might not entail any observational claim, and so cannot be confirmed or refuted by what we actually observe. However, there is some possible application of the hypothesis that does yield an observational claim, although it can only be tested by some observation that we might possibly make in the fullness of time and not one that we could test by what we have actually observed.

Here, then, are six virtues and one supreme aim of explanatory power that have been advocated by philosophers of science, along with a thumbnail sketch of what each virtue might be, and in some cases some reasons as to why we might adopt them. We have seen that some of the virtues can come into conflict with one another. And we have seen that often, behind some of these virtues, there is a more complex theory of method that is not initially evident. Why should we adopt these virtues? We have raised some queries about why some of these virtues, on some understanding, might not be so great. In other cases there is an appeal to a further theory of method to provide some rationale. But in all cases the justification of the virtue directly or indirectly lies with a theory of method in which it is embedded. Providing some justification is the topic of metamethodology.

2.4 Kuhn on values

Kuhn advocates some of the above values for science along with others. In *The Structure of Scientific Revolutions* he tells us that there is a "set of commitments without which no man is a scientist. The scientist must, for example, be concerned to understand the world and to extend the precision and scope with which it has been ordered" (1970a: 42). He goes on to mention the elimination of disorder and adds: "Undoubtedly there are still other rules like these, ones which have held for scientists at all times". Although Kuhn talks of rules here, these commitments can also be taken to be Kuhnian values. Despite other claims elsewhere in the first edition of his book, these are not paradigm-relative values but values for science at all times; moreover the word "must" can be taken in a strong sense to indicate that these values are constitutive of science. Kuhn endorses not only the aim of understanding, which we can take to include the aim of explanation, but also the values of precision (accuracy) and the scope of the theory in respect of the amount of the order possessed by the world that it captures. Although it is unclear what this last might mean, perhaps it comes close to the Duhemian value of systematicity of classification (see §2.6). In the "Postscript" to the 1970 edition of his book Kuhn adds to these values (*ibid.*: 184): accurate predictions, with a preference for quantitative over qualitative predictions; ability to form puzzles and provide solutions; simplicity; consistency, both internally and externally with respect to other theories. And in *The Essential Tension* (1977: ch. 13) he adds scope (in a different sense from that in the above quotation) and fruitfulness. Many of these are also on Hempel's list of desiderata mentioned earlier.

Kuhn endorses two alethic values: consistency (which we have met) and accuracy at the level of observations. Throughout his writings Kuhn advocated the value of accuracy, both qualitative and quantitative, with a preference for the latter where it is appropriate and available. This is not to be confused with the value of certainty. Scientific reports of observation and measurement generally come with some estimate of the degree of error involved in making them, so they are not certain (although a high degree of certainty may attach to the degree of error assigned to any measurement). Accuracy is important for Kuhn because it is needed for two other values, or aims, that Kuhn mentions only in passing, namely, explanatory and predictive power, "characteristics that scientists are particularly unwilling to give up" (*ibid.*: 323). Here perhaps Kuhn, like Quine and Ullian, is endorsing the high level value, or aim, of explanatoriness.

Accuracy is a value that comes in degrees and thereby gives rise to comparisons such as "theory T yields more accurate predictions than does theory T^*". How accurate must a theory be for it to exhibit the virtue? As a scientific discipline develops, more accurate ways of determining various quantities arise (such as the e/m ratio for electrons, or radioactive carbon-dating of archaeological artefacts). To apply a strict requirement of accuracy with fixed threshold degrees of accuracy would eliminate some hypotheses prematurely; minima for degrees of accuracy need to be flexible and dependent on the level of development of a science. Also for an account of degrees of accuracy we need not only a theory of error but also a theory of verisimilitude, however restricted to the observational claims of science or to measurable quantities. The theory of verisimilitude will tell us that even though two hypotheses may be erroneous, one hypothesis is more (or less) erroneous than the other, or more (or less) accurate, and so nearer to (further from) the truth.

The value of accuracy is strictly an alethic virtue pertaining to the closeness to the truth of our observations. Kuhn does not advocate either truth or verisimilitude at the theoretical level of science. He makes this clear in his comments against the view that as our scientific theories grow they get closer to the truth about what is "really there": "There is, I think, no theory-independent way to reconstruct phrases like 'really there'; the notion of a match between the ontology of a theory and its 'real' counterpart in nature now seems illusive in principle" (Kuhn 1970a: 206). Here Kuhn, as we shall shortly see, joins with Duhem and van Fraassen in rejecting the realist's value of truth and verisimilitude at the theoretical level; but they need to retain it at the observational level.

Oddly enough, Kuhn makes no explicit mention of epistemic confirmatory values that depend on some notion of degree of support by evidence. We often value the theory that has the highest degree of evidential support over its rivals; absence of support, or low support, is a vice. But he does advocate other values that are epistemic in character; so in an indirect way there is an emphasis on certain confirmatory values. He endorses the value of puzzle-formation and solution. Other things being equal, we are to value T over T^* if T forms a greater number of puzzles than T^*; and other things being equal we are to value T over T^* if T solves more of the puzzles that have been posed than T^* does. But the very idea that T solves (i.e. gets right) some puzzles carries with it the idea that T picks up confirmation in virtue of getting them right, while T^* does not do this, or do it to the same degree.

Kuhn's value of *breadth of scope* also appeals to confirmatory values. A theory "should have broad scope: in particular a theory's consequences should extend far beyond the observations, laws or sub-theories it was initially designed to explain" (Kuhn 1977: 322). The virtue of having excess true consequences over those assumed in a theory's initial design is standardly advocated within, and captured by, theories of confirmation. Kuhn also emphasizes a closely related confirmatory value of *fruitfulness* when he writes: "a theory should be fruitful of new research findings: it should, that is, disclose new phenomena or previously unnoted relationships among those already known" (*ibid.*). Whereas scope requires that a theory have consequences other than those it was designed to accommodate, fruitfulness requires that some of these consequences ought not to be known by the designer of the theory at the time it was designed. Although disputed by some, the requirement that theories lead to *novel* facts or laws is an important feature of many methodologies from Popper and Lakatos to the Bayesians; it is a value that can be given a rationale within their methodologies concerning theory choice.

Kuhn claims that his list of values can be shared by all scientists; and it is on this basis that they make their theory choices. But this is not enough to ensure sameness of choice, for two reasons: first, scientists can understand these values differently; secondly, they can apply them differently. Considering the first matter, when each value is clearly specified misunderstandings can be minimized. Simplicity can be understood in a number of different ways. It can be considered in respect of the number of entities postulated, or in respect of the number of *ad hoc* hypotheses adopted, or the degree and order of the equations under consideration. Copernicus's theory is more simple than Ptolemy's in the number of artificial equant points it proposed (unlike Ptolemy, Copernicus proposed none); but they are equally simple (or complex) as one another in the number of epicycles and deferents each employed. But once the kind of simplicity has been fully specified, there is little room for different understandings. Judgements about consistency ought to be quite sharp and unambiguous; and neither scope nor fruitfulness is open to great variation in understanding. Once any differences in the understandings of values are highlighted and ambiguities removed, scientists can still differ in the importance they attach to a given value; each value can be given an idiosyncratic weighting when assessing theories.

This leads to the second matter, and Kuhn's model of theory choice, understood not only as a description of how scientists have in fact made their choices, but also as a model that has normative force about how one ought to make choices. Scientists do not employ values one at a time in choosing theories; they employ them together. As we have seen in the case of generality and modesty, the values may not be all co-realizable; they can pull in different directions. Once a value is specified unambiguously, one scientist might be willing to downplay one in favour of another. Thus one scientist will favour accuracy over scope and/or fruitfulness while another does the opposite. Again, one scientist will downplay simplicity in favour of accuracy (e.g. they favour the more accurate function that captures a set of data points on a graph, which is often also the less simple); in contrast another scientist may do the opposite. And so on. Even though they may share the same values, they need not share the same *weightings* they give to each value. Thus Kuhn's model of theory choice is, for each scientist, a set of common values, but with a weighting for each value that can differ from scientist to scientist. Consensus will arise in the community of scientists over theory choice when there is sameness of weightings. It could also serendipitously arise even when there are different weightings; but more commonly there will be dissensus when there is difference in weightings.

This now raises what we might call *the problem of aggregation*. How do scientists aggregate the different values, given their respective weightings, to make a choice about theories? Here is a sketch of how this might be done. For a given theory T there will be some degree, or some measure, of the extent to which T realizes each value. Thus there are degrees to which T realizes simplicity, scope, fruitfulness, number of problems posed and solved and so on. (Consistency does not come in degrees, so it may be set aside.) It might be very difficult, if not impossible, to obtain absolute measures of the degree to which a value is realized on a scale from 0 per cent (not realized at all) to 100 per cent (fully realized). However, it might be less problematic to get comparative measures, as when we claim that T is more simple, or solves more problems and so on, than T^*. Let us suppose at a given time that each scientist endorses values $V_1, ..., V_n$, and let us suppose, somewhat idealistically, that theory T realizes these to some respective degree $D_1, ..., D_n$ (either absolutely or in comparison to some rival theory). Putting these together we need to suppose that there is a given degree to which T realizes each V_i; call this $(DV)_i$ $(i = 1, ..., n)$. Moreover, for a scientist to make an overall choice about theory T, we need to aggregate, or "sum", each $(DV)_i$ in some way. Let us represent this "sum" as $(DV)_1 + ... + (DV)_n$ (where "+" is an aggregation function that may or may not be numerical addition).

But more is needed. Any aggregation must employ each scientist's idiosyncratic weighting of each of their endorsed values. These weightings can vary over time for different scientists and for different theories they evaluate. If the weightings for scientist S considering theory T (at a given time) are w_1 to w_n, then the following function needs to be taken into account in determining the overall value of T for scientist S, that is, $V_S(T)$: $V_S(T) = w_1(DV)_1 + ... + w_n(DV)_n$. In some manner this function is supposed to yield an outcome that enables each scientist to make an overall ranking for each of the theories T, T^* and so on, between which a choice is to be made.

The idealized function $V_S(T)$ captures central aspects of Kuhn's model of theory choice involving more than one value, but also brings to the fore the problems in adopting it. In the ideal case, each scientist is required to estimate the degree to which each value has been realized (on some scale), and to have an explicit scale of weightings for each DV_i. It is hard to see how the process of constructing the scales and then performing the aggregation could be anything other than vague and ill-defined.[4] What might have initially seemed to be a plausible way to proceed turns out on closer analysis to be mired in problems. A final aggregation problem arises when each scientist's choice is used in some way to determine what the relevant scientific community takes to be their overall choice. Here there may be a weighting of each scientist's views since not all may be given equal consideration.

Does this in the long run entail relativism about theory choice? Consensus masks the fact that it seems to be just a matter of luck that the members of the scientific community reach the same conclusion. It is simply a brute fact that they reach consensus; there is no guarantee that they should reach agreement and no further rational basis is to be found for their collective agreement. Dissensus exposes the fact that different weighting can lead to different choices and there are no further rational grounds of appeal within Kuhn's model of weighted values to overcome the difference in choice. We say more on these matters in §11.1 on Kuhn.

2.5 Aims and values of science: Popper

The above will serve to illustrate some of the values that have been advocated in science. Here we shall consider some of the proposals that have been made to extract from various values a small core that constitute ultimate *aims* for science. But just as there might be disagreement over what values to adopt, so there might remain disagreement at the higher level of aims for science.

The sociologist of science Robert Merton proposed that one of the values of science is *organized scepticism*. (In fact he spoke of norms here; but as we shall argue in Chapter 3, values and norms in methodology are closely related.) In science we commonly value those beliefs that are open to critical assessment (even though they might not have actually been criticized) over those beliefs that are held to be immune from criticism on grounds that have to do with political conviction, religious faith, economic interests or whatever. Merton's value involves scepticism in that no belief is sacred and exempt from critical evaluation; nor is it to be accepted dogmatically and uncritically. All beliefs are to be open to examination by whatever appropriate means. This can even apply, for example, to the textual examination of the Bible (or any other religious book), a matter that has involved the controversial application of scientific methods since such examinations began in the mid-nineteenth century. Merton proposed the value of organized scepticism as an institutional value to be adopted by the community of scientists. Collectively they ought to leave no belief unexamined; if it is protected from critical assessment then that is tantamount to its being classified as unscientific.

There is also a methodological counterpart to this institutional value. Some, such as the young Popper, who grew up in the early 1920s, noted the profound changes taking place in science; not only did the new theories of Sigmund Freud and Karl Marx stand in need of evaluation, but there was also a profound revolution in physics in which the seemingly well-established theory of Newtonian mechanics was overthrown by Einstein's special and general theories of relativity and by quantum mechanics. Science is not a closed, static system of belief; it is open and dynamic, constantly undergoing revision and change through processes of critical enquiry. This led Popper to join with those who see:

> the distinguishing characteristic of empirical statements [scientific theories] in their susceptibility to revision – in the fact that they can be criticised, and superseded by better ones; and who regard it as their task to analyse the characteristic ability of science to advance, and the characteristic manner in which a choice is made, in crucial cases, between conflicting systems of theories. (Popper 1959: 49–50)

Here Popper endorses a fundamental aim that all science should strive to realize: being open to critical evaluation leading, where necessary, to revision or replacement. (What the canons of critical evaluation are is a controversial matter that can be set aside for the time being.)

In Popper's view science is a rational activity and as such must be governed by quite general aims; it is not an aimless activity. Popper also recognizes that some may have quite different aims for science other than the one just suggested. But it is hard to imagine what science would be like if it did not at least subject some claims to critical evaluation leading to (temporary) acceptance or revision and/or replacement. Not being open to such critical assessment is tantamount to not being science. Alternatively some might agree with Popper's aim of critical evaluation but disagree over the values that ought to be adopted in order to realize that aim. Here it is useful to draw a distinction that Popper does not fully make, namely, between a small set of values that are quite general and are regarded as *aims* constitutive of a certain conception or "image" of science and less general values, the role of which would be to bring about that aim. Here there might emerge differences in values since there is disagreement about the extent to which each value is efficacious in bringing about the agreed aim. But difference in values is thrown wide open if there is difference in aims.

To illustrate, consider Popper's own theory of critical rationalism or falsifiability as his preferred way of realizing the quite general aim of critical evaluation. In order to realize this aim he places a high value on falsifiability; and from this he draws out a number of other subsidiary values and rules that characterize his theory of scientific method. In this respect Popper thinks that these values, which are subordinate to the overall aim, are in conflict with inductivist and conventionalist values for science and their associated methodologies. Granted this, Popper famously writes of his proposal, which he calls his *criterion of demarcation* of science from non-science, that it "will accordingly have to be regarded as a *proposal for an agreement or convention* ... between parties having some purpose in common. The choice of that purpose must, of course, be ultimately a matter of decision, going beyond rational argument" (1959: 37). Here a combination of aims and values plays a quite fundamental role in determining what is to count as Popper's distinction between science and non-science. However, Popper does allow that there can be an incommensurability of aims and values for science. Whether there is no further way of deciding between rival sets of aims and their associated values and so their adoption is merely a matter of seemingly irrational decision is an important issue to be discussed within metamethodology: the theory of how we can decide between rival scientific methodologies that embody different aims and/or values (discussed further in §10.1.3).

As already mentioned, Popper also adopts another aim of science: to find satisfactory explanations. He also recognizes that explanatoriness can come in degrees in his talk of *explanatory depth*. Thus a theory T will be more explanatory than T^* if T unifies two disparate sets of laws or phenomena while T^* does not; or T will be more explanatory that T^* if it explains a law or theory by showing the limiting conditions under which T^* applies while T^* does not. (Thus the kinetic theory of gases has more explanatory depth than say, the Boyle–Charles law in that the former explains the limited conditions under which the latter applies.) The model of explanation Popper advocates is close to that of Hempel's deductive-nomological model of explanation (also extendable to non-deductive explanations and using statistical laws in the way advocated by Hempel). In Popper's view, what does the explaining will be satisfactory if it meets his criterion of demarcation, namely, falsifiability. So it would appear that explanatoriness is a subordinate aim while the aim of "criticizability", with its accompanying values and rules of Popperian falsificationism, is the more fundamental aim

2.6 Aims and values of science: Duhem

Duhem proposes an aim similar to Popper's, namely, explanation, when he asks: "What is the aim of physical theory?" But the similarity is superficial since he adopts a theory of explanation quite different from that of the Popper–Hempel theory. The two answers he canvasses are: (a) "A physical theory ... has for its object the *explanation* of a group of laws experimentally established"; and (b) "A physical theory ... is an abstract system whose aim is to *summarize* and *classify logically* a group of experimental laws without claiming to explain these laws" (Duhem 1954: 7). In Duhem's view answer (a) is committed to the following thought: "To explain (explicate, *explicare*) is to strip reality of the appearances covering it like a veil, in order to see the bare reality itself" (*ibid.*). In the light of this (a) is committed to the idea that the theory that does the explaining tells us what unobservable objects, properties and processes exist in reality, and that the laws of the theory correctly apply to this reality (or apply with some degree of verisimilitude). The aim of explanation is to put us in touch with this reality.

Understood this way, scientific realism is built into the aim of explanation. Here another quite general aim for science is at work, the alethic (or veritistic) aim of getting theories that tell us the truth about how the world is, not just at the level of what we can observe but also at the theoretical level (i.e. the theories have a high degree of verisimilitude). Duhem's characterization of (a) *via* its alethic aim is a feature of the Popper–Hempel theory of explanation since this requires the (approximate) truth of the *explanans* (which does the explaining). According to Duhem, this makes science, especially the physical sciences with which he was concerned, subordinate to metaphysics in that requirements that go beyond the experimental method, as he understood it, are imposed on what is to count as an explanation and what counts as getting at the truth. Once again what one counts as method in science plays a role in fleshing out what is to count as acceptable aims at least for physical theory.

Part (b) of Duhem's remarks above eschews such an account of explanation and uses another, thereby freeing science of the constraints of an allegedly undesirable metaphysics. It keeps something like the Popper–Hempel deductive link between what does the explaining and what is explained; and it keeps the nomological aspect in that the deductions link more fundamental hypotheses of a theory with experimentally determined laws. What is dropped is the requirement that the fundamental hypotheses be true of a hidden reality; they only have to be deductively linked to the experimentally determined laws. The hypotheses are true only in the sense that they deductively capture the experimental laws: "*Agreement with experiment is the sole criterion of truth for physical theory*" (*ibid.*: 21) Understanding the aim of science to be that of adequately capturing experimental laws (i.e. empirical adequacy) leads to a different set of subordinate values from that of the realist.

In the light of this overall aim, Duhem follows Ernst Mach in adopting the values of an "economy of thought" in which one chooses the theory that not only agrees with experiment but also has the following desirable features. The first is the value of unification: a large number of previously independent experimental laws and facts are unified in the sense that they are shown to be deducible from the few fundamental hypotheses of a theory (perhaps supplemented with auxiliary hypotheses). Since reduction in the number of independent laws and facts is central, there is a measure of unity in the following sense: theory T has greater unity than T^* if, with respect to the same scientific domain D, from T can be deduced more laws and facts in D than from T^*. The "psychological" value of "an economy of thought" is realized when the large number of independent laws and facts one has to grasp are replaced by a few fundamental hypotheses (and any required auxiliary assumptions) from which one can infer the larger number of independent laws and statements of fact.

Unity is an amorphous value that can mean many different things. Duhem's value of unity comes close to the Quine–Ullian virtue of generality. But it raises additional matters that need to be discussed. If the set of independent laws and singular observation statements to be unified is indefinitely large or infinite, then it might be difficult to construct measures of degrees of unity in which some theory T manages to unify more than some other theory T^* unifies. There is a clear case of greater degree of unification when the set of laws and singular claims that T^* unifies is properly included within the class that T unifies; otherwise measures of degree of unification are much harder to construct. Moreover, often in the process of unification the unifying theory corrects the laws to be unified. One of the classic examples of unification is that of the free-fall laws of Galileo and Kepler's laws of planetary motion by Newton's laws of motion; the laws to be unified are corrected in the process of their deduction from Newton's theory, thereby showing the limited conditions under which they apply. Here the notion of unification needs to be accompanied not merely by a theory of deduction but also a theory of deduction under limiting conditions or within some degree of approximation. Duhem makes much of the inconsistency between

Newton's theory and the laws of Kepler and Galileo; but he does not explicitly qualify his virtue of unity to allow for deduction under limiting conditions.

Suppose there is a failure of unification even under the less stringent conditions just mentioned. Then if some domain of laws and fact are not unified under looser conditions, is this a sign of lack of virtue, or even a vice, in a theory? Some who have a more "postmodern" understanding of science, or who are opposed to ideas of unity in science because they are anti-reductionist and advocate a more emergentist picture of science, would not see lack of unity as a vice but rather a virtue by their lights. A case for overall unity might be made on the basis of the fact that the various unified parts form a whole that realizes confirmatory virtues by obtaining greater confirmatory support as a result of forming a whole; also the unified theory has greater explanatory power. We shall see in §3.5 that Duhem's conception of the role of unity is more modest and does not include the ideal of overall unity. Surprisingly he allows for disunity, even the disunity of logical inconsistency. For Duhem, unity is a local, not a global, theoretical virtue.

Duhem also lists the virtue of generality discussed above as an economy of thought that brings together many instances under one law. There is also the value of systematicity of classification. In establishing the deductive connections between theory T and experimental laws, a structured grouping of laws (along with singular observational claims) can emerge. Laws originally thought to be disparate can be brought together into a new group owing to a similarity in their logical connections to T. The classic example here is the unification, by Newton's theory of motion, of laws of motion that were thought to obtain in distinct realms: the free-fall laws of Galileo, which applied in terrestrial regions, and Kepler's laws of planetary motion, which applied in the celestial realm. In contrast some laws originally thought to be closely related can end up in more distant groupings owing to their different logical connections to T. A theory will be more valuable the more systematic the classification it proposes (although there is the vexing problem of how degrees of systematicity of classification can be measured). Following from these values, the pragmatic values of beauty and elegance can also be realized through unity, generality and systematicity of classification.

Duhem wishes us to resist the urge to see in the increasing unity, generality and systematicity of our growing scientific theories the realization of the realists' goal of "tending towards a natural classification, thereby telling us about "bare reality". He claims that realists succumb to that temptation in thinking that theories that realize these values to greater and greater extents also realize the alethic value of truth about bare reality (even if they do not tell the whole story about bare reality). Although we might feel a strong pull in the realist's direction, it is something that transcends the legitimate bounds of what a methodology with Duhemian aims and values can deliver. This gives one reason for rejecting a value: its unrealizability, or our lack of a clear criterion of when we have realized it. In response the realist will have to specify a different theory of method that can reliably take us to the truth of our theories.

2.7 Epistemic and pragmatic values

The above difference between Popper and Duhem, and the many others who fall into one or other of these camps, raises the problem about rival aims for science. Realists advocate truth while anti-realists, from hard-core empiricists to more modulated constructive empiricists, reject or downplay this value. Both value theories that are true of all observable phenomena, no matter whether they are past, present or future. Such theories are said to be *empirically adequate*. (More accurately, since some constructive empiricists maintain that theories are sets of models, a theory is empirically adequate if and only if its models have sub-models that are isomorphic [or identifiable] with the phenomena.) To be empirically inadequate, that is to be false of some past, present or future phenomenon, is deemed by both to be a vice. However, realists want more than this; they also place a high value on those theories that give us truth about the unobservable realm commonly postulated in science, from claims about the existence of unobservables and their properties to law-like relations between them. If such truth is not available then realists might settle for theories that at least have some truth-likeness or verisimilitude. What is important for scientific realists is whether our theories are true or false of the world, or bear some similarity to it or represent it, not only in respect of what we can observe but also what we cannot observe but postulate in our theories.

In contrast constructive empiricists such as van Fraassen (1980) prescind from realist truth and aim only for empirical adequacy. They also add that when they accept a theory this does not entail that they believe it to be true. Rather, their acceptance of a theory indicates that they claim certain virtues for it that fall short of, and are independent of, the alethic value of truth as a concern for the full relation that a theory bears to the world. But not entirely, as included in their theoretical virtues are empirical adequacy, consistency and empirical strength. As has been indicated, the first two virtues do have an involvement with truth, but what of the third, empirical strength? The aim of constructive empiricists is to model the phenomena that we can observe; presumably the more phenomena modelled the better. Even in the case where two theories T and T^* are empirically adequate, T might model more phenomena than T^* does, and so have greater empirical strength. (More technically we can say of the models M of theory T and the models M^* of theory T^*, if every empirical sub-structure of M is isomorphic with some empirical sub-structure of M^*, then

T is *empirically at least as strong as T** [*ibid*.: 67]). If this is the case then theory *T* has the virtue of greater empirical strength than *T** and can be chosen on that basis. Putting this more loosely brings out the link to alethic values: *T* captures more of the truths about observational facts than *T** does.

For constructive empiricists there are important theoretical virtues that are not epistemic virtues. These are pragmatic virtues exhibited by a theory such as: mathematical elegance, beauty, simplicity, scope, unification and explanation. Of these van Fraassen writes: "In so far as they go beyond consistency, empirical adequacy, and empirical strength, they do not concern the relation between the theory and the world, but rather the use and usefulness of the theory; they provide reasons to prefer the theory independently of questions of truth" (*ibid*.: 88). Note that within constructive empiricism explanation is not taken to be an aim in the sense set out in §2.5; but it is nevertheless an important virtue. The virtue of having explanatory power need not be tied to the realist's notion of truth; but it can still serve the aims of the constructive empiricist's account of science if the explanatory hypotheses are empirically adequate, consistent and empirically strong.

What of confirmatory virtues for a constructive empiricist? Earlier, theoretical virtues were divided into two groups, epistemic and pragmatic, and the epistemic were further subdivided into the alethic and the confirmatory. This suggests a traditional view in which the confirmatory virtues play a role alongside alethic virtues in that the high confirmation of a hypothesis is linked to the idea of *H* being probably true. Constructive empiricists wish to sever such connections. The epistemic merits of a theory do not lie in its being true, but rather in its being empirically adequate and empirically strong and in whatever evidence we might have for this. But their position is more than this; they reject traditional accounts of confirmation with its rules of induction, the rule of inference to the best explanation, and the like. They opt for a quite different conception of epistemology that is probabilistic in character but without the baggage of much traditional epistemology.

This completes our survey of the notions of aims and values in science.[5] They play an important role in theories of method, but not necessarily an autonomous role as has been suggested. There are further aspects of methodology bound up with the notion of methodological rules – to which we now turn.

3. Rules and principles of method

In Chapter 2 a model of theory choice was presented in which values played a central role, but theory choice can also be governed by rules (alternatively norms, maxims or imperatives). In this chapter we shall discuss theories of scientific method understood as sets of rules of method or, as we prefer to say for reasons to be spelled out later, *principles* of method. Collections of such principles are commonly said to form theories of scientific method, and to embody the rationality of science. Section 3.1 sets out some commonly cited principles of method, some of the different kinds of principles there are, what connection there may be between values and principles and whether a principle or a value formulation of methodologies is preferable. Other historically proposed principles of method will emerge in §§3.3–3.5 and elsewhere throughout the book. Principles of method have some important features, such as reliability, robustness, power and speed. What these mean is spelled out in §3.2. Principles of method are not arbitrary and need to be justified in some way; this is the province of metamethodology, which is discussed in Chapter 4 (with further chapters setting out reasons for accepting or rejecting some putative principles of method). Features such as reliability, robustness, power and speed play an important role in critically assessing principles of method. After all, we do want reliable rules, we want them to apply in a wide range of possible epistemic situations and we want them to apply broadly to many theories and to be readily usable.

A principles-based approach to methodology has been common throughout the history of science and its accompanying theories of method. Although the focus of this book is not historical, the role of a principles-based approach to method can be readily illustrated by considering some of the principles that have been proposed in the past and that have been influential, some of which are still important. There is a rich history of putative methodological principles that helps put some flesh on the bones of more abstract considerations of principles. In addition some historically proposed principles have also embodied important criteria used in the demarcation of science from non-science. As a first illustration we consider briefly in §3.3 some of the principles that Descartes proposed in his *Rules for the Direction of the Mind*. In our selective treatment we pick out some of those rules that are intended to realize the aim of certainty in science; that is, the Cartesian principles of method illustrate hypothetical imperatives in which a rule is claimed to reliably realize something deemed of value, namely, certainty (a value rarely advocated in twentieth-century methodology). These principles also provide a criterion of demarcation for science based in certainty. In §3.4 we consider Newton's "Rules of Reasoning in Philosophy". Surprisingly in a subject that deals with the rationality of science, there is much rivalry between different theories of method, the Newtonian and Cartesian methodologies being no exception; we spell out a few of these differences. Newton's rules also played an important part in the actual constructions found in his "The System of the World" (*Principia*, Book III). We provide a brief sketch of this, thereby showing that methodological principles were an integral part of his science and not a distant influence on it. His rules are also important because they were taken up by subsequent scientists who wished to adopt some explicit account of scientific method (although they might not have followed such rules in their actual practice).[1] Finally we consider in §3.5 a number of principles of method proposed by Duhem, several of which still have their advocates today. There are many contemporary principles of method considered elsewhere in the book that are either the same as these historically proposed principles or are developments of them; hence their mention here as an introduction to a principles-based conception of methodology.

3.1 Values, rules and principles of method

For each value there is a closely associated rule telling us to follow certain paths of action such as (assuming all other things are equal): choose the simplest hypothesis; choose the most fruitful hypothesis; do not choose internally inconsistent hypotheses; make the most conservative change when inconsistency arises; and so on. Rules, like values, need not be followed one at a time; two or more rules may be conjoined, telling us to perform the action that conforms to them all. But, as with values, it may not be possible to follow all the rules at the same time since they offer inconsistent advice. Thus sometimes we may be able to follow two rules that say, in the case of finding the curve that fits given data, "choose the simplest hypothesis" and "choose the most accurate hypothesis". But sometimes we cannot follow both since they can select different hypotheses; the most accurate need not be the simplest and the simplest need not be the most accurate. There is an aggregation problem for rules just as there is for values. Nor is it clear whether there is a meta-rule that tells us how a trade-off between conflicting rules might be made. The *ceteris paribus* qualification "other things being equal" must also be heeded as the rules apply in different contexts where different matters may be relevant and where different rules may also have an application.

Principles of method will include the above rules. In general such principles can be understood as categorical imperatives that, like the Ten Commandments, are to admit no exception in any circumstance; they say "always one ought to do *X*", for example, "*always* one ought to choose the most accurate hypothesis". These are principles of obligation that tell us what we must do. But methodological principles can also be rules of permission that prescribe neither that we are obliged to do *X* nor obliged not to do *X*. In addition principles might be conditional and say "if condition *C* obtains then always one ought to do *X*", for example, "if a theory is in trouble and must be revised, then always one ought to adopt the most conservative alteration". One task in methodology would then be to spell out the conditions *C* that can obtain. Some conditions of application might be well known and can be set out in detail. But as Feyerabend often points out, other conditions might not be well known, or not envisaged at all, especially those that have not yet arisen but might in the future when we come to apply old principles in quite new circumstances. Such conditions might not only be lengthy but also incomplete, open-ended or indefinite, thereby leading to unwieldy imperatives that are difficult to express.

The following are a few examples of rules of method some of which can also be expressed as values. They are also examples of what we shall call methodological principles or *M-principles*.

1. One ought to accept only those theories that explain all the successes of their predecessors and repeat none of their failures; otherwise they are to be rejected.
2. One ought to avoid *ad hoc* theories.
3. Given some rival hypotheses and a large set of facts they all explain, then one ought to pick that hypothesis that best explains all the facts.
4. One ought to accept the simplest theory and reject those that are more complex.
5. One ought to avoid theories that postulate unobservables unless they have an operational basis. (This is a rule of strong empiricism, which does not eschew unobservables entirely.)
6. When a new theory replaces its immediate predecessor but also contradicts it, then one ought to adopt as the new theory the theory that contains the older theory approximately under certain assumptions of values of parameters of the new theory. (This is akin to Bohr's principle of correspondence.)

7. In conditions of experimentation on human subjects, one ought to prefer double-blind over single-blind experiments and never perform an unblinded experiment.

Another form that principles of method can take is that of hypothetical ought-imperatives in which the antecedent is a rule telling what we ought to do, and the consequent some value that is to be realized by following the rule. These are hypothetical ought-imperatives of instrumental rationality in which we ought to follow some rule in order to realize some value. They may have one or other of the following forms, where r is a rule we are to follow and v is a value to be realized.

Hypothetical imperative: One ought to follow rule r (in conditions C) if one wants to realize value v.
(Alternatively: following r always realizes v, or only n per cent of the time, where n is less than 100 per cent but is sufficiently high so that the principle is not entirely worthless.)

Comparative hypothetical ought-imperative: (in conditions C) One ought to follow rule r rather than r^* if one wishes to realize v.
(Alternatively: r leads to v all the time and r^* does not, or r leads to v n per cent of the time while r^* leads to v m per cent of the time where $n > m$ and n is high.)

Examples of hypothetical imperatives of method, or M-principles, are the following.
8. One ought to avoid *ad hoc* hypotheses (r) rather than accept *ad hoc* hypotheses (r^*) if one values highly refutable theories (v).
9. One ought to accept those theories that explain all the observational successes of their predecessors (r) since this is more likely to lead to truth [alternatively empirical adequacy] (v) than accepting those theories that do not explain all their predecessor's observational successes (r^*).
10. Where there is a conflict between theory T and what we observe, then one ought to form new theory T^* by making the minimum adjustments to T (r), since new T^* is more likely to evade falsification (v) than would any other theory in which the modifications are more than the minimum (r^*).
11. One ought to accept the theory that makes novel true predictions (r) since this is more likely to lead to the truth (v) than accepting any rival theory that captures the same observational information but makes no novel predictions (r^*).

Ought one to follow any of these principles of method? Are these just rules of thumb that are not to be dignified by calling them principles of method?

Nothing has been said about how we might address these questions; this a matter deferred to discussion in subsequent chapters about how metamethodologists attempt to justify such principles.

The above view of the form principles of method can take is to be found in philosophers such as Popper and Lakatos, but it has come into its own through the work of Larry Laudan (1996: pt IV). Laudan also argues that hypothetical imperatives are the main constituents of methodologies rather than categorical imperatives. These are often elliptically expressed, or suppress reference to specific values. Thus "follow rule r" ought more properly to be expressed as "you ought to follow rule r if you wish to realize value v", in which reference to some value is made explicit. While this may be true for values, it may not be correct for aims (see the aim–value distinction in §2.5). For some methodologists it might be hard to see how values, when they become highly general aims such as truth, explanatory power or empirical adequacy, can, when expressed in the form of categorical principles (such as "always one ought to seek truth"), have a further value added to them, turning them into hypothetical principles. However, for most categorical rules there is an implicit value that they realize that can, and ought to, be made explicit.

The above categorical and hypothetical imperatives of method need not always be understood to be universally applicable without exception. A more fruitful understanding is to allow them to be *defeasible*. A defeasible rule, or principle, is a generalization that specifies what one ought to do in normal or *standard* circumstances (although these are not set out in any antecedent clause). Importantly, defeasible principles allow for exceptions, but these do not lead to their rejection. Even though they can be defeated in particular circumstances that may not be specifiable in advance, they can still be accepted. In allowing that they be defeasible, principles of method resemble laws of nature. These can also have unspecified *ceteris paribus* conditions of constraint on their application, or *ceteris absentibus* conditions (other things being absent); but their defeasibility does not lead to their falsification and so rejection. It is also commonly said of moral obligations that we have a *prima facie* obligation to follow some moral rule, but in some circumstances the obligation can be defeated. The same can be said of principles of method; they also express *prima facie* obligations to make certain choices that can be defeated. In what follows we shall take the categorical or hypothetical imperatives of method to be defeasible.

As can be seen from the above, principles of method are quite broad; only a subset are directly equivalent to a formulation in terms of values. What is the difference between formulating theories of method in terms of values and in terms of rules? Kuhn, who addresses this question, writes: "the criteria of choice with which I began function not as rules, which determine choice, but as values which influence it" (1977: 331). Each value in Kuhn's model of weighted values influences the choice of theory without determining it. Values orient one in a field of possibilities of theory choice whereas rules tend to be more prescriptive and give one definite directives about what to choose. If rules are understood as exceptionless categoricals then, as Kuhn says, they will determine choices in all situations in which they are employed. But if they are understood as defeasible rules or principles, then they do not always determine choice but, like values, can influence it. Kuhn recognizes the affinity between values and rules when he writes: "my list of the values guiding scientific choice is, as nearly as makes any difference, identical with the tradition's list of rules dictating choice" (*ibid.*: 333). There is still a difference between influencing and dictating choice; but it is downplayed when Kuhn also adds that each scientist might flesh out the rules differently, as they do values. This is not quite the same as understanding rules as defeasible rather than exceptionless categoricals; but to so understand them is to make vanishingly small the difference between influencing/guiding on the one hand and determining/dictating on the other. It is also important to note that in concrete situations value-based and rule-based methodologies commonly lead to the same theory choices. Given the above considerations, contrary to Kuhn's position we can see no real difference between criteria of choice expressed as values or expressed as rules (where the rules are understood liberally as defeasible or conditional, and not always as strict categoricals).

In the literature on methodology the terms "principle" and "rule" are used interchangeably. Here we use the first rather than the second term to refer to the broad category of principles of method, with some principles containing rules as components. There are several sub-categories of methodological principles. The first contains the M-principles listed above; they may be rules that are categorical imperatives, or they may be mixed rule/value hypothetical imperatives. Since each value has an associated defeasible categorical rule, we can include, without too much strain, values and aims as a second sub-category within the broad notion of principles of method. A third sub-category of principles of method includes deductive and inductive rules of inference. We will also say: a scientific method is a set of such principles of method.

What is so great about the principles of method that have been proposed? What are the grounds for accepting or rejecting these? Are they no more than rules of thumb, or do they have more substance than this? On what grounds are they to be "validated", shown correct or justified? Often this is a matter to be settled within metamethodology (although in the case of rule 6 other matters also come into play, such as experimental discoveries about placebos). These are matters raised elsewhere. In what follows we discuss some desirable properties of principles of method; and we illustrate further principles of method through the prominence some have had in the history of methodology.

3.2 Some features of principles of method

There are some important features of many principles of method that need to be noted: reliability, robustness, power and speed. Hypothetical imperatives must be reliable in the sense that following *r* either realizes the associated value 100 per cent of the time, or more often than not. How might the reliability be established? One way is *a priori*; there is a proof that shows that following *r* realizes *v* (all or most of the time). Showing this would be part of the province of metamethodology and would be one of the best ways of guaranteeing reliability. Another way would be empirical; the task would be to show on empirical grounds that the method is 100 per cent reliable or exceeds a minimally acceptable degree of reliability (less than 100 per cent but above a minimum acceptable threshold). This is the approach suggested by Laudan (1996: pt IV) in his account of normative naturalism. But what empirically based method should one employ to determine reliability since establishing principles of method is the matter at hand? To show empirically that *r* realizes *v n* per cent of the time would require a theory of statistical method to establish the frequency of realization. But then the status of that bit of statistical method cannot be presupposed and needs to be examined. This raises questions about metamethodology in general (see Chapter 4) and normative naturalism in particular (§12.2).

Another matter concerns what might be called the *counterfactual robustness of principles of method*. We wish our principles of method to be sufficiently reliable in this world in which we use them. But what about other worlds, either like ours or worlds quite different from ours? A principle of method that was reliable in all possible worlds would of course be quite acceptable; it would be a necessarily true principle. If we include rules of deductive logic in the broad class of principles of method (as we have), then the valid deductive rules are 100 per cent *conditionally* reliable for the truth of their conclusions in this world, and in every other world. They are not absolutely reliable for the truth of their conclusions; if at least one premise is false then any conclusion could be true or could be false. But on the condition that all the premises are true, then valid rules of inference are 100 per cent reliable in yielding true conclusions. Moreover in all possible worlds in which valid deductive principles are used they are 100 per cent conditionally reliable; and there are proofs of this, one of which is based in the truth-table method for showing validity. We can say that the valid deductive rules are maximally robust in that they are 100 per cent conditionally reliable in all possible worlds.

What about inductive rules of inference? We wish them to be 100 per cent conditionally reliable in this world, or at least reach some minimal but high threshold of *n* per cent reliability. That is, given true premises then an inductive rule will yield a true conclusion (100 per cent of the time or at least *n* per cent of the time for high *n*). But inductive rules are not so reliable in all possible worlds;

there are many weird worlds in which they are not conditionally reliable and induction fails. Is our world one such weird world? This is something we cannot guarantee, and is part of the problem of justifying induction. Hume invited us to envisage the possibility that our inductions might well break down in the future; since this is a logical possibility inductive rules cannot be maximally robust in the way deductive rules are.

In contrast it would be sheer epistemic luck if there were very few worlds in which induction is reliable, and our world just happened to be one of them. We need more than sheer epistemic luck. Given our scientific investigations up until now, it is not fully clear to us which world we are in; there are many worlds that are compatible with what we have been able to discern given our ordinary beliefs and our scientific theories up until now. What we would like is for our inductive rules to be reliable in all of the possible worlds that are compatible with (much of) what we already know about our world. If the rules were not reliable, and our actual world turned out to be one of the worlds in which induction was not reliable despite appearances up until now, then induction would be a failure in our world. This suggests that we require of our inductive rules of inference that they be conditionally reliable in a sub-class of possible worlds that also includes our world. Thus if induction is reliable in our world it will not exhibit maximal robustness, but it will have some degree of robustness sufficient for us to keep using induction through all those worlds that are compatible with what we currently know.

Similar claims can be made on behalf of the M-principles of method we have sketched above that are not deductive or inductive principles of inference. We want them to be reliable in realizing in our theories whatever value might be associated with them. And we want them to be robust, at least to the extent that M-principles apply across a wide range of possible worlds; that is, they are contingent and not necessarily true.

We would also like our M-principles to be powerful. Some M-principles of a methodology might be quite narrow in the range of applications they can have, so they are hardly ever used to realize their associated values; but when they are used they are sufficiently reliable in realizing their associated values. More directly, M-principles are used in theory choice; but some might be quite narrow and rarely used in choosing theories. But when they are used they are sufficiently reliable in picking out theories with the desired value. Throughout the history of all the sciences there will be many cases in which choices between theories have to be made. But if the M-principles we employ are not powerful then there may be many cases where no choice can be made (even though they may be reliable in the cases of the few choices they do enable us to make). As a result the growth of science is quite slow since such M-principles leave us bereft of knowledge that we might otherwise have had if the principles we used had wider applicability and so were stronger. What we would like are M-principles that are not only reliable but are also powerful. That is, there is a sufficiently wide range of cases in which they are applicable and in which they do choose theories that reliably realize some value; they do not leave us in a relatively impoverished state due to their inability to make very many theory choices.

Finally, speed. We would like our M-principles to be usable in a reasonably short period of time. Principles that might take a very long time for us to use, so that few choices ever get made, would be less desirable than M-principles, which do take us to outcomes of theory choice in a much shorter period of time. However, quickly usable M-principles might not be very powerful, or even reliable. Some methodologists have thought of a methodology as sets of easily usable rules of thumb. While these might be speedy in application, they might not be very powerful, or might not be very reliable. So there is a trade-off here concerning some of the desirable features of M-principles, and more generally for any principle of method. These features of principles of method are metamethodological in character and play a role in their metamethodological justification. Given rival rules we may choose them on the basis of their reliability, robustness, power and speed of use.

3.3 Methodological principles from the history of science, I: Descartes

The history of science and philosophy is replete with examples of principles of method proposed as the core of various conceptions of science. Here we shall consider some proposals from Descartes, Newton and Duhem. The remainder of the book will focus on contemporary theories of method and their M-principles.

The twenty-one rules in Descartes's *Rules for the Direction of the Mind*, begun in 1619 but abandoned by 1628, are not the promising start to a theory of method that they seem, although, as they were reworked in his later *Discourse on Method*, they did influence subsequent conceptions of science and are part of a popular view in which certainty is the aim of science. The first two rules are categorical imperatives in which the aim of science is to at least obtain truths that are also certain or indubitable:

> *Rule 1*: The aim of our studies should be to direct the mind with a view to forming true and sound judgements about whatever comes before it.
> *Rule 2*: We should attend only to those objects of which our minds seem capable of having certain and indubitable cognition.[2]

While truth is still an aim of realists, perhaps the last philosopher to endorse certainty as an aim for science was Edmund Husserl. Although the aim of certainty has had a long history of advocates from the time of Aristotle onwards, its recent career has been much more chequered. It has been rejected by nearly all twentieth-century philosophers of science as a goal; if the strong variety of Cartesian certainty were to be adopted most science would fail to meet it. Since most theories undergo fairly constant revision over time, certainty cannot be an aim of science; theories open to revision cannot be certain. Much of science cannot be certain for a further important reason. Once science became a growing enterprise it was well recognized by the eighteenth century that its observations and measurements were always to be specified with a degree of error. In Book III of his *Philosophiae Naturalis Principia Mathematica* (*Principia*), Newton was well aware, when he was constructing the "system of the world", that certain values such as the distance between the earth and the moon could only be given mean values, and that there was an error factor in all measurements of, for example, the diameter of the earth. Methods for estimating means, or error factors, have become a central part of all science. There need to be more realistic aims for science that characterize it, rather than utopian aims such as certainty, which do not since they exclude most of science.

There are a number of realizable values with which certainty should not be confused, such as hypothesis *H* has a high degree of (probabilistic) support by evidence, or has passed tests, or has initial plausibility and so on. However, the criteria for Cartesian certainty are not merely that a person *A* has the best possible evidence at a time for belief in *H*, or that they have an overwhelming conviction about the truth of *H*. Cartesian varieties of certainty are much stronger, for example: *H* is (absolutely) certain (logically immune to doubt) if and only if it is logically impossible for person *A* to believe that *H* yet *H* be false; or, there is no evidence such that if it were to become available to *A* it would undermine *A*'s belief in *H*, and *A* knows that this is so. Since few hypotheses ever meet such stringent standards of certainty, including propositions about the existence of external objects, then science would surely fall foul of them, including Descartes's own science despite his attempts to found it in certainty. Our scientific beliefs are open to doubt in this strong sense; most recent characterizations make science fallible. This is an important change in our idea of the aim of science, of which Laudan writes: "this shift represents one of the great watersheds in the history of scientific philosophy; the abandonment of the quest for certainty" (1984: 83).

> *Rule 3*: Concerning objects proposed for study, we ought to investigate what we can clearly and evidently intuit or deduce with certainty, and not what other people have thought or what we ourselves conjecture. For knowledge [*scientia*] can be attained in no other way.

This rule can be understood to express Descartes's demarcation of science from non-science. He correctly rules out merely conjectural and untested beliefs as part of science; but it is unclear whether Descartes also wishes to rule out the role conjectures can play within the H-D method. What he recommends is a model of scientific knowledge based on: (a) the certainty of our intuitions, where these are whatever can be mentally apprehended, such as sensory experience, and, he argues, are certain; and (b) a chain of deductions that also fall within the category of certain intuitions. This rule recommends a classical foundational picture for science in which, on the basis of observations guaranteed to be certain, we deduce, also with certainty, the edifice of scientific theory. Since nothing else is to count as science this rule yields a Cartesian criterion of demarcation.

Rule 4 gives us the almost empty advice that "we need a method if we are to investigate the truth of things". But this becomes more significant when he tells us in the commentary that follows the rule: "by 'a method' I mean reliable rules which are easy to apply and such that if one follows them exactly, one will never take what is false to be true ... but will gradually and constantly increase one's knowledge". Descartes's thought is nicely captured by the conception of methodological principles introduced in the previous sections. He envisages methodology as comprising hypothetical imperatives or M-principles that have the goal of truth (verisimilitude?), or increasing knowledge; moreover they are to be reliable and easy to apply.

The next rule, which is intended to meet these criteria, gives only a general and somewhat unspecific directive:

Rule 5: The whole method consists entirely in the ordering and arranging of the objects on which we must concentrate our mind's eye if we are to discover some truth. We shall be following this method exactly if we first reduce complicated and obscure propositions step by step to simpler ones, and then, starting with the intuition of the simplest ones of all, try to ascend through the same steps to knowledge of the rest.

There is, first, a reductive or analytical step away from complex propositions to simple propositions of which one ought to have certain intuitions. This is followed by a reconstructive and synthesizing phase in which knowledge is arrived at that replaces the originally obscure propositions we entertained. These two processes remain very schematic; even though the general directive is clear there is no heuristic accompanying it that would enable one to apply it in particular cases. However, several of Descartes's remaining rules, which we shall not explore, do attempt to be more specific and are applied to sciences with which he was acquainted, such as optics and physics, thereby fleshing out the rules.

Finally there is an underlying directive that appears in his commentary on the rules mentioned above concerning the overall *unity* of science and of the world's *comprehensibility* to us. As he tells us in his commentary on Rule 1, it is a mistake to think, because we learn the sciences separately and they are often about different objects, that the sciences are disparate. Instead there is a unity to be discovered in all the sciences, although he does not say exactly what that unity is beyond claiming of the sciences that "they are all interconnected and interdependent". This is a claim about ontological unity. The directive to seek it out is accompanied by a cognitive claim about the extent of human wisdom and thought that underlies our ability to come to understand this unity. Given the way we are, and the alleged fact of ontological unity, it is possible for us human beings to aim for, and realize, comprehensibility in our scientific conception of the world as a whole. Here comprehensibility can be understood to at least involve the aims of explanation and understanding that would display the unity of the sciences. These two Cartesian sub-rules can also be expressed as values we wish our theories to realize, namely, unity and comprehensibility.

Descartes's rules conform to the conception of principles of method outlined at the beginning of this chapter. But they set out an image of science largely based in certainty; they make a proposal about demarcation by specifying that science ought to conform to a foundational view of the structure of knowledge of deduction from intuitions; and they entail directives about seeking unity in the sciences and in seeking comprehensiveness in our understanding. Although the rules move at a high level of generality in which it remains quite unclear how they are to apply to particular sciences, they still give us a broad, although limited, framework of principles that can be used to provide a methodologically based account of scientific rationality, and from this a specifically Cartesian image of science.

3.4 Methodological principles from the history of science, II: Newton

Newton proposed some influential principles of method in his *Principia*, Book III, "The System of the World". These are his four "Rules of Reasoning in Philosophy". They permeate his mathematical treatment of the solar system and his derivation of the law of universal gravity. In the third edition of the *Principia*, Newton's rules are formulated as follows.[3]

> *Rule 1*: No more causes of natural things should be admitted than are both true and sufficient to explain their phenomena.
> *Rule 2*: Therefore, the causes assigned to natural effects of the same kind must be, so far as possible, the same.

The first two are ontological rules of parsimony concerning causes. When it comes to postulating causes of phenomena, we are not to postulate too many, and when we do postulate some we should always assign to like effects like causes. (Note that Rule 2 is not the same as the less questionable causal principle that to like causes we should assign like effects.) Newton says little in justification of these rules. Concerning the first he merely writes that "nature is simple and does not indulge in the luxury of superfluous causes". This is an ontological claim about how the world is, and it is distinct from a methodological principle that tells us to be parsimonious in the postulation of causes. The ontological claim cannot support the methodological principle; but the successful adoption of the methodological principle can give us grounds for thinking that the ontological claim is true of how the world is. Taken together they can be viewed as propounding a version of the principle of common cause; that is, where effects are similar in similar situations, do not suppose different causes but suppose that the same kind of common cause is at work in each. Rules 1 and 2 are not universally strict but are defeasible; as Newton writes, they should be followed "as far as is possible".

Such rules may well be presuppositions that scientists make without further question across a range of different sciences. However, it is in large part due to Newton's clarity about how he was to argue for his theory of the world, particularly for universal gravitational attraction and laws governing its operation, that these rules are explicitly stated as principles employed in his reasoning. How do they do their work? Newton had a broad view of what he called "phenomena", which included phenomenal laws about how classes of objects behaved. Included as phenomena are two of Kepler's laws of planetary motion. Newton sets out phenomenal laws governing each of the known satellites in the solar system, namely, the planets as they orbit the sun, and the orbiting moons of these planets including the moon as it orbits earth. One law says that if a radius is drawn from each to its orbital centre, then each sweeps out equal areas in equal times in their orbital paths. Another law says that, for each satellite, if T is its periodic time and D is its mean distance from its orbital centre, then $T^2 \propto D^3$. On the basis of these phenomena Newton argues for the important proposition that the force acting towards the centre obeys an inverse square law.

The analysis Newton provided of the motion of an orbiting body requires two forces: one that brings about straight-line motion at a tangent to the orbit; and another directed towards the centre of the body about which it orbits, constantly pulling it out of this straight-line motion, called the *centripetal force*. In Propositions 1–3 of Book III of *Principia*, Newton shows, on the basis of their respective phenomenal laws, that the satellites of Jupiter, the sun and the earth (i.e. the moon) are each acted on by a centripetal force that draws the satellites out of their straight-line motion, and in each case the centripetal force acts according to an inverse square law. What is this centripetal force? Proposition 4 makes the then novel claim that in the case of the moon the centripetal force is nothing other than the earth's gravitational attraction: "The Moon gravitates towards the Earth and by the force of gravity is always drawn back from rectilinear motion and kept in its orbit". Such a proposition goes well beyond the mathematical derivations from the phenomena to the inverse square law found up to Proposition 3. It is here that the rules do their work.

Important background to Proposition 4 is the general acceptance by Newton's time of the belief that the earth and the planets are made of the same matter; they are not made of different substances as the Aristotelians supposed. It was also generally recognized that everyday objects close to the surface of the earth are "heavy" due to their gravitational attraction by the earth. Through Newton's laws of motion, it is also generally recognized that there are forces acting on accelerating bodies. Given this, the startling new claim of Proposition 4 is that the force that acts on familiar bodies close to the earth's surface and is responsible for their "heaviness", namely, gravity, is also the very same force producing the motion of a heavenly body well away from the surface of the earth, namely, the moon. The force that makes rocks fall also keeps the moon in its orbit! With this are laid the foundations of the idea of a gravitational field extending from the bodies about which satellites orbited, and then the more general idea that all bodies gravitationally attract one another.

In Proposition 4, and its scholium, Newton presents his argument explicitly citing Rule 1 and Rule 2. He envisages what it would be like for the moon to lack all motion except that due to the force pulling it to the centre of the earth. He also investigates the different measurements of the earth–moon distance (about 60.5 earth semidiameters) and then asks: how far would the moon fall in one minute when at that distance from the earth (assuming the previous propositions that the force varies with the inverse square of the distance)? He then compares this with the distance a terrestrial body would fall when close to the surface of the earth (where the inverse square forces would be much greater). This is an experimental result that had been well established by measurements by the Dutch scientist Christiaan Huygens (1629–95). What Newton then shows is that the distance the moon would fall in one minute from the height of its orbit when under the action of a force at that distance corresponds exactly to the distance a terrestrial object would fall in one second when close to the earth's surface and under the much stronger force acting at the closer distance. Given that these are mathematically similar effects obtained by applying the same inverse square law to the different bodies at different distances, what conclusion can be drawn about the forces at work? In the case of the terrestrial object the force is due to gravitation. But what about the force on the moon? Applying Rule 2, in which like effects are to be assigned like causes, Newton argues that the causes are the same, namely, gravitational.

But we need more than Rule 2 to establish this result more securely as it might be open to us to assign different causes. Newton invites us to consider two possibilities: (a) that the moon lacks any gravity and (b) its falling is due to another cause in addition to that of gravity. In the case of (a) we are in breach of Rule 1, which tells us not to introduce superfluous causes. To suppose the moon lacks gravity, yet falls in much the same way as other terrestrial bodies, is to suppose a curious kind of doppelganger force that acts, in the case of the moon, in much the same way as gravity, but is not gravity. This is ruled out by the parsimony of Rule 1, which tells us not to postulate a superfluity of causes. Considering (b), if the force acting on the moon is different from that of gravity, then Newton argues that it would be under the action of two forces and would fall much faster, in fact twice as fast as he shows; and this is contrary to anything that is experienced of falling bodies. Thus Rule 1 and Rule 2 play a crucial role in showing that the centripetal force is none other than gravity, and that the action of gravity on terrestrial bodies can be extended to the moon. None of this tells us anything about the nature of gravity itself, something about which Newton remained agnostic. But in showing that the moon's centripetal force is gravitational, Newton begins his extension of the action of gravity beyond the surface of the earth to the moon – and beyond the moon to the rest of the universe as he subsequently argues. The rules play a crucial role in the kind of theoretical unification that Newton made concerning terrestrial and celestial motions.

Without drawing on Rule 1 and Rule 2, either explicitly mentioned as in the case of Newton, or perhaps implicitly in the case of most others, no good argument is available to the conclusion that the moon is under the action of the same gravitational force of the earth as are all other terrestrial bodies. Rule 1 and Rule 2 embody certain metaphysical assumptions about causation, such as that in the causal structure of the world there is parsimony of causes that, on the whole, rules out the logical possibility of the same effects being due to two or more different causes. Also, Rule 2 is not without its false instances, as Newton's discussion of the rule reveals when he claims on the basis of it that we are to assign the same cause to the same effects of "the light of a kitchen fire and the Sun". The rule needs supplementation by restrictions on the kinds of effects to which it can be applied. The rules also express methodological constraints on what causes to postulate. As such they express in a simple but direct way a number of more elaborate considerations to be found in contemporary causal methodology about how we are to correctly specify the causes really at work, given the phenomena we observe.

The rules also function as principles of theory choice; they tell us which of rival causal hypotheses we are to choose. This becomes clearer in Newton's next two rules:

Rule 3: Those qualities of bodies that cannot be intended and remitted [i.e. qualities that cannot be increased or diminished] and that belong to all bodies on which experiments can be made, should be taken as qualities of all bodies universally.

Rule 4: In experimental philosophy, propositions gathered from phenomena by induction should be considered either exactly or very nearly true not withstanding any contrary hypotheses, until yet other phenomena make such propositions either more exact or liable to exception.

Following this there is the important addendum: "This rule should be followed so that arguments based on induction may not be nullified by hypotheses".

These two rules concern the use of inductive inference in science (broadly understood). Newton's worry underlying Rule 3 is: how do we know that the properties that we assign to bodies in our experiments done here on earth also apply to bodies elsewhere on earth, elsewhere in the solar system, or elsewhere in the entire universe, past, present and future? If there is no guarantee that what we postulate for objects here and now cannot apply at other times and places for similar objects throughout the entire universe, then science would be impossible. This was of acute concern to Newton since he wished to apply laws he had discovered here on earth to all bodies in the universe. And the only way to do this is to suppose some principle of induction. A rival view that the laws of nature could vary over time and space remains speculative. Perhaps some laws do have an unnoticed temporal parameter; but the question remains whether the most basic laws of nature are themselves temporally and spatially invariant. If so, then if the laws we discover to apply here and now are to be applied elsewhere in the universe, as they commonly are, then something like Newton's Rule 3 is at work.

For Newton, what we now call science was called *experimental philosophy*. One understanding of Rule 4 is to view it as Newton's demarcation principle distinguishing science from what he called "hypotheses", a term he increasingly used in a disparaging way. In the "General Scholium" to Book III of *Principia* he tells us: "whatever is not deduced from the phenomena must be called a hypothesis ... [and hypotheses] have no place in experimental philosophy". Scholars have spilled much ink on what exactly Newton means by "induction" and "deduced from the phenomena". Despite the several ways in which these can be understood (either broadly or narrowly), historically they provided a Newtonian demarcation criterion for science that was subsequently very influential. Our task here is to briefly indicate the way in which Rule 3 and Rule 4 entered into Newton's theorizing about the world.

In Proposition 5 Newton argues that each of the moons of Jupiter and Saturn, and the satellites of the sun, are also under the action of centripetal forces that obey an inverse square law. These are mathematically just the same as the motion of the moon about the earth. So Rule 2 is invoked to infer that their centripetal forces are none other than gravitational forces. Thus gravitational attraction is extended to all the bodies in the solar system. In the scholium that follows Proposition 5 he says: "For the cause of the centripetal force [i.e. gravity] by which the Moon is kept in its orbit ought to be extended to all the planets by Rules 1, 2 and 4". We have seen the roles that Rule 1 and Rule 2 play here. What role does Rule 4 play?

In invoking Rule 4 Newton issues a challenge to anyone who would deny the extension of the force of gravity from the case of terrestrial objects and the moon to all the other planets and satellites in the solar system. Whatever Newton means by "deduction from the phenomena" and "induction", his procedure is sufficiently illustrated by the way he arrives at the inverse square law from the phenomena. In addition he has promulgated the additional rules he needs to infer that all the centripetal forces at work are gravitational. If someone is to deny that gravity can be so extended, then Newton's challenge to them is not to idly hypothesize some alternative, but to do the hard work of "deducing" the alternative from some phenomena, either the same as he has used or different. Only then can an alternative hypothesis be taken seriously as a bit of experimental philosophy (science). Without this it remains a speculation not to be taken seriously. Thus Rule 4 is a strong backing for the hypothesis of universal gravitation; it is not to be undermined by any alternative hypothesis that is not arrived at by playing the game of science according to Rule 4. The use of Rule 4 as a challenge is somewhat negative; however, it makes positive recommendations about induction and "deducing from the phenomena" that Newton's science itself illustrates in Book III.

Finally to a use of Rule 3 that arises in Corollary 2 to Proposition 6 in Book III. Rule 3 tells us: if there is a certain set of qualities in bodies such that (a) they cannot vary (i.e. cannot be intended and remitted), and (b) are experimentally found in all bodies close to the earth, then infer by induction (c) all bodies everywhere in the universe have these properties. Although it is not clear exactly what Newton's medieval terminology of intention (an increase) and remission (a decrease) means, his examples are clear enough. Extension and hardness are such properties possessed by bodies; but the magnitude of these properties can vary from body to body. Since these properties, of whatever magnitude, satisfy (a) and (b), we can infer that bodies everywhere have them. A useful way of putting the matter is to think of constant parametric values.[4] The values of the magnitudes of extension and hardness are fixed in the case of some particular body under investigation; but different constant parametric values of these properties will obtain for different bodies.

In Proposition 6 Newton argues that conditions (a) and (b) are met by two further properties: the property of being "heavy" or gravitating towards the earth, and the property of the quantity of matter in a body or its inertial mass. And the same conditions are met by the ratio of the mass of a body to its gravitational attraction to the earth. Since this ratio is a parametric constant, as has been experimentally found for all bodies with respect to the earth, then by Rule 3 it is a constant for all bodies anywhere (terrestrial and celestial) with respect to the earth. The ground is now clear for the claim in Proposition 7 that "Gravity exists in all bodies universally and is in proportion to the quantity of matter in each".

There is an important ancillary effect of Rule 3, which is to provide considerations against the Cartesian model of science in which we are to admit only those notions into science that are clear and distinct. That all bodies possess extension passes the Cartesian test. But Newton's idea that all bodies possess gravity fails that test since it is not a clear and distinct notion; so on the Cartesian criterion of what counts as science, talk of gravity is not to be admitted. Many of his contemporaries found Newton's idea of gravity somewhat suspect, some for Cartesian reasons. But the rules, especially Rule 3, provide a way around these strictures that still enables one to do science, or at least science in accordance with Newton's rules.

It is the combined use of the four rules that provides a different conception of science, not based on clear and distinct ideas, and a goal of certainty that gets Newton to a notion of universal gravitation that would not be admitted by Cartesian rules. There is much more to the story of how Newton's rules are intended to be a counter to the rules recommended by Descartes than the one difference mentioned here.[5] But their different rules, understood as foundational principles of method, shape their respective conceptions of science.

3.5 Methodological principles from the history of science, III: Duhem

In §2.6 we discussed Duhem's anti-realist aim for science, namely, explanations that are empirically adequate rather then true of "bare reality"; and we also discussed some of the pragmatic values he endorsed, which involve an "economy of thought". As well as these values, are there any distinctive principles of method that Duhem endorses? Yes, and a few are reviewed here. But first there are some well-known claims that Duhem makes that underpin his principles of method.

The first is his criticism of Newton's inductivist methods expressed in his four rules. Duhem's central claim, and in this he is followed by Popper and Lakatos, is that any Newtonian inductive method faces an insurmountable hurdle: "*The principle of universal gravity, very far from being derivable by generalisation and induction from the observational laws of Kepler, formally contradict these laws. If Newton's theory is correct, Kepler's laws are necessarily false*" (Duhem 1954: 193). Such a contradiction between premises and conclusion would be a serious barrier to any kind of inference, including the inference from Kepler's phenomenological laws about planetary motion to Newton's law of universal gravitation. Even allowing for the fact that in Newton's time expressions such as "deduction" and "induction" did not have quite the same meanings as we now give them, Duhem's claim is only partially correct. We cannot enter into the dispute here. But as some have pointed out in making a case against a position such as Duhem's,[6] Newton's procedure does use methods of approximation and idealized models (see §1.5) and does make assumptions about the constancy of certain parameters that, as his theory advances, can be removed. This helps remove the sting in Duhem's claim that any inductive inference is impossible.

Suppose we were to agree with Duhem's case against Newton. Does this show, as many assert, that Duhem is anti-inductivist? All that follows is that there is one case where Newton's methodological rules could not have worked in the way he claimed to arrive at theory. Duhem also criticizes André-Marie Ampère's alleged use of Newtonian methods in electrodynamics (*ibid.*: pt II, ch. VI, §5). On the basis of these two cases Duhem draws the conclusion: "we have recognized that it is impossible to construct a theory by a purely inductive method. Newton and Ampère failed in this" (*ibid.*: 219). Setting aside ambiguity between discovery and justification in talk of "construction", this general conclusion can only be arrived at by an inductive argument. If Duhem adopts a rule prohibiting inductivist methods, at best it only applies to Newton's method for arriving at theoretical laws, especially Rule 4. It does not apply to experimental laws, which play an important role in establishing the empirical adequacy conditions for any theory. These experimental laws need to be justified in some way, and it is hard to see what might do this other than induction of the sort championed in other Newtonian rules.

Duhem also makes some important methodological claims: "An experiment in physics can never condemn an isolated hypothesis but only a whole theoretical group" (*ibid.*: §2). The restriction to physics makes his claim narrower than the oft-cited Quine–Duhem thesis, which is quite general; but both turn on the same logical point. Suppose T is a theory (which may be a finite conjunction of laws, etc.), and A is the conjunction of all the auxiliary hypotheses and conditions of application of T. Suppose also that C is a test consequence logically deduced from them: $(T \& A) \vdash C$ (where "$\vdash$" stands for logical consequence). Then if C is false one is only *permitted* to infer, by *modus tollens*, the falsity of the whole conjunct $(T \& A)$; one is *not permitted* to infer the falsity of the conjuncts separately, particularly that T is false and/or A is false. Nor is one permitted to infer the falsity of any of the component conjuncts within T, or within A; we cannot get inside the whole conjunction to infer the falsity of any internal conjunct. Here we have some principles of method, founded *a priori* by appeal to logic, which set out what we are permitted, and not permitted, to infer concerning theories under test. We say more on the Quine–Duhem thesis later.

Duhem also tells us: "A 'crucial experiment' is impossible in physics" (*ibid.*: §3). The reason follows from the above. We do not pit one theory T against another T^* and then compare them with an experimental outcome. Rather, there are auxiliaries for each theory so that we compare $(T \& A)$ and $(T^* \& A^*)$

with the experimental outcome. (T & A) as a group may pass while (T^* & A^*) as a group may fail; but we cannot get inside each group and infer that T is the correct theory and T^* is the false rival theory, for reasons already given. Understood this way, crucial experiments are not crucial; any allegedly crucial verdict can be reversed if any of the auxiliaries are revised. The classic case Duhem discusses is the alleged crucial experiment of Léon Foucault in the 1850s to test the rival hypotheses of wave and corpuscular theories of light (see also §8.2). On the wave theory, light should travel faster in air than in water, while for the corpuscular theory the opposite follows. Foucault devised an experiment to test the difference, the outcome being that light travels faster in air thereby supporting the wave theory; but the test is not definitive in favour of the wave theory and a version of the corpuscular theory later came to be adopted.[7] We could turn this into a negative principle of method that prohibits certain inferences that many had thought were permissible: in conditions in which theories T and T^* are rivals, and they are compared in contexts of application (T & A) and (T^* & A^*) with some experimental test outcome, and the test favours the conjunct (T & A) but not the conjunct (T^* & A^*), then do *not* infer that a crucial experiment has been performed in which T definitively passes and T^* definitively fails.

Is there anything Duhem recommends about what changes in the above two situations one ought to make to the theories to bring them into accordance with experiment? Although there is a need to make some modification, no particular modification in either T or A is recommended: "It leaves to the physicist the task of finding out the weak spot that impairs the whole system. No absolute principle directs this inquiry, which different physicists may conduct in very different ways without having the right to accuse one another of illogicality" (*ibid.*: 216). In the absence of any methods here, it looks as if "anything goes"; different scientists can go in different directions. What Duhem correctly rejects is the idea that there is any algorithm, or method, for discovering what change to make; instead he appeals to "*bon sens*": good sense. This can be rare, even in Duhem's own case.[8] Good sense does not impose itself in the way logical considerations do; and there is something vague and uncertain about it when it is made an ultimate court of appeal that methodologists, with their desire for rules, find unsatisfactory.

Although there is no algorithm, or other method, for discovering the changes to be made, once a modification is made it is possible to appraise it using values and principles. Duhem does not propose anything like Quine's maxim of minimum mutilation to apply to these changes, but he already has in his list of the pragmatic virtues of unity, generality and systematicity of classification the means for assessing the overall outcome of any changes that a physicist may propose.

In Duhem's view, logic itself is not powerful enough to impose particular kinds of choices on physicists in situations of theory revision; his anti-inductivism enters in at this point with his rejection of any method such as Newton's that might be imposed here. But he suggests that, for theory revision, there are three "conditions logically imposed on the choice of hypotheses to serve as the basis of our physical theory" (*ibid*.: 220). The first is that any hypothesis or theory "shall not be a self-contradictory proposition". The second is a principle of external consistency with the rest of physics, which is also a step in the direction of realizing the virtue of unity: "the different hypotheses ... shall not contradict one another". Theory is not to be "a mass of disparate and incompatible models; it aims [at] ... a logical unity". The third condition is logical only to the extent that it involves deduction. It requires that from hypotheses "*taken as a whole* mathematical deduction may draw consequences representing with sufficient degree of approximation the *totality* of experimental laws". Apart from these constraints "the theorist enjoys complete freedom ... to construct in any way he pleases" (*ibid*.).

It might appear that Duhem puts great store on the values of unity and consistency, but surprisingly the historian in Duhem leads him away from this ideal picture to one in which science grows by a piecemeal evolution in which the requirements of overall logical consistency and unity are relaxed; in this evolutionary process disunity can be allowed, including the disunity of contradiction. In each science one is always confronted with a vast amount of observational data and a large number of experimental laws extracted from some of the data; and this is to be logically captured by theory. In the evolution of science, the above three constraints of "logic" are not sufficient to help with the complex task of developing theory to capture the laws and data; and they may not even be necessary.

Duhem asks whether we ought to adopt the following rule of method arising from the third condition mentioned above: "Physical theory has to try to represent the whole group of natural laws by a single system all of whose parts are logically compatible with one another" (*ibid*.: 293). Call this the *rule of global unity*; it clearly involves consistency. Is this a reasonable rule to adopt in the long run? Duhem argues against it as a short-term rule; to adopt it would cripple science and its evolution. Duhem offers no proof against adopting it in the long run; but he does think that the commonly hoped for ideal of global unity, in which there is a time at which a theory captures all experimental laws and data, cannot be realized. Instead he locates the grip this ideal has on our minds in our propensity to adopt a realist understanding of theories. As mentioned in §2.6 this is to suppose that science tends towards a "natural classification" that tells us something of "bare reality". For anti-realists such as Duhem these are tendencies we are to resist; and in doing so there is no need to adopt anything like the rule of global unity even as a long-term ideal.

Instead Duhem recommends a rule of permission that allows us to construct theories that admit localized unities (which presumably are internally consistent), but taken overall are logically inconsistent. He asks:

Is it permissible to symbolize several distinct groups of experimental laws, or even a single group of laws, by means of several theories each resting on hypotheses incompatible with the hypotheses supporting the others?

To this question we do not hesitate to answer: *If we confine ourselves strictly to considerations of pure logic*, we cannot prevent a physicist from representing by several incompatible theories diverse groupings of laws, or even a single group of laws; we cannot condemn incoherence in physical theory. (*Ibid.*: 100–101)

What Duhem says "pure logic" permits is the following within a single science. For two sets of experimental laws, L and L^*, there can be two theories, T and T^*, such that: (a) T logically captures L and T^* logically captures L^* (i.e. each is locally empirically adequate); and (b) T and T^* are incompatible with one another. Moreover, he allows a case of under-determination in which for any set of laws there can be two theories, T and T^*, that logically capture the laws of the set yet T and T^* are inconsistent with one another. In place of the hopelessly unrealizable ideal rule of global unity, there ought to be a rule permitting local unities with the overall disunity of inconsistency. As such Duhem's rule goes against the rules and values of many others such as Kuhn, but it comes closer to others such as Feyerabend or Lakatos. Finally he recommends we "quarantine" T and T^* from one another when inferences are to be made, since he recognizes that contradictions entail anything.

Since the unity that theories T and T^* provide for their respective laws is local only, and the under-determination he envisages is also local, there is no reason why the overall inconsistencies of disunity cannot be overcome with the growth of science. Thus there may emerge novel evidence that removes the local under-determination and favours, say, T^* over T. Or, since T and T^* are within the same science, there may emerge evidence that supports one over the other thereby undermining the local empirical adequacy of one of the theories. But for Duhem these appear to be merely stages in the growth of science in which old local unities (which taken together can exhibit disunity) are replaced and new local unities – and a new overall disunity – reasserts itself. There is no reason to suppose the permissive rule of local unities should be dropped and the obligatory rule of global unity be adopted in its place.

Elsewhere Duhem emphasizes his permissive stance when he writes: "There is a right of the physicist to develop a logically incoherent theory" (*ibid.*: 294). Duhem makes this claim when discussing metamethodology: "No scientific method carries in itself its full and entire justification; it cannot through its principles alone explain all these principles" (*ibid.*: 293). Whether or not there is a metamethodological justification of methodological principles is a matter we raise in Chapter 4. But here Duhem stakes out for himself the position that says that some metamethodological principles are unjustified justifiers; they lack any justification even though they might be used to justify lower-level methodological principles. But the main grounds for Duhem's adoption of a rule permitting only local unities comes from a Feyerabendian consideration based in the actual investigation of the history of science: the rule that imposes global unity would cripple the evolutionary growth of science. Duhem's rule of permission is one that realizes the value of growth in science much more effectively than the rule of global unity.

Duhem's permissive stance towards disunity is assisted by his anti-realism. For Duhem the task of theorizing in physics is not to obtain truths about the nature of "bare reality"; it is to obtain empirically adequate theories that also realize the values of an economy of thought such as unity, generality and systematicity of classifications. Granted the anti-realist stance, there is no reason to always maximize on these values; we could satisfice instead, or even give way on one of these. There is no metamethodological constraint to prohibit this. It leaves open the possibility that these pragmatic virtues, if they apply, should only apply locally and not globally. Duhem claims that it is realists who ought to be scandalized by the possibility of a range of contrary theories each locally adequate; they would be the first to be repelled by this kind of logical disunity because their realist axiology demands that theorizing be directed towards uncovering "bare reality", and there is only one truth about that. However, realists need not be too scandalized; they can adopt Duhem's more permissive stance and look for other arguments for their realism. But Duhem's position gives new meaning to his distinction between his two kinds of genius exemplified by strong but narrow minds and ample and flexible minds (*ibid*.: pt I, ch. 4). No methodological prescriptions are to rule out freewheeling, ample and flexible minds; they are to be tolerant towards disunity, even the disunity of overall inconsistency.

The interpretation of Duhem that we have just presented is one in which Duhem adopts a permissive attitude towards disunity in science. However, Duhem's position may be open to an alternative interpretation. According to this alternative interpretation, while Duhem allows that disunity occurs in science, he is opposed to it. Instead, he favours a requirement of global unity in science that involves the overall consistency of theories. However, Duhem denies that the requirement of global unity can be grounded in an appeal to logic. It must be based instead on common sense and intuition (*ibid*.: 104). In our view, while this may be an acceptable interpretation of Duhem, the attempt to ground a requirement of unity in common sense and intuition fails because it does not provide a sufficiently powerful justification of the need for unity and consistency in science. It is to questions about the nature of such metamethodological problems of justification that we turn in Chapter 4.

4. Metamethodology

In Chapter 3 we presented a case for saying that principles of scientific method are generally of the following sorts: deductive and non-deductive principles of inference; values by which theory choices can be made; and methodological M-principles, which govern theory choice and can include values. On what grounds do we think that any of these are correct? There is some controversy about the grounds on which the rules of deductive logic are to be justified; some argue that they involve circularity since they are employed in their own justificatory arguments (see §6.1). Even more controversial are the grounds for accepting inductive inferences, values and M-principles. It seems appropriate to call the investigation into principles of method and their justification *meta-methodology*. This chapter explores what this might be, and what grounds it can offer for accepting principles of scientific method.

In §4.1 we set out a "three levels" picture of the sciences, methods and meta-methods. Objections have been made to metamethods on the grounds that their justification involves either circularity or an infinite regress. In §4.2 and §4.3 we outline some of the *a priori* and empirical approaches to metamethodology found in the philosophy of science that either circumvent these objections or show us how to live with them. In §4.4 we evaluate one common metamethod-ology: reflective equilibrium. This has been advocated by some methodologists as a way of bringing particular judgements about good theory choices into accordance with principles of a theory of scientific method. The historical turn in recent philosophy of science uses these particular judgements to criticize theories of method for being too *a prioristic* in failing to reflect accurately what has actually transpired in the history of science. In §4.5 we examine how aspects of the history of science can be brought into relation with methodological principles and what metamethodological presuppositions are made in using history of science critically to evaluate methodologies.

4.1 A three-tiered relationship between science, methods and metamethod

For as long as there has been science from the ancient Greeks onwards, there have also been reflections on the nature and methods of science. Theories of scientific method begin with some remarks of Presocratic philosophers and in Plato's more Socratic dialogues. The first systematic treatise on science and its methods and character is Aristotle's *Organon* (literally "the instrument", or "tool", the common Greek use of the term being for instruments used in, say, farming, in contrast to Aristotle's special sense of instruments to be used in organized thought). Ever since then there have been a large number of theories of method about science proposed by scientists and philosophers. We have already mentioned a few: Descartes, Newton and Duhem. More contemporary methodologists appear elsewhere in the book. The general picture of the relationships between the various sciences and theories of method that we wish to work with is depicted in Table 4.1.

Level 1 contains the actual, historical sequence of scientific theories proposed about some domain. Consider the domain of dreams. The actual historical

Table 4.1 Hierarchy of scientific theories, scientific methods and metamethods.

Level 3 Metamethodologies	*A priori*: transcendentalism, logicism, etc. *Empirical*: historical intuitionism of later Popper and Lakatos; reflective equilibrium; varieties of naturalism (Laudan); etc. *Conventionalist*: early Popper *Pragmatist*: Quine, Rescher *Decision theoretical*: Bayesian decision theory *Nihilistic*: sociology of science, postmodernism, scepticism, relativism
Level 2 Scientific methodologies	Aristotle's *Organon*; ...; Bacon's *Novum Organon*; Descartes's *Rules for the Direction of the Mind*; Newton's "Rules of Reasoning in Philosophy"; ...; Duhem's aims and rules; Popper's critical rationalism; Lakatos' scientific research programmes; Kuhn's weighted values; Feyerabend's methodological pluralism; Bayesianism; decision-theoretic methods; etc.
Level 1 Historical sequence of scientific theories in some domain	*1. Theories of dreams*: Homer, Bible, ..., Aristotle, ..., Freud, Jung, ..., Crick, Hobson, etc. *2. Theories of motion*: Aristotle, ..., Kepler, Galileo, Descartes, Newton, ..., Laplace, Lagrange, Hamilton, ..., Einstein, etc. *3. Others*

sequence of theories about the nature and causes of dreams begins with the works of Homer, the Bible and Plato. Aristotle seems to have been the first to propose a theory about the causes of dreams that did not appeal to spirit-like entities and that has affinities with modern scientific theories.[1] Skipping the intervening centuries, the twentieth century began with the psychoanalytic theories of Freud and Jung; the more recent theories of Francis Crick and J. Allan Hobson and are based on the neurophysiological functioning of the brain. Considering a different domain, such as motion, there has been an equally long sequence of theories, most prominent of which are those of Aristotle, Kepler, Galileo, Newton, Laplace, Lagrange and Einstein. Similarly for other domains of investigation in all the sciences. The idea that there is a historical sequence of scientific theories is fairly uncontroversial; it yields the raw material to which the two higher levels are to be applied.

Among all the possible theory choices scientists might have made at any time, what has led to the actual historical sequence of changes in theory? The word "change" is used deliberately since talk of growth, development or improvement in our choices involves appeal to a methodology to provide criteria for such growth, and so on. Let us pick one such criterion and say that the historical sequence of theories on the whole displays over time the desirable feature (or value) of increase in *instrumental success*, where such success is either our increased ability to explain, or to predict, or to manipulate the natural and social worlds to our own ends. Refining the above question we now can ask: what explains our choice of a sequence of theories which yield such instrumental success, given that there are many other pathways through all the available theories over time that would not yield such success?

Is the successful sequence of theories due to luck, or to the tacit incommunicable "feel for the right thing" that some such as Polanyi (1958; 1966) alleged is indicative of scientific genius? Methodologists suggest that it is neither luck nor the incommunicable insights of genius; a better explanation is the use (tacit or explicit) of principles of scientific method in choosing the successful theories. At this point sociologists of science enter the field and offer their own empirically based explanation. They not only reject appeal to luck or tacit "feel", but also the appeal to principles of method. Their rival explanation is in terms of our sociopolitical and cultural circumstance, or our interests in these. Which of the four suggested explanations ought we to adopt?

Our non-cognitive personal, professional and political interests are often such that we do value having theories with high instrumental success. But is it very probable that merely having such interests would, on the whole, lead us to choose the very theories that, when we examine and apply them, turn out to realize the value of instrumental success, thereby realizing our interests? Personal, professional and political interests seem, on the face of it, to be quite randomly linked to whether the theories chosen on the basis of such interests are also those that are successful in the defined sense. Methodologists would, in contrast, argue that something much more efficacious intervenes, producing the sequence of theories that do have instrumental success. These are principles of method that, when applied, reliably produce theories with the value *instrumental success*. Here we shall simply assert that there are Level 2 theories of scientific method to consider, and that they offer the best explanation of why we have our actual sequence of successful Level 1 scientific theories.

Just as there is a historical sequence of scientific theories at Level 1, at Level 2 there is a historical sequence of theories of scientific method. The various scientific methods are at a higher level only in the sense that principles of method at Level 2 have as their object of application scientific theories at Level 1. In Table 4.1 we list just a few of the many theories of scientific method that have been proposed from the ancient Greeks to our own time.[2] Philosophers and scientists have suggested a number of scientific methods. Not to be overlooked is the significant contribution made by statisticians to the development and application of scientific method to many sciences. This will only be touched on here since our focus is largely on the contribution made by philosophers through their accounts of methodology, deriving as they do from general epistemological considerations, and not the immediate practical needs of scientists.

4.2 Metamethodology: what is it and is it possible?

We have already raised some metamethodological matters in §3.2 when considering desirable features that principles of method ought to have, such as reliability, robustness, power and speed. There are other desirable features of scientific methods such as: they are internally consistent (the list of principles does not contain contradictory directives or lead to inconsistent adjudications of theories); they can be finitely stated as a set of directives; and so on. However, metamethodology is primarily directed towards the following matter: given that historically a large number of different theories of scientific method have been proposed, which should one choose, if choose at all? In Table 4.1 there is a downward link from Level 2 scientific methods to the Level 1 sciences between which they are to adjudicate. Analogously, there is also a downward link from Level 3 metamethods to Level 2 scientific methods; if there are rival theories of scientific method then one needs metamethods to make a choice between them to determine which scientific method one should use to apply to scientific theories.

We have now ascended to the quite rarefied atmosphere of metamethodology, the task of which is to provide ways of adjudicating between, or justifying or legitimizing, theories of scientific methods. There are several reactions to the possibility of metamethodology. The first is the quite negative stance of sceptics, relativists, sociologists of knowledge and postmodernists: there is no such thing. The second, discussed in the next section, is more positive in that there is such a thing as metamethodology, which can play some kind of justificatory role. There are expressivist and descriptivist approaches to metamethodology, the second of these dividing further into *a priori* and empirical modes of justification.

Some might argue that the atmosphere at Level 3 is so rarefied that there is nothing there at all. There are no metamethods; or if there are, they are purely ornamental and cannot perform any task of adjudication, justification or legitimization. The reason is this. Level 2 contains all the principles of method that there are, from rules of deductive and inductive reasoning to values and M-rules. The whole idea of metamethodology is that there is some distinct principle (or set of principles), P, the task of which is to adjudicate between scientific methods. If principle P is to carry out this task, either it is *sui generis* at Level 3 and has no counterpart within Level 2 scientific methods, or it has to be elevated from Level 2 to Level 3. But there is nothing about any putative P that can give it such a privileged role, for two reasons.

The first is that P is used to justify other principles of method without being justified itself. P might be able to justify all the other principles at Level 2; but P itself remains unjustified since the relation of justification is not reflexive in that no principle can justify itself on pain of circularity. The second objection is that if a justification is to be provided for P, then one cannot appeal to P; one has to appeal to another principle of method P^*, which is distinct from P. Now a regress of justifications threatens: P^* justifies other methods including P, but not itself; so it stands in need of further justification by some other method P^{**}, and so on. If the idea of metamethodology is to have any justificatory role, these two objections of circularity or regress need to be circumvented in some way. Ways of doing this will be discussed below.

The above objection has it roots in ancient Greek scepticism about meta-justifications. Such sceptics often adopt a philosophical position of nihilism about metamethodology; there is no principle to do the required philosophical work of justification on pain of circularity or infinite regress. There is another reaction that is also nihilistic, but for different reasons, namely, relativism. On this view there may well be different putative scientific methods but they are all equally correct and there is no method or metamethod that is privileged in any way so that it can carry out any task of justification.

For others, any meta-principle is alleged to be purely ornamental; or it is a mask for what is really at work in theory choice. On this view there is no Level 3 meta-principle; so there can be no justifiable Level 2 scientific methods. This in turn helps expose the purely ornamental character of scientific methods that do not play the role alleged of them in adjudicating between Level 1 scientific theories. Worse, since there is no justifiable scientific method, then no Level 1 scientific theory can have any justification. What plays the real role in theory choice, say some sociologists of scientific knowledge who adopt this position, are sociopolitical cultural factors, or interests in these. If principles of scientific method are used then there is nothing strongly justificatory about them; they are what the community of users of such principles, such as scientists, endorse or socially sanction or arrive at by negotiation. Moreover, what is endorsed, sanctioned or negotiated is relative to different groups at different times and places.

In adopting this stance, the sociologists are aided and abetted by postmodernists who follow Jean-François Lyotard's declaration: "I define *postmodern* as incredulity towards metanarratives" (1984: xxiv). Here the metanarratives are akin to the attempts to find Level 3 principles of metamethod. Any incredulity towards them extends down to the Level 2 scientific methods themselves, and ultimately to all of science itself. What, if anything, plays the major role of generating our actual historical sequence of theories in the sciences? If there is any explanation at all, no appeal can be made to any methodological principles; without these all semblance of the rationality of science seems to have drained away.

The sceptical objection to metamethodology is a familiar one in discussions about the lack of a justification for induction. In the three-level schema in Table 4.1, rules of inductive inference, such as the simple rule of enumerative induction, find their place as Level 2 principles of an inductivist scientific method to be applied to the observational and other claims of science at Level 1. The Humean sceptical challenge that induction cannot be justified is itself a Level 3 metamethodological claim, albeit a negative one, about the status of Level 2 inductive principles. For sceptics, even though we do make inductive inferences, there is no rational basis for making such inferences. The failure to find a metamethodological justification is at the core of Humean scepticism about induction. Attempted philosophical rebuttals of Hume's view also have the character of metamethodological arguments; these are discussed in Chapter 6.

Attempts to justify induction have parallels in attempts to justify non-inductive methods using some non-inductive metamethodology. As will be shown in §10.1.3, Popper uses his Level 2 methodology of falsification as a Level 3 metamethodology to adjudicate between the rival theories of method at Level 2, including his own. Lakatos also uses his Level 2 methodology of scientific research programmes (SRPs) in a similar way (§10.2.2). In general, a methodology can appear at both Levels 2 and 3; from the stance of Level 3 it can be used to adjudicate between all the rival scientific methods at Level 2, including itself. While this appears to be circular, there are ways in which the circularity problem might be finessed through a discussion of the non-vicious nature of rule-circularity.

4.3 *A priori,* empirical and expressivist approaches to metamethodology

Setting aside the nihilist position, there is a range of metamethodological approaches to justification. One approach is to show that Level 2 principles are necessary rather than contingent truths. Techniques for showing claims to be necessarily rather than contingently true abound in philosophy, and they afford one way of circumventing the problems raised above for the justification of any metamethodology. A case can be made for the principles of deductive logic being necessary truths, and we shall assume this here. But no similar case can be made for the principles of inductive reasoning or M-principles; these are contingent.

A different kind of justification is based in considerations that show that methodological principles are either *a priori* or empirical. This looks more promising; and it also affords a way of avoiding the problems that beset justifying metamethodologies. We shall argue in §11.1.3 that Kuhn wished to show that, for the values he endorsed, there is an *a priori* justification; more strongly, he thought that the justification was quasi-analytic in character, depending on the holistic semantic links between the various values he endorsed and the meaning of the term "science". This is one of the few attempts to show that a methodology can be justified on *a priori* grounds that are also broadly analytic; we argue that this is failure.

There are several other kinds of *a priori* accounts of the status of methodology and metamethodology. The principles of deductive reasoning can, on certain views of the nature of logic, be given an *a priori* justification. Can the principles of scientific method also be given an *a priori* justification? In Part III we shall consider the probability calculus as a source of principles of scientific method. Can an *a priori* justification be given of the probability calculus and its theorems, such as Bayes's theorem? Although we shall not argue it here, a good case is made by Abner Shimony (1993: ch. 6, §3, §5) for the axioms themselves having an *a priori* (and even analytic) justification; this *a priori* status flows from the axioms to all the theorems that follow, such as Bayes's theorem.

A second *a priori* approach is as follows. Consider the simplest version of Bayes's theorem: $P(H, E) = P(E, H) \times P(H)/P(E)$. Are the posterior and prior probabilities that make up the theorem known *a priori* or *a posteriori*? If we could establish *a priori* the numerical values of $P(E, H)$, $P(H)$ and $P(E)$, then there would be a totally *a priori* argument to the value of $P(H, E)$, and thus, it might seem, an *a priori* probabilistic methodology for science. Such a position arises naturally for those, such as Carnap, who think of expressions such as $P(H, E)$ on a model of partial entailment, with total entailment being the special case of logical deduction. On this account deductive logic will tell us when it is appropriate to claim that E logically implies H. Similarly an inductive logic will tell us when E *partially* logically entails H. That is, it ought to be possible to provide a theory of a confirmation function that will give us a quantitative value for r in expressions such as $P(H, E) = r$. Carnap argues that the status of these confirmation expressions is analytic; and so an *a priori* justification can be given for them.

It is now well known that the programme of finding *a priori* a numerical value for expressions such as $P(H, E)$, explored by John Maynard Keynes, Carnap and others for any H and E, faces so many difficulties that this quasi-logicist justification of a probabilistic methodology for science has little hope of success (see e.g. Salmon 1967: 70–79). Most present-day advocates of probability in methodology (a position that Carnap also explored) are Bayesians. Bayesians take a quite different subjectivist approach in which the key issues of justification turn on quite different matters (see §8.6). But this does not preclude the *a priori* approach of someone like Shimony, who is also a subjective Bayesian.

A final *a priori* approach is a modification of the above. Consider a hypothetical imperative of some scientific method of the form: rule r will, when correctly followed, realize value v. What kind of "proof" can be given of the claim: *if one wishes to realise value* v *then one ought to follow rule* r? One task of metamethodology would be to show that rules are reliable realizers of certain goals; and this reliability might be established on *a priori* grounds. Suppose the theoretical value v is "increased support for a theory". And suppose rule r says: one ought always to take into account new evidence that is unexpected in the light of known evidence. Is there a proof that following r will always realize v? Such a proof arises in the probability calculus from Bayes's theorem in the form (where H is the hypothesis under test, E is evidence and B any background information): $P(H, E \& B) = P(E, H \& B) \times P(H, B)/P(E, B)$.

Under certain conditions (in which the numerator on the right-hand side remains fixed), $P(H, E \& B)$ is inversely proportional to $P(E, B)$, that is, the expectedness of new evidence E with respect to old evidence B. (On the use of the term "expectedness" see §8.2, Bayes's theorem, version 1.) If the expectedness is high, that is, $P(E, B)$ is close to 1, then the goal of increased probability will be realized, but only to a very small extent. However, if the expectedness is low, that is, $P(E, B)$ is close to 0, then the goal of increased probability will be realized in a quite striking way. Using the probability calculus in this way, an *a priori* proof can be given of an important principle of many scientific methods, namely, that new unexpected evidence will realize the goal of increase in confirmation of our hypotheses; but there is an additional boon in that the proof sets out conditions under which the principle holds.

In contrast to the above *a priori* approaches to the problem of justification, there are several empirical approaches that show methodological principles to be contingent and open to empirical investigation. In fact, many of these approaches fall within the scope of attempts to "naturalize" the norms of method. One well-known approach along these lines is Laudan's normative naturalism. The norms of method are shown to be empirically based in the means–ends strategies that scientists have employed in using rules to achieve any of a wide number of theoretical values; we discuss this in §12.2. To illustrate, if the principle of method is a norm of the form "if you wish to realize v then follow r", then what is subject to empirical test against the historical record, rather than *a priori* proof, is an associated declarative hypothetical "always following r realizes v". Empirical testing can show this to be generally true, or to have a high probability, or to be disconfirmed by counter-examples.

This empirical approach presupposes that there are some principles of method that can be used to test the declarative hypothetical; but these presupposed methods are the very objects of investigation within normative naturalism. Here issues of circularity or infinite regress come to the fore, and it is the task of any naturalistic approach to avoid them. Pragmatic approaches to the justification of scientific methods also have naturalistic and empirical aspects, for example those of Quine (§12.1) and Nicholas Rescher (§12.3). These pragmatic metamethods must also meet the twin objections of circularity or regress.

Other approaches are not so overtly empirical and are called "quasi-empirical" by Lakatos. He quite explicitly elevates his Level 2 scientific method, the methodology of SRPs, to a Level 3 meta-principle and tests his own methodology against the record of episodes in the history of science reconstructed according to each of the rival theories of method; he then compares these to determine which has the more progressive historiographical research programme. Lakatos's position is discussed in §10.2.2. His approach bears many similarities to that of Popper. For Popper the principles of his Level 2 scientific method are regarded as conventions. But he recognizes that there can be different conventions that rival his own. So he elevates to Level 3 his own method of falsification and provides an empirical test basis for it. This is discussed in §10.1.3. Both approaches need to show that their rule-circularity is not vicious.

In both cases there is an appeal to an "empirical basis" for purposes of test. This comprises intuitive, but well-considered, singular judgements about what is or is not a rational move in the game of science when one theory is chosen over its rivals. These intuitions about particular cases play an important role in assessing methodologies such as those of Popper, Lakatos, Laudan (at an earlier period) and many others. In the next section we consider these judgements and the role they play in a version of the metamethodological principle of reflective equilibrium applied to the case of scientific methods.

A quite different approach to issues concerning the meta-justification of the rules, or norms, of scientific method is one that arises from the norm expressivism of Allan Gibbard; a similar position is advocated by Hartry Field as a form of epistemological evaluativism.[3] It is commonly assumed, in appraising some item x (whether it be an act, or a rule of logic, method or morality) as *rational*, *reasonable* or *justified*, that these are descriptive or factual properties of x. An alternative view is that, despite surface grammatical appearances, evaluative terms such as "rational", "reasonable" and "justified" are strictly not predicates at all. So they do not refer to descriptive properties of these items; they are not factual properties, or not fully factual properties. Instead they are expressive of attitudes or stances, or they are non-factual and evaluative. This approach might be classified as *nihilistic* in that it denies that there is any substantive justification of the kind sought by metamethodologists.

Expressivism is a view that has traditionally had its place in moral philosophy. When actions or moral norms are appraised as "right" or "good", this is not to be understood as attributing any kind of naturalistic property to the action or rule; rather it is expressive of a stance. The doctrine can be extended to epistemology and methodology. To call principles of method "rational", "reasonable" or "justified" is not to ascribe a property to the rule, or to say something of it that is truth-evaluable or factual; rather it is non-factual, or not truth-apt, but expressive of an attitude. On this view, issues concerning the meta-justification of principles of method take on a new and much less urgent character. The principles will still have descriptive properties such as reliability, robustness, power and speed (see §3.2). However, there are no further descriptive or factual features of principles of method to uncover that could constitute their justification. Rather, their justification, such as it is, is to be given in ways that do not turn on any descriptive properties of the principles. The position is one that gives a role to both descriptive or factual matters and evaluative non-factual matters. Some disagreements about principles of method will turn on factual matters; but other kinds of disagreement are fundamentally non-factual in character and turn on attitudes and values. Gibbard's and Field's analysis presents the factual and the non-factual not as separate elements, as is common in earlier versions of non-factualism, but as aspects of a single analysis in terms of possible-world semantics (a matter not pursued here). The outcome of their approach is that the metamethodological project of finding a rational ground for methodological principles, or of justifying them, cannot get a purchase at all because of their largely evaluative or non-factual character.

Gibbard's own account of norm expressivism is not directly about what it is for a norm to be rational, or justified; that is to be settled by what norms we do adopt. Rather, it is about what we *accept as, call, believe to be* or *regard as* rational, and this he puts as follows:

> To call something rational is to express one's acceptance of norms that permit it. ... Normative talk is part of nature, but it does not describe nature. In particular, a person who calls something rational or irrational is not describing his own state of mind; he is expressing it. To call something rational is not to attribute some particular property to that thing ... (Gibbard 1990: 7–8)

To say "x is rational" is to express acceptance of norms or principles that permit (or prohibit) x. As we understand this, any deliberate use of some principle of method by a person is assumed to be an expression of acceptance of the principle by that person. Accepting the x that the norms permit is just to accept that x is rational, or justified, or reasonable. In giving an account of the rationality of some x, where the range of x can include norms of method themselves, there can be no further court of appeal to some further descriptive fact of the sort commonly supposed by those who adopt a descriptivist stance. This is because it is a mistake to think that there is a further property to be uncovered that is the rationality, or reasonableness of principles of method. There is no such property; there is only a non-factual expression of acceptance (or rejection) of the principles.

There are some further additions to the account of norm expressivism that attempt to avoid the purely personal, idiosyncratic or subjective in norm acceptance. The position allows that, with respect to the same norms N, one person expresses their acceptance of N while another expresses their rejection of N. So there can be a deep rivalry about the norms to be accepted or rejected. But there are at least two restraints on this. First there are higher-order norms that tell us what lower-order norms we ought to accept. This would be important in the case where the norms are principles of method; but of course the same rivalry can arise for norms at a higher level. Secondly, there is a "conversational demand" that accompanies one's acceptance of norms through the addition of the extra demand that goes along with acceptance, namely, "you do the same as well!" (*ibid.*: chs 8, 9). But such additional constraints are not sufficient for a full objectivism for principles of method in which it is required that there be a fact of the matter about which principles are right or wrong. But this is precisely what the norm expressivist denies. Can this save us from a full-blown relativism about methodological principles? This is an issue faced by Field in discussing his version of evaluativism, which we need not address here.[4]

The importance of the expressivist or evaluativist stance for the position outlined in this chapter is that it brings into question aspects of the three-level view of the sciences, their methods and the metamethods used to adjudicate between methods and to justify some of them. For the expressivist, the level of metamethods can be dispensed with. All the work that needs to be done is simply in the use of Level 2 methods; their mere use is tantamount to an expression of their acceptance. Alongside the expressivist stance is the claim that there is no further natural property to be captured that constitutes their rationality or their justification.

A rival view to expressivism claims that, despite the normativity of the properties of being rational or justified, these are descriptive properties. Moreover, these properties supervene on other purely descriptive properties. Thus the properties a principle of method might have of being justified could be found to supervene on other purely descriptive properties within some supervenience base such as being reliable (i.e. having high truth ratio), being robust, being powerful and so on for the many descriptive properties they might have or acquire through the application. Supervenience is a relation of dependence: in this case the dependence of the normative on the descriptive. The normative properties of principles of method, such as being rational or justified, do not float free of the descriptive properties of the supervenience base. Rather they are dependent in the sense that there can be no change in normative appraisal of principles of method without change in some aspect of the descriptive supervenience base. This kind of dependence rules out the kind of free-floating independence, inherent in a relativism about principles of method, in which two or more sets of different principles of method can be adopted despite the descriptive facts being just the same. The idea that there is a property of justification and that it supervenes on other purely descriptive facts is not a matter we can explore here,[5] but it is one that challenges the kind of relativism that appears to be inherent in the expressivist position.

4.4 The metamethodology of reflective equilibrium

Reflective equilibrium has commonly been employed in moral theory as a way of bringing into accordance, and so justifying, particular considered moral judgements and general principles of morality. We have, on the one hand, quite strong gut intuitions about when some action is right or wrong; and on the other hand we also endorse general principles of morality. Either the intuitions fit the general rules or they do not. If not then we either modify our general moral rules or revise what we formerly took to be a strong intuition about the rightness or wrongness of some action in order to bring the rules and the particular judgements into accordance.

The doctrine of reflective equilibrium has its origins in some remarks by Nelson Goodman concerning particular considered judgements about particular (deductive and inductive) inferences we would be willing to accept and much more general rules of inference: "rules and particular inferences alike are justified by being brought into agreement with each other. *A rule is amended if it yields an inference we are unwilling to accept; an inference is rejected if it yields an inference we are unwilling to amend*" (1965: 64). This is not a claim about the justification of the rules of deductive logic that we accept,[6] but in what follows we shall go along with it.

There are six different aspects of reflective equilibrium to consider. The first concerns the existence of particular considered judgements (about a person's actions, or about particular inferences); call these *J*. The second concerns the existence of some general principles (either of morality or of reasoning); call these P. The third concerns the method of bringing these into accordance with one another. This process of reflection or equilibration must involve some meta-principles about how the processes are to be carried out in bringing J and P into accordance (which we can take to at least involve consistency). The fourth concerns the important claim that the reflective process can come to an end at some time at which balance or equilibrium is achieved between J and P. The fifth concerns the goal state of equilibrium itself. It is assumed that J and P form an acceptable coherent set. The coherence lies in not merely the consistency of J and P but in the mutual support they give one another, or the mutual explanations they offer. Finally it is assumed that reflective equilibrium provides a justification of both J and P rather than mere equilibration. In this respect reflective equilibrium is akin to coherence theories of justification in which a body of beliefs is said, in some sense, to cohere; and this in turn provides a justification of the body of beliefs, which in some cases may be strong enough for the beliefs to count as knowledge.

The metamethod of reflective equilibrium can be usefully extended from the spheres of morality and logic to scientific method. Reflective equilibrium can be taken to be a Level 3 principle that plays the role of bringing together considered judgements in quite particular cases of theory choice (J) and Level 2 principles of method (P). Many who work in the sciences and philosophy of science can have strong considered intuitions, or judgements, about whether a particular choice of a theory or a hypothesis is rational; they also say that a particular move in the game of science is a rational one to make. Without putting too much weight on the notion, we could say that they have an untutored "rational sense", in part cultivated in their training as scientists, in much the same way as, in the case of reflective equilibrium applied to morality, we might be said to have a "moral sense". Label the particular considered judgements deemed to be rational Y for "yes". Equally for other moves, there are strong considered judgements that these moves are irrational; call these cases N for "no". Finally there may be further moves in the game of science for which there is no strong intuition one way or the other. Call these cases U for "unsure either way". The overall class of particular judgements J to be employed in reflective equilibrium is simply the union of Y and N, the definitely rational and the definitely irrational moves in the game of science.

These judgements may be made by individuals, or they may be summed up collectively for a given community of scientists; we consider that it makes no difference for the purposes here. Such a classification into Y, N and U of judgements about particular cases of theory choice in science may alter over time and differ from community to community and from individual to individual. In making these particular judgements a scientist should not apply some theory of scientific method; otherwise the particular judgements would cease to be relatively methodology-free and could not be used in a reflective equilibrium exercise.

In contrast, general principles P of method are relatively easy to come by; they are furnished by the many Level 2 methodologies that have been proposed throughout the history of science.

Given J and P, how does the process of reflection work so that these are brought into accordance with one another? Is reflective equilibrium a *sui generis* metamethodological principle, or does it depend on the employment of other principles of method? Our verdict will be that reflective equilibrium is not *sui generis* and turns on other principles of metamethod that we have already met in their other guise of Level 2 methodological principles. Finally, it is not obvious that in the process of reflection some equilibrium, or balance, can be reached. If equilibrium cannot be reached, then the claim that reflective equilibrium can provide any justification becomes problematic.

Consider three possible ways in which the process of reflection can take place. The first is the case where all and only the Y judgements are captured by the principles P while all and only the N judgements are ruled out. The P might also rule in some of the U and rule out others; but this is of no concern as the fate of the U judgements is not a crucial matter. Such a case would be ideal in that just a little bit of reflection shows that the J and the P are in accordance, that is, equilibrium or balance has been effortlessly achieved. They are in accordance on grounds of consistency between P and Y and inconsistency of N and P. Here the virtue of consistency plays a role in reflective equilibrium. But we might need more than this if such a process is to *justify* either P or J, or both. There is nothing about reflective equilibrium so far that concerns justification. To achieve this we need to appeal to some principles of confirmation of the sort commonly proposed in the philosophy of science. We need principles of instance confirmation that tell us that the particular cases of Y strongly support P, and that P's ruling out the Ns also supports P.

Such effortless realization of equilibrium on reflection is rare; more often there are imbalances that the process of reflection has to remove. The next two cases concern two kinds of disequilibrium: the P are too narrow to capture the J, or there is inconsistency between P and J. Consider the case in which the principles P are rather weak because there are some particular Y judgements that they should capture but do not; such Y judgements can be consistent with P but Y and P are logically independent of one another. Again, the P are weak because there are some N judgements that they should rule out but do not. Combining both cases, there is some relevant evidence, some of the Y and N judgements, about which the P ought to adjudicate but they do not. We have already met in §2.3 the virtue of generality championed by Quine and Ullian. One way of understanding this is by considering the complementary vice of narrowness. A theory or hypothesis lacks generality, that is, it is too narrow, when there is some evidence that is relevant to it but about which it says nothing; it is neither supported nor refuted by the evidence and remains neutral. This fits the case of principles P that fail to adjudicate either way on particular Y or N judgements; they remain neutral. If the process of reflection is to do its work, principles P must exhibit the virtue of generality; they cannot exhibit the vice of narrowness.

If the P have the vice of narrowness then there is a problem about what to do next. Should we discard some of the Y judgements (respectively some of the N judgements) so that the blemish of narrowness is removed from the P? Or should we keep these judgements but revise principles P so that they are no longer narrow? Here we might need to invoke another Quine and Ullian virtue, that of conservativeness, or the associated rule, the maxim of minimum mutilation: make the minimum revisions in P and/or J (assuming we know what the minimum is). We now land in the thick of principles of belief revision in order to overcome the lack of accordance between J and P. Once again it would appear that reflective equilibrium is not a *sui generis* metamethodological principle but one that depends on a large number of other such principles.

Consider now the case of inconsistency between P and J. Principles P rule out some of the Y judgements; alternatively P permits some of the N judgements. In both cases P is inconsistent with some of the Y but consistent with some of the N. Do we give weight to the Y and the N judgements and reject P? Or do we give weight to P and revise our Y and N judgements? Such revision can take place by putting the recalcitrant Y and N judgements into U, the class of unsure judgements. Or more radically those Y judgements inconsistent with P could be completely revised by taking them out of the Y class and relegating them to the N class; conversely the N judgements sanctioned by P could be relocated in the Y class. Which do we do? Reflective equilibrium does not tell us. But if we appeal once more to the virtue of conservativeness, or the maxim of minimum mutilation, we do have a way of proceeding to restore at least consistency.

The above are ways in which Level 2 principles of method might be brought into accordance with intuitive, but considered, judgements about particular cases of theory choice when they fail to accommodate one another because of narrowness or inconsistency. But more needs to be said of the process of equilibration. This raises the following six further matters.

The first matter concerns the kind of principles P we are to employ. The business of science is complex enough, and the methodological rules governing it should reflect some of that complexity. However, we cannot be assured that we have discovered the appropriate principles that are to act as norms governing the activity. And when we do we need to be sure that we have an adequate formulation of them. So the first problem is that of having a minimally adequate set of principles on which reflective equilibrium can operate in the first place; reflective equilibrium is not a method for discovering those principles in the first place even if it is a method for modifying and thereby improving them.

Secondly, following on from this, there is the issue of whether the principles are strictly universal or not. We allowed that some of the principles may not be 100 per cent reliable; and we even allowed that they can be defeasible. If the principles are strictly universal, then there are much clearer criteria of when they are, or are not, in conformity with our particular judgements and so whether a process of reflection needs to take place. However, if the principles are defeasible this is much less clear. We may not know whether a process of reflection ought to take place or not, since it is not clear when defeasible principles and particular judgements are in conflict; there is much slack because of the defeasible character of the rules. The possibility could also emerge that, given the defeasible character of the rules, there are two or more ways in which accommodations could be made with particular judgements. It is unclear whether reflective equilibrium ought to allow that there be two or more points of equilibrium for bringing defeasible principles and our particular judgements into accordance; that is, there are two different endpoints for resolving prior conflict, which has the undesirable result of producing two different sets of defeasible rules and judgements. Perhaps a decision could be made in such cases based on parsimony of principles, or an overall simplicity of principles combined with particular judgements. But in this case methodological considerations of simplicity seem to be playing the major role with the methodology of reflective equilibrium adding nothing new.

This leads us to a third difficult point. What is it for the J (the set of definite Y [yes] and N [no] judgements) and the P to be in equilibrium? A first pass at this is that all the J fall under, or are instances of, principles P (we leave it open as to whether P also captures or rules out any of the U [unsure] judgements). What we need is a guarantee that for any discord between some initial J and P, we can arrive at some revised J^* and P^* such that J^* and P^* are in equilibrium. Is there a guarantee that there exists such a pair J^* and P^* for us to arrive at, or to arrive at after a finite time has passed over which reflection has taken place? The answer to this question is an important one in the context of belief-revision theory, which does consider processes such as reflection, since reflection appears to be nothing but the revision of our beliefs in J and P. The answer to the equilibrium question is in general no (a matter we shall not pursue here, but see the discussion in Bonevac 2004: esp. §IV). Whether there exists an equilibrium point is a different matter from whether or not putative equilibrium points are static; we might allow that they change as the process of reflection continues when it deals with new particular judgements and/or new possible general principles to bring into accordance.

A fourth matter concerns the number of cases of misfit that we have to consider at any one time; occasionally they might be few but more commonly they might be indefinitely large. One approach would be to deal with these singly, case by case. An alternative procedure might be to consider all the cases of lack of fit all at once in a more holistic revision procedure. It is not clear that the endpoints would necessarily be the same for the case-by-case approach and the holistic approach; within belief-revision theory the matter of which path is taken in revision is important and cannot be set aside.

A fifth point focuses on the diachronic aspect of belief revision rather than just its synchronic aspect. Whichever way we proceed, it may well be the case that any earlier resolutions of lack of fit we have achieved will have to be revised because of later reflections on newly uncovered cases of lack of fit. These are important issues discussed in belief-revision theory that any process of reflective equilibrium will have to draw on.

A sixth point concerns the fact that reflective equilibrium appears suited to dealing with only one scientific method at a time; it cannot compare scientific methods. To compare them using reflective equilibrium, one needs first to investigate the extent to which each scientific method is capable of bringing its Ps and the Js into agreement and, secondly, to be able to compare scientific methods according to the extent to which they are able to do this. But to do the latter, the metamethodological reflective equilibrium needs supplementing with a further principle about how well each scientific method produces its agreements; that is, we need not merely reflective equilibrium, but the *best overall* reflective equilibrium. It is the notion of which *best overall* reflective equilibrium and not reflective equilibrium *simpliciter* that will do most of the work in determining which scientific method we should adopt.

Reflective equilibrium has become a significant methodological approach in logic, ethics and epistemology. It has also been extended to scientific method, where it plays a role at the level of metamethodology in seeking justifications for some Level 2 scientific method, Feyerabend's work being just one example (see §11.2). So what is it about it that provides justificatory force? The claim of justification is a significant addition on top of the merely factual claim that the particular J and the general P are in agreement. However, agreement is neither necessary nor sufficient for justification (see Siegel 1992).

It would be helpful to consider Harvey Siegel's cases in logic as an illustration. Can a principle of reason be justified but not capture some of our intuitive judgements about what is correct inferential practice? As empirical research in cognitive psychology shows, there are many cases in which our inferential practices involve "principles" such as the following three: affirming the consequent; accepting poll results on the basis of who phones in to the host of a television show; or the gambler's fallacy. Here there is simply the failure to reason in accordance with justified principles (for the time being set aside questions about where the justification comes from). So bringing into agreement is not necessary for justification. Conversely, can we formulate principles that capture our inferential practices, yet not have these principles justified? Yes, we can accurately codify our (bad) inferential practices, as illustrated in the above three principles, yet these principles lack justification. So codification into principles is not sufficient for justification.

The above examples concerning logic are fairly clear-cut in severing the link between equilibrium and justification. We know of ways of justifying principles of logic that do not depend on achieving equilibrium (such as constructing truth-tables, forming axiom systems, constructing models for these systems and the like). These independent ways help in constructing the above counter-examples. In methodology matters are not so clear, since we have little in the way of independent access to what justifies the norms of method and what makes particular cases worthy of attention in a reflective equilibrium exercise. But it may well be that some of our scientific practices mislead us as to what are the genuinely correct particular judgements (many non-scientists are wrong about astrology while some scientists are, controversially, wrong in their intuitive judgements about the worth of intelligent design theories over the theory of evolution). And some codifications into principles of method are wrong because of the wrong particular cases they capture. Yet all of these bad particular judgements and wrong general principles could come into some equilibrium.

This brings us to the final matter, which concerns the very status of the following claim: X is justified if and only if X passes the reflective equilibrium test of achieving equilibrium.[7] We can ask: is this claim an analytic truth, true in virtue of the words that make it up? At best it is synthetic; the very meanings of "reflective equilibrium agreement" and "justified" are not so linked. We can ask: is this a necessary truth, that is, a truth that holds in all possible worlds? At best it is contingent as there are obviously possible worlds in which X is justified yet X fails some reflective equilibrium test, and conversely. The examples from logic illustrate this clearly; the cases from methodology are no different. There can be justified principles of method without equilibrium (in fact there is no guarantee that equilibrium can always be found). And one can be right about particular cases yet have bad codifications of what the principles are (a position that Feyerabend often endorses on the basis of his investigations into the history of science). Finally we can ask: is this claim something we can know to be *a priori* true? We might know this, but only in the case in which we simply stipulate that the claim is true. And this seems to be what gives reflective equilibrium its justificatory force; it is a truth by fiat. If one does make such a stipulation, then the claim is at best empirical. One way to understand the claim empirically is that X's passing the reflective equilibrium test is good, or at least not unreasonable, evidence for X's being justifiable. But even in this case X's passing the reflective equilibrium test need not always be reliable for X's justifiability.

In exploring the idea that reflective equilibrium might serve as a metamethodological principle, what is wanted is a principle that: (a) is itself justifiable; (b) is able to justify principles of scientific methods at Level 2; and (c) can play a role in selecting these principles. If the above considerations are correct then reflective equilibrium cannot meet the requirements of either (a) or (b); (c) has been weakly formulated so that a limited role can be assigned to reflective equilibrium pointing to many, but not all, principles of method that are worthy of further consideration. Finally, as has been mentioned, reflective equilibrium is not a *sui generis* principle of method or metamethod at all; it appears to be the name of a group of other values and rules of method that collectively taken together spell out what constitutes reflective equilibrium.

4.5 The historical turn, methods and metamethods

From the 1960s a "historical turn" was inaugurated in the philosophy of science by philosophers such as Hanson, Toulmin, Kuhn, Feyerabend and Laudan along with many others including historians of science, in which there was a strong focus on the history of science as a source of principles of methodology. In what way can the history of science be a "source" for methodology? A historical approach to science will tell us much about scientists' choices of, or attitudes towards, various theories, and their many different practices. But how can these facts of history lead to anything normative such as principles of method, or even a theory of rationality? There appears to be an unbridgeable "is–ought" gap that makes it hard to see how facts from the history of science could have any constitutive or evidential bearing on principles of method that are intrinsically normative and not factual.

A way around this might be the following. If one assumes that the history of science is a vast repository of the best of human rationality when it comes to considering our beliefs and practices, then one could require of any theory of scientific method or rationality that it ought to fit that history; the best theory of method would be the one that gives maximal fit, thereby making most of the moves in the history of science "rationally" explicable in terms of methodology. This is an approach taken by some philosophers such as Lakatos and, in a different way, Laudan. Just how close the fit ought to be is left open since it cannot be assumed that all episodes in the history of science have a rational basis in methodology. But it would certainly do much better than, say, a similar attempt to fit principles of deductive and probabilistic reasoning with human practices of reasoning; as much research in cognitive psychology shows, we are not very rational when it comes to conforming to the rules of reasoning.

What needs to be explained about the historical turn in respect of matters methodological is just how history of science can be a source of, or has any bearing on, normative methods. Here three issues need to be addressed. (i) The first concerns what elements of the history of science are to be used. For example, are we to take as the historical material the judgements of scientists themselves as to what are acceptable and unacceptable moves in the history of science? Or are other historical materials to be used? (ii) The second issue concerns the Level 2 principles of method themselves. Here we need to consider matters to do with the discovery of principles of method versus the justification of principles of method. The history of science may have played some role in leading (in whatever fashion) to the discovery of principles of method. But many have been discovered in an *a priori* manner, such as through the exercise of the human intellect. Let us grant that several different sources can play a role in the discovery of principles of method, the history of science being just one of them. Once some principles of method have been proposed, how are they to be justified? It is here that the history of science can play a critical role in that the proposed principles either do or do not fit episodes in the history of science. This critical role has been one of the main features of the historical turn. (iii) But for it to play this critical role a third matter must come to the fore: that of metamethodology. Metamethodology plays its role by bringing the materials from the history of science into relationship with Level 2 principles of method, thereby enabling history of science to play its critical role.

As we shall see, methodologists have been keenly aware of the role of metamethodology in enabling the history of science to play its critical role. This is particularly the case for Laudan's normative naturalism with its use of a meta-inductive principle as a Level 3 metamethodology (§12.2). And it is also the case for Feyerabend (see §11.2.3), who, we argue, employs something like the metamethod of reflective equilibrium mentioned in the previous section. These considerations are also true for Popper (§10.1.3) and Lakatos (§10.2.2); each employs his own Level 2 theory of method elevated to Level 3 metamethodology to adjudicate between the history of science and the principles of some theory of method. It is even true of subjective Bayesians, who put strong emphasis on the idea of coherent personal degrees of belief. It would be the role of a philosophically and Bayesian minded historian of science to consider the subjective degrees of belief of various scientists and to use this in the explanation of why they held particular scientific beliefs (see §§8.5–8.7 on subjective degrees of belief and an application in the case of the Quine–Duhem problem in §9.7).

The case of Kuhn is somewhat different. He certainly played a role in the historical turn; his book *The Structure of Scientific Revolutions* is replete with examples from the history of the natural sciences. But his model of science is largely descriptive. It provides a framework for viewing large chunks of the history of science under the following categories: normal science → normal science with anomalies → period of crisis → revolution and paradigm change → establishment of a new normal science. There is a considerable amount of vagueness as to what each of these categories might mean. For example, from a broad perspective it might appear as if a science is undergoing a revolutionary change of paradigm, but at a closer look there are often more continuities than discontinuities. And in normal science often there can be changes that move in the direction of revolutionary paradigm change. What are needed are sharper criteria for the identity conditions for each of the categories in his model of scientific change.[8] What are important for our purposes here are the principles of method that are to be critically evaluated against the history of science. The first edition of *The Structure of Scientific Revolutions* makes some negative comments about the role of theories of method in science. But in the "Postscript" to the second edition his methodology of weighted values comes to the fore as part of a modified account of what is a paradigm. In later writings Kuhn gives a metamethodological justification of his chosen values in terms of their semantic holistic (i.e. quasi-analytic) links to the notion of science (see §11.1). How does the rich material of the history of science relate to Kuhn's proposed methodology of weighted values? In part the values are those that are traditionally mentioned in the history of science, although his list of values is hardly complete. But Kuhn provides little in the way of the critical evaluation of his methodology of weighted values with that history. This is a task in which others have engaged. In this respect Kuhn is like most other methodologists; he presents us with a methodology, that of weighted values, while downplaying its assessment against the history of science.

Advocates of the historical turn have been critical of the attitude that methodologists, such as Popper and Lakatos, and earlier positivists, such as Carnap and Reichenbach, have had towards the history of science. They may have used episodes from the history of science to illustrate their methodologies; but given their strong leanings towards their own theories of method, the history of science was often used to illustrate their methodology rather than be a source for it; or it was used for rhetorical purposes to bolster their preferred theory of method. Some advocates of the historical turn argue that they in fact falsified the history of science in order to squeeze it into their methodological moulds. Lakatos was quite aware of the way in which different methodologists found particular episodes from the history of science more amenable to their methodological purposes than others. In illustration of this he shows, in his "History of Science and its Rational Reconstructions" (1978: ch. 2), how four methodologies (inductivism, conventionalism, falsificationism and his own methodology of SRPs) exploit certain episodes in the history of science as examples that fit each methodology and downplay those episodes that do not fit so well, or not at all. Famously Lakatos begins this paper with his Kantian quip "Philosophy of science without history of science is empty; history of science without philosophy of science is blind" (*ibid.*: 102). This indicates that history of science ought to be taken seriously by methodologists. But the way that Lakatos expects methodologists to go about their task has been found deeply unsatisfactory by many historians of science and historically inclined philosophers of science.

In "History of Science and its Rational Reconstructions", Lakatos deploys one version of the internal–external distinction to show that internal history of science is to be written in accordance with the principles of some theory of method while external science inherits the leftovers, which are to be explained by means other than those that appeal to principles of method. This gives bite to Lakatos's notion of a "rational reconstruction of history of science". In an internal history of science, actual episodes in science would have to be "massaged" so that they could be made to fit the principles of some theory of method; once they were made to fit then the episode could be explained rationally in terms of the adoption of some methodological principle. This depends on a "rational" model of explanation that answers the question: why does some scientist believe (accept, adopt, etc.) hypothesis H? In providing the answer the explanans must mention some principle of method M that shows that H is the best hypothesis to adopt. The explanans must also claim that the scientist either explicitly employs M in arriving at the belief that H is the best hypothesis, or can be construed to have implicitly done so (in the light of Lakatos's views about the "rational reconstruction" of episodes in the history of science).

This approach makes methodology the main explanatory driver of scientific progress. But it allows rational reconstructors such as Lakatos too many liberties with actual history. This is something that Lakatos openly admits when he discusses the activities of the nineteenth-century chemist William Prout. Lakatos says of his rational reconstruction of this episode, which he calls the "Proutian programme": "The Proutian programme is not Prout's programme" (*ibid*.: 119). By this Lakatos means that the kind of story he wishes to tell of this episode may contain elements that one might not find in the actual historical episode, or as thoughts that Prout actually entertained. Lakatos's reconstruction is very much along the lines of a Popperian "third world" item and not a "second world" item of, say, the actual thoughts passing through the minds of scientists.

Historically minded philosophers of science reject this approach despite Lakatos's Feyerabendian advice to those who wish to write a historical case study: "(1) one gives a rational reconstruction; (2) one tries to compare this rational reconstruction with actual history and to criticize both one's rational reconstruction for lack of historicity and the actual history for lack of rationality" (*ibid*.: 52–3). But this does raise issues (i), (ii) and (iii) for those who wish to give episodes in the history of science a much more prominent role. Despite what some historians would regard as his cavalier attitude to the history of science, Lakatos does raise some of the central issues concerning the manner in which actual history of science is to be brought into relationships with principles of method, and what role a metamethodology is to play.

Let us turn to issue (i) concerning the elements that are to be extracted from the history of science and used in any comparison with principles of method. One kind of element is suggested by Lakatos. We are to extract from episodes in the history of science particular judgements of the relevant scientific elites about what is or is not a "rational move" in those episodes. We are not to ask the elite how they make the judgement; we simply accept the judgement they do in fact make. Here it is assumed that the historical and/or sociological investigation that is to take place does come up with a consensus on this matter and that there are agreed judgements J_1, J_2, and so on for different episodes. Once we have these basic judgements of each scientific elite then they can be used critically to evaluate different sets of principles of method. The previous section discusses how the metamethodology of reflective equilibrium can be used to make the evaluation; this, we suggest, is the procedure Feyerabend recommends (§11.2.3). Lakatos also requires such judgements; but he uses a different metamethodology, namely, his own theory of the methodology of SRPs elevated to Level 3. This determines which of the different sets of Level 2 methodological principles maximizes the "rationality" of science (see §10.2.2).

Different kinds of materials can be extracted from the history of science. In the above the history of science is used to extract the judgements of the scientific elite about what are the "rational moves" in the game of science. This allows the possibility that the elite make the right judgements (in that they do in fact, say, lead to progress in science), but they do this for wrong or bad reasons. Further research into the history of science is to tell us something about their reasons for making their judgements, perhaps codified as maxims or as methodological rules of thumb. These reasons then become the material on the basis of which the evaluation of methodologies is to be made. Consider an example. Copernicus was very critical of the use of the equant point by Ptolemaic astronomers when they constructed their geocentric models of planetary motion, so he did not use them in his own (heliocentric) models. Some of the scientific elite at that time, but many more later, may well agree that this was a good move. But what were Copernicus's reasons? What he disliked was the fact that the equant point represented an abandonment of the Platonic heuristic that all motions in the heavens were to be explained by uniform circular motions about a given central point (and not an equant point displaced from the centre). How can this episode be used to evaluate principles of method?

Here it might be useful to adopt a distinction between maxims and principles that Kant makes in the context of his moral philosophy. A maxim on which an individual acts has the general form: in theoretical situation S, doing A will bring about goal G. A general principle incorporates this maxim but goes beyond the particularities of the theoretical situation in being far more general and more widely applicable. Applying this to the case of Copernicus we need to specify something about the scientific context in which he was working (geometrical models of planetary motion) and the goals he had, such as producing "better" models of planetary motion (but still using the deferents and epicycles of his predecessors). His maxim might be: do not make moves in the construction of models that go against the basic principles (involving uniform circular motion about a centre) for the construction of those models. Perhaps the maxim might employ the notion of being *ad hoc*; but this is a notion that is best employed when we move to the general principle of which the maxim is an instance. The general principle might be an anti-*ad hoc* rule telling us not to make any adjustment whatever to our theories and models that simply preserve their fit with the observable phenomena, especially where these adjustments undermine one of the core postulates with which one works.

What this procedure requires is a research programme in the history of science that looks to the maxims of action of scientists in their particular problem contexts. It tries to uncover the goals that the scientists have and the methodological means that they employ to achieve them. The history of science is used as a vast repository of cases in which particular means are employed to reach particular ends. The task of metamethodology would then be to bring these maxims of action into accordance with some Level 2 principles of method. Once again the metamethodology of reflective equilibrium might be employed to perform this task. But Laudan, who advocates an approach like this, recommends using as a metamethodology either the straight rule of induction or the H-D method (see §12.2).

As mentioned, subjective Bayesians would need to go to the history of science for quite different materials in order to test the correctness of probabilistic rules of method. What they want from the history of science are some numbers, or very small interval ranges, in the overall interval [0, 1], which represent each scientist's coherent degree of belief in some hypothesis or evidence. These numbers are then used in probabilistic principles to show that there is a fit between actual behaviour of scientists in, say, accepting or rejecting theories, and the rules of probability that make this behaviour "rational", or coherent. This requires a quite different investigation of the materials of the history of science in order to establish the "rationality" of Bayesian principles.

Other ways might be suggested as to how the history of science is to provide materials for the evaluation of principles of method. But they will all involve the elements of (i), (ii) and (iii) listed above. And, as has been indicated, not all methodologists will, when equipped with appropriate materials from the history of science, adopt the same metamethodological stance. While the historical turn in the philosophy of science has had a salutary effect, by itself it can tell us nothing about what are the principles of method one ought to adopt. It may not even be a source of those principles if what is meant by this is that it provides a means for discovering principles of method; to do this it would have to employ some methods of discovery. But once furnished with some principles of method it can play a role in critically evaluating these principles, providing some metamethodological procedure is already available for doing this.

II. Inductive and hypothetico-deductive methods

5. Induction in science

The idea that science involves inductive inference was first adumbrated by Aristotle in his *Organon*, where he speaks of a way of getting knowledge of the universal by induction from our knowledge of particulars, his term being *epagoge*, literally meaning "to lead on". Our term "induction" comes from the Latin "*inducere*" meaning much the same. Francis Bacon, in his *Novum Organum*, also gave pride of place to induction in science, although he did not think much of the rule of enumerative induction as an example of it (see §5.3). In contrast, as we have seen in §3.4, Newton's third and fourth rules appeal to induction. However, nobody thought that induction was a deeply problematic form of inference until Hume sharply formulated an argument that shows that all inductive inference lacks justification, thereby challenging a deep philosophical assumption. The problem of justifying induction is discussed in Chapter 6; in this chapter we shall be concerned with some of the different kinds of inductive inference used in science.

Scientific methods are intimately bound up with rules of inference. Few would characterize science so narrowly as to say that it is only the collection of the perforce finite number of disparate reports we make about what we can directly observe. Such a naive view of science has no role for inference-making. In recognizing the need to transcend the meagre amount of data we can collect, we must make inferences, drawing out two broad kinds of conclusion. The first concerns the potentially infinite number of particular claims about states of affairs, past, future and elsewhere, that we do not, or cannot, directly observe. We wish to know what the rest of the world is like outside the small spacetime region to which our lives are confined, the only region of which we can have direct observational access through our senses. The second kind of conclusion concerns our inferences to the laws and theories that go beyond what we can observe and that, we hope, give us a deeper cognitive insight into how the world really works. Even if we are more imaginative and start not from observations or data but from observation-transcendent conjectures, laws, hypotheses or theories, we still need to make inductive inferences to bring our conjectures into a relation with observational data as a "reality check" against our conjecturing.

In Chapter 7 we discuss how we may bring our theoretical conjectures into a relation with what we can observe using the *H-D method*. As its name indicates, it uses deductive modes of inference. But inductive modes are also central to this methodology. We infer not only downwards by deduction from our conjecture to what we might observe, but also upwards to discover how well what we observe supports or undermines our theoretical conjectures. The upwards path is crucially inductive and not deductive. In some of the non-empirical sciences deductive methods are the principal methods employed, Euclidean geometry being a prime example. Many of the empirical sciences have a similar deductive structure in so far as much science involves making deductions from more fundamental laws and theories to the less fundamental; or deductions from the applications of laws to predictions and evidential tests for them. But in order to make tests, inductive modes of inference must be involved to evaluate our conjectures by telling us how well or badly they are supported by test evidence.

Science has been pre-eminently successful in getting us knowledge of the world and ourselves. But can inductive methods also bask in that success as the means whereby it has been obtained? Some would say so, as the many books on statistical methodology and probabilistic inference attest. However, others, especially philosophers who delve into the foundations of such modes of inference, are not so sanguine about our understanding of induction in science, despite the success of science. We use induction, but it is philosophically problematic and hard to justify. In Chapter 6 we consider the longstanding meta-methodological problem of the justification of inductive inference, a topic on which there is a vast literature, only some of which we survey.

This chapter sets out some of the kinds of inductive inference there are. Section 5.1 begins with the difference between deductive and inductive modes of inference and ways of characterizing induction. Section 5.2 makes a link between inductive inference on the one hand and probability and confirmation on the other. Section 5.3 focuses on simple enumerative induction, while §5.4 considers some of the different ways of characterizing abduction or inference to the best explanation. There are also some deep problems that inductive inference faces due to the "grue" problem and issues to do with curve-fitting; these are discussed in §5.5 and §5.6 respectively.

5.1 Deduction and induction

In science as elsewhere, we wish to make valid inferences from premises to conclusion; these are sanctioned by the rules of deductive logic. Broadly speaking, we can say that logic is the study of the support that the premises of an argument give its conclusion. The best possible support is given in the case where the premises, A_1, A_2, ..., A_n, have as a *logical consequence*, or *entail*, the conclusion C; or C *follows logically* from the premises. We shall write this as "$A_1, A_2, ..., A_n \vdash C$", where the turnstile symbol "$\vdash$" stands for the relation of logical consequence, or deduction of the conclusion from the premises.

We can also characterize the connection between premises and conclusion semantically, invoking the notion of truth. One of the desiderata of principles of method is that they be reliable for the truth (see §3.2). Valid deductive inferences are highly reliable, on the condition that their premises are true. That is, they are 100 per cent conditionally reliable in the sense that if the premises are true, then valid deductive inferences give the best possible guarantee of the truth of the conclusion. There is an equivalent semantic account of what it is for a conclusion to be a logical consequence of some premises: it is logically *impossible* for the premises to be true and the conclusion to be false. There are many senses of the word "possible"; here the one intended is that of logical possibility, a notion that is spelled out in texts on logic.

The theory of deductive logic also tells us when a conclusion does not follow from the premises, that is, the argument is deductively invalid. Not all non-deductive arguments are necessarily bad. Although invalid, there is a range of arguments that do give some support for the conclusion, although not as good as the support given by deductively valid arguments. The support comes in degrees. As will be indicated, the degree of support can be measured on a scale from 0 to 1 with a limiting case at the top of best possible support (i.e. valid deduction), and then descending to high, middling and then quite low support (the bottom limiting case of zero support arises when the premises contradict the conclusion). Alternatively the support may be comparative, as when two arguments are characterized as better or worse according to the support the premises of each give to their respective conclusions. These are *non-deductive* forms of argument or, equivalently, *inductive* forms of argument.

There is another way of characterizing the difference between the two broad kinds of argument. Deductive arguments are said to be *non-ampliative* in that the content of their conclusions does not "go beyond", or amplify, the content contained in their premises. In contrast the contents of the conclusions of inductive arguments do "go beyond" the content contained in their premises. In so far as nearly all our theories transcend the observations or data that might support them as evidence (they say much more than the evidence), then any inference from evidence to theory will be ampliative.

One of the major tasks of a theory of inductive inference is to say what degree of support the premises can give a conclusion. In the case of valid deductive inference, the degree of support is 100 per cent conditionally reliable in that it takes us from true premises to true conclusions. In addition, forms of deductive inference (such as *modus ponens*) are reliable not only in this world but in all possible worlds. In contrast, for inductive inference the degree of support is not always 100 per cent conditionally reliable. Moreover inductive inferences are not reliable in all possible worlds; it is always possible that the premises be true and the conclusion false. But we would like our preferred modes of inductive inference to be highly reliable in the actual world in which we exist in that they reliably take us from true premises to true conclusions. For example, when we inductively infer from the premise "on each day that we have observed the sun has risen" to the conclusion "tomorrow the sun will rise", then we wish the argument to be reliable in that it takes us from true premises to true conclusion. Finding a guarantee for this is a large part of the metamethodological issue of justifying modes of inductive inference addressed in Chapter 6.

Paralleling the definition of what it is for an argument to be deductively valid we can propose the following characterization of a *strong* inductive argument: although the argument is logically invalid, it is *improbable* for the premises to be true and the conclusion is false. The difference lies in the difference between the words "impossible" and "improbable". Similarly we can say that an argument is *weakly* inductive if and only if (iff) it is *probable* that the premises are true but the conclusion is false.

5.2 From induction to probability and confirmation

The above characterization of inductive inference strongly suggests that there is a relation of *inductive probability* between any single statement or conjunction of statements that serve as premise(s) A, and any statement C that is an alleged conclusion, or more generally between any pair of statements whatsoever. This we can write as "$P(C, A)$" where "P" stands for the (inductive) probability relation and the expression is read as "the (inductive) probability of (conclusion) C given (premises) A". This is a *conditional* probability, in that we speak of the probability of C on the condition of A. Alternatively we can speak of the *relative* probability, the probability of C relative to A. Finally we can speak of the *posterior* probability of C in the literal sense of the probability of C "coming after" the premises A that serve as evidence for C.

We can also make the following two important suppositions, which have far-reaching consequences: for any pair of propositions A and C, (a) there is a well-defined measure of the degree of inductive support that A gives C, and

(b) this can be expressed as a probability, understood in terms of the probability calculus. Making these suppositions enables us to say, for any propositions A and C, $P(C, A)$ lies in the interval $[0, 1]$, that is, $0 \leq P(C, A) \leq 1$. There are two limiting cases to consider. When $P(C, A) = 1$, we have the best possible support in which C is a logical consequence of A. When $P(C, A) = 0$ we have the worst possible support when A contradicts C. (Both of these results can be established within the probability calculus.) For the other cases in which $0 < P(C, A) < 1$ there are varying degrees of inductive probabilistic support that (premise) A gives (conclusion) C.

If we think of the premises of our arguments as being evidence E and the conclusion being a hypothesis (law, theory, conjecture, etc.) H, then we can rewrite the above as follows: $0 \leq P(H, E) \leq 1$. We understand this to mean that any hypothesis can be given the best or the worst support by evidence E, or any degree of support in between. The formulation here is quite general. Hypothesis H can be a generalization, a putative law of nature, a conjunction of laws or a theory. The evidence E can be a collection of data or observations, or other laws and theories. Kepler's laws of planetary motion or Galileo's laws of free fall, or the evidence for these, can all constitute evidence E for Newton's laws of motion as hypotheses H. H can also be a particular claim, as when a doctor formulates singular hypothesis H, for example, that his patient is suffering from haemochromatosis; the evidence E for H is based in symptoms and medical tests. Again, a detective can form a hypothesis H about who has committed an offence on the basis of various kinds of forensic evidence E. The account here is meant to be quite general in that any (consistent) proposition can count as evidence, and any other (consistent) proposition can serve as a hypothesis.

The above suggests that in determining the degree of inductive support A gives to C, we can find some number r such that $P(C, A) = r$ and $0 \leq r \leq 1$. Is there a general procedure for doing this? One of the grand goals of Carnap's *The Logical Foundations of Probability* was to find such a number for what he called his "c-functions" or *logical probabilities*, that is, for any proposition C and A there is a confirmation function such that $c(C, A) = r$. Carnap's programme of determining logical probabilities is akin to the problem of finding the degrees of inductive support, as in $P(C, A) = r$. Unfortunately Carnap's programme has been rejected by many since it cannot be easily completed and there are many technical problems that remain unsolved; important as it is we shall not discuss it further.[1] This is not to say that there are not other methods for determining the value of r (within some range of error) for $P(C, A) = r$. Some methods use empirically determined frequencies. Thus if C is the conclusion "the next toss of the coin will yield heads" but the evidence that serves as the premise acquired by experimental observation is "on 1000 previous trial tosses there were only 200 heads", then there are good grounds for claiming $P(C, A) = 0.2$. Quite different approaches will be examined in Part III when we consider Bayesianism.

Given the above considerations of inductive support in terms of probability, it is now possible to introduce the notion of *confirmation*. First a notion of *absolute confirmation*:

E confirms H iff $P(H, E)$ is high, or at least $> \frac{1}{2}$.

E disconfirms H iff $P(H, E)$ is low, or at least $P(H, E) < \frac{1}{2}$.

E is confirmatorily *neutral* with respect to *H* (i.e. neither confirms nor disconfirms *H*) iff $P(H, E) = \frac{1}{2}$.

It is possible to give more refined notions of confirmation in terms of the increase or decrease in confirmation that can arise when new evidence comes along. But first we need to introduce the notion of a prior, or absolute, or unconditional probability, which we shall write as "$P(H)$". One simple way to introduce this suitable to our purposes here is to consider the case in which the premises of the argument that serve as evidence are not empirically contentful but are merely tautologous truths of logic. We shall refer to these as "*Taut.*"; and in place of "*E*" we can write "$P(H, Taut.)$". This expression tells us the probability of *H* in the presence of only tautologies and in the absence of any contentful evidential claims; that is, it is a *prior* probability, prior to any evidence other than contentless tautologies. Looked at in this light we can abbreviate "$P(H, Taut.)$" as "$P(H)$". We also need the idea of background evidence, *B*, which is already present as new evidence *E* comes along; *E* can be considered to be a new premise to be added to the premises *B* that concern earlier or old evidence. In the limiting case *B* can be empty, that is, just tautologies.

We can now introduce the idea of *incremental* confirmation in which new evidence *E* added as an additional premise either increases or decreases the confirmation of *H* over what confirmation it had before given only *B*.

E increases the confirmation of *H* with respect to *B* iff $P(H, E \,\&\, B) > P(H, B)$.

In the limiting case of *B* as tautologies we have: $P(H, E) > P(H)$; that is, there is an increase in probability when *E* is considered over the probability before any evidence is entertained.

E decreases the confirmation of *H* with respect to *B* iff $P(H, E \,\&\, B) < P(H, B)$.

In the limiting case of *B* as tautologies we have: $P(H, E) < P(H)$; that is, there is a decrease in probability when *E* is considered over the probability before any evidence is entertained.

Finally there is no increase or decrease and *E* is *confirmatorily neutral* with respect to *B*: $P(H, E \,\&\, B) = P(H, B)$; or in the limiting case $P(H, E) = P(H)$.

111

Here confirmation is not an all-or-nothing affair; as would be intuitively expected, it admits of degrees and increases and decreases with E, or with new evidence E against a background of previous evidence B.

So far we have only spoken of the degree of (inductive) support that a conclusion H gets from its evidential premises E. Now we turn to an issue that follows on from this, namely, whether we are entitled to detach the conclusion from the argument and simply assert "H" or, equivalently, "H is true". Such detachment is commonplace in deductive reasoning. There is a rule of detachment for deductive logic that licenses us to detach the conclusion from the argument and assert it as true. Alternatively, if we know, or justifiably believe, the evidential premises E, then we also know, or justifiably believe, the conclusion H. (This follows from some plausible closure principles.)

Is there a parallel detachment rule for inductive reasoning? In inductive reasoning, the premises E that serve as evidence for a conclusion H are commonly true, or we know them to be true, or we justifiably believe them. Granted this, and granted that the evidence E strongly favours H, then can H be detached and added to our body, or corpus K, of scientific knowledge? (Here the term "knowledge" is used in the etiolated sense of the best we are able to do in our science up until now and is open to revision, and so is not necessarily truth-entailing.) There are opposing views as to whether we should adopt any rule of detachment for inductive reasoning.

Hempel, along with many others, is a "detacher" and gives us the following rule of detachment or acceptance into K, and rejection from K:

Tentative rule for inductive acceptance: Accept or reject H, given E, according as $P(H, E) > \frac{1}{2}$, or $P(H, E) < \frac{1}{2}$; when $P(H, E) = \frac{1}{2}$, H may be accepted, rejected or left in suspense.[2]

For detachers, this rule is an important principle of methodology concerning the acceptance of hypotheses into the body of scientific knowledge K, along with rules for the acceptance of evidential claims such as observational reports, reports about data, and the like. This does not mean that all the statements in K are true; rather their presence in K is sanctioned by methodological principles formulated as rules of acceptance and rejection. The goal of such acceptance or rejection is that of pure enquiry: we want to know which propositions reach sufficiently high epistemic criteria to be included in the corpus K of science.

In contrast, there are the "non-detachers", and even "anti-detachers", who do not adopt rules of detachment, or are opposed to them. They are content to remain with whatever support current hypotheses get from current evidence, merely keeping track of that degree of support as evidence comes in without detaching the hypotheses and saying they are to be accepted or rejected.

Consequently they downplay the theoretical goals of detachers in favour of more pragmatic goals of action, with specific applications that require not that *H* be true, but only the degree of support *H* has at a given time, namely, $P(H, E)$. Of course, the acceptance envisaged by a detacher is an action of sorts; but the action is directed towards the goals of pure enquiry concerning what we are to put into the corpus *K* of scientific knowledge. Those who reject detachment have different actions in mind. As Richard Jeffrey insists:

> it is not the business of the scientist as such ... to accept or reject hypotheses. ... the proper role of scientists is to provide the rational agents in the society which they represent with the probabilities for the hypotheses which in the other account [i.e. that of detachers] they simply accept or reject. (1992: 26)

Here we adopt the stance, and the reasons, of Hempel (2001: chs 18–20) along with many others who advocate a role for rules of detachment; they are an important addition to the principles of scientific method. Non-detachers recommend a quite different approach to methodology that employs decision theory.[3]

5.3 Enumerative induction

There are many forms that inductive inferences might take. One form is the simple statistical syllogism in which the universal quantifier "all" has been replaced by a percentage as in the following:[4]

About 90 per cent of people in rapid-eye-movement (REM) sleep have dreams;
person *P* is in REM sleep; [90 per cent]
∴ *P* is having a dream.

Here the wavy line indicates that an inductive argument is intended (as opposed to a straight line, which indicates that a deductive argument is intended). But what is the degree of support that the premises, with the statistical first premise (of the form "*n* per cent *P* are *Q*"), give the conclusion? Following Hempel (1965: 380–400) we can claim that the degree of support is 90 per cent, that is, the same percentage as in the statistical first premise. This is indicated on the wavy line to show that it is the premise–conclusion link that is so qualified and not the conclusion.

Another common form is that of inductive analogy, a good example of which is the argument from design for God's existence proposed by William Paley on the basis of an analogy of the order and intricacies of a watch, which evidently has a designer (a watchmaker), with the order and intricacy of the entire world:

A watch is orderly, intricate and law-governed, and has a designer;
the world is similarly orderly, intricate and law-governed;
─── [*n* per cent]
∴ the world has a designer.

The argument is clearly not deductive and is based on a number of similarities between the watch and the world. What degree of support do the premises give the conclusion? Following a suggestion by Sober (1993: 34) we can say that the degree of support is to be estimated by taking into account the overall similarities and differences between a watch and the world, which might be high, middling or low. Such inductive analogies have a considerable role in science, in particular the case that Darwin made for natural selection on analogy with domestic selection.

Enumerative induction is a form of inductive inference based on the enumeration of observed cases (or more broadly known cases, which may not have necessarily been directly observed). Bacon criticized enumerative induction, writing that it "is a childish affair, unsafe in its conclusions, in danger of a contradictory instance, taking into account only what is familiar, and leading to no result" ([1620] 1994: 21, 111). Although Bacon is right about those inductions that ought to have a proper randomly chosen sample, his claim is too harsh since in some cases enumerative induction is all we have; thus inferences to the sun rising tomorrow or our mortality are both based on enumeration of past cases that do not permit randomization of the sample.

Why do we think that we are mortal, that is, that all people now alive will die at some time in the not too distant future? Because of the very large number of particular past cases in which a person who was born at an earlier time died at a later time. This is an *inductive prediction* about particular cases, namely, each person now alive. We can use the same evidence to make the general claim that all persons alive at any time in the past, present or future will die at some time. This is an *inductive generalization* about all people, observed and unobserved. Enumerative induction is clearly a source of much of our everyday belief, whether as a prediction about the next case or as a generalization.

Inductive inferences are also an important part of the methods of science. The conclusions we draw on the basis of them constitute a central aspect of our scientific beliefs, especially the laws, theories and hypotheses of science. Newton's Rule 3 (see §3.4) expresses an important role for enumerative induction. We make experiments and observations in our laboratory, or out in the field; then we wish to know if the outcomes of the experiments and observations would be the same at other places and times, past or future. For example, suppose we perform the Eötvös experiment in a laboratory using a simple torsion balance with a plumb bob made of a given substance. We discover, as did Roland Eötvös in 1889, that the ratio of the gravitational mass to the inertial mass of substances is the same to an accuracy of 1 in 10^8 (improved results have been obtained since then). There are two inductions here. The first concerns the bob itself. We perform the experiment using bobs of a few different substances (lead, iron, etc.). But does the result apply to all other substances out of which the bob can be made (e.g. oxygen)? The second induction involves other places and times. We wish to know if what we observe in the laboratory holds elsewhere, say at the South Pole, or on the moon, or in the next galaxy; but we are not able to repeat such experiments unless we practice space travel. Again we wish to know if these results also held in the past, and will hold in the future, but perforce we cannot travel in time to make such investigations. But by the method of simple enumerative induction we can make an inference and draw the conclusion that the result of the Eötvös experiment will hold for all other substances, times and places. Enumerative induction expresses the idea that even though we inhabit a very small region of spacetime, we can infer that what we observe holds elsewhere in spacetime. Whether we infer justifiably is another matter considered in Chapter 6.

A rule for enumerative induction formulated for both inductive prediction and generalization runs:

Inductive rule for enumerative induction: From information (observational or otherwise) that *n* instances of *P* are also *Q*, infer all *P*s are *Q*s (or the next *P* is a *Q*).

As part of the methodology of applying the rule we can add to it the proviso that a wide variety of cases of *P* should be observed. We can assume that the reference to "all observed *n*" means that no *P* was observed not to be *Q*. We also allow that the information need not be obtained only by observational means. So the rule for enumerative induction applies equally as well to cases that are about items that are unobservable, such as the unobservable objects of physics (e.g. electrons) and their unobservable properties (e.g. inertial mass, negative charge, spin, etc.). Thus, on the basis of empirical investigations, as in the Millikan oil-drop experiment, which determines that when a finite number of electrons are investigated they have a given mass/charge ratio, we can infer that all the electrons in the cosmos have the same mass/charge ratio.

The above rule is not the only rule that might be adopted. The counter-inductivist rule tells us to take past observational information as a guide to what will not happen in the future:

Counter-inductivist rule for enumerative induction: From information (observational or otherwise) that *n* instances of *P* are also *Q*, infer the next *P* will not be a *Q* (or not all *P* are *Q*).

Another rule that could be adopted is one that says that the observed cases have no bearing at all on the cases we have not observed. This is the position of neither the inductivist nor the counter-inductivist since both pay careful attention to the past, but make different inferences from it. The "indifferentists" (we might say) claim that the past is irrelevant and adopt the following indifference rule of enumerative induction:

Indifference rule of enumerative induction: From information (observational or otherwise) that *n* instances of *P* are also *Q*, do not infer anything about the next *P* being *Q*, or that all, or no, *Ps* are *Q*.

Most people are inductivists and not counter-inductivists (although the gambler's fallacy often leads us astray) or "indifferentists". This is evident when we next reach for water to quench our thirst because water has quenched our thirst in the past; when we remain in our room and do not think that the ceiling will fall in, because that is what has happened in the past; when we act to get away from oncoming buses, based on past evidence of human collision with buses; and so on for countless other cases that (inductively) support Bishop Butler's remark "To us probability is the very guide of life" (see Carnap [1950] 1962: 247). For those who are not inductivists, life may well be, as Hobbes said in another context, "poor, nasty, brutish and short". But do we have a justification for the rule of enumerative induction that also shows that the two envisaged rival possibilities lack justification? This is Hume's famous sceptical challenge, which, he argued, cannot be met. It will be discussed in Chapter 6.

The premises of an enumerative induction are not always amenable to controlled experimental investigation; like the rising sun or our mortality, we can only observe the regularities as they happen. Nor do all enumerative generalizations lead us to a perfectly general conclusion; some may lead us to a statistical regularity. For example, in the first publication on the experimental investigation into REM sleep and dreaming, Hobson (1988: 142) reports that between 90 per cent and 95 per cent of subjects awoken from REM sleep accompanied by rapid eye movement reported dream experiences (the independent criteria for dreaming having been specified in advance). REM sleep is identified by characteristic brainwave patterns (registered by an electroencephalogram) during which there are bursts of rapid eye movement (registered on an electrooculogram). In different experimental circumstances there was a drop to about 70 per cent of subjects awoken during REM sleep without rapid eye movement but who reported dreaming. In contrast only 5–10 per cent of those woken from non-REM sleep reported anything that could be taken to be dreaming.

These percentages are based on the frequencies determined on the basis of the experimental investigation of a small number of subjects selected randomly from the population as a whole. What can we say about REM sleep and dreaming for the total human population? (A similar question can be asked about REM sleep that occurs in all mammals and most vertebrates.) Should we take the percentages discovered for the small number of experimental subjects to be the same for people as a whole? If so, the following inductive rule for statistical generalization captures this thought:

Rule for statistical generalization 1: From *n* per cent observed *P*s are *Q*s, infer *n* per cent of all *P*s are *Q*s.

If *n* per cent is 100 per cent then the rule of enumerative induction is a special case of this rule. If we use Hobson's data on REM sleep, then from the test group in which 90–95 per cent of a small population of *N* people who are awoken from REM sleep during bursts of rapid eye movement report dreams, we can infer that 90–95 per cent of human beings at large behave similarly. There are cases where we make inferences when *n* = 0. Thus we have never observed that drinking water leads to raging thirst; so we infer that 0 per cent of the time water leads to raging thirst.

The rule is defective as it stands. It says nothing about sample size but only what percentage of *P*s are *Q*s. If the number *N* of *P*s investigated is, say, 10, and 90 per cent of them are *Q*s then we might feel that the sample size is too small. A better argument would be one in which, say, *N* was 100, or even 1000; then we would have greater confidence in the claim that 90 per cent of all *P*s are *Q*s. We would have even more confidence in the conclusion if we also know that the sample of *N* people of whatever size has been chosen randomly. Also important is the variety of experimental circumstances in which the statistical regularity has been found to hold. It is not easy to incorporate all these requirements and express them in a rule of the above sort. Although we say little about it here, the requirement is tantamount to the rule being set in the context of an adequate account of statistical inference. Some of these points lead to the next rule, which is slightly more general.

Psephologists sample the opinions of eligible voters as to political party preference, often using a sample size of 500–1000 people. From this they infer the voting habits of the population as a whole, which may involve several million people. The statisticians recognize that there may be errors due to the small sample size. (The smallness is often due to the costs of making such random samplings or the short period of sampling.) There are well-established, powerful statistical techniques for determining what the error is. This is usually expressed in terms of a number n and another factor ε, the error factor. This leads to the next rule, an improved version of the previous one:

Inductive rule for statistical generalization 2: From n per cent observed Ps are Qs, infer $(n \pm \varepsilon)$ per cent of all Ps are Qs.

The rule as formulated says nothing about how the value of $\pm \varepsilon$ is to be determined; this is a matter left to theories of statistics. But by adding to n the error factor due to ε, this rule presupposes a setting within theories of statistical reasoning. Understood this way the rule is the widely used form of inductive inference. The rule of enumerative induction, widely discussed by philosophers, is a special case of this rule of statistical generalization (2), in which $\varepsilon = 0$ and n is set at 100 per cent.

Finally, Reichenbach proposed a rule of enumerative inductive inference, known as the *straight rule*, which is more general than the rule of enumerative induction in that it is based on frequencies. Suppose we have a finite sequence of n trial events A (such as n tosses of a die), which have chosen feature B (such as a six resulting m times), so that the Bs occur m times among the n As. That is, the frequency of the Bs among the As is m/n, which we can write as "$F^n(A, B) = m/n$". What we wish to know is what is the frequency of the Bs among the As, either in the long run or as they continue to infinity. Reichenbach's suggested rule of enumerative induction in this case is:

Straight rule: If $F^n(A, B) = m/n$, then in the limit as $n \to \infty$, $F^n(A, B) = m/n$.

The rule assumes that the frequency is based on all the trials that have been observed. If more trials are subsequently undertaken and a new frequency is established, the straight rule assumes that we adopt that new frequency. The new observed frequency is then to be projected to all the unobserved cases and is taken to be the frequency in the limit. What limiting frequency might we adopt other than the one we have observed up until now? It might appear that any frequency in the neighbourhood of m/n could be adopted. Clearly the straight rule stands in need of justification, as do all the other enumerative induction rules listed. This we leave to Chapter 6.

5.4 The rule of inference to the best explanation

In this section we shall discuss a common, but controversial, form of inductive inference generally known as *inference to the best explanation* (IBE). That a theory is able to explain some facts is regarded as one of its virtues; it is a vice of a theory that it explain nothing or very little. If theory T is able to explain more relevant facts than any other theory T^*, or explain the same facts better, then T exhibits more of this virtue. This in turn leads to a principle of theory choice: other things being equal, if T explains more, or better, than T^*, then this is a reason for choosing T over T^*. For some (see §2.5, §2.6), being able to explain is not merely a virtue but one of the aims of science. As an aim it could be understood to override other virtues in that when it comes to choosing between T and its rivals, T's ability to explain more outranks consideration of other virtues that any rival T^* might exhibit but T does not.

Some philosophers would like to draw important conclusions from a theory's ability to explain facts, understood either as a virtue or, more strongly, as an overriding aim. If we grant as premises some facts, and grant that T explains these facts much better than any of its available rivals, then the following conclusions can be inductively drawn: either T is true, or it is reasonable to believe in the truth of T, or T has greater verisimilitude, or T has greater probability, than its rivals, or T ought to be accepted for whatever purpose (including belief). This is the core idea behind IBE. Expressed as a hypothetical imperative it says: given a set of rival hypotheses, if you want to realize truth (v), then, if you are going to make any choice at all from that set, you ought to choose the best explainer. Clearly much more needs to be said about the inferential rule of IBE concerning its premises, its conclusion, the kind of inference that links premises and conclusion, the conditions under which it is to be applied and whether there is always a uniquely optimal, best explanatory hypothesis (there might be several tied for first place). Such a rule would be opposed by those who think that explanatoriness is a pragmatic virtue of a theory that is not linked to the alethic virtue of truth; they allege we can have explanation without being automatically committed to truth.

IBE has long been recognized as a form of inference and has gone by several other names, such as *method of hypotheses* or *abduction*. It has been advocated within the sciences that have developed since the eighteenth century, and well before in other contexts. It is a form of inference currently adopted in many sciences as a Level 2 methodological principle. There is also much literature in artificial intelligence and theories of computation that use and explore IBE and its applications in different areas from medical diagnosis to jury deliberation.[5]

As an illustration, consider the use of IBE in establishing the theory of natural selection against its creationist rival. Darwin begins the final chapter of the sixth edition of *The Origin of Species* with: "As this whole volume is one long

119

argument, it may be convenient to the reader to have the leading facts and inferences briefly recapitulated". He continues using a version of IBE:

> It can hardly be supposed that a false theory would explain, in so sat-
> isfactory a manner as does the theory of natural selection, the several
> large classes of facts above specified. It has recently been objected that
> this is an unsafe method of arguing; but it is a method used in judging
> common events of life, and has often been used by the greatest natural
> philosophers. The undulatory theory of light has thus been arrived at;
> and the belief of the revolution of the Earth on its own axis was until
> lately supported by hardly any direct evidence.
>
> (Darwin [1972] 1962: 476)

The large number of facts that Darwin lists in the final chapter that require
explanation include: the sterility of hybrid species; the geographical distribution
of species; variability in natural and domesticated species; the existence of atro-
phied organs in animals; the facts concerning embryology; and many others.
Natural selection offers all these facts a much better explanation than does, say,
creationism (which some allege offers little or no explanation). He concludes
that, given that it offers a better explanation than its main rival, the theory of
natural selection can hardly be said to be false; less tentatively he could say that
it is true, or truthlike. Unsafe or not, the idea that from greater explanatoriness
one can infer truth is at the core of IBE. Darwin also thinks the same for other
theories, such as the wave theory of light or the theory of the daily rotation of
the earth about its axis. All of these offer a better explanation of their domain
of relevant facts than any of their rivals.[6]

How is IBE to be characterized? C. S. Peirce claimed that there is a kind of
inference that is important in science that is in his view neither inductive nor
deductive. He called it *abduction* and characterized it by the following argument
form (Peirce [1901] 1955: 151):

(1) The surprising fact, C, is observed;
(2) But if A were true, C would be a matter of course,

(3) Hence, there is reason to suspect that A is true.

Here there is a fact to be explained (said to be surprising, but this is not
essential to characterizing IBE). The second premise is expressed as a subjunc-
tive; but it can be understood to be an explanatory relation between a suggested
explanans A and the *explanandum* C. We can agree with Peirce that the argument is not deductively valid but disagree when he claims that it is not inductive (but what degree of support the premises give the conclusion is unclear).

Since it is strictly inductive, in characterizing it as abduction, Peirce can only be picking out a special subclass of inductive arguments for our attention, namely, those in which we argue to the (suspected) truth of an explanatory hypothesis as conclusion. The conclusion of Peirce's abduction is unusual; it introduces an epistemic operator not found in the premises so that the conclusion is not "*A* is true" but "*there is reason to suspect that A* is true". Without the addition of the operator the argument can be understood as a version of the fallacy of affirming the consequent (in which *C* is affirmed). For Peirce, IBE has uses both in the context of discovery and context of justification; here we are concerned only with the latter.

Gilbert Harman, who introduced the phrase "inference to the best explanation" (1965), had a project that is opposed to that of Peirce, namely, to show that all legitimate inductive inferences can be reinterpreted as a form of abductive inference, or IBE. As we shall shortly see, some construe IBE as a deductive form of inference. Our stance is that it is non-deductive and is one of several forms of inductive inference, and so is ampliative. In enumerative induction, from given facts one can infer a general conclusion, namely, that some hypothesis is true; in IBE, from the same facts and the hypothesis that best explains those facts, one infers the conclusion that the hypothesis is true. The enumerative induction is then reinterpreted as an instance of IBE.

Harman's version of IBE is close to that of Lycan (1988: 129); we take this to be our second form:

(1) $F_1, \ldots, F_n$ are facts;
(2) Hypothesis H explains $F_1, \ldots, F_n$;
(3) No competing hypothesis explains the F_i as well as H does;
(4) $\therefore$ [probably] H is true.

Again the argument is not deductive but inductive, with the bracketed word "probably" best understood as qualifying the "therefore" sign to indicate probabilistic inference. The conclusion is simply "*H* is true" (but it gets at best only a high degree of probabilistic support from the premises). Lycan adds that the word "explain" is to be understood in a non-success sense; it is not as if *H* is the correct explanation but, rather, it would explain if true.

The first premise sets out the facts to be explained and is not problematic. However, the second premise does need to be qualified. Not any old explanation will do; we need to assume that *H* and its competitors pass some threshold of adequacy for counting as good explanations. Concerning the third premise, we have yet to say what counts as the best explanation; we shall return to this later.

A third construal of IBE takes on board the point about minimal adequacy conditions for being admitted as an explanation, but presents IBE as a deductive argument. There has been a long tradition of treating inductive arguments as enthymemes because they have missing premises. A task then arises of providing the missing premises and at the same time turning the argument into a deductive one, thereby avoiding problems that arise for the justification of induction. The inductive version of IBE is no exception; it too can be put in deductive form. One suggestion along these lines has been made by Alan Musgrave (1999: 285):

(1) It is reasonable to accept as true the best available satisfactory explanation of any fact;
(2) F is a fact;
(3) Hypothesis H satisfactorily explains F;
(4) No available competing hypothesis explains F better than H does;

(5) ∴ it is reasonable to accept H as true.

The argument is now deductively valid, and it makes essential use, as does Peirce's original account of abduction, of an epistemic operator in the conclusion. When we replace the variables H and F in the above argument by specific hypotheses and facts, we may well have instances of the valid argument that make it sound. Consider now the premises. The third premise sets out the minimal adequacy requirement for any explanation and tells us that H meets it. For the time being let us grant the fourth premise, which supposes that one explanation is better than another and there is a unique best (and to make the argument not just sound but also usable we have ways of being able to tell this).

What can we say about the first premise that expresses an epistemic principle that would be common to all the instances of IBE so understood? It may be the case that our best explanation, H, is false. In Musgrave's view this does not falsify the conclusion; it is a common occurrence that, for some p, it is reasonable for us to accept p as true but, unbeknown to us, p turns out to be false. The falseness of p does not always undermine the reasonableness of the acceptance of p. Countless cases from everyday life and detective stories illustrate this. Episodes from the history of science also show this, for example the claim, made at times prior to the emergence of Einstein's special theory of relativity, that there is no upper bound to the velocity of moving bodies, or Darwin's oft-repeated claim that all evolutionary processes exhibit gradual transformation rather than exhibit punctuated equilibria, and so on. For similar reasons the first premises can be accepted; even though the best explanatory hypothesis is false, it may well not have been unreasonable to accept it.

However, there is a problem with the conclusion which gets us only to "it is reasonable to accept that H is true". The deductive argument does not get us to the further conclusion "H". And it is the conclusion "H", rather than the conclusion "it is reasonable to accept that H is true", that we want to use in predicting other facts, in explaining other facts, in making applications of H, and so on. We need to detach "H" and use it; but such detaching is not reliable for the truth of H.

There are other forms of IBE that differ in the kind of conclusion that can be drawn. From the fact that H is the best explainer, Rescher argues that we should not draw the conclusion that H is true, or that it is reasonable to suspect that H is true. Rather, we should conclude only that H has greater verisimilitude than its rivals.

> The most we can claim is that the inadequacies of our theories – whatever they may ultimately prove to be – are not such as to manifest themselves within the (inevitably limited) range of phenomena that lie within our observational horizons. ...
>
> In general, the most plausible inference from the successful implementation of our factual beliefs is not that they are right, but merely that they (fortunately) do not go wrong in ways that preclude the realization of success within the applicative range of the particular contexts in which we are able to operate at the time at which we adopt them.
>
> (Rescher 1987: 69)

This is a quite weakened form of IBE that needs to be supplemented by a theory of the degree to which our theories are right and wrong.

The above outlines some of the different forms that IBE can have and the different conclusions that can be drawn. What we need to address now is what is meant by being a better explanation. After that we shall consider some of the objections that can be made against IBE. There is also the important issue of how it is to be reconciled with Bayesianism; this is a matter we leave to §9.5.

The notion of likelihood (or inverse probability) is often used as an important part of the account of greater explanatoriness. Schematically we can express this by saying the following, where H and H^* are rival (non-trivial) explanatory hypotheses (each is a part of a pair of rival *explanans*) and E is a description of the happening or state of affairs to be explained (the *explanandum*): H explains E better than H^* if E is made more probable given H than it is given H^*. For example, if E is quite probable given H, but E is quite improbable given H^*, then H would provide (if true) a much better explanation of E than H^*. We can express this as follows using probability:

H is a better explanation of E than H^* if $P(E, H) > P(E, H^*)$

The right-hand-side likelihoods are expressed as probabilities, but they are not to be confused with similar but quite different probabilities, $P(H, E)$ and $P(H^*, E)$. They capture one aspect of being a better explanation. The account allows for better explanation even when both probabilities are quite low but one is higher than the other. An approach through likelihoods plays a large role in statistical thinking, in which the best explanation is said to be the one that maximizes what statisticians call the "likelihood function". (In the expression $P(E, H)$, E is treated as fixed while H is treated as a variable, and then methods are found for determining which particular H maximizes the likelihood [Lindgren 1976: §4.5].)

Another aspect to take into account is the initial plausibility of each of the rival hypotheses. That is, we need to consider $P(H)$ and $P(H^*)$ as well. For example, consider two hypotheses purporting to answer the question: "How come E?", where E = "Michelangelo was able to get high up to paint the Sistine Chapel ceiling each day". Two possible hypotheses are:

H = he built scaffolding and each day climbed up.
H^* = he levitated daily up to the ceiling and supported himself there.

Both H and H^* make E probable, that is, $P(E, H)$ and $P(E, H^*)$ are high. As Peirce would put it, if it were true that he could levitate, then Michelangelo's painting of high ceilings would be a matter of course. However, $P(H^*)$ is much, much lower than $P(H)$. Why so?

We can say that one hypothesis is plausible while another is implausible. We can arrive at the plausibility of each hypothesis by considering a matter so far not mentioned; this is the background knowledge K we have from elsewhere in science or everyday life. On the basis of our background knowledge K, levitation simply does not occur; that is $P(H^*, K)$ is zero or close to zero. In contrast, the building of scaffolding to reach heights is commonplace; so $P(H, K)$ can be high. Here we assess the initial, or prior, plausibility of the two hypotheses; they are initial or prior in the sense that they are what we know of H and H^* before their consideration in respect of E. So, a further consideration alongside likelihoods that needs to be taken into account in determining the best explanation is the comparative merits of $P(H, K)$ and $P(H^*, K)$. If the background knowledge K is common to the rival hypotheses whose plausibility we are considering, we can drop explicit reference to K and formulate the above more simply as follows: a further consideration alongside likelihoods that needs to be taken into account in determining the best explanation is the comparative merits of the prior probabilities $P(H)$ and $P(H^*)$. In many cases we might think that, considered in themselves, two rival hypotheses are equally plausible, in which case the burden of cashing out greater explanatoriness falls on the likelihoods alone.

There are many different models of explanation that can be used to determine when one explanation is better than another. Hempel's inductive-statistical model of explanation tells us that statistical laws (call these collectively L) in conjunction with initial conditions (C) make probable some appropriately described event E, which is to be explained. Using the above account of better explanation just in terms of likelihoods (and setting prior probabilities aside), then if $(L \& C)$ and $(L^* \& C^*)$ are rival *explanans*, we have:

$(L \& C)$ is a better explanation of E than $(L^* \& C^*)$ if $P(E, (L \& C)) > P(E, (L^* \& C^*))$

Hempel's more widely known deductive-nomological model of explanation is a special case of the above, in which $(L \& C)$ deductively entails E. Let us suppose that we have two rival *explanans*, $(L \& C)$ and $(L^* \& C^*)$, which both explain E in the sense that they both deductively entail E. Here we are to understand "explains" not in its success sense, but in the sense that L and L^* are potential explanations in the sense of "would explain if true". But in the account of "better explanation" above inequality cannot hold; $P(E, (L \& C)) = 1 = P(E, (L^* \& C^*))$ when both $(L \& C)$ and $(L^* \& C^*)$ entail E. So if we focus on likelihoods only, all deductive-nomological explanations that properly meet the condition of being deductive are just as good as one another. One way out of this problem would be to focus on the plausibility of the hypotheses in the *explanans* (as well as their likelihoods). Another might be to query whether or not there genuinely are deductive-nomological explanations.

What is not widely known is that in his later writings Hempel came to think that there were no purely deductive-nomological explanations. One important feature of all deductive-nomological and inductive-statistical explanations is an assumption that they are complete, in that they take into account all the factors that bring about some event E. That is, they involve what Hempel calls *provisos* (see Hempel 2001: ch. 12). The proviso makes ontological assumptions of the following kind. Suppose that we assume that some real system of, say, binary stars obeys Newtonian mechanics, N, and we conjoin to N information about the state of the binary system at one time to deduce its state at a later time. Then we make the ontological assumption that Newtonian forces are the only forces acting and enter a proviso to that effect, thereby excluding electric, magnetic, frictional forces, radiation pressure, angelic and diabolical forces, and the like. Importantly, some of these provisos may not even be expressible in the language of theory N; this is the language in which the laws of N are expressed, as well as conditions from which the deductions are made. This is true for both the inductive-statistical and the deductive-nomological models of explanation; both involve provisos.

In general we can say that there are ontic provisos concerning the boundary conditions of the applications of theories such that, in their appearance in explanations of phenomena, they undermine the purely deductive model of explanation. The need to take into account such provisos leads to a modification of Hempel's account of explanation that is important for our purposes. It removes the awkward case in which pure deductive-nomological explanations do not seem to leave room for one deductive explanation being better than another in the sense specified. If provisos play an important role in explanation, then the deductive-nomological model needs to be modified so that the deductive relation between *explanans* and *explanandum* is replaced by a probabilistic one. And this is something that the likelihoods used in the account of better explanation can take into account.

There are other ways in which one explanation can be better than another. Consider the range of relevant facts that two theories can be expected to explain. Suppose hypothesis H, when applied in conditions C, explains a class of facts, F (which is the set of particular facts $\{f_1, f_2, \ldots\}$). Its rival H^*, applied in conditions C^*, also explains a set of facts F^* $(= \{f^*_1, f^*_2, \ldots\})$. If the two sets of facts are the same, then no comparison of H with H^* on the basis of the facts they explain can show that one explanation is better than the other. One would then have to fall back on the likelihood of the hypotheses. Suppose now that F and F^* differ. There are two cases to consider.

Case 1. If F^* is a proper subclass of F, then H clearly explains at least one more fact than H^*. More interesting is the second case where F^* is just one of the many different classes of fact that F contains. To illustrate, consider the case of theories of light in which there are classes of fact concerning reflection and classes of fact concerning diffraction that need to be explained. There may be one theory H^* that explains just the facts of reflection (this is F^*) and another H that explains not only the facts of reflection, but also those of diffraction as well (this is F). H would clearly be the better explainer on account of explaining at least one more class of facts to do with light than its rival H^*.

The nineteenth-century methodologist Whewell made much of this when considering the support theories get from their evidence. He spoke of the *consilience* of inductions, literally a "jumping together" of different classes of fact such as the class of refraction facts and the class of diffraction facts. A theory is *consilient* if it brings together two different classes of fact under its scope; the more consilient it is, the better (i.e. it "jumps together" several different classes of fact). Consilience is a mark of a better explanation.

Case 2. The second case to consider is where the number of different classes of fact in F is much greater than the number of classes of fact in F^*. This is not the same as the first case just envisaged. F^* can be properly contained in F (the case just envisaged), or they can overlap (the case being considered now). The number of classes of fact in F can be much greater than the number in F^*; but there may be one class of fact in F^* not in F (i.e. F^* is not a subclass of F even though they largely overlap). In such a case one might say that H is a better explainer than H^* on account of H explaining a greater number of classes of fact than H^* explains. But now consider the one class of fact in F^* but not in F that H does not explain. Perhaps this one class of fact that H does not explain is outweighed by the many more classes of fact that it does explain; so H is the better explainer. But this verdict can be reversed. Suppose the single class of fact in F^* but not in F are very important facts to explain. Then a weighting of the importance of a class of fact to be explained against the number of classes of fact explained can make a difference as to whether H is a better explainer than H^* or not. In the light of these considerations the degree of consilience brought about by rival explanatory hypotheses, along with the importance of the facts explained, are matters to consider in assessing which is the better explainer.[7]

Under this heading one can consider not merely the number of classes of fact a theory explains to determine whether it is the best explainer; one could also consider the number of laws it explains as well. Thus when Newton's theory was introduced it was a better explainer than its contemporary rivals because (on limiting assumptions) it explained the laws of terrestrial motion proposed by Galileo, and it also explained the celestial laws of planetary motion of Kepler (and much else). Here such consilience of laws is one of the considerations that makes Newton's theory a better explainer than its rivals.

In the light of the last example, some methodologists might appeal to the greater unity that Newton's theory provides compared with the lack of unity of a large number of less general laws; or they might appeal to the greater systematization it provides compared with the lack of systematicity of explanation provided by its rivals. But the virtues of unity and systematization are vague at best. One way of understanding them is in terms of the above considerations, in which being a better explainer is spelled out in terms of the notions of likelihood, consilience and importance of facts and laws to be explained. Understood this way, some content is then given to the notions of unity and systematization through the notion of greater explanation; this contrasts with an approach in which these notions are given an independent account that is then used to determine what counts as a better explanation. (Of course this might not be the only way to spell out the vague notions of unity and systematization.)

Some appeal to other virtues to give an account of what it means to be a better explainer. We began this section by saying that greater explanatoriness is a virtue, and we assessed the hypotheses used in the explanation on this basis in relation to matters such as likelihoods and consilience. But we can also assess explanatory hypotheses in ways that do not relate only to these. This approach can be found in Peter Lipton's book *Inference to the Best Explanation*. His analysis of IBE is based on two pairs of distinctions: the distinction between actual and potential explanation; and the distinction between the likeliest and the loveliest explanation. The first distinction is one between the explanation that is in fact a correct explanation of some phenomenon, and the various alternative explanations that might be proposed of the phenomenon (Lipton 2004: 57–8). The set of potential explanations may include an actual explanation, but it will typically include a number of inadequate explanations as well. The purpose of IBE is to attempt to identify an actual explanation from the set of potential explanations.

The next matter concerns the selection of the best explanation from among the potential explanations. Here Lipton distinguishes between the explanation that is most likely to be true on the basis of evidence, and the explanation that best displays explanatory virtues and is therefore the loveliest explanation. Lipton argues that IBE can be thought of as inference to the loveliest potential explanation (*ibid.*: 61). He seeks to show that considerations of explanatory virtue or loveliness, along with likeliness, are a guide to the best explanation.

Lipton suggests that IBE is best thought of as proceeding in two stages (*ibid.*: 148ff.). At the first stage a set of potential explanations is generated, while at the second stage the best explanation is selected from among the potential explanations. Explanatory merit is relevant at both stages of the process. Rather than consider all possible explanations, only plausible explanations that fit with background knowledge are included at the first stage of the process. Explanation plays a role at this initial stage in so far as the background knowledge is itself the product of earlier inferences based on explanatory considerations. Background information, as we have already noted, is an important consideration in determining the initial plausibility of a hypothesis and plays a role alongside the likelihood of the facts to be explained; and we have already noted the need to admit only explanations that meet some threshold of adequacy.

In the second stage two different ways of understanding IBE come to the fore. Inference to the best explanation is inference to the *likeliest* explanation, where likeliness (not to be confused with likelihood) concerns the support an explanatory hypothesis gets from available evidence, including background information. Alternatively, inference to the best explanation is inference to the *loveliest* explanation, in which theoretical virtues come to play a significant role. These could select the same hypothesis (the likeliest hypothesis is also the loveliest). But they can select different hypotheses in which being likely and being lovely are in competition and have to be played off against one another in some way in order to arrive at the best explanation.

Talk of the loveliness of an explanation requires criteria on which to base judgements of loveliness. Lipton appeals to a range of familiar theoretical virtues, frequently cited in discussion of theory choice, such as "mechanism, precision, scope, simplicity, fertility or fruitfulness, and fit with background belief" (*ibid.*: 122). Here, talk of a mechanism goes beyond explanations couched in terms of *what* is the cause to *how* the cause operates. In so far as how-explanations (which answer the how-question, e.g. "*how* does the heart pump blood?") specify underlying mechanisms, then these are to be preferred over explanations that do not. We have also previously recognized the role that background beliefs can play. But there is also an appeal to virtues such as simplicity, scope, fertility and fruitfulness that are advocated by Kuhn and Quine (see Chapter 2).

These virtues, along with others such as unity and systematicity, can also provide criteria for what is to count as a best explanation in ways that are, of course, independent of matters such as mechanism, likelihood and consilience.

Putting together all the considerations about best explainer canvassed in this section, we now have three different ways for determining what that is: likelihood along with consilience and importance of facts explained; likeliness; loveliness. The question now arises as to whether one of these can trump the other in arriving at the best explanation; or whether all the criteria we have mentioned must be taken together to determine the best explainer. If there is no good reason as to why some criteria should trump others, then the second alternative in which all criteria play a role raises the problem of how they are to be aggregated. This is a problem we have already met in discussions of Kuhn's recommended values (§2.4); he admits a large number of differing values that can conflict, and so there is a problem of how all the weighted values are to be aggregated to determine which theory is to be chosen. The same issue arises when multiple criteria are used to determine the optimal explainer; some criteria will pull in opposite directions, or be incompatible.[8] This means that relative to some criteria and their respective weightings, explanatory hypothesis H might be the best explainer; but relative to some other criteria and their respective weightings, H is not the best explainer but some rival is. So there is no fact of the matter as to there being a unique optimal explanatory hypothesis.

Having set out some of the different accounts of what IBE is and what is meant by being a better explanation, we can ask: what justification can be given for IBE? If it is an inductive inference, then it faces the same problems that the justification of any inductive inference faces. And this is especially so if IBE is thought of as a *sui generis* principle of inference that can account for other forms of inductive inference. One can also ask if it is a reliable form of inference. That it is reliable, especially when used to argue for realism in science (see Chapter 14), is strongly contested by Laudan (1984: ch. 5). There are also other objections that have been made to IBE, a few of which we now outline.

Suppose that at a given time the set of hypotheses that are available for consideration is $\{H, H^*, H'\}$; from this set we are to select our best explainer. But there is no guarantee that what is available to us at any one time is a good explainer, even though it might be the best in the set. This is the "best of a bad lot" objection. We have tried to counter this by requiring that each member of the set is plausible, given what else we know, and that each ought to meet a threshold of minimum satisfactoriness (which can be set quite high) for what is to count as an adequate or an admissible explanation. What the advocate of IBE has to show is that in selecting H, none of the other hypotheses (such as those not selected or that we have not even considered and so are not included in the set) is a better explainer than H. If the conclusion of IBE is to be the truth of H, then this can be problematic for IBE. But if the conclusion is along the lines of

Peirce and Musgrave, namely, that it is reasonable to accept, or suspect, that H is true, then IBE is less problematic. But it might not be a helpful conclusion to end up with, since a further step of detaching H has to be made.

A further objection is that there is no guarantee that the true hypothesis is in the currently available set, even if the first objection has been met. The set is not exhaustive of all possible explanatory hypotheses and so can leave out the true one. But we can make the set exhaustive by including a fourth "catch-all" hypothesis H^+ = neither H nor H^* nor H'. Now the set comprising the four hypotheses $\{H, H^*, H', H^+\}$ is logically exhaustive and so the truth has been included in the set. Although this logical dodge does construct a set that contains a true hypothesis, it cannot be said that a hypothesis such as H^+, which is rather empty of content, will provide any explanations that meet a minimum threshold of satisfactoriness. This raises a problem for the conclusion drawn from IBE that H^+ is true; it may explain badly. As van Fraassen, who makes these two objections, notes, "to take it that the best of set X will be more likely to be true than not, requires a prior belief that the truth is already more likely to be found in X than not" (1989: 143). We cannot overcome these objections by claiming that there is something special about being a scientist (such as education, God's good grace, or natural selection), and that it is this that makes scientists disposed to hit on the truth, thereby guaranteeing that the true hypothesis will be in the set. The track record of scientists shows that they are not always reliable for the truth in this way, and that historically the pathway of science is littered with false theories that were once given credence. So, there is no good reason to assume that the truth is to be found in the set of theories available to any scientist at a given point in time.

These, and several other objections not mentioned here, have been raised against IBE by van Fraassen (1980: ch 2; 1989, ch. 6.4) and others. One of van Fraassen's important objections is that IBE, when compared with Bayesianism and its updating procedures, is either superfluous or lands us in incoherence (1989: ch. 7.4). We shall consider this in §9.5 in the discussion of Bayesianism and its links to IBE.

5.5 The problem of grue

The simple rule of enumerative induction formulated in §5.3 makes two presuppositions: the first is that there is a unique hypothesis supported by the evidence "n observed Ps are Qs"; the second is that given such evidence we can readily determine what hypothesis fits the evidence, namely, "all Ps are Qs". But these two presuppositions do not hold generally. For many kinds of evidential data, especially quantitative data, we cannot readily determine the correct hypotheses;

more problematically there may be more than one hypothesis equally supported by the data. The Humean problem of induction concerns the justification of the inference leading to a hypothesis as conclusion (to be discussed in Chapter 6). The issues raised here pose the question: which hypothesis is supported by the evidence? Both presuppositions are undermined by the problem of curve-fitting and the ingenious argument from Goodman about the predicate "grue". Both in their different ways are deep problems for which any satisfactory theory of inductive inference ought to provide an answer. They show that there must be more to the rule of enumerative induction than the simple formulations they are given. In particular, if the rule of enumerative induction is to be formulated in the manner of §5.3, one needs to know what are to be admitted as legitimate substitutions for the predicate letters "P" and "Q". So far no restriction has been imposed, but Goodman's "new riddle of induction" (1965: ch. III, §4) can be taken to raise just this problem, among others.

Goodman introduces two new predicates, "grue" and "bleen", as follows:

- "grue" applies to all things examined before T (a time in the future, say 3000CE) just in case they are green, but to other things (examined at T or after) just in case they are blue;
- "bleen" applies to all things examined before T just in case they are blue but to other things (examined at T or after) just in case they are green.

Consider the case of observing, before T, n emeralds that are noted to be green. Then using the simple rule of enumerative induction we infer "all emeralds are green". But given the definitions introduced above, the observation, before T, of n green emeralds can be equivalently described as the observation, before T, of n emeralds that are grue. From this the simple rule of enumerative induction licenses the inference "all emeralds are grue". A situation has now arisen in which the very same observations entail two hypotheses that are inconsistent with one another about what we shall observe at, or after, T. The first hypothesis is that all emeralds are green; and this entails that any emerald examined at, or after, T will be green. The second hypothesis is that all emeralds are grue; and this entails that any emerald examined at, or after, T is blue. Given the evidence, the rule of enumerative induction sanctions two inductive predictions inconsistent with one another. And on the same evidence it also sanctions inferences to two equally well supported hypotheses inconsistent with one another. Is there something wrong with the rule of enumerative induction in these cases?

Some responses to this paradox suggest that we ought to dismiss predicates such as "grue" because they appear to be gerrymandered, or because they mention a time T in their definition. But this is not an adequate response. Goodman is well aware of such objections and shows, by introducing the predicate "bleen" defined above, that there is perfect symmetry between the definition of "grue" and "bleen" in terms of "green" and "blue" and a time, and the definition of "green" and "blue" in terms of "grue" and "bleen" and a time. In addition we do admit grue-like predicates into science, such as when we say "x is a solid and is at a temperature of 0°C or less, or is a liquid and is between 0°C and 100°C, or is a gas and is above 100°C" (where a temperature scale takes the place of a time scale).

Goodman's own solution is to add a further requirement to the evidential information that supports, but does not violate, a hypothesis, and for which there are still some unexamined cases to consider, namely, yet to be determined predictions or retrodictions. Such hypotheses are said to be *projectible*, and there may be a large number of them to consider, including the grue-some ones. Which one of these hypotheses should we actually project? Goodman's answer is to consider the predicates that occur in the hypotheses. If a predicate such as "green" has survived many more successful actual projections of the hypotheses in which it occurs than the projections in which "grue" occurs, then "green" is said to be better *entrenched* than the predicate "grue". Goodman's proposal for distinguishing the correct projection from those that are incorrect is to adopt the hypothesis that contains predicates that have been better entrenched in our language. This is not to rule out new predicates that are introduced into science, such as the newness at one time of "is an electron". Instead it is to say that such predicates would be ruled out if the hypotheses in which they were projected were overridden by hypotheses containing better entrenched predicates. The extra requirements of projectibility and entrenchment, Goodman argues, are needed to supplement the simple rule of enumerative induction if the grue problem is to be solved. This additional requirement is linguistic in character; as Goodman puts it "the roots of inductive validity are to be found in our use of language" (*ibid.*: 120). For some, such a relativity to language is an unsatisfactory solution if a more robustly objective extra condition is to be found (as will be indicated shortly). Whether or not one accepts Goodman's resolution of his new riddle of induction, peculiar predicates such as "grue" remain an obstacle to any simple rule of enumerative induction.[9]

Goodman's riddle can be illustrated by setting out the normal "green" hypothesis and its rival grue-some hypothesis by means of two graphs that are functions of colour and time (Figure 5.1). Let the y-axis represent colours in the order of the rainbow from violet (of shorter wavelength beginning at 3800Å) to red (of longer wavelength ending at 7600Å). The colour green will be at a higher level (at about the 5300Å mark), while the colour blue is at a lower level (at about the 4700Å mark). The crosses in both graphs represent the same evidence of the colour (green) of emeralds observed before time T. The lines represent the hypotheses that might be projected. That all the evidence (as crosses) supports the hypothesis that all emeralds are green is represented by the straight line. That all the evidence (as crosses) supports the hypothesis that all emeralds are grue (i.e. green if examined before T but blue if examined at or after T) is represented by the discontinuous line.

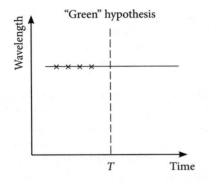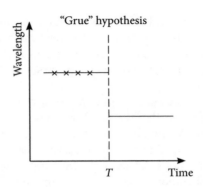

Figure 5.1 Rival green and grue hypotheses.

Goodman's example of the rival green and grue-some hypotheses concerns qualitative hypotheses only. However, in 1939 Harold Jeffreys (1961: 3) showed that quantitative laws of the sort found in physics are also involved in issues closely related to Goodman's later "grue" problem; and unlike the grue-some hypothesis, which involves a discontinuity, these functions can be continuous. Consider the law of free fall under gravitational attraction in which s is the distance travelled in time t and where a is the initial displacement at $t = 0$, u is the initial velocity (at $t = 0$) and g is the acceleration due to gravity:

$$s = a + ut + \tfrac{1}{2}gt^2 \qquad [1]$$

Suppose we discover that the following n pairs of data concerning distance s and time t fit the law:[10]

$$<s_1, t_1>, <s_2, t_2>, \ldots, <s_n, t_n> \qquad [2]$$

That is, the n pairs of pieces of data fit the following equation:

$$s_i = a + ut_i + \tfrac{1}{2}gt_i^2 \quad (i = 1, 2, \ldots, n) \qquad [3]$$

Now it is possible to propose a "grue"-like quantitative law that fits the same data given in [2] as equation [1] does (and so yields the same information as in [3]), but differs at other times in its prediction from [1]. Select any function $f(t)$ and add it to [1] accompanied by further factors, as indicated:

$$s = a + ut + \tfrac{1}{2}gt^2 + f(t)(t - t_1)(t - t_2)(t - t_3)\ldots(t - t_n) \qquad [4]$$

At all the data times, $t_1, t_2, \ldots, t_n, f(t)$ will be multiplied by zero, and so the added factor is zero. It can be readily seen that [1] and [4] agree for the evidential data given in [2]. However, they will differ for all other times. These other times can be later than t_n or at any time between $t_1, t_2, ..., t_n$. Finally, there are a very large number of different forms that the added function $f(t)$ can take. So there is an infinity of rival hypotheses to the free fall law [1] that fit the data equally as well.

The above applies not only to the free fall law but to any quantitative law of science that is a function of time (or, for that matter, any set of variables). The following question now arises for any quantitative hypothesis of science (and any qualitative hypothesis as Goodman's grue problem shows): how ought we to choose between the indefinitely large number of rival hypotheses (of which the above example is just one instance) since data seem not to determine a unique hypothesis?

5.6 Simplicity of equations

Along with many others, Jeffreys suggests that the answer to the question posed at the end of the previous section requires an appeal not only to evidence but also to a criterion of simplicity. The appeal is not to be made, as in the case of Duhem (see §2.6), to an "economy in the description or thought", or to the ease with which an equation can be used, or to conventions, or to some peculiarity of human psychology concerning simplicity that has been bequeathed to us by evolution, and so on. Rather, Jeffreys makes a substantive proposal in what he calls the *simplicity postulate*, in one aspect of which: "the simpler laws have the greater prior probabilities" ([1939] 1961: 47). How is the link between simplicity and prior probability to be established?

First, some preliminaries. Consider the linear equation $y = a + bx$. The x and y are variables that range over the real numbers. The a and b are fixed numerical values called *parameters*; given fixed parameters a single straight line is generated for variable x and y. But the parameters can also be made to vary so that for different fixed numerical values for a and b other straight lines are generated. The parameters are said to be independently adjustable. This gives rise to a family of linear equations that we may call LIN, each member of the family differing from any other according to the choice of parameters. Similarly the parabolic equation $y = a + bx + cx^2$ also generates a family of parabolic curves as the three parameters, a, b and c, are allowed to vary. This family of curves we can call PAR. Finding the simplest curve then becomes a two-step procedure: first select one family of curves (LIN, PAR, etc.); then from that family find particular values for the parameters to determine the equation that best fits the data. In the statistical literature the task of finding the right family of curves is called the problem of *model selection*. This approach to the problem of curve-fitting can be found in Jeffreys's original work. How does this contribute to matters to do with simplicity?

Other things being equal, scientists tend to judge that a theory is more complex if it has more adjustable parameters. Thus a circular path of an orbiting object is judged to be simpler than an elliptical path. In Cartesian coordinates (with the figures centred at the origin) the equation for a circle is $x^2 + y^2 = a^2$ while that of an ellipse is $x^2/a^2 + y^2/b^2 = 1$. The circle equation has one adjustable parameter, a, while an ellipse has two, a and b; moreover, the circle equation can be obtained from the ellipse equation by setting the eccentricity to zero, in which case $a = b$. Which of the two equations is the simpler? The intuition commonly employed here is that special cases of equations in which an otherwise free parameter is set at zero are simpler; so, the circle equation is simpler than the ellipse equation on account of the larger number of independently adjustable parameters in the ellipse equation.

A generalization of this leads to the idea that the number of independently adjustable parameters in equations is an indicator of the degree of simplicity. Since these can be easily counted, this yields a measure of simplicity in which the fewer adjustable parameters the simpler the equation. Jeffreys adopted aspects of this view of simplicity, saying that it is also the view commonly adopted by scientists. At different times he gave different accounts of how parameters related to simplicity; sometimes he says that we should consider their absolute value, on other occasions we should just consider the number of parameters.[11] We shall consider only the latter here.

Jeffreys also considers the *degree* of the equation as a factor in determining simplicity. The degree is the highest power of a variable, or the sum of the powers of the variables when they are multiplied together. To illustrate, the linear equation above is of the first degree; the parabola, circle and ellipse equations are all of the second degree; $x^3y^2 = a$ has degree 5; $y = ax^n$ has degree n; and so on. The magnitude of the degree of an equation is also taken to be a mark of simplicity. If, in the parabola equation, which is of degree 2, parameter c is set at zero, then it becomes a linear equation of degree 1. Which is the simpler equation? Here the same intuition about setting parameters to zero comes to apply, along with the intuition that the equation with fewer terms is simpler. Finally Jeffreys restricts the equations under consideration to those that can be expressed as differential equations. These can come in different *orders* according to the number of times differentiation takes place. For example the order of the differential in the free fall law expressed as the differential equation $d^2s/dt^2 = 0$, is 2. This yields a further mark of simplicity: the lower the derivative order of differentiation of the equation, the simpler it is.

Jeffreys's overall measure of simplicity for equations brings together these three intuitions. To arrive at a measure, the equation must first be expressed as a differential equation. Next, all roots and fractions are to be cleared away.

Then the degree of simplicity of an equation (expressed in differential form) is a function of the following three factors: the order, the degree and the number of parameters (and sometimes their absolute value). Given this, for Jeffreys paucity of parameters alone does not give a measure of simplicity. Commonly the numerical values of the order, degree and absolute value are summed to obtain the required degree (*ibid.*), but other functions could be considered. Whatever function one adopts, suppose the numerical values of these factors yield a number m. Then Jeffreys proposes a way of obtaining the prior probability of the equation; it is 2^{-m}. Thus the simplest hypothesis, that is, the lowest m, has the highest prior probability; more complex hypotheses will have a larger m and thus a lower prior probability.

The importance of Jeffreys's idea is that it attempts to deal with a notoriously difficult problem: that of providing a measure of prior probabilities, or at least an ordering of them, which is objective and not subjective. But it is not without its problems. As noted, one of Jeffreys's important discoveries is that an indefinitely large, even infinite, number of mathematical functions can fit given data. Before one considers the evidence, ought all hypotheses be treated equally, that is, should the prior probability of each be the same? For various reasons Jeffreys rejects the idea of a uniform prior probability distribution. Instead, functions are to be ordered according to their simplicity, in the way just described, yielding a decreasing and convergent sequence of functions. But a problem, of which he was well aware, is that these hypotheses might have a number that is infinitesimally small, and in some cases zero, for their degree of simplicity; for these no amount of evidence might be able to lift the posterior probability of a hypothesis much beyond its initial prior probability. One might try to lessen this difficulty by considering not all possible hypotheses but some manageable subset of actually proposed hypotheses. But as can be seen from the infinite number of equations that can fit given data, the actually proposed hypotheses that are to be admitted into a simplicity ordering might not contain the correct one.

Jeffreys also recognized other difficulties for his proposal (*ibid.*: 48). Many different hypotheses might have m as the same measure of their degree of simplicity; so the ordering is partial and many (even an infinite number of) quite different equations have the same degree of simplicity and thus prior probability. Also it is not clear how transcendental functions such as $y = \cos x$ or $y = e^x$ are to be ordered for simplicity. In addition some principles in some sciences, for example, genetics, are not expressible in terms of differential equations and so are excluded from any simplicity ordering. (In fact in later writings Jeffreys realized that this requirement is too strong.) An objection that Jeffreys did not note is that intuitive judgements of simplicity may well be relative to the coordinate system in which the equations are expressed, thereby echoing Goodman's claim that the roots of inductive inference lie in our language. Thus in polar coordinates the equation of a circle of radius 1 centred on the origin is the simple $r = 1$ when compared with the more complex Cartesian equation $x^2 + y^2 = 1$. In contrast the line $y = a$ is, in polar coordinates, the intuitively more complex $r \cos \theta = a$. In addition, the polar expression of the circle appears to be simpler than the polar straight-line equation, thereby reversing the simplicity ordering of the two equations expressed in Cartesian coordinates. Although Jeffreys has posed a deep problem about rival equations being equally well supported by the same evidence, the additional simplicity hypothesis he advocates is limited in its use and cannot provide a general solution to the problem he raises.

Independently of Jeffreys's second thoughts, the simplicity postulate is subject to a serious objection noted by Forster (1995: 407–8) if the simplicity measure depends on paucity of parameters alone. Hypotheses with fewer parameters entail hypotheses with more parameters. Thus if hypothesis C says that planets move in circles, then hypothesis E follows, namely, that planets move in ellipses (since a circle is a special case of an ellipse in which both axes are of the same length). But if C entails E then the probability of C is less than the probability of E; and this follows from a fundamental theorem of the probability calculus. However, on Jeffreys's measure of paucity of parameters alone, C, the circle hypothesis, is simpler than E, the ellipse hypothesis. Applying the simplicity postulate, the simpler is more probable; so C is more probable than E. Thus, we have the contradiction that C is both more and less probable than E. It is not clear that taking into account Jeffreys's other criteria for simplicity, such as order and degree of equations, can overcome this simple and decisive objection.

Jeffreys's intuitions are not shared by all, especially not Popper, who argues the opposite, namely, the simpler equation has the greater prior *im*probability (Popper 1959: ch. 5). Both agree about the paucity of parameters being a mark of simplicity. But while Jeffreys connects this to simplicity understood as high prior probability, Popper connects this to simplicity understood as high prior *im*probability. For Popper the simpler equations are those that are easier to falsify while the more complex are harder to falsify. On this intuition a measure of the simplicity of a hypothesis is identified with the degree of falsifiability of the hypothesis. And as will be seen in §10.1.1, Popper's notion of the degree of falsifiability of a hypothesis, and also the notion of its empirical content, is inversely linked to the prior probability of the hypothesis. This supports Popper's claim that simplicity goes along with prior improbability rather than Jeffreys's prior probability; and also his claim that simple hypotheses tell us more in the sense that they have greater empirical content.

Both Jeffreys's and Popper's accounts of simplicity rely on intuitions that are not clearly articulated. We have seen that Jeffreys's intuition can lead us astray; and so does Popper's, as Hempel (1966: 44–5) shows by constructing a counter-example. In some cases Popper is correct; a strong theory such as Newton's theory of gravitational motion has a higher degree of falsifiability and thus higher content, and so is simpler, than the many unrelated laws of motion of more limited scope that it entails (or shows hold under limiting conditions). But intuitively greater content does not always go along with simplicity. Consider any two unrelated laws, such as Hooke's law (concerning the deformation of a spring under different loads) and Huygens's laws of optics. When these are conjoined they do tell us more in the sense of having greater empirical content than either conjunct. But the conjunction of such disparate laws cannot be simpler than each law taken separately. In this case a criterion of simplicity based on amount of content is all too readily satisfied by the mere conjunction of laws that are otherwise irrelevant to one another; but being irrelevant to one another, and so disparate, counts against their conjunction being simple. Having greater content, and so falsifiability, need not always guarantee greater simplicity. Here intuitions about simplicity pull in opposite directions, so that a given theory of simplicity can satisfy one intuition but not another.

5.7 Simplicity and curve-fitting

The important problem Jeffreys raises is illustrated in Figure 5.2, in which a small number of data points are given, and then it is shown that many curves can pass through them, three of which being the straight line, the saw-toothed "curve" and a wavy curve. In setting out Jeffreys's problem, we assumed that the many curves are accurate and pass through the data points. Some curves can be eliminated for very inadequate fit to the data. A problem to be solved concerns the further selection among the many curves that fit the data to an acceptable degree. Simplicity, however it is measured, is then invoked to solve this problem.

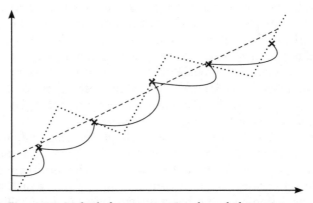

Figure 5.2 Multiple functions passing through data points.

But what happens if we drop the unreal assumption that the curves accurately fit the data? Instead the data is "noisy", using a radio metaphor. There is a genuine "signal" to be found (the correct hypothesis) but it is overlaid with "noisy" inaccuracies due to measurement errors, or unknown causal factors for which there was no control, and the like.

This brings us to the real-life situation in science in which data is collected but is inaccurate.[12] Should we then find a curve that fits all the data accurately? Such curves can be found but they may be very complex and have an extremely large number of adjustable parameters and be of a very high degree. By focusing on just one desideratum, accuracy of fit, the danger of curve *overfitting* emerges. The problem with an overfitting curve is that it is a vice and not a virtue; it fails to discriminate between "noise" and the real underlying "signal" that one is trying to discover. In many cases it is an error of scientific method to overfit accurately every data point; simplicity considerations must constrain overfitting. This gives rise to a need for a trade-off between two values (or desiderata): accuracy and simplicity (or parsimony as it is also called in the literature). Such a trade-off is advocated by Hempel, Kuhn and others (see Chapter 2). For example, Kuhn's response to the trade-off problem is to appeal to an idiosyncratic weighting of values adopted by each scientist. But these are not always rival values and can be applied together in ways that need not be subjective, that is, one can have objective criteria for both goodness of fit and simplicity.

The following quip is commonly attributed to Einstein: "Everything should be made as simple as possible, but not simpler". Having an equation that is too simple is as much a fault as is overfitting to maximize fit with data. The goal of scientific methodology here is to get at the "signal" while eliminating the "noise". There are some notable attempts to do just this (Forster & Sober 1994; Forster 2001; Sober 2001). They build on the results of statisticians who have devised quantitative methods with precise numerical values for accommodating goodness of fit with simplicity. Here only a brief overview of their approach can be given, omitting details that are too technical. What will be outlined are some principles of method that realize different values through a consideration of different functional relationships between simplicity (which in turn is a function of parameters) and amount of data.

Let D be the data, which can be represented as the data points on a graph; and let N be the number of pieces of such data. Suppose also that we are given an equation L_i chosen from some family of equations in, for example, the family of linear equations (call it LIN). (To illustrate, L_i could be the linear hypothesis $y = 6 + 5x$, which is a member of the infinite class of linear equations LIN.) In the light of data D, we can then ask what is the likelihood of each of the L_i, that is, $P(D, L_i)$. For those L_i near the data it will be high; for those L_i away from the data it will be low, or even 0. Now turn to the family of equations LIN, and ask, in the light of data D, what is the likelihood of LIN, that is, $P(D, \text{LIN})$ which is the probability of data D given that LIN is the right family. Following Sober (2001: 28) we accept the following answer to this question:

$$P(D, \text{LIN}) = \sum_{i=1}^{n} P(D, L_i) P(L_i, \text{LIN})$$

What is the last factor $P(L_i, \text{LIN})$ on the right-hand side? It is the probability that L_i is the right law, given that the family is LIN. Statisticians who consider this problem usually give those straight-line hypotheses in LIN that are close to the data D an extra weighting over those hypotheses that are further away. And the same can be done within other families of curves such as the family of parabolic curves. When the average likelihood is calculated it can turn out, for example, that the average likelihood of LIN is greater than, say, the average likelihood of the family of parabolic curves. Generalizing, let F be any family of curves (such as LIN, parabolic curves, etc.); then in the light of evidence D consider the likelihood of the family, that is, $P(D, F)$. To develop the theory further, we need to consider logarithms of the likelihoods. To express this let $L[(F_k)]$ be the likeliest curve in the family F_k (with number of parameters k). This leads to the expression "log-likelihood$[L(F_k)]$". Now if N is the number of pieces of data, and k is the number of adjustable parameters for the family F of curves, then the following are two proposals for selecting the best member from the family of curves (or model as is more commonly said).

The first is a rule based on a Bayesian information criterion (BIC).

> BIC rule: Select the family that has the highest BIC value as determined by log-likelihood$[L(F_k)] - k\log[N]/2N$

The second is a rule based on the Akaike information criterion (AIC) (named after the statistician Hirotsugu Akaike).[13]

> AIC rule: Select the family that has the highest AIC value as determined by log-likelihood$[L(F_k)] - k/N$.

Which rule should we use to solve the original problem of curve-fitting? In the two functions in each rule the first factor is the same. They differ only in their second factors. These second factors are a function only of the number of data points N (i.e. sample size), and number of parameters k. In both cases their respective second factors provide two different ways of estimating which curve fits best as a function of only k and N, that is, the trade-off between simplicity (understood as related to the number of parameters) and fit with data, including the amount of data. In both cases as the amount of data N becomes large the second factor becomes negligible. However, in intermediate stages the BIC rule gives extra weighting to simplicity by a factor of $\log[N]/2$ when compared with the AIC rule.

To highlight what these two rules entail, Forster (2001: 106–7) asks us to consider two other extreme rules in contrast. The first is the "always-simple" rule, which tells us always to select the simplest hypothesis downplaying or ignoring any fit with data. This is the kind of rule that rationalists might tell us to adopt when they prize simplicity well above fit with data. The other extreme rule is the "always-complex" rule, which tells us always to select the hypothesis that fits the data best. This is the kind of rule the empiricists would tell us to adopt when they prize fit with data well above simplicity. But following such a strongly empiricist rule will lead us to the vice of overfitting; such a curve will be quite complex with a high k as an indicator of that. In contrast, following the "always-simple" rule leads us to the vice of lack of accuracy or lack of empirical relevance. These two extreme rules are unacceptable since they downplay or ignore the trade-off that is necessary between goodness of fit and simplicity. But they can act as a foil for the AIC and BIC rules; these are a much more plausible *via media* than the two suggested extremes. But owing to their differing second factors, the BIC rule is slightly closer to the "always-simple" rule but avoids its rationalistic extremism; in contrast the AIC rule is slightly closer to the "always-complex" rule but avoids the extremism of naive empiricism.

The AIC and BIC rules are two ways of treating the trade-off problem that have an element of objectivity not found in approaches to simplicity that are said to be entirely linguistic in character (as in Goodman's response to the grue-problem), or turn on an idiosyncratic weighting of values (as Kuhn suggests). However, are the AIC and BIC rules inconsistent since they could make differing recommendations? This question can be finessed by indicating the different values that the rules can be taken to reliably realize when they are put in the form of hypothetical imperatives.

The AIC rule aims to maximize predictive accuracy. Forster (2002) makes a useful distinction here between *interpolative* accuracy (in which predictions are made within the domain from which the data were sampled) and *extrapolative* accuracy (in which the predictions are outside the domain from which the data were sampled). The hypothetical imperative "follow AIC if you value predictive accuracy" is more reliable when the kind of accuracy is interpolative predictive accuracy rather than extrapolative predictive accuracy (where it may not be very reliable at all). In contrast it is claimed that the BIC rule best realizes a different value, that of the probable truth of the selected hypothesis. Looked at in this way, the AIC and BIC rules are not incompatible. If each is to be treated as a principle of scientific method, then each is best expressed as a hypothetical imperative that associates a given rule with an appropriate value. What Sober and Forster usefully show is that the different rules of AIC and BIC need to be associated with a particular value, interpolative accuracy or probable truth.

But more than this, it can be provably shown that they are reliable means for realizing these specific scientific values.

The two approaches of the AIC and BIC rules do not solve all problems in connection with curve-fitting; and they do not solve the grue problem. But they do open up new avenues for investigation that take us away from naive forms of the rule of enumerative induction. It is clear that the rule of enumerative induction needs supplementing in different ways. Important here is the need to take into account goodness of fit along with simplicity. The two criteria must go along with one another and cannot be easily traded-off against one another in an unprincipled manner. And even if there appear to be different ways in which the trade-off can be made, as the AIC and BIC rules illustrate, this is to be seen in the context of what other values each best realizes.

6. Some justifications of induction

In Chapter 5 we showed that there is a wide range of different kinds of inductive inference employed in the sciences. Although the simple rule of enumerative induction needs supplementation, it is a central case of induction with key features in common with most other varieties of induction, so it will be the focus of this chapter. The question to be answered is: on what grounds are we justified, from the premises of enumerative induction (or the premises of any inductive inference for that matter), in inferring its conclusion? This is a Level 3 meta-methodological question that asks for a justification of a core Level 2 principle of method, namely, the rule of enumerative induction. Since the same question can be asked about the justification of deductive inferences, §6.1 has a brief discussion of how a metamethodological justification of deductive inferences might proceed and problems for this. Hume was the first to clearly formulate the problem of justifying induction and to argue for the sceptical conclusion that it could not be justified. Although we have, and should keep, the habit of making inductive inferences, there is no rational justification for this practice. In this chapter we shall not discuss Hume directly but set out an argument that reflects the sceptical position.

Since scepticism about the justification of induction while employing induction is a difficult and uncomfortable position to maintain, there has emerged a huge literature in an attempt to provide a justification, only a very small part of which will be addressed here.[1] Section 6.1 considers a parallel problem for the justification of deduction, while §6.2 sets out the sceptical argument concerning the lack of justification of induction. In §6.3 we shall consider attempts at an inductive justification of induction; this illustrates nicely the different levels at which induction is employed as a metamethodology to resolve problems of justification of inductive principles of method at a lower level. Section 6.4 concerns Reichenbach's attempted vindication of induction. In §6.5 some of the previous considerations are drawn together in reliabilist or externalist justifications of induction. Some, such as Popper, accept Hume's sceptical conclusion about justifying induction but bypass it, claiming that the methods of science can do without it. Since there have been many who have criticized this position saying that Popperian methodology needs at least a "whiff" of induction, we shall not pursue these matters here. However, in §9.6 we will consider what Bayesianism says about the problem of induction.

6.1 Attempting a justification of deduction

In science both deduction and induction play prominent roles. But while it is widely acknowledged that there is a problem concerning the justification of our inductive rules of inference, it is not so widely recognized that there is a parallel problem about the justification of deductive rules of inference. Here we shall have a brief look at the problem for deductive rules of inference since the same problems also apply to inductive rules of inference.

Consider the common rule of inference *modus ponens*: $\alpha, \alpha \supset \beta \vdash \beta$ (where "$\vdash$" stands for the relation of deductive consequence and "$\supset$" is the standard way of representing the conditional "if ... then ..." in propositional calculus). Often this is presented in the metatheory of logical systems, where it is sometimes called the *rule of detachment*, which licenses inferences between the (well-formed) formulae in the system. Among the formulae in the system will be: $[p \& (p \supset q)] \supset q$. While this looks like the rule of *modus ponens*, strictly it is not a rule. First, it is a well-formed formula expressed in the object language in which the axioms and theorems of the system are expressed. Secondly, it is a provable theorem in standard axiomatizations of classical propositional calculus. It is also a tautology since it can be shown that whatever assignments of truth-values True and False to the component propositions p and q, the whole formula turns out to be always true. On the whole, for every rule of inference there is a counterpart formula that is provable. It might now be asked: is there a circularity in the claim that the rule of *modus ponens* is used to deduce the formula $[p \& (p \supset q)] \supset q$, which corresponds to the rule of *modus ponens*? Not really, as there is the important distinction between the metatheory in which the rule is formulated (along with any other rules) and an object language in which are expressed the axioms and all the formulae provable as theorems from the axioms.

What justification can be provided for systems of logic, such as propositional calculus? To answer that we need to distinguish (a) syntactic matters concerning the rules of the system used and the theorems proved from the axioms by the rules, and (b) semantic matters to do with the truth or falsity of the axioms and theorems when given their standard interpretation (an example of which is the method for establishing the truth or falsity of the theorems and axioms using truth-tables). A justification for the system can then be given by showing that the system as a whole is sound and complete. The idea of completeness is, roughly, that all the truths of (a system of) logic can be shown to be provable from the axioms and rules of inference. The idea of soundness is the converse, namely, that all the axioms and provable theorems are true (and that no falsities follow). That a system is both sound and complete does provide some positive grounds for the justification of our rules of inference, such as *modus ponens*, that the system employs.

Another thought about the problem of justification is the following. There are a large number of rules of inference. Suppose that there are some rules that are more basic than others in the sense that there is a set of basic rules, **B**, that serve to justify all the other rules; and, further, no member of **B** provides a justification of any other member of **B** (if it did, the justified rule would have to be removed from **B**). Do the rules in **B** thereby lack a justification so that they are unjustified justifiers? One way of responding to this is to find some meta-rule to provide a justification for each member of **B**. A second kind of justification is to consider the coherence of the members of the set **B**; however, it is not easy to say what such justificatory coherence is like. Thirdly, the rules might be self-intimating or self-evident (although these days this is hardly a popular way of proceeding because of the obscurity of what this might mean); or alternatively the rules are, in some manner, self-justifying.

The first and second alternatives raise, in their different ways, a problem for any justification. If the set **B** is genuinely basic, then any argument for the justification of **B** cannot employ any non-basic rule outside the basic set **B**; at best it can only employ some rule(s) in **B**. But to employ a rule in **B** is contrary to the idea that **B** is basic. The appeal to a meta-rule can overcome this; but this then raises a question about the justification of the meta-rule. If a hierarchy of rules and meta-rules is formed, the meta-rule is an unjustified justifier that itself stands in need of justification. And from this an infinite regress of meta-rules threatens. Whether such a regress is seriously problematic or stops at a rule that has an *a priori* justification then becomes an issue. Here we shall consider the last possibility, that of self-justification. To make matters simple, suppose **B** has just one rule, R, which is the justifier of all other rules; but it is not unjustified since it is supposed to be self-justifying. What might this mean? One suggestion is the following: there is a satisfactory justificatory argument for the correctness of rule R, which employs an instance of R as the form of the justificatory argument. On the face of it, this is circular; but is it vicious?

To deal with this question a number of authors distinguish between *premise-circularity*, which is vicious, and *rule-circularity*, which is not obviously so. Some regard rule-circularity as benign while others find that, whatever other problems it might have, it fails to yield any satisfactory justification.[2] Consider premise-circularity first. The logical law of identity licenses as deductively valid reasoning of the following form: from premise P infer conclusion P (i.e. $P \vdash P$). But one would hardly use this as an argument to justify belief in the conclusion P. Although valid, it involves a fallacy of reasoning. If P is the conclusion of an argument that is to justify P, to appeal to P as a premise is to beg the question in favour of the conclusion, or to reason in a blatantly circular manner. This is an explicit form of what is known as *premise-circularity*, or *epistemic-circularity*. Sometimes premise-circularity is less explicit; it might be the case that the only way to come to have a justifiable belief in some premise Q that, in conjunction with other premises, leads validly to P, is via proposition P. Either way, premise-circularity involves an unacceptable mode of justification for a conclusion.

In contrast some argue that rule-circularity is not necessarily vicious. In the following we give an example of an argument for the truth-reliability of a particular rule of inference R (it shows that the conclusion drawn from true premises is always true), but importantly the argument itself is an instance of the very rule R. This is to be contrasted with a different case that is problematic, namely, the argument against a particular rule of inference R that is itself an instance of R. This does invite the charge of incoherence. The case we are considering at least has the virtue of coherence between the argument for the correctness of R and the form of the argument that is an instance of R.

To illustrate rule-circularity, consider an example from Haack (1996: 186) in which a justificatory argument for R is itself an instance of the rule R. Suppose R is the rule of *modus ponens*. The task is to discover whether *modus ponens* is truth-preserving, and so is valid. Suppose we consider the table that defines the symbol "$\supset$"; this along with the table for conjunction "&" is used to show, in the standard way, the validity of *modus ponens*. In working our way through it we use the following justificatory argument based on the lines of the table. From the truths given in the two premises "'A' is true" and "'$A \supset B$' is true", we can draw the conclusion that "'B' is true", and thereby show that *modus ponens* is truth-preserving:

(1)   "A" is true, and "$A \supset B$" is true   [by supposition]
(2)   If "A" is true and "$A \supset B$" is true,
      then "B" is true   [by inspecting the table for "$\supset$"]
(3) $\therefore$ "B" is true.   [(1) and (2) and the rule of *modus ponens*]

The conclusion of the argument is not the proposition *that modus ponens is truth-preserving*, or *that modus ponens is valid*. But the argument shows that *modus ponens* is truth-preserving, and so valid, for given (1) we arrive at (3). However, the form of the argument used to get from (1) and (2) to (3) is itself an instance of *modus ponens*. An argument to justify a rule based on information gleaned from the table for defining symbol "⊃", employs an instance of the rule as the justificatory argument. This appears to be an example of rule-circularity. But is it problematic?

Not all are agreed as to what rule-circularity is. Salmon defines it for arguments saying that the argument "exhibits a form whose validity is asserted by the very conclusion that is to be proved" (1967: 15). This does not accurately characterize the argument above as the conclusion concerns the reliability of the attribution of truth to "B"; but the argument as a whole does have a bearing on the truth-reliability of *modus ponens* itself. Since rule-circularity is involved with matters of justification, van Cleve formulates rule-circularity epistemically as a justificatory argument that "is sanctioned by a rule of inference that one could know to be correct only if one already knew that its conclusion was true" (1984: 558). This imposes a necessary condition on our knowledge of the correctness of a rule, namely, that we know that the conclusion of an argument of the form of *modus ponens* is true. For Salmon this is too strong since, as he correctly points out, there are many other ways available in logic for knowing about the correctness of *modus ponens*. But the story we are considering is slightly different. We are envisaging that for the rules of inference there is a basic set B of unjustified but justifying rules, and that B contains just one rule, which we suppose is *modus ponens*. There is little else that could justify *modus ponens*; the only other information we have is the definition of "⊃" in the form of a table. In such a case could we accept a justifying argument that is rule-circular in the way indicated in the above argument concerning the rule *modus ponens*?

The problem with this kind of self-justification is that it lets in far too much as justified when it should not. Consider a further example from Haack (1996) of rule-circularity that is intended to be a justification of the rule of affirming the consequent (AC): β, α ⊃ β ⊢ α. In line with the story we have been telling, suppose that the basic set B of unjustified justifiers contains just the rule of AC. We now argue in a similar fashion as for the rule of *modus ponens*:

(1) "$A ⊃ B$" is true; "B" is true   [by supposition]

(2) If "$A ⊃ B$" is true, then "B" is true   [from (1) and the corresponding
line in the table for "⊃"]

(3) If "A" is true, then if "$A ⊃ B$" is true
then "B" is true   [by inspecting the table for "⊃"]

(4) ∴ "A" is true.   [(2) and (3) and the rule of AC]

What the above shows is that an argument, with the form of AC, establishes the correctness of AC (it shows "'A' is true" can be reliably arrived at from true premises). Moreover, the self-justificatory argument for AC is the same as the self-justificatory argument for *modus ponens*. Now, of course, given what else we know about logic (such as the completeness and soundness of various systems), we reject the rule of AC but accept the rule of *modus ponens*. But in the story envisaged about the basic set **B**, all we have is a rule that stands in need of justification (along with a definition for the symbol "⊃"). And the rule could be taken to be *modus ponens*, or AC. We cannot appeal to the fact that the rule of *modus ponens* is valid while the rule of AC is invalid; this is the very matter that is to be decided in considering any member of the basic set **B**. The problem is that the self-justificatory argument makes no distinction between the two rules in equally justifying both. So the culprit here must be the rule-circular self-justifying argument itself. The charge against rule-circularity is not so much that it is vicious; rather it is profligate in justifying too much given what else we know about logic.

Rules of deductive logic do stand in need of justification. But one seemingly plausible way of justifying them suggested above does not work, and other ways need to be found. We shall see when we come to consider rules of induction that the same fault emerges when we try to justify them inductively.

6.2 A sceptical argument against the justification of induction

Although Hume was the first to provide a sceptical argument against the justification of induction,[3] we will not follow his actual argument through a textual examination. But we do follow his strategy, which appeals to a *principle of the uniformity of nature* (PUN), which he expresses as the claim "*that instances, of which we have had no experience, must resemble those, of which we have had experience, and that the course of nature continues always uniformly the same*" (Hume 1978: 89). Bertrand Russell alternatively expresses this as: "everything that has happened or will happen is an instance of some general law" ([1912] 1959: 35). But it cannot be that the future resembles the past in all respects. As Russell famously writes: "The man who has fed the chicken every day throughout its life at last wrings its neck instead, showing that more refined views as to the uniformity of nature would have been useful to the chicken" (*ibid.*). A person falling down the side of the Empire State Building who argues "ninety-nine windows have gone by and no accident has befallen me, so when the hundredth window goes by no accident will befall me" will not be around much longer to make too many further inferences of this form. This conveys a useful image in that as we, too, fall through spacetime, there is no guarantee that the future will conform to the regularities we have already observed.

We follow Carnap's suggestion ([1950] 1962: 179) that PUN can be improved somewhat by reformulating it to take into account the following:

1. The uniformity in the world is high (and not low or zero);
2. If a uniformity has been noted between *A* and *B* (in that the frequency of

*A*s among the *B*s is high, say *r* per cent) then in the (future) long run the frequency remains the same (a version of Reichenbach's straight rule).

To what extent is our world uniform? And if so, in what respects? There is a possible world in which the uniformity is maximal (i.e. uniform in all respects, a seemingly static, changeless world). Secondly, there are possible worlds in which the uniformity is zero, in which case any observed uniformity ultimately fails. Such a world need not be chaotic; rather it is just that regularities that do hold over a period of time, and that we observe through our local window on the world's happenings, ultimately break down in the future (or did not hold in the past or do not hold elsewhere). In performing any induction, we do not know in advance the extent of the uniformity of our world, if it has any. More problematically, the negative existential "there are no uniformities of nature" is not verifiable. Thirdly, if the world is uniform to some extent, we do not know in what respects it is uniform. Like Russell's chicken or the person falling, we might have latched on to the wrong respects. However, if we do latch on to the right respects Carnap's second point can help us with matters concerning the degree of the uniformity (which need not be 100 per cent).

Minimally, let us take PUN to be a multiply existentially quantified claim. First there exists some uniformity in the world, that is, there exist two or more respects in which the world is uniform; secondly, there is some degree, *r* per cent (which is sufficiently high), to which the uniformity holds. Clearly such a version of PUN is a contingent claim and not a necessary truth; there are possible worlds in which PUN holds and other possible worlds in which it does not hold. Further, we come to know it on empirical rather than *a priori* grounds.[4] More needs to be said in making PUN precise; but this will be enough since the upshot of the sceptical argument is that nothing like PUN will help justify induction.

What is the point of an appeal to PUN? In any theory of inductive reasoning we wish to know what degree of support the premises of an inductive argument give the conclusion. If some version of PUN holds not only for what we have observed but for the unobserved (whether past, future or elsewhere), then this supports the claim that there is a class of inductive arguments that are highly reliable in that, most of the time, from true premises about past observed regularities they yield true conclusions about unobserved regularities. Granted this, justifying many inductive arguments boils down to showing that PUN holds. Subsequently we shall show how some attempts at justifying induction bypass any appeal to PUN.

The following is a version of the sceptical argument that shows that PUN lacks justification; from this it follows that inductive arguments that depend on PUN lack justification.

(1) If PUN can be justified, then the argument for its justification will be either deductive or inductive (i.e. non-deductive).

(2)   PUN is a contingent and empirical claim about the world and what uniformities hold in the world at all places and times past, present and future.

(3)   In any deductive argument to conclusion PUN, if a contingent and empirical conclusion is drawn then at least one premise must be contingent and empirical.

(4)   The only available relevant contingent and empirical premises are those concerning information about the uniformities that have been observed.

(5)   But it is logically possible that this information be true and PUN false.

(6)   So, PUN cannot be justified by a deductive argument from those premises.

(7)   All correct inductive arguments assume the truth of PUN.

(8)   So, any inductive argument for the truth of PUN would assume PUN.

(9)   No argument for a principle that assumes the correctness of that principle can provide a justification for that principle.

(10) So, there is no inductive justification for that principle.

(11) So, there is no deductive or inductive justification for PUN.

The argument above is deductively valid. The final conclusion (11) about the lack of justification of PUN, and so inductive forms of argument, follows from interim conclusions (6) and (10), and these are obtained validly from the two alternatives specified in (1). So it remains to inspect the truth of the other premises. Note that although the conclusion expresses scepticism about the justification of induction, none of the premises on which it depends rely on standard doctrines of scepticism in philosophy.

Criticisms of the second half of the argument from (7) to (10) are discussed in subsequent sections. Some downplay the role of PUN or attempt to bypass it altogether. Premise (9) involves a charge of circularity. Section 6.3 considers the possibility of an inductive justification of induction, in which the circularity is avoided. Section 6.4 considers the extent to which Reichenbach's vindication of induction provides a reply. Section 6.5 considers the reliabilist or externalist attempt to reject scepticism about induction that among other things questions (6), the role of PUN as a premise in a justificatory argument.

Consider the first half of the argument. Conclusion (6) can be obtained in several different ways. The version above turns on premise (2), the contingent and empirical status of PUN (some reasons for this have been canvassed above). Premise (3) is a feature of deductive arguments since they are non-ampliative and require contingent premises if contingent conclusions are to be drawn. Premise (4) sets out the only relevant contingent premises that are available, namely, the part of PUN that specifies the uniformities we have already observed; it does not include those that are essential to the full formulation of PUN, that is, the uniformities that hold in the unobserved cases whether past, future or elsewhere. The only information we have about our world is simply what we have already observed; there is no further information to which we can appeal. This information can be true, yet PUN false; and since this is what we mean by deductive invalidity we fail to deductively justify PUN. So the argument to (6) is sound as well as valid.

Some might challenge the overall sceptical argument by claiming that there are really no inductive arguments; it is claimed that when analysed properly they are deductive arguments with missing premises (i.e. they are enthymemes). The missing premise is usually a metaphysical principle such as PUN. We can set this out as follows:

(1) All observed *P*s are *Q*s,
(2) PUN [the future resembles the past to some degree and in some respects]
(3) (1) is an instance of PUN
(4) ∴ the next *P* to be observed will be *Q*; or,
(4*) ∴ all unobserved *P*s are *Q*s.

There are two problems with this. One is that the deductive reconstrual helps itself to PUN, a principle that stands in need of justification. Even if either conclusion is true, we cannot validly infer that PUN is true. Secondly, if the conclusion turns out to be false, it might appear that PUN has been shown false; but this does not logically follow. What is falsified is (3), the claim that the future resembles the past in the respects set out in (1). PUN escapes refutation because the uniformities it alleges exist are taken not to include uniformities about *P*s and *Q*s. So PUN is a principle that freeloads on those cases where the conclusion turns out to be successful; but where the conclusion is false it escapes any responsibility for the falsity. PUN escapes because it is unspecific about what uniformities there are beyond the claim that there are some somewhere. But this claim, since it is unrestrictedly existential, is not falsifiable; and nor is it verifiable since if we think we have latched on to a uniformity, tomorrow can reveal that it fails. In sum, while inductive inferences can be viewed as enthymematical, the missing premises that turn them into deductive arguments will not make them sound since the premises are somewhat suspect, or empty.

Scepticism about induction not only shows that there is no sound, valid deductive argument to the conclusion that PUN is true, it also shows that there is no argument to a conclusion about the *probable* truth of PUN. (This is also a striking point that Hume initially made.) The claim that inductive inferences are not deductive is of long standing and is generally recognized to be correct. Granting this, the sceptical argument shows that no justification is available for believing that the conclusions of inductive arguments are true (although they may in fact be true). But it shows more than this; inductive arguments do not even confer on their conclusions the probability that they are true. The sceptical position about justifying induction is of very wide scope and includes not just inductive arguments but also what are sometimes called *inductive probabilistic* arguments. The reason is much the same as that given in the reconstruction of the argument above. PUN is at best a contingent, and not a necessary, claim; moreover it is logically possible that the course of nature changes from what we have observed in the past. As with ordinary inductive arguments, so with probabilistic inductive arguments; only our past experience can lead us to confer on the conclusions drawn one probability rather than another. But which should we confer? Whichever probability we confer, there will be a lack of justification since any justification presupposes the very principle under consideration. So even inductive probabilistic arguments are unjustified, even though we might, as a matter of habit, use them.

6.3 The inductivist justification of induction

In this section we shall focus on criticisms of the second half of the argument that question premise (9), namely, there can be no form of inductive justification of induction. This section develops the positive line that it is possible to have an inductive justification of induction while avoiding problems due to vicious circularity.[5] What is this approach, and how successful is it?

Consider instances of the rule of enumerative induction, which we apply both in everyday life and to what we observe in science, as illustrated in the following two arguments, A1 and A2:

A1 We have observed each day that the sun has risen,
 ∴ every day the sun will rise.
 Or ∴ tomorrow the sun will rise.

A2 90 per cent of examined patients woken from REM sleep have dreamt,
 ∴ 90 per cent of people waking from REM sleep have been dreaming.

And so on for many other such arguments. They all have the form of a simple rule of enumerative induction. In the system of levels distinguished in this book, this is a Level 2 methodological rule applied to the subject matter of Level 1 scientific laws, theories and observations, which can appear as premises or conclusions in arguments such as A1 and A2. To indicate its Level 2 methodological status we shall subscript it as rule$_2$ of enumerative induction (EI). As an inductive generalization it has the following form:

A3 Rule$_2$ of EI n per cent of observed As are B
∴ n per cent of all As are B.

The number "n" could be 100 per cent, as in A1, or it could be less than 100 per cent, as in A2. To overcome problems due to inadequate testing in the use of rule$_2$ of EI, assume that the observations have been made over a sufficiently wide number of cases (so that the sample is not too small), and that a wide variety of test situations have been considered. That is, where appropriate rule$_2$ of EI is to be understood along the lines of the *inductive rule for statistical generalization 2* (see §6.2).

The above makes a fundamental supposition that some question, namely, that there are inductive rules and that they can have a form that can be understood along the same lines as the notion of form in deductive logic. The standard characterization of deductive logic, it is argued, is an unsatisfactory model for inductive reasoning. On this model, in the case of rule$_2$ of EI we must specify what are legitimate substitution instances for its symbols "A" and "B". A1 and A2 contain plausible instances of rule$_2$ of EI. But one would want to rule out the possibility of grue-like properties being instances of "A" and "B". This is part of the very problem raised by Goodman concerning the language in which we are to express regularities. Given the problem of grue, it is hard to see how a distinction can be drawn between supposedly legitimate instances of A1 and A2 and all the illegitimate grue instances. There is also a further challenge to the idea that there are inductive rules. It is not that we have not yet formulated adequate rules of inductive inference that get rid of unwanted grue-like instances. Rather, there are no rules to be found at all! Even though we do form beliefs that go beyond some given data, we are not to suppose that this is a rule-governed process. The process has been wrongly characterized as following a rule of inference; but there is no rule and perforce no inference.[6] We shall return to these matters in §9.6, where we consider a Bayesian response to the problem of justifying induction. For the purposes of this section we shall assume that there are rules of inductive inference, that they can be set out as quasi-formal-looking rules and that suitable (but admittedly unclear) restrictions are to be placed on admissible instances of "A" and "B".

Continuing with the inductive justification of induction, suppose we examine a large number of arguments that are inductive predictions, as in the first conclusion of A1. We survey them like a statistician and find that on the whole they are successful in the sense that from true premises a true conclusion is reached. We could then perform an induction over these cases of inductive prediction and draw a conclusion about the success of the next inductive prediction, or most future inductive predictions we make. More generally, consider the following instance of the rule of enumerative induction, which takes as its subject matter the Level 2 rule$_2$ of EI:

A4 Rule$_3$ of EI   Most past uses of rule$_2$ of EI have been successful,

∴ the next use of rule$_2$ of EI will be successful.
Or, ∴ most uses of rule$_2$ of EI are successful.

Here we go metamethodological and use a Level 3 rule about the use of Level 2 rules, of which rule$_2$ of EI is an instance, and arrive at the conclusion of a Level 3 argument, which is about a Level 2 methodological rule. By "successful" we mean that when the premises of the various instances of rule$_2$ of EI have been true, then the conclusion has been true, or mostly so. The conclusion of the argument is that the use of rule$_2$ of EI is successful in getting us from true premises to a true conclusion. Alternatively we can say that Level 2 rules, such as rule$_2$ of EI, are *conditionally reliable* in getting us to true conclusions in *r* per cent of uses (where *r* per cent is 100 per cent or quite high). Being highly conditionally reliable is one of the desiderata of rules of inductive inference.

How does the Level 3 rule$_3$ of EI differ from Level 2 rules, such as rule$_2$ of EI? As far as the general form of rules of enumerative induction is concerned, both seem to be of the same form. Moreover rule$_3$ of EI will suffer from the problem of lack of restriction on what are admissible substitution instances in the same way as rules at Level 2 (e.g. rule$_2$ of EI, which is to apply to the objects and properties examined in science at Level 1). But it is possible to stipulate a difference. Rule$_3$ of EI is to take as its subject matter only rules at the next level down, Level 2, an example of which is rule$_2$ of EI. So we can restrict the substitution instances of rule$_3$ of EI to be those that are about the rules at the next level down and their properties such as success or lack of success. This does distinguish between rules at different levels and establishes a hierarchy of rules with their respective subject matters.

If we recognize that there can be different levels at which inductive rules are employed so that a rule at a higher Level 3 justifies a rule at lower Level 2, and we accept the conclusion of argument A4, then there is a response to the sceptical objection made in premise (9) in the argument against the justification of induction (see §6.2). The formulation of (9) is not cognizant of the different levels at which rules are to be employed. Once this is taken into account, (9) is no longer the strong objection that it seems. There is a non-circular justification of rules of induction employed at Level 2 when used on Level 1 subject matter. The justification is metamethodological in that a Level 3 rule provides the justification of Level 2 principles of method such as rule$_2$ of EI. But in bypassing (9), do other difficulties arise?

The justification of the use of rule$_2$ of EI is by appeal to a rule$_3$ of EI. But what of the justification of rule$_3$ of EI itself? Could one appeal to the use of a rule$_4$ of EI to investigate statistically the successes in the use of Level 3 rules such as rule$_3$ of EI, in much the same way rule$_3$ of EI was used to investigate the successes in the use of Level 2 rules such as $rule_2$ of EI? This suggests that there is a hierarchy of rules of inductive reasoning such that for a rule at Level i, $rule_i$ of EI, there is another rule at Level $i + 1$, $rule_{i+1}$ of EI, that justifies the rule immediately below.[7] In this way an entire system of inductive rules at different levels in the hierarchy can be given a justification. Note that none of the rules in the hierarchy justifies the use of a rule at one level by appeal to a rule at the very same level; rather, the justification uses a different rule at the next level up. It is the system as a whole that provides justifications for rules employed at any level in terms of the rules at the next level up.

Although PUN is not a premise used in the justification, at each level of the hierarchy there is a recognition of PUN, the claim that nature is uniform in some respects. But the uniformities at each level will differ. Thus at Level 2 the uniformities that PUN says hold are about the world. At Level 3 they might also be said to be about the world, but only a small aspect of it, namely, uniformities about our inductive practices at Level 2. And so on for higher levels; the uniformities that are supposed at the higher level concern our inductive practices at the next level down.

It is important to note that in the above considerations no rule is used to justify itself; so strictly there is no rule-circular argument involved in the justification. Not to observe the hierarchy of rules is not to be scrupulous about subscripting the rules of enumerative induction according to their level and wrongly treating them all on a par. Failure to observe this leads to the following version of the previous schema:

A5 Rule of EI   Most past uses of rule of EI have been successful,

$\therefore$ most uses of rule of EI are successful.

This introduces rule-circularity in that the rule licensing the alleged justificatory argument is the very same rule (and at the same level) that is said in the conclusion to be successful. Is such rule-circularity problematic as it was in the case of attempting to justify deduction? Whatever one's view about the vicious or benign character of rule-circularity, *prima facie* the distinction between levels of inductive rules helps avoids circularity of the sort just envisaged.

In avoiding the circularity charge of premise (9), has the idea of a hierarchy of inductive rules resolved one problem at the cost of another because it leads to an infinite regress of different levels of justificatory inductive rules? Some might feel that this is an Achilles heel in the attempt to justify the use of any rules of enumerative induction within a methodology at Level 2. We avoid the problems of circularity at the cost of a regress; and either the regress is infinite (so there is no endpoint justification) or it stops at the point at which we simply accept a mode of inference and so it lacks any justification). It is important to note that those who have investigated an inductivist justification of induction do not claim the following: "no inductive argument ought to be regarded as correct until a philosophical justification has been provided" (Black 1954: 191). This would exclude any inductive argument for justifying induction; but it would also be too strong in excluding the possibility that any inductive argument in science or ordinary life could be deemed correct until a justification has been found. Rather, some inductive arguments are correct, and we are right in relying on them. This is a point that those who advocate a reliabilist approach to induction emphasize (see §6.5). In providing justifications that employ deductive reasoning, we do not require that such arguments also be justified at the same time; we simply rely on them in the justification. Similarly we can take a reliabilist approach in our use of inductive rules at whatever level; we simply rely on them in the justifications we make.

For those with a coherentist approach to justification, the infinite regress of justifications need not be a problem. Coherentists tend to reject the idea that there is a linear justification for our beliefs with an endpoint in some foundational beliefs that have a special epistemic status that provides other beliefs with justification. Rather, they take on board an initial set of beliefs B that is coherent, and ask of any further belief whether or not it coheres with B; if so it can be admitted, if not rejected (or adjustments can be made to B). The same considerations can apply to the hierarchy of rules of inductive inference. Given an initial coherent of rules then, if any new rule is introduced, such as one further up in the hierarchy that coheres with the other rules, then this can provide grounds for its justification.

There is a further problem about the inductive justification of induction. Such an approach can be used to justify some weird inductive rules since it uses a style of justification that is too profligate in what it will allow to be justified. Sometimes some of us adopt a different system of inductive reasoning and argue counter-inductively. For example, a gambler might argue, "I have lost at the roulette wheel all evening, so I shall win next time I bet". This, however, is not a reasoning strategy that we generally employ. Less commonly we might adopt a further system of inductive rules, a rule of indifference in which whatever we have observed in the past about, say sun risings, we can infer equally justifiably either that tomorrow the sun will rise, or that it will not. Indifferentists and counter-inductivists are rare; we normally employ the standard system of inductive reasoning along the lines of A1, A2 and A3. However, it is useful to consider a rival system of inductive reasoning in order to explore the virtues of the standard system more fully. Granted a rival system of inductive rules we can now ask which might be best justified. That is, just as standard inductivists might use A5 to justify induction, can counter-inductivists also use a similar rule-circular argument to justify counter-induction? Unfortunately, yes, so the style of justification is too permissive in what it will admit.

Counter-inductivists adopt a rule of counter-enumerative induction, which, in general form, is a Level 2 principle to be applied to Level 1 scientific or everyday matters. Since they adopt a quite different inductive policy towards what they have observed, they propose a quite different set of inductive rules from those of the inductivist. Those who adopt the rule of enumerative induction assume that nature is to some extent uniform. Those who adopt rules of counter-induction do not make any such assumption, but rather the opposite, namely, that the future will not be like the past. Counter-inductivists adopt the following rule of counter-induction:

A6 Rule of CEI   Most observed As are Bs
$\therefore$ the next A is not B;
or, most unobserved As are not Bs

Counter-inductivists also argue from the failure of a regularity as follows:

A7 Rule of CEI   Most observed As are not Bs
$\therefore$ the next A will be B;
or, most unobserved As are Bs.

When it comes to justifications of their rules, counter-inductivists can give the following rule-circular justification for their counter-inductive practices:

A8 Rule$_2$ of CEI   Most past uses of rule of CEI were unsuccessful
$\therefore$ the next use of rule of CEI will be successful.

The situations in A5 and A8 are, in one important respect, similar to that in which a circular argument is used to justify rules of deduction. But as was noted in §6.1, such an argument can justify both the acceptable rule of *modus ponens* and the unacceptable rule of AC. Turning to induction, in A5 there is a justification of induction using the rule of enumerative induction that is itself inductive in form (and uses the rule of enumerative induction). In A8 there is a similar rule-circular justification of the rule of counter-induction which uses the rule of counter-induction as the justificatory argument. So it would appear that rule-circular arguments can justify two different systems of inductive rules, one of standard induction and the other of counter-induction. Both cannot be correct. When a similar situation arose for the case of deductive logic an appeal was made to other facts that we know about deductive logic; this showed that rule-circular justifications were ineffectual in that they failed in the task of discriminating between valid and invalid deductive inferences. What independent grounds can we appeal to in the case of the rival justifications of induction and counter-induction? There do not appear to be any weighty independent facts about induction to which one can appeal as in the case of the justification of deduction. There are simply our inductive practices and their success or lack of it.

What would happen if we were more scrupulous and ask the counter-inductivist to indicate the different levels of justification that parallel the case of the hierarchy of inductive rules. In A7 we would then have a Level 2 rule of counter-inductivist methodology, $rule_2$ of CEI, which is applied to what we observe in science and everyday life, and which is about the alleged lack of uniformity in the world. A8 would then be altered to include a Level 3 meta-methodological $rule_3$ of CEI about the rules at the next level down:

A9 $Rule_3$ of CEI   Most past uses of $rule_2$ of CEI were unsuccessful

∴ the next use of $rule_2$ of CEI will be successful.

By the lights of the counter-inductivist (but not the inductivist) this is a strong argument. The counter-inductivist is not in the least perturbed by the failure of his Level 2 inductions; in fact, the failures are recorded in the premise of A9. And this, by $rule_3$ of CEI, gives strong support to the conclusion that the next use of $rule_3$ of CEI will be successful. If we go up the hierarchy of rules the same goes for a $rule_4$ of CEI, which is about the success and failures of $rule_3$ of CEI at the next level down. It would appear that just as there can be a consistent hierarchy of inductivist rules, so there can be a consistent hierarchy of counter-inductivist rules.

Although the counter-inductivist system of rules seems weird to us, none-theless such rules can receive the same kind of justification that our normal inductive rules do. If we are to exclude such weird alternatives, something extra is needed to justify our normal system of inductive rules.[8] What this may be remains a continuing problem for the inductivist justification of induction. This aside, what the inductivist justification of induction shows is that premise (9) in the sceptical argument of §6.2 against the justification of induction is not satisfactory as it stands; there are different levels at which rules of induction can apply. However, while suggesting new avenues to explore, it has not been successful in undermining the sceptical conclusion, as the above remarks about the justification of counter-inductive rules show.

6.4 The pragmatic vindication of induction

At the end of §5.2 we gave a further refinement of the simple rule of enumerative induction, in the form of Reichenbach's straight rule of induction. This says that suppose we discover that the frequency with which the feature B turns up in the class of As is m/n (e.g. m heads (B) on n coin tossings (A)), which we can abbreviate as $F^n(A, B) = m/n$; then we should infer that in the long run the frequency of Bs among the As is also m/n.

Straight rule of induction: If $F^n(A, B) = m/n$, then in the limit as $n \to \infty$, $F^n(A, B) = m/n$.

It is useful to employ the notion of a limit to the sequence of frequencies. Suppose there is a limit L as n increases. Then for any small arbitrarily chosen number ε, one can find a number N in the sequence of frequencies, $F^N(A, B)$, such that for any other n greater than N the difference between L and $F^N(A, B)$ becomes even smaller than ε. Expressed mathematically as a limit, for any chosen small ε, there is a number N of trials of A such that for any $n > N$, $|F^n(A, B) - L| < \varepsilon$. In this case the frequencies *converge* on limit L. If there is no such convergence on any limit then the sequence of frequencies is said to *diverge*.

Reichenbach accepted that the sceptical problem of induction was a genuine problem and that there is no deductive, inductive or probabilistic inductive justification for induction. However, he wished to vindicate our inductive practices by showing that if any method we employ is going to be successful, then induction will be successful; but if induction fails, no methods will be successful. This is Reichenbach's *pragmatic justification of induction*, the significance of which we examine here.[9]

Reichenbach's position is commonly and conveniently set out as in Table 6.1. PUN is the usual principle of the uniformity of nature and M is any other method other than the straight rule of induction that we might employ. M could be a weird method such as reading tea leaves, throwing a die, consulting a guru or soothsayer or adopting counter-induction; or it could be a seriously proposed method of science that is not inductive. We do not know whether PUN is true or not; but it is possible to explore what happens with respect to scientific methods when PUN holds, and when it does not.

Table 6.1 Matrix for pragmatic justification of induction.

	PUN holds	PUN does not hold
Straight rule of induction used	Success	Failure
Other method (M) used	Success or failure	?

The table sets out a number of metamethodological considerations about the use of induction, in this case the straight rule of induction, with and without PUN. Consider the second line in which the straight rule of induction is used. If PUN holds, then the persistent employment of the straight rule of induction will be successful (where success is taken to mean that there is a limit for a sequence that the straight rule of induction uncovers that can then be used to show that there is an instance of PUN that in turn backs the claim that in some inductive argument a true conclusion follows from true premises). But if PUN does not hold, induction will fail in the long run. Consider the bottom line. If PUN holds then it is possible that some other method M will uncover what uniformities there are; but it is also possible that it will not.

The crucial alternative is the box on the bottom right, in which there are no uniformities in nature and the world might even be chaotic. Suppose that some method M is used and it is successful in the usual sense in that it gets us to correct conclusions (M might be a method for reading tea leaves, or getting revelatory or intuitive insights about correct conclusions). Importantly, M does this when nature is not uniform and PUN does not hold. After all, why should there be a requirement that for some method M to be successful PUN must hold? Reichenbach the inductivist now turns the tables on M and asks: how do we know that M is correct? There is at least one obvious uniformity in the world, namely, the observed successes of M. Given past successes of M, induction is needed to infer that M is the correct method to use the next time, or that M is correct *tout court*. There may be no other uniformity in the world that the straight rule of induction can uncover; but the straight rule of induction is needed to show that M is correct. It would then appear that if any method M is successful then induction is successful, and where induction fails so must any other method M. Thus induction is vindicated.

There are some problems concerning the argument about the bottom right-hand box. In the case we are considering induction has been quite unsuccessful while M has been successful; the only success that induction seems to have is when it is applied to Level 2 method M. However, this ignores matters raised in the previous section about the different levels at which principles of method apply. M is a Level 2 methodological principle applied at Level 2 to Level 1 sciences; so we should tag it appropriately to indicate that it is a Level 2 principle of method, that is, M_2. Now, if we note a uniformity about the success of M_2, the inductive argument pointing out this success is of the following form:

Method M_2 has been reliable in the past (despite PUN not holding)

∴ Method M_2 will be reliable in the future.

It is important to note that this inductive argument does not employ a rule of induction at the same Level 2 as M_2; it employs induction at the next level higher up at Level 3. That is, a meta-rule of induction, rule$_3$ of EI, is employed to tell us about the success of M_2 at Level 2. What we do not employ is a rule of induction rule$_2$ of EI at the same Level 2 as M_2. Once this point is made, it can be readily seen that the above argument for what goes into the bottom right-hand box is not convincing. If PUN does not hold, some other method M_2 could be successful without induction also holding at the same level as M_2, that is, a Level 2 principle of scientific method. But to establish that M_2 is correct it would appear that an inductive rule is needed at the higher level since its subject matter is rules at the next level down, unless there is a version of method M, so far unspecified, that could do the work of justification at Level 3. This last suggestion is that methods M of revelation might themselves be employed at a higher level to adjudicate between rules at the next level down. But as with the case of the inductive justification of induction, circularity and regress need to be avoided in the justification of M, which needs to be successful at all levels of use.

There is an alternative way of expressing Reichenbach's argument that overcomes these problems and does not use PUN but the notion of a limit as specified in the straight rule of induction. If we apply the straight rule of induction, then, in the limit as $n \to \infty$, either $F^n(A, B)$ has a value or it has no value, that is, there is convergence or no convergence. The task of any other method M of science would also be to determine what that value is. The alternatives to investigate are as shown in Table 6.2.

Table 6.2 Matrix for pragmatic justification of induction (modified version).

	Value exists at the limit	No value at limit
SRI	Value determined	No value determined
Any other method (M)	Value may or may not be determined	No value determined

This is a more precise way of expressing Reichenbach's position. The task of the straight rule of induction is to find the limit in the case of statistical regularities that we have noted, particularly relative frequencies, as in the case of the frequencies of the Bs among the As specified in $F^n(A, B)$. Either as $n \to \infty$ the sequence of $F^n(A, B)$ converges on some limit, or it does not. Clearly if there is a limit to be found then if one perseveres with the straight rule of induction one will find it and determine its value. However, some method M other than the straight rule of induction might, or might not, be successful in determining the value at the limit. But if there is no limit to be found, then neither the straight rule of induction nor any other method M will find it. Thus it would appear that the straight rule of induction is vindicated in its use while other methods are not.

Is this a good response to the sceptical argument about induction? In some ways it gives us more interesting features of induction not encountered in the sceptical argument. But it is not a full reply for the following reason. We need a reason for claiming that if $F^n(A, B) = m/n$ for finite n, then in the limit as $n \to \infty$, $F^n(A, B) = m/n$; it seems quite possible that these frequencies have different values. This is an issue of which Reichenbach was well aware as there can be other proposals about what values to assign the frequencies. We have already noted the oddities of counter-inductivists; they say that if the observed frequency is m/n then we should suppose in the long run that the frequency is $(m - n)/n$. Further, there are those who might say that past evidence has no bearing on the future and that one should only consider *a priori* probabilities. Thus if one is tossing a six-sided die to determine the frequency of, say, getting a six, then this will simply be $1/6$, regardless of what one has already observed. In such cases observed frequencies are not a direct guide to the limiting frequencies.

Given any observed frequency arising from an initial, finite segment of a sequence, for example the n members of the sequence that ends at $F^n(A, B)$ and that has the value m/n, there is no guarantee that in the limit this will converge; it could diverge. In one sense this is an aspect of the problem of induction. If there is convergence then the straight rule of induction has latched on to one of nature's uniformities; it is a regularity if $m = n$, but more commonly $m < n$, in which case the uniformity is statistical. However, Reichenbach realized that the straight rule of induction is not the only rule that could be adopted to determine the limiting frequency, where it exists. He envisages an infinity of alternatives to the straight rule of induction of the following form: if the observed frequency arising from an initial, finite segment of a sequence yields $F^n(A, B) = m/n$, then we could pick just about any number as the frequency in the limit as $n \rightarrow \infty$. One kind of limit can be expressed as $F^n(A, B) = m/n + c_n$, where c_n is a function of n that converges to zero as $n \rightarrow \infty$.

This yields a class of "asymptotic rules" in which the value of the observed frequency and what one then takes to be the limiting frequency can differ everywhere except in the limit. In Reichenbach's own version of the straight rule of induction, $c_n = 0$. But there are a host of other functions where $c_n \neq 0$. Suppose we persist in the use of any of these rules for larger values of n, say $2n$; and we observe the initial finite segment of the sequence up to $2n$, which also yields frequency of m/n; then the new limiting frequency is $m/n + c_{2n}$. All such rules do find the limit if there is one; but what is taken as the limiting frequency, based on the observed frequency and the associated rule, will differ for each asymptotic rule in all cases except the limiting case. There needs to be a principled reason for preferring the straight rule of induction to all the other asymptotic rules; without this Reichenbach's justification does not justify one unique rule, but a whole family of rules. Perhaps there are other criteria that could be used to select a narrow subset of rules within the family, but many of the suggestions, such as Reichenbach's own descriptive simplicity, either do not work or are hard to get to work, or go beyond what one would intuitively envisage as a rule of induction.

There are other kinds of rules that concern predictive induction about unobserved cases. Laplace seems to have been one of the first to link induction with probability through his rule of succession, which we can express in the following form: if we have observed $F^n(A, B) = m/n$, then for any other unobserved case the frequency is $(m + 1)/(n + 2)$. To use an example of Laplace, who assumed that the earth was created about 6000 years ago, the sun has been observed to have risen on about two million days. Then the frequency of the next rising of the sun is 2,000,001/2,000,002. This is not quite the same as a version of the straight rule of induction used to determine the next case, which would yield 2,000,000/2,000,000 = 1. For much smaller numbers of trials Laplace's rule and the straight rule of induction will differ much more markedly in the values they yield.

Carnap ([1950] 1962: 568) proposes his own rule of enumerative induction. His confirmation functions yield the formula $(m + w)/(n + k)$ where m and n are as before, and w and k are fixed real numbers such that $0 < w < k$. (The letter k stands for a function of the number of primitive properties [more strictly predicates] being considered in the formation of Carnap's confirmation functions and w is the "logical width" of the properties.[10]) At the beginning, before observations are made and m and n are zero, Carnap's rule reduces to the purely "logical" factor w/k, which arises from considerations due to the framework of languages in which Carnap sets his theory of inductive logic. But as values are determined for m and n, the empirical factors due to the number of trials and the frequency m/n begin to dominate. As the number of trials increases, Carnap's formula converges on the ratio m/n. But at other than the limit, Carnap's rule will give different values to those given by the straight rule of induction. Given such differences between his own rule and the straight rule of induction, Carnap is able to criticize the straight rule of induction for ignoring the k and w factors. Finally, as Carnap points out, Laplace's rule of succession emerges as a special case when $k = 1$ and $w = 2$.

Although Reichenbach's straight rule of induction tells us something new and important about induction and frequencies that go beyond the sceptical argument, it finally does not provide an answer to scepticism about the justification of induction. We are left with a plethora of inductive rules between which we cannot choose. To resolve this Reichenbach sometimes appealed to simplicity to support the straight rule of induction and eliminate the many rival rules that could be adopted. While this is an important extra consideration (different kinds of simplicity consideration can be found in §5.6), there needs to be a guarantee, not obviously forthcoming, that the number of rival inductive rules will be reduced to a unique single rule if the problem of induction is to be solved.

6.5 Externalism and the warrant for induction

Perhaps the first reliabilist about induction was Frank P. Ramsey, who wrote in a 1926 paper:

> We are all convinced by inductive arguments, and our conviction is reasonable because the world is so constituted that inductive arguments lead on the whole to true opinions. We are not, therefore, able to help trusting induction, nor if we could help it see any reason why we should, because we believe it to be a reliable process. ... An indispensable means for investigating these problems [of induction] is induction itself, without which we would be helpless. In this circle lies nothing vicious. (Ramsey 1990: 93–4)

In Ramsey's view, induction is a useful habit to have. Not to have it is not to infringe any laws of logic, but it is to be unreasonable. In his remark there are some themes we have already met, such as the use of induction to justify induction, which is said not to be vicious. But there are some new themes that Ramsey introduces, including that induction is a reliable process because "the world is so constituted". If the world were not so constituted then inductions would fail, as has been illustrated in the previous section concerning the use of the straight rule of induction.

Is this an appeal to PUN? Not directly. For reliabilists, inductive inference can be reliable, but PUN need not be used as a premise in any justification of the inference. This leads to an important aspect of the reliabilists' "justification" of induction. A better name than "reliabilist" for Ramsey's position might be "externalist", in that the kind of justification sought for induction is not the standard kind in which a justifying argument is presented with or without PUN as a premise; as we have seen such justifications get caught up in problems such as the regress of justifying principles or of self-justifying rules. Instead these matters are avoided through reliance on how the world works, or is constituted, as Ramsey put it. In a certain sense it is the world that tells us when our inductive practices are *warranted*; but the world itself does not, and cannot, provide a justificatory argument for induction. The ways the world warrants our inductive practices (rather than justifies them) is something that we can investigate like any science. As Ramsey suggests, the externalist can adopt a strategy of the sort adopted by those who attempt an inductive justification of induction by using inductive rules at a higher level to investigate inductive rules at the next level down to determine the extent to which they are reliable in producing true conclusions. And such an investigation will be necessary if we are to inspect and renovate our inductive practices; just as our cars need to pass a check for roadworthiness, so our inductive practices need to pass a check for reliability. However, a regress of justifications is avoided because the kind of justification provided for our inductive rules is not by means of justificatory argument; rather, the *warrant* for the rules is determined by how the world is constituted. In this section we shall explore the difference between justification and a warrant (here we follow Mellor [1991: ch. 15], where a warrant for induction is advocated).

Suppose we are given some premises *A* from which follows conclusion *C* according to some inductive rule *R*. The attempt to show that induction is warranted can be understood in the following way: rule *R* is reliable iff from true premises *R* will yield true conclusions, always or most of the time. *R* is not highly reliable *tout court*; rather, *R* is highly *conditionally* reliable in the sense that for input of true premises it will yield output of true conclusions most of the time. Some externalists put this point in terms of chance (*ibid.*: 264). If the premises are true the conclusion has some chance of being true, and where the chance is high enough the conclusion is warranted, in the sense that what is warranted is the truth of the conclusion.

But what is the warrant for our inductive habits or practices, which we may suppose can be codified in inductive rules? Consider cases where properties have been noted to be correlated: thirst quenching with water drinking, or sun rising and setting with 24 hours passing. Following Ramsey's suggestion, the warrant for our inductive practices is to be found in how the world is constituted. Suppose that there are simple laws of nature linking water drinking with thirst quenching; or in the case of the link between sun rising and setting with the passing of 24 hours of time, suppose there is a derived law-like link from a more complex set of laws of motion, gravitation and so on, which operate under the conditions that prevail in our solar system. Our inductive practices get their warrant from such external laws, either simple or complex, and the conditions in which they operate. In making our inductions we rely on such laws and their conditions of operation, whether we know them or not.

The fact that there are such laws on which the inductivist relies explains why non-inductivist strategies, like those of the counter-inductivist, are doomed to failure. There are no laws on which their inductive practices can rely (i.e. there is no law linking water drinking and thirst continuing); so there is no warrant for their non-inductive practices. But this explains why inductivist strategies will succeed; there are laws, known or unknown, that warrant our inductive practices. Of course, as considerations of the sort raised by Reichenbach show, if there are no relevant law or laws, then induction will have no warrant either. So, for Reichenbachian reasons, if there are laws of nature, whether we know them or not, induction will get us to them, and having inductive practices will be a good thing. But if there are no such laws (and so PUN fails), then, whether we know this or not, induction will not be successful, from which it follows that there will be no good practices, inductive or non-inductive, to be had. The same considerations of warrant will apply to both deterministic and statistical laws of nature. Given the complexity of the conditions in which the laws of nature operate and the nature of the laws themselves, so our inductive practices, and their codification into rules, will have to reflect this complexity by paying attention to matters such as diversity of cases, sample size, randomness of selection of sample and the like.

Externalists put considerable weight on the fact that we need not know that the external conditions on which one relies actually prevail, in this case that the relevant laws of nature hold. But even if we do know this, we need not know it for induction to be warranted; it just is warranted. This undercuts an alleged circularity that would arise if one were to insist that one knows that there is a law underlying the induction. Let us suppose that, in order to know that my inductive inference is warranted, I need to know that there is a law that warrants it; but to know that there is a law I need to have used induction successfully. The problem here is the over-strong requirement that one has to know that there is a law warranting one's inductive practice, rather than the weaker requirement, which is merely that there is such a law (which one may or may not know).

Consider those who have the habit, or disposition, to reason inductively. Suppose a person has a justified belief in premises A. (Alternatively this could be strengthened to say that the person *knows* the premises A; nothing is lost in considering only justified belief). This is commonly taken to be sufficient for having a justified belief in conclusion C. But some might object to this, claiming that it is not sufficient. They claim that a person must also have a justified belief in a further matter, namely, rule R itself, which provides the inductive link between premises and conclusion. This is a quite strong *internalist* requirement imposed on what it is for a person to have a justified belief in conclusion C; they must not only justifiably believe premises A and conclusion C, but must also justifiably believe the rule of inference R linking A with C. It is internalist in the sense that the light of rationality must shine so brightly within the person's noetic structure that they have a justified belief in the laws of logic, and even more strongly justifiably believe the very reasons for their being the laws of logic. And this applies not only to deductive rules but also inductive rules such as R.

In contrast, those who adopt an *externalist* requirement simply require that the rule R *be* a correct rule, not that a person justifiably believes it to be correct. On this stance, having a justified belief in the premises A is all that is required to have a justified belief in the conclusion C (providing, of course, the person has the inductive habit to reason in conformity with R in reaching C from A). This holds equally whether R is a deductive or inductive rule. All that is needed is the more relaxed externalist requirement that R *be* a reliable rule, not that R *be justifiably believed* to be reliable.

We are justified in believing that the next time we drink water it will quench our thirst; the sufficient ground for this is our justified beliefs about past observed cases of water drinking and thirst quenching. It is not necessary to invoke an inductive rule as part of the justification of our belief about what will happen next time, any more than it would be necessary to invoke a deductive rule if the inference were deductive in character. We simply rely on the correctness of this inductive rule. And this rule is, as Ramsey says, reliable because of the way the world is constituted. That is, the world is such that there is a law-like connection between water drinking and thirst quenching, and this warrants the induction.

Is this an appeal to PUN? Strictly, no, despite the fact that there is reliance on law-like uniformities. For many, a significant role for PUN is to turn an inductive argument into a deductive argument, thereby hopefully justifying induction. But as van Cleve (1984: 557) points out, this is strikingly irrelevant. What we are concerned with are inductive arguments that, obviously, we do not claim to be deductive. So the manoeuvre of adding extra premises to inductive arguments to turn them into deductive arguments is beside the point. Rather, we want to know one of two quite different things: (a) whether the non-deductive, that is, inductive, argument is justified; or (b) whether we can, given our justified belief in the premises, have a justified belief in the conclusion (to some extent). It is the matter raised in (b) that the reliabilist approach addresses. And it addresses it by not requiring that we have a justified belief about matters raised in (a), although it does require that there be such an inductive argument with a high chance of producing true conclusions (otherwise the reliance is baseless). Some have taken the sceptical argument against the justification of induction to concern (b) rather than (a); so what the sceptic is taken to have shown is that we are not justified in believing the conclusion of any inductive argument. This is not the same as the issue addressed in (a), namely, that no argument could make its conclusion probable (although some do understand the sceptic as showing this as well). The externalist's warrant concerns matters raised in (b); there is a warrant that the externalist can provide that is different from the internalists' justification (which, if the sceptic is right, is not available).

Not any old inductive habits will do. The habits can, and must, be refined by taking sufficiently large samples, by considering a variety of evidence and the like. That is, our habits must ideally be in conformity with the best methods of statistical analysis. In taking note of this, some of our inductive habits will have to be improved. (Empirical research into how badly we reason inductively shows a need for improvement.) Every once in a while it will be useful to practise some mental hygiene by studying rules of induction, just as we can study the rules of deductive logic to ensure our mental hygiene concerning deductive inference-making. That is, we need to be responsible externalists who ensure that our processes of belief formation, using either deduction or induction, are in good working order by getting a warrant of fitness for them. But this does not mean that in every case of forming a justified belief we have to justifiably believe that we are using reliable processes of belief formation; it still remains that the processes we use, in this case inductive inference, need only be reliable.

But an externalist can be asked about whether or not they have a justified belief in induction itself, and for this they have an answer, but an externalist one. Like any good statistician they could survey their Level 2 inductive inferences as applied in science or everyday life and go metamethodological by arguing as follows, taking care about the appropriate level of their rules of inference:

A4 Rule$_3$ of EI   Most past uses of rule$_2$ of EI have been successful,

∴ most uses of rule$_2$ of EI are successful.

Earlier we noted some defects concerning the use of such higher-level rules; either there is a hierarchy of them that leads to an infinite regress, or they apply to themselves thereby inviting the charge of rule-circularity. But the externalist need neither suppose that there is such a hierarchy nor use rule-circular arguments. Importantly, externalists need not know, or justifiably believe, that rule$_3$ of EI is correct; all they need is that the rule is correct. As Ramsey puts it, there is a small portion of our world, namely, our refined and tutored inductive practices, which is so constituted that such practices are reliable for the truth. And if that is so then the externalist has given, by their lights, a "justification" for their use of rules of induction at Level 2. And this is as much as any internalist might give for their justification of the use of deductive rules that lead to justified beliefs in conclusions of deductive arguments (in which, let us suppose, they also have a justified belief in their premises). It is internalist hankerings after a justification for the use of rule$_3$ of EI that might lead one to question whether the externalist does have a satisfactory reply to the sceptic about induction; but it is a hankering that internalists do not satisfy when it comes to the use of deductive rules of logic in forming justified beliefs. The externalist tells us why we do not need to give in to this hankering.

Has the externalist provided an answer to the sceptics' question "Are we justified in believing the conclusions of inductive inferences?" only by shifting the goalposts about what counts as a justification? To some extent the talk of warrant rather than justification does reflect a difference in the requirements of externalism as opposed to internalism. But note that the externalist does have a reply to the matter raised in (b) above. They do not, however, have an answer to the matter raised in (a) above, nor need they. It should not be expected that an externalist epistemology should address matters concerning the correctness of rules of inference; this is the province of logic. Externalist epistemology is not required to show that the rules of deductive logic are valid or provable or justifiable, any more than an internalist epistemology is so required. It leaves, as it should, these matters to other domains of philosophy. If this is also understood to be an issue raised by the sceptic about induction, then part of the answer will lie in attempts by others to give an account of the correctness of our inductive rules of inference. The externalist reply about justification concerns only the reasonableness of the beliefs we form when we rely on such inferences, that is, the matter raised in (b). This is not the same as the matter raised in (a), although the sceptical argument raised against induction has been taken to concern this as well.[11]

There are many other attempts at the justification of induction that are not covered here. But in Part III we consider one further kind of justification for induction to be found within a Bayesian context once we have set out the main features of probabilistic reasoning.

7. The hypothetico-deductive method

As the name indicates there are at least two parts to the hypothetico-deductive (H-D) method: a *hypothetico* part in which a hypothesis or theory, arising from whatever source, is proposed for test, and a *deductive* part in which test consequences are drawn from the hypotheses. Unmentioned in the name of the method is a crucial third part in which consequences are deduced and compared with experiment or what we can observe. The consequences pass or fail when the comparison is made. In some cases the hypothesis might be invented to account for some already known fact(s); it is then tested by deducing further consequences from it, which are then subject to test. An important question arises about how the pass or fail verdict is transmitted back to the hypothesis; this creates problems for the H-D method, as will be seen. The test consequences need not be obtained only by deduction; if the hypotheses are statistical then the consequences are inferred by non-deductive, or inductive, reasoning. So a better name might be *the hypothetico-inferential method*, to cover both cases of deductive and non-deductive inference.

The method has had a long history from the time of Plato when it went by other names in his dialogues such as "the method of hypothesis". It was applied to science in medieval times and since then has had a long involvement with scientific method. It became central in the nineteenth-century debate over method between Whewell and J. S. Mill. Some say its day has now come and its involvement in methodology is largely over. The task of this chapter is to spell out the nature of this method, and its strengths and weaknesses.

Huygens was a strong advocate of the H-D method in his *Treatise on Light* (1690). He had developed a number of principles of a theory of light in which light is conjectured to be a large number of very small wavefronts advancing through space in the direction of propagation. But like all theoretical claims about unobservables, this is not something that is directly amenable to test; as

Huygens realized, the only way to test such a theory is by examining its consequences. So he proposed the following method for examining his principles about light in the "Preface" to his *Treatise*:

> There will be seen in it [i.e. the following *Treatise*] demonstrations of those kinds which do not produce as great a certitude as those of Geometry, and which even differ much therefrom, since whereas the Geometers prove their Propositions by fixed and incontestable Principles, here the Principles are verified by the conclusions to be drawn from them; the nature of these things not allowing of this being done otherwise. It is always possible to attain thereby to a degree of probability which very often is scarcely less than complete proof. To wit, when things which have been demonstrated by the Principles that have been assumed correspond perfectly to the phenomena which experiment has brought under observation; especially when there are a great number of them, and further, principally, when one can imagine and foresee new phenomena which ought to follow from the hypotheses which one employs, and when one finds that therein the fact corresponds to our prevision. But if all these proofs of probability are met with in that which I propose to discuss, as it seems to me they are, this ought to be a very strong confirmation of the success of my inquiry; and it must be ill if the facts are not pretty much as I represent them.
>
> (Huygens [1690] 1962: vi–vii)

The contrast is with the method of exposition of Euclidean geometry, in which consequences, the theorems and lemmas, are drawn deductively from axioms that appear to be absolutely certain. However, in his science of light, the "axioms", or principles as Huygens says, of the theory of advancing wavefronts are not certain at all; they are very much hypothetical and need to be confirmed. For Huygens the H-D method seems inescapable; there is no other way to examine his principles about light except by examining their consequences. Huygens also talks of verifying his principles. This cannot be right if "verify" means "show to be true". The principles cannot be shown true for two reasons; they are about unobservable entities and properties and there are a potentially infinite number of rays of light to check for these properties. Huygens, who also wrote an early treatise on probability, more correctly says his principles might be shown to be probable. In §8.4 we shall show that the best aspect of the H-D method is a special case of Bayes's theorem. Huygens also talks of two types of consequences: those that fit already known observable facts and those that anticipate something we do not know but are given a "prevision" of what might be the case (i.e. a novel prediction). Confirmation by known and by novel facts is an important part of the theory of H-D confirmation; but this is better captured within Bayesianism. As will be seen, the H-D method does not come equipped with a theory of confirmation; one has to be added on.

7.1 The structure of the H-D method

Hypotheses are never tested by themselves since nothing follows from a hypothesis of the form "(x)[if Px then Qx]" except, by the rule of instantiation, its instances such as "if Pa then Qa". Only if we are given additional information about the conditions in which the hypothesis applies, such as Pa, can we then infer Qa, and then compare this with what we can observe. More realistic cases of H-D do not have this simple form. Here we describe a more general schema for H-D testing of some target hypothesis H. H may itself be a conjunction of many hypotheses or laws, such as in the H-D test of Newton's three laws of motion and the law of universal gravitation. But H could also be a singular hypothesis such as the hypothesis formed by a detective that a particular suspect committed some crime (and then the detective tests this using the H-D method); or a doctor forms the hypothesis that a patient has such-and-such a condition (and then he H-D tests for this using diagnostic and other procedures). No restrictions need be placed on the kind of hypothesis H that is the target of testing.

As indicated, the testing of H cannot take place by itself. What additional information needs to be added to H in order for the H-D method to work? In what follows we list a number of different items, at least some of which must be present.

1. H usually needs to be applied to some system S; for this, information about S is necessary. For example, to apply Newton's theory of motion to the planetary system, information is required about the system, such as the number of planets and their distribution in space relative to one another and so on. It was missing information about the planetary system that led to faulty calculations when nineteenth-century physicists applied Newtonian dynamics to the orbit of the planet Uranus (which had been discovered in the previous century). It was assumed that there were just seven known planets in S. However, due to the work of nineteenth-century astronomers and mathematicians, an eighth planet, Neptune, was discovered outside the orbit of Uranus that perturbed its orbit. Thus the model S of the solar system had to have an eighth planet added to it.

    Missing information may not be the only way in which S (say, a model of the solar system) fails to model correctly a real system R (the real solar system). S may be deliberately proposed as an ideal model that fits a real system with differing degrees of fit. Ever since Galileo and Newton, physics has used the method of idealized models. For example, real friction forces are commonly set aside in the case of Galileo's theories about bodies rolling down inclined planes; and the rolling bodies are assumed to remain perfectly spherical as they roll. Similar idealizing assumptions are made about the simple pendulum: it is not subject to friction forces due to the air or to the point about which it swings; the angle of swing is assumed to be small; the centre of gravity is assumed to be where the bob is; and so on. In such cases the hypotheses H about motion are applied to an idealized system of bodies S and consequences are drawn from them that can then be compared with the actual observable behaviour of the real system R. The predicted data deduced from H as applied to S and the actual data observed of the real system will commonly differ. This does not mean that H, as applied to S, has been refuted; model S can be changed to S^* to remedy the disparity so that H as applied to S^* is more accurate. There is a procedure whereby idealizing assumptions can be dropped about S so that the revised ideal model approaches more closely the real system it purports to model (see §1.5 on Lakatos's account of the sequence of idealized models proposed by Newton). In this way S is made more "concrete" in the move to S^*. Here the H-D testing of H is done in conjunction with idealized S. If their test consequences fail, then the concretization of S to S^* can yield more acceptable test consequences while H remains unchanged.

2. As is well known in dynamics, and elsewhere, a particular kind of information is needed about any idealized or real system S, namely, its state at a given time. Often the state of a real system at any one time determines (either fully or with a high degree of probability) the state of the system at another time. Suppose we possess hypotheses about the evolution of a system over time. Then, given relevant information called *initial conditions* (I) of system S at any one time (idealized or not), we can deduce what state the system will be in at a later time, or in some cases retroduce what state it was in at an earlier time.

3. Often other background theories T need to be employed in making deductions from the H under test but are themselves not under test. Thus if one were to test theories of drag on an object when it falls in a medium such as air, then a background theory of dynamics is required in working out that part of the object's motion that is due to gravitational attraction and not friction or impact with the medium. The background theory is essential in making any deductions about the motion of the object, but it is not the target of any testing.

4. Often an assumption is made that there is *sufficient isolation* of the system S (the "SIS" assumption) from any other external effects. Hempel (2001: ch. 12) discusses such assumptions in his talk of *provisos* as assumptions about completeness. Using Hempel's example, Newton's theory of motion can be applied to a system S that is a pair of binary stars moving about

one another. It is possible to deduce, using Newton's theory, the state of the binary system at a later time from its state at an earlier time. The proviso here is that the only forces acting within system S are Newtonian forces; this is, in effect, an ontic assumption that Newtonian forces are the only forces acting. However, this may well be an incomplete account of the system. The kind of incompleteness envisaged is not epistemic in that there is more information we could have provided about S but did not. Rather, it is a kind of ontic incompleteness in that there are forces at work that have been sidelined by the proviso. Thus electric and magnetic forces have been ignored as have pressure forces due to radiation, and other forces (Hempel even imagines diabolic and angelic forces). What is missing here is the full list of the actual "nomically relevant" causal factors that do affect the behaviour of the binary system. The assumption that the SIS condition has been satisfied is closely related to Hempel's proviso assumption about the completeness of the specification of all the kinds of forces acting, whether Newtonian or not.

5. The consequences drawn from H are to be compared with information from elsewhere. This we denote by "E" (for evidence). Sometimes this can be obtained by observation. Sometimes it is obtained by experiment, in which case one has to take into account any background theory employed in the experiment; call this theory of the experiment "T_E". Thus in archaeology one might propose rival hypotheses about, say, whether agriculture was transmitted across Europe from the Middle East or developed locally. Suppose, further, that when one of these hypotheses is applied to a site it entails that one kind of artefact ought to be earlier than some other kind of artefact. The only way to test this may be to use radioactive isotope carbon-14 (^{14}C) dating techniques. But this presupposes further matters such as a theory about the radioactive decay of ^{14}C, information about the prevalence of ^{14}C in the atmosphere in prehistoric times (this changes and is dependent on sun-spot activity) and the like. Any fault in T_E can undermine E used in any H-D test.

The H-D schema of Figure 7.1 represents factors involved in deducing a test consequence C from not just H alone, but H in conjunction with at least some of S, I, T and SIS, with T_E also playing a further role. For convenience denote the four additional factors by "A", which stands for the *auxiliaries* that are employed in the *application* of H. In addition there is a logical condition to impose. C should not be deducible from A alone; H must do work in being one of the premises from which C follows. We can now express the inference that is made in the following way: $(H \& A) \vdash C$ (where "$\vdash$" stands for the relation of logical consequence).

What is the test consequence C? This may be a singular observational claim to the effect that, say, a planet is in position P at time t. Or it could be a functional law. Often functional relations between a number of variables can be deter-

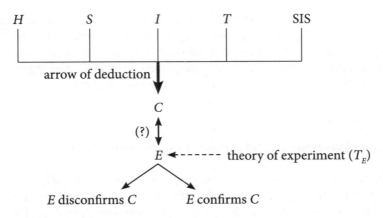

H S I T SIS

arrow of deduction

C

(?)

E ◄------ theory of experiment (T_E)

E disconfirms C E confirms C

Figure 7.1 Flow diagram for H-D method.

mined by inductive methods such as curve-fitting and the like. What is then of interest is how these experimentally determined laws are to be fitted into a theory. It is here that the H-D method comes into its own in showing how, from some theoretical principles, experimental laws can be deduced. This was the role that Huygens envisaged for his principles concerning the many unobservable, advancing wavefronts supposed in his theory. From them he was able to show how one could deduce the already known experimental laws concerning reflection, diffraction and the double refraction of Icelandic Spar, and so on. An added boon would be if deductions to new and previously unknown laws could be revealed by the H-D method – and then these laws subsequently be shown by empirical investigation to be correct.

Much the same kind of unification of Kepler's laws of planetary motion can be made by their H-D deduction from Newtonian dynamics (along with some idealized assumptions about their conditions of application). Thus from Newtonian dynamics it is possible to deduce that: the orbit of a planet is an ellipse when under the action of only the central force of the sun; a line joining the orbiting planet to the sun sweeps out equal areas (A) in equal time intervals (t), $A \propto t$ (Kepler's area law, or second law of planetary motion); the cube of a planet's (average) distance from the sun, D, is proportional to the square of its period, T, $D^3 \propto T^2$ (Kepler's third law of planetary motion). Newton's theory also provides an example of Huygens's "prevision"; from the theory Newton was able to predict that the earth was an oblate spheroid slightly flattened at the poles and bulging at the equator (by about 40 km); this was later confirmed by experimental observation. Again, the same can be said for the use of the H-D method by Bohr in his early "planetary" model of the atom, in which he was able to deduce the already known Balmer and Paschen laws concerning series of wavelengths in the electromagnetic spectrum. Deducing functional relations like these is one of the main roles of the H-D method in bringing theoretical principles and experimental laws into one deductive system. But as will be seen, there are problems for the H-D method when it comes to confirming the theoretical principles from which the deductions flow. These and other problems for the H-D method are the topics of the next two sections.

7.2 Refinements of, and problems for, the H-D method

The H-D method does not come equipped with any theory of confirmation or disconfirmation; one needs to be grafted on to it. This absence reveals some of the limitations of the H-D method along with some problems for it. So far what the H-D method has provided is a deductive consequence C, which is to be compared with evidence E. In what follows, suppose that we accept E (along with any theory of the experiment T_E). Then there are three possibilities to consider, two of which are set out in Figure 7.1:

1. C and E might be logically irrelevant to one another, in which case the H-D method cannot be applied.
2. Within limits of error, E can be the same as C, or E entails or gives support to or confirms C. In this case C passes its test against E. Can we go on to say that H has also passed its test, or that H is confirmed or even true? No, what we have is that $(H \& A) \vdash C$; if C is true we cannot infer the premise $(H \& A)$ since this would be to commit the fallacy of affirming the consequent. Setting aside the faultiness of the inference, we could not even confirm H, but at best the conjunction $(H \& A)$. One can only say derivatively that the conjunction $(H \& A)$ has passed a test. But this is not yet to provide a theory of confirmation. We shall see in §7.3 what principles of confirmation would be needed so that the confirmation of C could be transmitted back up the flow of Figure 7.1 to reach inside the conjunction $(H \& A)$ to confirm H alone.

    Suppose $(H \& A)$ has several test consequences $C_1, C_2, ..., C_n$, which pass their comparison with the evidence and there are no fails. By induction we can infer that $(H \& A)$ will pass the next test C_n+1. Alternatively, we could appeal to $C_1, C_2, ..., C_n$ as inductive support for $(H \& A)$. But again none of this enables us to break through the conjunction and affirm that one of the conjuncts H has inductive support.
3. Again within limits of error, E can be inconsistent with C, or E disconfirms C. But it does not follow that H is false. At best we can only say, using *modus tollens,* that the conjunction $(H \& A)$ is false. Here we have an illustration of the Quine–Duhem thesis,[1] which says that it is not possible to sufficiently isolate a hypothesis in order to test it; such testing can only be

of a group of hypotheses. Thus we can only infer the falsity of at least one, or several or all, of H, S, I, T, SIS and C; but we cannot infer which is false. For the same reasons, if H itself is a conjunction of further hypotheses or laws, one cannot determine which internal conjunct is false. In addition, if C is disconfirmed by E, to show that H is disconfirmed we need further principles of disconfirmation to reach inside the conjunct (H & A) to show that H is the culprit. In the next section some plausible principles of disconfirmation will be examined, but they prove to be of little use.

If all of H, S, I, T, SIS and T_E are inconsistent with one another then the source of the inconsistency can lie anywhere. However, if there are quite independent grounds for accepting that each of the auxiliaries S, I, T and SIS (we can include T_E here) are correct then we can be in the position to infer correctly that H is the culprit. Such independent grounds could arise from other methods of test that do not involve the target hypotheses H under scrutiny here. So the Quine–Duhem thesis is not always an insurmountable obstacle.

In many experiments there is an issue of ensuring that the SIS condition holds. As an illustration consider the case of the solar neutrino experiment and the problem that emerged of "the missing solar neutrinos" (Franklin 2001: esp. ch. 8). The earth is bombarded with different kinds of emanations from the sun, including cosmic rays and billions of neutrinos every second. A theory was developed about the nature of the (assumed) mass-less and charge-less solar neutrinos produced by the sun's nuclear reactions that needed testing (this is hypothesis H under test). In detecting them on earth it is necessary to screen off all effects that might be due to other sources, such as the cosmic rays that also bombard the earth's surface. To achieve this the neutrino detection apparatus was sunk about 1.5 km deep in a mine shaft where there would be few cosmic rays penetrating that deeply; it was also surrounded with a battery of detectors to ensure that this was so. Without this precaution the SIS condition would have been violated. Even though the SIS condition was thought to be satisfied there still remained a contradiction between what the solar neutrino theory H predicted and the results obtained by T_E. Depending on the experiment, less than a third to half the number of solar neutrinos was detected than were predicted. Which of H, S, I, T, SIS and T_E is at fault?

One of the first prediction devices was a 390,000 litre tank of a liquid akin to dry-cleaning fluid, tetrachloroethylene (C_2Cl_4). Each molecule has, on average, a particular isotope of chlorine. Neutrinos hardly interact with anything but the chlorine isotopes are sensitive to their presence and both will interact to produce radioactive argon gas. The relatively inert gas is allowed to build up over a period of several weeks or months in the tank; the argon gas molecules are then swept up from the liquid using helium gas and their number counted. This is a complex experiment that depends on many factors, such as the kinds of neutrinos that will enter into reaction with the chlorine in the tank (not all will), the production of the radioactive argon and its rate of decay, the means whereby the argon is swept up by the helium, their subsequent separation and the method whereby they are counted. Also to be controlled is the possibility that sub-nuclear particles simulate the interaction of the neutrinos. Here the background theory, T, and the experimental theory, T_E, play a big role in the test of H.

The problem of the missing solar neutrinos raised the following issues. Is the background particle physics wrong (i.e. T)? Is the model of the interior of the sun whereby neutrinos are produced wrong (this reflects information about system S)? Is there some unknown interference (SIS is not satisfied)? Are the experiments in error (i.e. T_E)? Initially some of the background theory and techniques used in T_E were found to be faulty and were subsequently rectified; but the problem of the missing neutrinos did not go away. When different kinds of experiments also showed a similar deficit between prediction and theory, the focus of attention shifted away from revising T_E to other matters, such as the model of neutrinos to be adopted (an element within T). The case of the solar neutrino experiment illustrates nicely the issues that arise when at least one of H, S, I, T, SIS and T_E are at fault.

There are several other problems for the H-D method, some of which are linked to a lack of a theory of confirmation. The H-D method falls victim to what is known as the "tacking" paradox, or the paradox of irrelevant conjunction. Suppose we say, on the basis of (i) $(H \& A) \vdash C$, and (ii) C passes its test when compared with E, that $(H \& A)$ picks up what we can call H-D *confirmation*. Then tack any irrelevant proposition X on to $(H \& A)$. By the law of monotonicity of classical logic, it follows from (i) that $[X \& (H \& A)] \vdash C$. So C also H-D *confirms* $[X \& (H \& A)]$. Suppose one of the hopes of a theory of confirmation to supplement the H-D method has been realized and that there is some way of distributing confirmation inside a conjunct; then not only does $(H \& A)$ get some confirmation but also the irrelevant X does. It is not good news for the H-D method that totally irrelevant and arbitrary claims such as X can get confirmation. This is an extra obstacle for the H-D method to surmount.

The H-D method can only deal with one target hypothesis H at a time; it has no way of comparing two or more hypotheses that might be up for consideration. There is a simple model of a crucial experiment that could be construed as H-D in character. Suppose there are two rivals H and H^* with their associated auxiliaries A and A^* and test consequences C and C^*: $(H \& A) \vdash C$, and $(H^* \& A^*) \vdash C^*$. Suppose that evidence E supports C^* while it undermines C. For the reasons already given, there can be no decisive refutation of H and confirmation of H^*. So either the very idea of a crucial experiment is wrongheaded (as Duhem would insist), or the H-D schema cannot capture it. (Compare this with the end of §8.2, which sets out the way Bayes's theorem can give an account of crucial experiment.)

The H-D method inherits a problem connected with the issue of finding curves that fit a given data set. Suppose we are given a number of data points on a graph, and that this constitutes evidence E. Now it is well known that two or more curves can fit the data equally well (see §5.5). Consider the case of just two experimentally determined, but logically contrary, laws, L and L^*, that fit E equally well. Suppose also that we have the following two H-D schemata in which H and H^* are rival hypotheses from which, along with their respective auxiliaries, L and L^* can be deduced: $(H \& A) \vdash L$, and $(H^* \& A^*) \vdash L^*$. Now evidence E fits both L and L^*, and so confirms both. Suppose we also help ourselves to one of the desiderata of a theory of confirmation that allows us to say that H and H^* are H-D confirmed by passing tests when compared with E. Then E confirms both H and H^*. That is, E confirms both of a pair of rival hypotheses. This has been called the *problem of alternative hypotheses*.[2]

This is hardly a satisfactory state of affairs. We want a theory of confirmation to distinguish between rival theories, but in this case it cannot. And this disability is endemic to the situation of H-D testing. If there are always rival pairs of laws L and L^* for whatever data E that might be envisaged, then there can always arise a situation in which rival hypotheses H and H^* are confirmed by E. If one were to relieve this problem by appealing to other methodological matters such as simplicity of H and H^* then one would have moved outside the ambit of the H-D method, as traditionally understood.

There is one final objection to consider. If we put emphasis on the deductive side of the H-D method, then it has no way of dealing with statistical hypotheses or any non-deductive inference. This could be dealt with by not requiring that the H-D method always be deductive; non-deductive inferences can also be allowed. As already suggested, it could be renamed as the *hypothetico-inferential method*, or the *hypothetico-inductive method*. Although this is a plausible move and does expand the method to allow for different kinds of laws and inference, it raises even more serious problems for the issue of a theory of confirmation and disconfirmation of such hypotheses, to which we now turn.

7.3 Problems for H-D confirmation

The core idea behind the H-D method is simple enough; if (some of) the consequences C of a hypothesis H are made true by evidence E, then while this does not prove H to be true (to so infer is fallacious), at least there is something to be said for H. However, as is well known, any false H can have true deductive consequences. If we aim for less, can it be said that H receives some qualitative confirmation, albeit weak, even though no quantitative or comparative confirmation is acquired? In Hempel's (1945) "Studies in the Logic of Confirmation"

(Hempel 1965: ch. 1) there is a careful investigation of these matters that leads to a negative verdict for the H-D method as far as confirmation is concerned. He lays down some simple adequacy conditions for any theory of confirmation that the H-D method does not meet:

> The *entailment condition*: If any observational or evidential claim E (deductively) entails a hypothesis H, then E confirms H (*ibid.*: §8).

> The *consequence condition*: If any evidence E entails a class of propositions K then it confirms any consequence of K.

> A *special consequence condition* (arises from the consequence condition as a special case): If $E \vdash H$, and for any H^* such that $H \vdash H^*$, then E confirms H^*. The idea here is that, if by the entailment condition E confirms H, then the confirmation is transmitted down the line to anything that logically follows from H.

> The *equivalence condition*: If E confirms H then it also confirms any proposition equivalent to it.

These seem plausible conditions to impose on any notion of confirmation, but they do not help the H-D method as this requires some notion of a converse relation of confirmation going back up against the flow of the relation of deduction, as presented in Figure 7.1. Hempel proposes such a condition and calls it the *converse consequence condition*.

> The *converse consequence condition*: If E confirms H^*, and H is any proposition such that $H \vdash H^*$, then E also confirms H.

Granted this principle confirmation can flow back up against the direction of deduction. As an example, suppose that E confirms some general law L (such as Kepler's elliptical law of motion); and suppose further that some theory T (such as Newton's theory of dynamics) entails L; then the evidence E confirms T as well as L. Even though the example has some plausibility, it does not follow that the general principle to which it conforms is also correct.

It would appear that in the H-D method we do need something like the converse consequence condition. We need to get from the true consequence C (suppose it to be the same as evidence E) back up to H. But note that in any version of the H-D method worth its salt, it is (H & A) that is confirmed and not H alone. We have not yet developed any principles that enable us to penetrate the conjunction and confirm one of the conjuncts, namely, H. In order to do this we need to suppose that the converse consequence condition holds in order to say that (H & A) has been confirmed.

Hempel's startling result is that we cannot even do this much. It turns out that the converse consequence condition is inconsistent with the other three conditions on confirmation (see §7.4 for the proof). Which of the four we abandon is unclear, but Hempel suggests we drop the converse consequence condition.[3] With this we lose a crucial principle that is needed to supplement the H-D method with some principles of confirmation. In the light of this result Hempel does develop some more restricted principles of confirmation that we shall not explore here.[4] Hempel also argues that the H-D method falls foul of the ravens paradox (see §7.4 and Hempel 1965: ch. 1). But the ravens paradox is not merely a problem for the H-D method; it is also a problem that any theory of confirmation must solve.

The upshot of the treatment of the H-D method is that while it does capture the deductive aspects of the applications of theories in some context, and does give a pass/fail verdict when compared with evidence, it does not come equipped with a theory of confirmation and one must be added to it. But the most plausible principles that one might add face considerable difficulties. We will see that Bayes's theorem does capture the good deductive aspects of a theory as a special case; but since it also comes equipped with a theory of probabilistic confirmation then it proves to be superior to the H-D method (see §8.4).

7.4 Appendix on some paradoxical results of confirmation theory

In this appendix we set out two paradoxes of confirmation in which, paradoxically, intuitively seemingly irrelevant claims can contribute to confirmation of some hypothesis. Both can be found in Hempel (1965: ch. 1).

The first paradox concerns the converse consequence condition. Suppose that E is any evidence and H any hypothesis whatever.

(1) As a special case of the entailment condition
     since $E \vdash E$, then E confirms itself.
(2) $(H \& E) \vdash E$ [by the classical law of simplification]
(3) E confirms $(H \& E)$ [by (1), (2) and the
                                                 converse consequence condition]
(4) $(H \& E) \vdash H$ [by the classical law of simplification]
(5) E confirms H [by (3), (4) and the consequence condition]

But result (5) is unacceptable. E and H are any chosen propositions whatever; so what (5) says is that any proposition confirms any other proposition. This must be an unacceptable result for any theory of confirmation. The result shows that three plausible principles needed for the H-D method lead to an unacceptable result. Whichever one rejects, the H-D method is in trouble as it seems to need them all. In Hempel's view the converse consequence condition is the culprit.[5]

The second paradoxical result concerns the paradox commonly called the ravens paradox as set out by Hempel (1965: ch. 1, §§3–5). The paradox arises not only in the case of the simple model set out below; it also arises for confirmation within the H-D method.

Suppose we are given a law L, which we can represent logically as follows:

(L)   All A are B, or $(\forall x)[Ax \supset Bx]$ (e.g. using Hempel's illustration "all ravens are black").

Let us also grant what Hempel calls the *Nicod criterion* (N) for confirmation (named after Jean Nicod who proposed it). It says:

(N)   If n is a particular object, then (i) An & Bn confirms $(\forall x)[Ax \supset Bx]$ but (ii) An & $\neg Bn$ disconfirms $(\forall x)[Ax \supset Bx]$.

There is an important equivalence condition for confirmation, which says:

(E)   Whatever confirms (disconfirms) one of a pair of equivalent hypotheses, also confirms (disconfirms) the other (this is mentioned in §7.3).

Now consider another law L^*, which is logically equivalent to L, namely,

(L*) $(\forall x)[\neg Bx \supset \neg Ax]$ (that is, all non-black things are non-ravens).

On the basis of (N) it follows that a particular item m such that $\neg Bm$ & $\neg Am$ confirms L^*, that is, $(\forall x)[\neg Bx \supset \neg Ax]$. Using Hempel's example, some particular thing m that is not black and not a raven will confirm "all non-black things are non-ravens". That is, this piece of white paper, or the red sun or the blue Pacific Ocean, being non-black non-ravens, will confirm "all non-black things are non-ravens".

Granted principle (E) it follows that item m such that $\neg Am$ & $\neg Bm$ will also confirm $(\forall x)[Ax \supset Bx]$.

The paradox now emerges. Not only does An & Bn confirm $(\forall x)[Ax \supset Bx]$, but also anything that is non-B & non-A will confirm $(\forall x)[Ax \supset Bx]$. That is, this piece of white paper, or the red sun or the blue Pacific Ocean, and a host of other things, also confirm $(\forall x)[Ax \supset Bx]$. But there is a strong intuition that these items should *not* count towards the confirmation of L; at best they should be neutral, neither confirming nor disconfirming the law.

Given this paradoxical conclusion, one might subject to scrutiny the assumptions on the basis of which the inference is made, particularly (N), (E) and the assumption made in (L) that a minimal necessary feature of laws has been captured by their expression in first-order logic. But if these are granted (as they commonly are), then Hempel has raised a serious paradox not only for the simple model of confirmation discussed here, but also any notion of H-D confirmation that employs this model. The task for any theory of confirmation will be to remove the paradox.

III. Probability and scientific method

8. Probability, Bayesianism and methodology

The theory of probabilistic inference has come to occupy a prominent place in methodology. Over the past fifty years subjective Bayesianism has been regarded (by many but not all) as the leading theory of scientific method. Here and in Chapter 9 we set out what this theory is, how it comes to encompass many of the aspects of method explored elsewhere in this book and what its strengths and weaknesses may be. Section 8.1 sets out the axioms of probability along with some of their more important consequences. These lead quite naturally to Bayes's theorem, a result discovered by the eighteenth-century cleric Thomas Bayes, which is central to all probabilistic thinking. The theorem comes in many different forms several of which are mentioned in §8.2 in order to bring out the different ways in which it can be applied. Once this is set out it is possible to outline a theory of the confirmation of a hypothesis by evidence (§8.3). In §8.4 it is shown that the H-D method can be placed in this setting; its good aspects turn out to be special cases of Bayes's theorem. This setting also provides a theory of confirmation for the H-D method, something that it lacks.

There are a number of different ways in which the probability calculus can be interpreted. Some interpret it in an objectivist way, for example Jeffreys in his attempt to show that there is an objective way of assigning prior probabilities to hypotheses (see §5.6). This is to be contrasted with the widely adopted alternative view in which probability is understood as a coherent subjective, or personal, degree of belief. This position is explored in the remainder of this chapter beginning with §8.5, which sets out the subjectivist position, taking its cue from the work of Ramsey. Coherent subjective degrees of belief are those that ought to be in conformity with the probability calculus. If they do not conform then there is an argument that says that a "Dutch book" can be made against a person such that they can never win in their bets against nature. This is an important result in the metamethodology of subjective Bayesianism, which lays the foundations for the normativity of the rules of the probability calculus; §8.6 outlines some of the metamethodological issues involved here. Another important aspect of subjective Bayesianism is the rule of conditionalization (§8.7). These three sections provide the core of the subjectivist Bayesian approach.

In Chapter 9 we consider a range of further matters to do with Bayesianism such as: whether the rules of the probability calculus need supplementation in order to provide a theory of scientific method; the problem of priors; its account of new and old evidence; the extent to which it can accommodate aspects of inference to the best explanation; what justification of induction it can provide; and its account of some of the values and rules mentioned in Part I. Although there are some successes, there are also some shortcomings to note. Whatever the verdict on Bayesianism as an overall theory of method, it is the pivot around which much current work in methodology turns.

8.1 Principles and theorems of probability

We commonly speak of *the probability of a hypothesis* H *given evidence* E, and abbreviate this as "$P(H, E)$" (some write this as "$P(H/E)$"). This is sometimes called *relative* probability, the probability of H relative to E. More commonly it is called the *posterior* probability (following Laplace's terminology); it is the probability of H coming after the evidence. It is also called the *conditional* probability, the probability of H on the condition of E.

This is to be distinguished from another probability, $P(E, H)$, in which the order of E and H is the reverse of that given in $P(H, E)$. This used to be called *inverse probability*, but following Fisher's usage it is more commonly called the *likelihood* of hypothesis H in the light of evidence E (and is sometimes written as $L(H, E)$).

The difference between the two forms can be illustrated as follows. If we think of hypothesis H as given and fixed and we let E vary over different kinds of evidence $E_1, E_2, ..., E_m$, then $P(H, E_i)$, $i = 1, 2, ..., m$, will represent the different probabilities of the same hypothesis for different evidence. That is, from the stance of the same hypothesis H, different pieces of evidence will make H probable, less probable or more probable. Now think of E as a constant and let H vary in $P(E, H)$ (or in $L(H, E)$). That is, H varies over the hypotheses $H_1, H_2, ..., H_n$, thereby yielding various likelihoods $P(E, H_i)$, $i = 1, 2, ..., n$. We can now ask: how probable do the various H_i make the same evidence E? Or, how likely are the H_i in the light of E? $P(E, H_i)$ represents various *likelihoods* that different hypotheses H_i confer on the same evidence E. From the stance of the same evidence, different hypotheses will make that evidence more likely, less likely or unlikely.

H and E can be any propositions whatever. The hypothesis H can be taken quite broadly to be any of the following: a theory (e.g. in the case of Newtonian mechanics the conjunction of the three laws of motion and the law of universal gravitation); a single law or generalization; a singular hypothesis of the sort to be determined in courts of law (e.g. whether or not some person is guilty as charged); a medical hypothesis about the cause of a patient's symptoms; or a singular claim of history (e.g. Napoleon was poisoned with arsenic when exiled in St Helena). Similarly, what counts as evidence E can be broad, from a singular report of observation, a conjunction of many pieces of data, lower-level laws, and the like.

We can also consider the probability of a hypothesis H all by itself in the absence of any evidence. This we shall write as: $P(H)$. Sometimes this is called the *absolute* probability, or the *unconditional* probability (as opposed to *conditional* probability given above) in that no conditions of evidence are required. More commonly it is called the *prior* probability, that is, prior to considering any evidence. This can also be represented as a *relative* probability. If we let "$\mathfrak{I}$" stand for only logical truths or tautologies, then we can write "$P(H)$" as "$P(H, \mathfrak{I})$". That is, we consider the probability of H given only logical truths and not any empirical and/or contingent evidence.

What is the connection between prior and posterior probability? Posterior probability is commonly defined in terms of prior probability as follows:

Definition: $P(H, E) = \dfrac{P(H \,\&\, E)}{P(E)}$, providing $P(E) \neq 0$

The rationale behind this definition can be seen with the help of the Venn diagram below (Figure 8.1) to represent probability relations.

Consider the rectangle, which properly contains two oval figures each of a given area. The area of each oval over the total area of the rectangle yields a fraction between 0 and 1. Let the ovals represent hypothesis H and evidence E; their *prior* probabilities can then be given as one of these fractions (of the respective oval area over the area of the whole rectangle). H and E overlap in the area

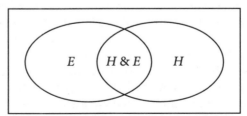

Figure 8.1 Venn diagram for definition of posterior probability in terms of prior probability.

(*H* & *E*). Suppose that one throws a dart at the rectangle and hits the evidence area *E*. (The supposition makes no sense when the evidence area *E* is zero.) Then we can ask: what is the probability that the dart also hits the hypothesis area *H*? It could only do so if it hits the overlap area of *H* & *E*. So, what is the probability that, given that the dart hits *E*, that it also hits *H*? In effect we are asking: what is the probability of *H* given *E*, that is, $P(H, E)$? Looking at the diagram we can work this out. It is the fraction obtained from the intersection area (*H* & *E*) over the total area of *E*. Since the areas are proportional to probabilities we can say that it is given by the ratio of $P(H \& E)/P(E)$.[1]

The following sets out what are commonly taken to be the three axioms of the probability calculus, and some of the important principles or theorems that follow from them, which have a central role in scientific reasoning and method.

Axiom 1: $0 \leq P(H) \leq 1$

That is, the (prior or absolute) probability of a hypothesis *H* lies between 0 and 1, and includes 0 and 1 as lower and upper bounds. The same axiom also holds for conditional probabilities: $0 \leq P(H, E) \leq 1$.

Axiom 2: $P(\mathfrak{I}) = 1$ (where $\mathfrak{I}$ is a tautology)

That is, any tautology or logical truth has probability 1, the upper bound for probabilities. Given other theorems mentioned below it is easy to show that $P(\mathcal{C}) = 0$, where $\mathcal{C}$ is any contradictory proposition. A similar axiom also holds for the case of conditional probabilities: $P(\mathfrak{I}, E) = 1$. Given some of the theorems below, it can then be shown that $P(\mathcal{C}, E) = 0$.

Axiom 2 can be taken to apply not only to tautologies but any claim that is quite certain, 100 per cent sure or holds beyond any (Cartesian) doubt whatsoever. Propositions that are certain need not be tautologies or necessary truths, but all tautologies and necessary truths are certainties. If we extend Axiom 2 to such certainties we can write: $P(\text{Certainty}) = 1$. Similarly for conditional probability $P(\text{Certainty}, E) = 1$.

Axiom 3: $P(H_1 \lor H_2) = P(H_1) + P(H_2)$ (providing H_1 and H_2 are inconsistent, that is, they mutually exclude one another)[2]

This is also known as the *additivity rule* since it concerns the addition of probabilities: the probability of a disjunction of mutually inconsistent propositions is the sum of the probabilities of each of the propositions taken singly. It is also known as the *principle of finite additivity* when it is extended to a finite number *n* of hypotheses H_i where *i* = 1, 2, …, *n*. It can also be extended to a *principle of countably infinite additivity*, in which the number of hypotheses is countably infinite. In what follows we shall consider only the finite case.

There is a more general additivity rule that does not have the above proviso and applies to any pair of hypotheses whether exclusive of one another or not:

General addition principle: $P(H_1 \lor H_2) = P(H_1) + P(H_2) - P(H_1 \& H_2)$

The difference between Axiom 3 and the general addition principle can be explained with the help of the following two Venn diagrams (Figures 8.2 and 8.3) in which the probabilities of the two hypotheses are represented by a fraction formed by the area of each oval divided by the area of the containing rectangle. The same applies in Figure 8.3 for the fraction obtained by dividing the overlap area of H_1 and H_2 by the area of the rectangle. In the case of Axiom 3 the pair of hypotheses $\{H_1, H_2\}$ is mutually exclusive; so there is no overlap area of the two ovals as illustrated in Figure 8.2. To obtain $P(H_1 \lor H_2)$, simply add the fractions of the two hypotheses represented by $P(H_1)$ and $P(H_2)$. But if there is overlap, as in Figure 8.3, then in adding $P(H_1) + P(H_2)$ the common area of the probability due to $P(H_1 \& H_2)$ has been added twice; so there needs to be a deduction of $P(H_1 \& H_2)$. And this is what the general addition principle says in subtracting the factor $P(H_1 \& H_2)$.

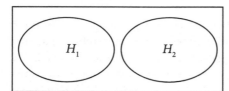

Figure 8.2 Venn diagram for addition principle.

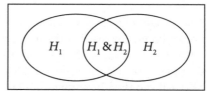

Figure 8.3 Venn diagram for total probability principle.

There are some special cases of Axiom 3 that are of interest. Consider the pair of hypotheses $\{H, \neg H\}$. Since these satisfy the proviso of Axiom 3 of mutually exclusivity then:

Axiom 3 (special case): $P(H \lor \neg H) = P(H) + P(\neg H)$

Since "$(H \lor \neg H)$" is a tautology, then by Axiom 2 the following theorem readily follows:

Theorem 1: $P(H \lor \neg H) = 1$

From Theorem 1 and the special case of Axiom 3 we can readily show the following two further results:

Theorem 2: $P(H) + P(\neg H) = 1$

Theorem 3: $P(H) = 1 - P(\neg H)$

That is, as the prior probability of one hypothesis goes up or down in value, that of its negation goes in the reverse direction. These are important results when considering two rival hypotheses such as H and its negation $\neg H$.

Using conditional probability we can prove a version of Axiom 3 that is important in science for adjudicating between rival hypotheses with respect to the same evidence E:

Theorem 4: $P([H_1 \vee H_2], E) = P(H_1, E) + P(H_2, E)$ (providing E entails not both (H_1 and H_2); that is, $\{E, H_1, H_2\}$ is an inconsistent set)

A special case arises for the mutually exclusive pair $\{H, \neg H\}$:

$P([H \vee \neg H], E) = 1 = P(H, E) + P(\neg H, E)$

As the posterior probability of H goes up or down on evidence E, so the posterior probability of its negation $\neg H$ goes down or up on evidence E.

Theorem 4 raises an important matter when adjudicating between an exhaustive and mutually inconsistent set of hypotheses, such as the sets $\{H_1, \neg H_1\}$, $\{H_1, H_2, \neg(H_1 \& H_2)\}$, and so on. Suppose instead of the second set we consider only the pair of rival hypotheses $\{H_1, H_2\}$. There is no guarantee that these two hypotheses exhaust all the logical possibilities of hypotheses even though they exclude one another. In fact the correct hypothesis may be neither of H_1 or H_2; that is, $\neg(H_1 \& H_2)$ is the correct hypothesis. Often when applying probabilistic considerations to rival hypotheses we require them to be not only mutually exclusive but exhaustive as well. So a further hypothesis has to be added to, for example, the exclusive pair $\{H_1, H_2\}$, in this case $\neg(H_1 \& H_2)$. This is often called the *catch-all hypothesis*. It is not a positive hypothesis like H_1 or H_2. Rather it simply states that some third hypothesis that is neither H_1 nor H_2 is the correct hypotheses. Although a catch-all is needed there is a problem in that, unlike the other hypotheses, we do not know what empirical content it has.

Equivalence principle: For any two propositions that are logically equivalent, then their prior and conditional probabilities are the same.

For example, if A is logically equivalent to B (symbolically $[A \equiv B]$), then $P(A) = P(B)$. Similarly for conditional probability where $H_1 \equiv H_2$, and $E_1 \equiv E_2$, then $P(H_1, E_1) = P(H_2, E_2)$.

191

If premise A entails conclusion B (in the sense that B is a logical consequence of A) then the following important principle holds:

Entailment principle: For any propositions A and B (except where A is a contradiction), if $A \vdash B$ then $P(B, A) = 1$.

The restriction that A cannot be a contradiction is important. In classical logic (presupposed here) from a contradiction any proposition validly follows. In the above if the contradiction $\mathcal{C}$ is substituted for "A", we have both $P(B, \mathcal{C}) = 1$ and $P(\neg B, \mathcal{C}) = 1$. Substitution in Theorem 4 shows that the sum of the two probabilities is $P(B \vee \neg B, \mathcal{C}) = 2$. But this result violates Axiom 1; hence the restriction on the entailment principle. However, it is permissible for B to be a contradiction; but in this case $P(\mathcal{C}, A) = 0$.

Since the entailment principle holds for any two propositions, it also holds for the case where evidence E entails a hypothesis H; that is, if $E \vdash H$ then $P(H, E) = 1$. Although it is not common for evidence to entail hypotheses, sometimes it does. More commonly, hypothesis H will entail evidence E; that is, if $H \vdash E$ then $P(E, H)$ (a likelihood) is 1. This situation arises for the H-D method; if hypothesis H, along with whatever auxiliaries A that are needed, entails evidence E, then $P(E, [H \& A]) = 1$.

The equivalence principle also leads to the following result, which tells us what happens when the evidence contradicts the hypothesis: if $E \vdash \neg H$ then $P(\neg H, E) = 1$. From this it can be readily shown that $P(H, E) = 0$ (this result follows from the theorems above). That is, where the evidence contradicts the hypothesis then its probability on the evidence is zero. The different aspects of the entailment principle capture within the probability calculus several intuitive ideas in methodology concerning deducibility and refutation that are important in the H-D method.

The next principle concerns the probabilistic relations between propositions A and B, where B is a logical consequence of A, that is, $A \vdash B$:

Logical consequence principle: $A \vdash B$ iff $P(A) < P(B)$

In the limiting case where A and B are equivalent, $A \vdash B$ iff $P(A) \leq P(B)$. But generally A is the logically stronger proposition because it entails the logically weaker B (but B does not entail A). Note that the probability relations are in the reverse order of those of logical strength. The logically stronger A is less probable than the logically weaker B, which is more probable.

The logical consequence principle tells us something important about the connection between a hypothesis and its evidence:

If $H \vdash E$ then $P(H) < P(E)$

A related result holds for conditional probabilities involving two hypotheses and any evidence that obtains for both. It says that any evidence cannot make the logically stronger hypotheses more (or equally) probable than the logically weaker:

Given any E, if $H_1 \vdash H_2$, then $P(H_1, E) < P(H_2, E)$

Consider the logical consequence principle in two cases involving the rule of simplification of deductive logic, namely, $(A \& B) \vdash A$ and $(A \& B) \vdash B$. Then it follows that $P(A \& B) < P(A)$, and $P(A \& B) < P(B)$. Thus the prior probability of a conjunction is never greater than the prior probability of each conjunct taken separately. Putting these two results together we have:

$P(A) \geq P(A \& B) \leq P(B)$

There is an important rule known as the total probability principle that in its simplest form can be expressed as follows:

Total probability principle: $P(E) = P(H)P(E, H) + P(\neg H)P(E, \neg H)$,
where $0 < P(H) < 1$

Suppose a particular case in which evidence E is the claim that a person is cured of their cold (abbreviated as "cure") and the the hypothesis H is the claim that taking large doses of vitamin C cures colds (abbreviated as "VC"). Here E is being examined against the background of a partitioning with respect to the hypotheses H and $\neg H$ (in more general cases of the principle the partitioning can be with respect to three or more hypotheses). In the particular case of "cure" and "VC" we have:

$P(\text{cure}) = P(\text{VC})P(\text{cure}, \text{VC}) + P(\neg\text{VC})P(\text{cure}, \neg\text{VC})$

The right-hand side concerns the prior probability of the claim that taking large doses of vitamin C cures colds, the likelihood of a cure given that vitamin C has been taken and the likelihood of a cure given that vitamin C has not been taken. When values for the right-hand probabilities are obtained, the probability of a cure can be calculated.

A Venn diagram (Figure 8.4) can be used to explain this principle and suggest a proof. Assume, as with the earlier Venn diagrams, that propositions E, H and $\neg H$ have prior probabilities represented by the fractions of their associated areas divided by the total area of the encompassing rectangle. The top portion gives the prior probability of H, the bottom portion gives the prior probability of $\neg H$ and the circle gives the prior probability of E. Given the partition of E by

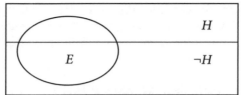

Figure 8.4 Venn diagram for total probability principle.

H and $\neg H$, the area of E can be represented as the sum of the areas represented by the intersection of E and H, and the intersection of E and $\neg H$. (One can readily envisage that E be partitioned by three or more hypotheses.) Given that the areas in the Venn diagram represent probabilities then we can say: $P(E)$ is given by the sum $P(E \,\&\, H) + P(E \,\&\, \neg H)$. By using the appropriate form of the definition of conditional probabilities in terms of unconditional probabilities, the principle follows.[4]

There is also a form of the total probability principle for conditional probabilities that, under partitioning by rivals H and $\neg H$, is as follows:

$$P(E, B) = P(H, B)P(E, H \,\&\, B) + P(\neg H, B)P(E, \neg H \,\&\, B)$$

Axiom 3 provides an addition principle for the probability of disjoined hypotheses in terms of the addition of the probabilities of each disjunction. There is also a rule for the probability of conjoined hypotheses in terms of the multiplication of probabilities of each conjunct. In a simple form it says:

> *Multiplication or conjunction principle*: $P(H_1 \,\&\, H_2) = P(H_1) \times P(H_2)$, where H_1 and H_2 are independent of one another.

To illustrate, suppose a pair of fair dice is rolled; since the rolling of each die is independent of the rolling of the other the principle applies. If H_1 = "die 1 produces a 6" (so $P(H_1) = 1/6$) and H_2 = "die 2 produces a 6" (so $P(H_2) = 1/6$), then by the principle the probability that a pair of sixes is rolled is $P(H_1 \,\&\, H_2)$ = $1/6 \times 1/6 = 1/36$. The rule also provides a condition for the probabilistic independence of H_1 and H_2 from one another.

Expressed as conditional probabilities the corresponding principle says that the probability of the conjunction of two hypotheses, given evidence, is equal to the probability of the first hypothesis given the same evidence multiplied by the probability of the second hypothesis given that the same evidence *and* the first hypothesis is true:

$$P([H_1 \,\&\, H_2], E) = P(H_1, E) \times P(H_2, [E \,\&\, H_1])$$

Put more generally we can express the multiplication principle as follows:

$P(H \& E, F) = P(E, F) \times P(H, E \& F) = P(H, F) \times P(E, H \& F)$

We shall not explore the principle further, except to note that if we consider "F" to be a tautology we can effectively eliminate expression "F" and arrive at a special case of the multiplication principle, which, rearranged, is the definition of conditional probability in terms of unconditional probability:

$P(H \& E) = P(H, E) \times P(E)$

This is important in that it leads directly to a form of Bayes's theorem. The proof is simple, and depends also on the equivalence principle and the definition of conditional probability (a special case of the multiplication principle).

(1) $P(H \& E) = P(E \& H)$ [by equivalence principle]

(2) $P(H, E) \times P(E) = P(E, H) \times P(H)$

This is obtained by two substitutions in (1), one for the left and one for the right, of the definition of conditional probability as expressed just above, observing carefully the order of H and E in (1). By suitable rearrangement we get the first simple form of Bayes's theorem:

(3) $P(H, E) = P(E, H) \times P(H)/P(E)$, providing $P(E) \neq 0$

A paper by Thomas Bayes (1702–61) on probability was published posthumously in 1763. Although the exact form of (3), which we now commonly call *Bayes's theorem*, is not to be explicitly found in it, Bayes established a result that has come to be at the heart of our understanding of probability theory.

8.2 Bayes's theorem in some of its various forms

Bayes's theorem comes in many forms, some simpler than others. Here we shall consider five versions, revealing different applications of the theorem (other versions will appear elsewhere). The first and simplest version is based directly on the last proof given above:

Bayes's theorem, version 1

$$P(H, E) = \frac{P(E, H) \times P(H)}{P(E)}, \text{ where } P(E) \neq 0 \qquad [1]$$

The left-hand side tells us something we commonly wish to know, namely, the probability of a hypothesis H given evidence E. The right-hand side has three probabilities in it; if we know the value of these then we can work out what we want to know, namely, $P(H, E)$. Do we ever obtain the right-hand-side values? Sometimes, and that is helpful. But often we do not, or have only one of them. Still we can learn a lot from this version of the theorem, as we shall see, by considering its comparative forms.

The three expressions on the right-hand side are as follows. The expression $P(E, H)$ is the *likelihood* of H in the light of E. The expression $P(H)$ is the prior probability of H, that is, prior to the evidence E. Finally, the expression $P(E)$ is called the initial or prior probability of the evidence E. Sometimes (following Carnap [1950] 1962: 327) it is called the *expectedness* of the evidence.

Putting all of this together, the first simple form of Bayes's theorem may be expressed in words as follows:

$$\frac{\text{posterior}}{\text{probability } (H, E)} = \frac{(\text{likelihood of } H \text{ on } E) \times (\text{prior probability of } H)}{(\text{expectedness of } E)}$$

Throughout the various forms of Bayes's theorem given in this section, the factor $P(E, H)/P(E)$ will appear in various guises. It is known as the *Bayesian multiplier* and its role will be spelled out further in §8.3 and §8.7. In effect it is the ratio of the likelihood that H bestows on evidence E over the probability of evidence E. As it goes up or down, so the ratio $P(H, E)/P(H)$ goes up or down, that is, the ratio of the probability of H given E over the probability of H in the absence of evidence E. As will be seen in §8.3, the ratio $P(H, E)/P(H)$ tells us about the degree of confirmation or disconfirmation of H by E. And this is the same as the Bayesian multiplier, which involves likelihoods.

Bayes's theorem, version 2

$$P(H, E \& B) = \frac{P(E, H \& B)P(H, B)}{P(E, B)}, \text{ where } P(E, B) \neq 0 \qquad [2]$$

Here we have simply added to version 1 an expression "B", which stands broadly for "background information". If we think of this background information as old evidence, $E_1, E_2, \ldots, E_n$, and E as new evidence, then we have a way of assessing the probability of H on the total evidence, old and new. It is given by the expression on the right-hand side. Alternatively we could take B to be any background to H, including a theory. What we are then considering is the probability of hypothesis H given evidence E relative to a background theory B.

Bayes's theorem, version 3

As is often the case, we wish to compare several rival hypotheses against the same evidence. This we could not readily do with the H-D method since it deals with only one hypothesis at a time. Version 3 of Bayes's theorem considers the comparison of the pair of rival hypotheses, $\{H, \neg H\}$. In addition we substitute for "$P(E)$" (assuming it is not zero from now on), its equivalence based on the total probability principle in version 1 of Bayes's theorem. (The same considerations also apply to version 2 of Bayes's theorem by substituting for $P(E, B)$ its equivalence based on a conditional probability version of the total probability principle.) This yields:

$$P(H,E) = \frac{P(E,H)P(H)}{P(E,H)P(H) + P(E,\neg H)P(\neg H)} \qquad [3]$$

$$P(\neg H,E) = \frac{P(E,\neg H)P(\neg H)}{P(E,H)P(H) + P(E,\neg H)P(\neg H)} \qquad [4]$$

Equations [3] and [4] provide a way of calculating the probabilities of two rival hypotheses on the same evidence E. This version of Bayes's theorem is useful in all contexts where we need to see just how well each of a pair of rival hypotheses are doing on the basis of the same evidence E. The two equations can be placed one over the other, thereby eliminating the common denominator factor: $P(H, E)/P(\neg H, E) = P(H)/P(\neg H) \times P(E, H)/P(E, \neg H)$. That is, the ratio of the degree of confirmation of the rival hypotheses by the same evidence E is given by the ratio of the prior probabilities of the rivals multiplied by the likelihood of the two rivals, or in other words the ratio of the degree to which each rival predicts the evidence.

Bayes's theorem, version 4

This is a further generalization of version 3 in which not merely two rival hypotheses but n rival hypotheses can be considered together:

$$P(H_k,E) = \left[P(E,H_k)P(H_k) \right] \Big/ \sum_{i=1}^{n} P(E,H_i)P(H_i) \qquad [5]$$

where H_k is any one of n hypotheses, $k = 1, 2, \ldots, n$, and where these are exclusive and exhaustive of the range of rival hypotheses (to make them exhaustive a *catch-all* hypothesis may have to be included).

This version allows the comparison of n hypotheses through a set of n equations, each yielding a value for $P(H_k, E)$, $k = 1, 2, .., n$. This helps illuminate an old idea within scientific methodology, that of *eliminative induction*. It is not always clear what eliminative induction might mean; but version 4 gives us a simple way of understanding this. Suppose that a set of rival hypotheses is being compared with evidence E. Some hypotheses get very low probability, and even increasingly low probability as more evidence E comes in, while others get increasingly high probability. In such a case we can, as the differences become greater and greater, say that some hypotheses have been eliminated as serious candidates while others can be kept. Bayes's theorem in this version gives us a simple understanding of what might be meant by elimination; all hypotheses in a set that is exclusive and exhaustive are compared with one another on the basis of the same evidence, with some being eliminated from the set while others are retained (with some of these being eliminated in the light of further evidence).

Bayes's theorem, version 5

Finally we mention one further version of Bayes's theorem. The following version has been called the *Bayesian algorithm for theory preference* (see Salmon 1990: §7; Salmon 1998a: §7) since it arises from version 2 of Bayes's theorem (although a more complicated version of it can be considered based on version 3). Consider version 2, but for two different equations involving two different hypotheses, H_1 and H_2. In both there will be a common factor $P(E, B)$ that will cancel out when we put one equation over the other and obtain the following ratios:

$$\frac{P(H_1, E \,\&\, B)}{P(H_2, E \,\&\, B)} = \frac{P(E, H_1 \,\&\, B)}{P(E, H_2 \,\&\, B)} \times \frac{P(H_1, B)}{P(H_2, B)} \qquad [6]$$

The left-hand side is the comparison of the probabilities of two hypotheses, H_1 and H_2, in the light of evidence E, and the background of B. The right-hand side tells us that this is a function of two factors, the *ratio of the likelihoods* of the hypotheses with respect to evidence E (and background B), and the *ratio of the prior probabilities* before evidence E is considered (i.e. in the absence of E but in the presence of the common background B). This version of Bayes's theorem allows the comparative evaluation of a pair of hypotheses in terms of the ratio of their likelihoods and their prior probabilities, an important matter when it comes to considering the evidential support of a pair of rival hypotheses. Another way of considering equation [6] is the following (in which likelihoods are a measure of the extent to which hypotheses predict or explain data): the ratio of the probability of two hypotheses on the same data is equal to the ratio of the prior probabilities of the two hypotheses multiplied by the ratio of the degree to which each hypothesis predicts that data.

This version of Bayes's theorem also yields an understanding of crucial experiment. Consider two rival hypotheses H_1 and H_2. (The catch-all that is neither of these hypotheses can be set aside since we are considering ratios as in equation [6]). The rivals are compared with the same evidence E provided by a crucial experiment designed to test between them. Equation [6] yields a way of comparing the two hypotheses. However, the situation in crucial experiments is usually more complicated than this since the rival hypotheses H_1 and H_2 will have their own respective background assumptions B_1 and B_2. This yields the following version of equation [6]:

$$\frac{P(H_1, E \& B_1)}{P(H_2, E \& B_2)} = \frac{P(E, H_1 \& B_1)}{P(E, H_2 \& B_2)} \times \frac{P(H_1, B_1)}{P(H_2, B_2)} \qquad [6^*]$$

Understood this way, crucial experiments need not be all that crucial, and their outcome over time can depend on the nature of the background assumptions made in the crucial experiment.

A nice example of the way changing background assumptions can affect the verdict of a crucial experiment is set out by Hempel (1966: 25–8). Two early theories of light were the classical particle theory of Newton (H_1) and the wave theory of light (H_2) as developed by Augustin-Jean Fresnel and Thomas Young from the beginning of the nineteenth century. It was soon realized that, on the wave theory of light, its velocity should be greater in air than in water, while the opposite should be the case on the particle theory of light. In 1850 Léon Foucault proposed an experiment in which the velocities in air and water could be directly compared; the outcome was in favour of the wave theory of light. But is the result decisive? The particle theory supposed not only the core hypothesis H_1 that light is a stream of particles, but also adopted a quite definite background theory, B_1, about the nature of the classical particle. But at the turn of the twentieth century, due to the work of Einstein and others, a modified corpuscularian account of light emerged yielding a new background theory, $B_1{}^*$. (In the new "corpuscularian" theory, light was now understood to be light quanta or photons.) Once the old "corpuscularian" core hypothesis was accompanied by the new background theory, $B_1{}^*$, of what the "corpuscles" were like, there was a reversal of the outcome of the earlier crucial experiment. This does not mean that the wave theory of light was then refuted. Rather, the crucial character of so-called "crucial experiments" is really not that crucial and their outcome can be reversed given the changing background theories that can be employed. The above version of Bayes's theorem contributes to our understanding of how this can occur.

8.3 Bayesian confirmation

In §5.2 we introduced the idea of confirmation. This can now be given a setting within the above theory of probability. Put simply, evidence E *confirms* hypothesis H if and only if the posterior probability of H on evidence E is greater than the prior probability of H; and E *disconfirms* hypothesis H if and only if the posterior probability of H on evidence E is less than the prior probability of H. Otherwise, in the case of no change in probability there is neither confirmation nor disconfirmation. These three claims can be expressed as follows:

H is *confirmed* by E if $P(H, E) > P(H)$;

H is *disconfirmed* by E if $P(H, E) < P(H)$;

E is *neutral* in respect of the confirmation of H if $P(H, E) = P(H)$.

Consider the ratio $P(H, E)/P(H)$, which arises as a simple consequence of the definition of confirmation given above; it is greater or less than 1 as H is confirmed or disconfirmed. Write the first version of Bayes's theorem as follows: $P(H, E)/P(H) = P(E, H)/P(E)$. As mentioned in §8.2, on version 1 of Bayes's theorem, the right-hand side is the Bayesian multiplier. What this tells us is that the ratio expressing the degrees of confirmation of H by E is the same as the Bayesian multiplier, that is, the ratio of the likelihood of H on E over the probability of E.

If background information B is included (as in version 2 of Bayes's theorem), then the above definitions can be modified to include the idea of confirmation or disconfirmation of H by E *relative to B*. Note that the above definitions do not say what degree of (dis)confirmation H gets on E, nor how the degree might be measured; they introduce only a qualitative notion of confirmation and their comparison. But the above definitions do suggest a measure of the degree of confirmation E bestows on H as some function of $P(H, E)$ and $P(H)$. The most obvious and simplest function (but not necessarily the best) is to consider the difference between the two expressions. This gives rise to a difference measure: $d(H, E) = P(H, E) - P(H)$. However, within the Bayesian framework the above definitions of confirmation are not the only ones that are possible. Thus one can also propose: H is confirmed by E if $P(H, E) > P(H, \neg E)$; that is, one compares the probability of H when E is true and when E is false. This gives rise to a slightly different measure of degree of confirmation, the simplest being: $d^*(H, E) = P(H, E) - P(H, \neg E)$. Also, a notion of confirmation of H by E can be given in terms of likelihoods such as: H is confirmed by E if $P(E, H) > P(E, \neg H)$. This gives rise to a measure of degree of confirmation in terms of a ratio of likelihoods $P(E, H)/P(E, \neg H)$. In the light of these (and other[5]) accounts of confirmation, Bayesianism shows that there is not just one notion of confirmation and there is not just one measure of degree of confirmation; rather, there are several, each of which can be employed for different purposes.

A question can be asked about whether or not such definitions capture our pre-analytic notion of what confirmation is. Some Bayesians may not be very interested in whether or not any single pre-analytic intuition is captured at all. Given the above different accounts of confirmation and degree of confirmation, Bayesians could declare that there can be no unique pre-analytic notion to capture. It may well be the case that our intuitions are not very clear and that there is nothing, or no single thing, to be captured. Suppose that there is some pre-analytic notion to capture, and it differs from what is given above. Then Bayesians can become reformists and allege that they are laying the foundations for a theory of confirmation that is better and more systematic than that with which we have hitherto worked. But for some the above definitions are taken to capture some of our central intuitions about confirmation.[6]

These considerations also apply to a common case in science in which not only a single hypothesis H is under test but a number of hypotheses or laws conjoined together to form theory T, in conjunction with whatever auxiliary assumptions A that may be used in conjunction with T (as is set out in the H-D method). In this case what we are interested in is the increase or decrease of $P([T \& A], E)$ with respect to $P(T \& A)$ in the absence of E. Then the definitions of confirmation can be added to the H-D method, since that method does not specify any account of confirmation beyond saying that its test consequences either pass or fail when compared with the evidence. However, note that what is confirmed or disconfirmed is the conjunction $(T \& A)$ and not T by itself. Since it is T itself that is the intended target, the H-D method, even when put in the setting of the above notions of confirmation, falls short of its goal. More will be said of the H-D method in a Bayesian setting in the next section.

Version 3 of Bayes's theorem can be transformed in an interesting way to tell us something further about the confirmation of H by E. Consider only hypothesis H and its negation $\neg H$:

$$P(H, E) = \frac{P(E, H)P(H)}{P(E, H)P(H) + P(E, \neg H)P(\neg H)}$$

If we divide top and bottom by the factor $P(E, H)$, then we have the following expression:

$$P(H, E) = \frac{P(H)}{P(H) + P(\neg H)\dfrac{P(E, \neg H)}{P(E, H)}}$$

Using the theorem that tells us that $P(\neg H) = 1 - P(H)$, the above expression turns out to be a function of only two factors: the prior probability of H, $P(H)$; and the *likelihood ratio* (LR) of $P(E, \neg H)/P(E, H)$. This is evident when we transform the above expression to become:

$$P(H, E) = \frac{P(H)}{P(H) \times (1 - \text{LR}) + \text{LR}}$$

What does this mean? It shows that the probability of H given E varies with respect to just two factors. Suppose we keep the likelihood ratio constant; then as the prior probability increases so does $P(H, E)$, and conversely. Now keeping $P(H)$ constant, how does the likelihood ratio affect $P(H, E)$? The likelihood ratio will be smaller the more likely H makes E than does $\neg H$. For example, if E is all the times we have observed sun risings in our locality in the morning, and H is the claim that always the sun will rise in our locality in the morning, then the likelihood ratio of $P(E, \neg H)/P(E, H)$ will be small indeed. It follows from this that as the likelihood ratio becomes smaller, so $P(H, E)$ increases and tends in the direction of 1. On the other hand, the likelihood ratio will be greater the more likely $\neg H$ makes E than does H; it follows from this that $P(H, E)$ will decrease.

In the light of this, the above expression tells us something important about the confirmation of H by E. It tells us that $P(H, E)$ varies directly with the prior $P(H)$; and $P(H, E)$ varies inversely with the likelihood ratio $P(E, \neg H)/P(E, H)$, or, equivalently, varies directly with the likelihood ratio $P(E, H)/P(E, \neg H)$. From an intuitive point of view, this seems to be what one would expect in the light of induction. Not only does this version of Bayes's theorem ground this intuition, but it also spells out an important aspect of our understanding of inductive inference and provides one important link between induction and Bayes's theorem (see also §9.6).

8.4 The H-D method in a Bayesian context

The basic idea of the H-D method set out in Chapter 7 is that a hypothesis H under test, in conjunction with whatever auxiliaries A, entails a test consequence C, which we can suppose is identical to some evidence E. That is $(H \& A) \vdash E$; so by the entailment principle, $P(E, [H \& A]) = 1$. Granted this we can say that $(H \& A)$ passes one test, that is, its test against E. There are two further requirements on the H-D method. First, it is crucial that H is present and does some work in deducing E, and that E does not follow from A alone. Secondly, neither the target test hypothesis H nor evidence E is known, on the basis of auxiliaries A alone, to be true or false. That is $1 > P(H, A) > 0$, and $1 > P(E, A) > 0$.

Now consider version 2 of Bayes's theorem:

$$P(H, E \& A) = \frac{P(E, H \& A)P(H, A)}{P(E, A)}$$

Bayes's theorem in this form is quite general and allows, as the H-D method generally does not, that there be a non-deductive, or inductive probabilistic, relation between $(H \& A)$ and E, that is, $P(E, H \& A) < 1$. But given that the H-D method is intended to be deductive, $P(E, H \& A) = 1$; so the equation reduces to:

$$P(H, E \& A) = P(H, A)/P(E, A)$$

But the factor in the denominator is less than 1 and not zero, since $0 < P(E, A) < 1$. So it follows that $P(H, E \& A) > P(H, A)$. And by the definition of (incremental) confirmation, this says that there is confirmation of H by E with respect to the background of auxiliary theory A. One of the problems with the H-D method is that it does not come equipped with a theory of confirmation, and one has to be grafted onto it. However, in the setting of Bayes's theorem, the H-D method is a special case; and that setting automatically equips the H-D method with the theory of confirmation it would otherwise lack.

However, placing the H-D method in a Bayesian setting reveals one of its shortcomings: it can only deal with hypotheses one at a time. In contrast versions 3 and 4 of Bayes's theorem show how rival hypotheses can be compared two or more at a time. Also version 5 shows how Bayes's theorem can handle rival hypotheses in a crucial experiment; in contrast the H-D method needs to be gerrymandered to give an account of a crucial experiment between two hypotheses.

Setting the H-D method within the theory of probability and Bayes's theorem also overcomes an embarrassing problem that it faces: the problem of *irrelevant conjunction*, also known as the *tacking problem*. Suppose $(H \& A) \vdash E$, and E confirms H with respect to the background theory A. Suppose X is any genuinely irrelevant proposition that can be "tacked on" to $(H \& A)$ to form $(H \& A) \& X$. (For example, if H is a hypothesis in physics then X could be a hypothesis in Bible scholarship about who authored what chapter.) Now $(H \& A) \& X \vdash (H \& A)$, and $(H \& A) \vdash E$; so $(H \& A) \& X \vdash E$. Thus E confirms X, with respect to the background of $(H \& A)$. But it is undesirable that any irrelevant proposition X, concerning, say, Bible scholarship, should piggyback on the confirmation of hypotheses in physics.

To this problem there is a standard response made by many Bayesians that allows that X may be confirmed, but it turns out to be less well confirmed than H. A quick way to see this is to bear in mind the logical consequence principle, which says:

Given evidence E, if $H_1 \vdash H_2$, then $P(H_1, E) < P(H_2, E)$

Since $(H \& A) \& X \vdash (H \& A)$ then $P(((H \& A) \& X), E) < P((H \& A), E)$.

So even though $(H \& A) \& X$ with its "tacked on" irrelevant X does, as a whole, pick up confirmation from E, it must be less than the confirmation that E bestows on $(H \& A)$ (whatever unknown but absolute degree of confirmation each may obtain).[7] These considerations apply even though the irrelevant X is not sufficiently isolated from its context so that it can obtain confirmation by itself.

This last point raises the Quine–Duhem problem for the H-D method. This is the problem that even H cannot be sufficiently isolated from its context $(H \& A)$ of auxiliary hypotheses A and be subject to confirmation or disconfirmation all by itself. Thus we have spoken of the confirmation by E of H *relative* to B, and not the confirmation of H *tout court*. This is also true of any hypothesis H that is itself a conjunction of a number of laws, for example, Newton's laws of motion conjoined to the law of universal gravitational attraction; no single conjunct of the theory can be sufficiently isolated from the whole conjunction so that it, and it alone, can be subject to confirmation and disconfirmation. Can a Bayesian approach assist with resolving the Quine–Duhem problem? Some ways of dealing with this will be discussed in §9.7.

8.5 Subjective degree of belief as a probability

The principles and theorems set out in §8.1 and §8.2 partially constrain how we are to understand the probability functions "$P(-)$", or "$P(-, -)$", but they do not fully determine how we are to understand them. There are several "interpretations" of probability that attempt to spell out what this further understanding might be such as: classical *a priori*; frequency; propensity or objective chance; logical, or partial entailment; and subjective, or personal degree of belief. The first three interpretations we can set aside as not germane to our purposes. Our main focus will be on the last interpretation listed; but a little will be said of the fourth, partial entailment, account.

There is a tradition, of which Keynes and Carnap are prominent members, in which an attempt is made to think of probability as an objective logical relation between H and E in much the same way as there is an objective logical relation of entailment between the premises and conclusion of a valid argument, except that the entailment is partial and comes in degrees[8] with full entailment being a special case. The task would be, given any H and E, to discover the degree to which E partially entails H. That is, for E and H there is a number r ($0 \leq r \leq 1$) for a confirmation function c such that $c(H, E) = r$. However, the programme for working out the c-functions ran into some serious problems. It gave way on certain claims to objectivity (the confirmation functions as developed by Carnap were relative to the languages in which they were formulated); there was not always a uniquely specifiable number r for each $c(H, E) = r$; in some cases where r could be uniquely specified, particularly in the case of laws of nature, r turned out to be zero, something that many found unintuitive; the confirmation functions were difficult to develop for more than the simplest languages. There are now few attempts to develop this programme further.

During the same period in which Keynes was developing his interpretation of probability, Ramsey, and later Bruno de Finetti, were laying the foundations for the subjective or personalist interpretation of probability. De Finetti put the issue starkly when he claimed "Probability does not exist" (1974: x).[9] In de Finetti's view, objectivism about probability ought to go the way of belief in phlogiston, the cosmic ether and so on: "Probability, too, if regarded as something endowed with some kind of objective existence, is no less a misleading conception, an illusory attempt to exteriorize or materialize our true probabilistic beliefs" (*ibid.*). Ramsey and de Finetti make probability personal or subjectivist. In his later work it transpired that Carnap was not inimical to aspects of the subjectivist approach.[10] The big difference is that whereas on the partial entailment approach an attempt is made to found a probability logic on objective relations into which propositions can enter (in deductive logic these concern logical relations such as consistency, deducibility, etc.), on the subjective approach this is entirely eschewed in favour of a more "psychologistic" understanding of probability in terms of each person's attitude of belief in a proposition and the degree of that belief.

Knowledge is an all-or-nothing affair that does not admit degrees. For any person A, either A knows that p or A does not know that p, and there is no halfway position. Any wavering is an indication that A does not know. In contrast belief can come in degrees, from high to middling or low. At a coarse-grained level, some might only admit a three-part distinction between belief, suspension of belief or disbelief. But a more fine-grained approach is available in which differing degrees of belief are represented by the real numbers in the interval $[0, 1]$. Thus we can say that A's degree of belief (or credence) in p at a time $t = r$ (where $0 \leq r \leq 1$); this can be abbreviated to "$\mathrm{Bel}_{A,t}(p) = r$". The values, r, of $\mathrm{Bel}_{A,t}(p)$ can fluctuate over time for the same person A; and it will vary over persons A, B and so on; and it will vary according to the propositions p, q and so on, that are believed. In this sense $\mathrm{Bel}_{A,t}(p)$ is a personal or subjective degree of belief, relative to a person, a time and a proposition. There is some idealization in supposing that r is a precise number. In some cases it might be. But in other cases r could be replaced by a very short range of values with an upper bound r^+ and a lower bound r^- so that $\mathrm{Bel}_{A,t}(p)$ is in the very small range $[r^+, r^-]$ well contained within the much wider range $[0, 1]$. In yet other cases no number, or even a small range, can be realistically determined. However, it might still remain open that there are comparative relations such as: $\mathrm{Bel}_{A,t}(p) < \mathrm{Bel}_{A,t}(q)$; $\mathrm{Bel}_{A,t}(p) > \mathrm{Bel}_{A,t}^*(p)$; $\mathrm{Bel}_{A,t}(p) = \mathrm{Bel}_{B,t}(p)$; and so on.

To some extent the phrase "personal degree of belief" is a philosophers' term of art, although attempts can be made to link it to ordinary usage. To escape ordinary connotations of the term "belief" we could equally as well use the more technical "degrees of credence". We should not always think that the value r that is assigned to $\text{Bel}_{A,t}(p)$ results from an actual measurement made of A's degree of belief. Rather, there is some point in finding a way to *represent* degrees of belief using numbers. To adapt an example due to Hacking (2001: 156), who draws the distinction between *measuring* and *representing*, a person may place their degrees of belief in three propositions in the following decreasing order: a fair coin tossed today yields seven heads in a row for the first seven tosses; it snows somewhere in New Zealand today; a fair coin tossed today will yield eight heads in a row for the first eight tosses. That is, $1/128 < A$'s degree of belief that it snows somewhere in New Zealand today $< 1/256$. Here A's degree of belief that it snows somewhere in New Zealand today can be *represented* by a number in the range 0.0039 and 0.0078, say, 0.006; but there is no claim here that the degree of belief has been measured or could be measured as precisely as the numbers indicate.

Since knowledge involves belief we could give this very special sub-class of beliefs the highest number on the scale, 1. We can also do this for beliefs that meet strong Cartesian standards of certainty, that is, are beyond any possible doubt. Some suggest that we ought to admit the notion of *full belief*, which takes the value 1 as well.[11] Despite the conceptual distinctions that can be drawn between *certain belief, full belief* and *knowledge*, all are accorded 1, at the top of the scale. *Partial* belief that p is less than *full* belief that p and, along with partial disbelief that p, can be represented by the open interval (0, 1), with full disbelief that p at 0 (which is the same as full belief that $\neg p$).

What is measured when we talk of "degrees of personal belief"? Degrees of belief are akin to unobservable entities, or theoretical postulates, for which an "operational definition" is required. In a 1926 paper Ramsey first suggested that we take the idea of degrees of belief seriously, and suggested several different ways in which we might operationally measure them (Ramsey 1990: ch. 4, §3). We can set aside Ramsey's jocular but graphic suggestion that degrees of belief might be measured by a device such as a psycho-galvanometer (*ibid.*: 57). His next suggestion is one in which we attempt to measure something that is perceptible to a person when they believe: "beliefs differ in the intensity of a feeling by which they are accompanied, which might be called a belief-feeling or a feeling of conviction, and that by degree of belief we mean the intensity of this feeling" (*ibid.*: 65). This importantly recognizes that for the same person and the same belief the intensity might change over time, and that different beliefs can have quite different intensities accompanying them; also for any two people who believe the same proposition, their intensities of belief can differ.

To some extent this does capture an important psychological aspect of belief; but it faces two serious difficulties if we use it as a way of measuring degree of belief. The first is that it is quite unclear how we might measure intensities and assign numbers to them in order to set up a scale of degrees of belief (we lack intensity psycho-galvanometers!). The second, as Ramsey points out, is that, from a phenomenological point of view, there are beliefs that have nothing in the way of a feeling of intensity associated with them, yet these are beliefs we simply take for granted and would not readily abandon; so there can be high strength of belief without an inner accompanying "intensity of feeling". You can be certain that you are reading a page of print but have little in the way of inner intensities accompanying the certainty.

Rather than focus on measuring inner states, Ramsey looked for something more external, objective and measurable, for example our actions, to get a measure of degrees of belief. He used the idea that many of our actions are prompted by our beliefs (along with our desires). To illustrate, if one is standing at a bus stop, to what degree does one believe that a bus will arrive in the next five minutes? One may or may not have an inner belief intensity about this. But in Ramsey's apt phrase, a belief is "a map of neighbouring space by which we steer" our lives (*ibid.*: 146). Our action of waiting at the bus stop is steered by the belief that a bus will come within five minutes. If one really believed that a bus will not arrive in five minutes, then one would not wait, thereby steering one's life differently.

Ramsey focuses on a particular kind of action we can perform: our betting behaviour. We can ask of person A waiting for a bus: what odds would A bet on the truth of the proposition that a bus will arrive in the next five minutes? Although the odds need not be all that precise, in general we can say: where the odds a person gives for betting on the truth of a proposition are m to n (or $m:n$), then the degree of belief we ought to assign is $m/(m + n)$. (Since there might be a range of odds A is willing to bet, Ramsey took the lowest odds as the measure of degree of belief.) Thus if A is willing to bet and gives odds of 4 to 1 that a bus will arrive within the next five minutes (p), then $Bel_{A,t}(p) = 4/5$. But if A gives odds of 1 to 3, then $Bel_{A,t}(p) = 1/4$. (Note that if A is willing to give odds of $m:n$ on p being the case, then this is the same as being willing to give odds of $n:m$ against p being the case.)

Taking the odds a person is willing to bet on as an indication of their degree of belief, especially when understood operationally and behaviouristically, is not without its problems, as Ramsey noted. Person A may not be willing to bet at all, yet they still hold some degree of belief in p. They may be coerced into betting and so not reveal their true degree of belief. They may be unsure what to bet and offer a somewhat vague range of odds. More problematically, what they bet may have little relation to their actual degree of belief. They might bet only if they think they will win. Or they might bet below their degree of belief because of the risk of losing. There is also a problem of diminishing marginal utility; the poor might resist betting if the money at stake is more than, say, £10, while the wealthy might think little of bets in hundreds of pounds. To overcome some of these problems one could investigate betting behaviour in idealized experimental situations in which people bet using, say, matchsticks, the goal of the betting game being to see who ends up with the most matchsticks at no monetary cost to anyone.

Despite some of these problems, Ramsey says of the betting analysis of degrees of belief: "This method I regard as fundamentally sound; but it suffers from being insufficiently general and from being necessarily inexact" (*ibid.*: 68). So to develop a more general and exact account of how degrees of belief might be measured, Ramsey turned to a theory of utility and developed a theory of both utility and probability in conjunction with one another. Many have followed Ramsey in this respect. Here we shall stay with the method Ramsey regarded as "fundamentally sound" and measure degrees of belief in terms of the odds one is willing to bet. Ramsey's two approaches remain at the heart of many aspects of theories of degrees of belief.[12]

The idea of personal degrees of belief leaves us only at the empirical level of psychology; what is of greater *normative* interest concerns *coherent* degrees of belief. Ramsey spoke of the interpretation of degrees of belief in terms of the probability calculus "as a calculus of consistent partial belief" (*ibid.*: 83). Talk of *consistency* is akin to talk of a theory of *coherent* degrees of belief; both carry with them certain norms or epistemic values in contrast with degree of belief in the empirical and psychological sense.

To illustrate, consider a case that results in an unsatisfactory outcome that we could label "incoherent". Person A (at a bus stop) believes that the bus will come in five minutes (p). Suppose we discover that the odds A is willing to bet on the truth of p are 4:1; then $\mathrm{Bel}_{A,t}(p) = 4/5$. Suppose we investigate A's beliefs further and we discover that the odds on which A is willing to bet on the falsity of this belief, namely, that the bus will *not* come in five minutes, are the same odds of 4:1; so $\mathrm{Bel}_{A,t}(\neg p) = 4/5$. Intuitively some might find this peculiar. Surely, one might say, if $\mathrm{Bel}_{A,t}(p) = 4/5$, then $\mathrm{Bel}_{A,t}(\neg p)$ *ought* to be $1 - 4/5 = 1/5$, and not $4/5$. That is, $\mathrm{Bel}_{A,t}(p) + \mathrm{Bel}_{A,t}(\neg p)$ *ought* to total 1. Alternatively, if $\mathrm{Bel}_{A,t}(\neg p) = 4/5$ then $\mathrm{Bel}_{A,t}(p)$ *ought* to be $1 - 4/5 = 1/5$, and not $4/5$. Is A is free to distribute degrees of belief as A wishes? Yes, and no. Even though A is free to assign any values to particular degrees of belief, their overall distribution must be coherent. What does this mean?

Pursuing the above example further reveals an incoherence in A's arrangement of bets, and a penalty that stems from it. Suppose, as above, that the odds on which A is willing to bet on p, and bet on $\neg p$ are both $4:1$. (This accords with the fact that A's degree of belief that p and A's degree of belief that $\neg p$ are both $4/5$.) Now get A to place two bets at the same time, one on p and the other on $\neg p$. (For simplicity, using single units of money, since A's odds are $4:1$, A makes two bets of £4). Suppose that p is true: the bus does arrive within five minutes.

Then on the first bet A gets £4 back plus a further £1, that is, wins £1; but on the second bet A loses £4. So the overall loss is £3. Now suppose that $\neg p$ is true: the bus does not arrive within five minutes. Then on the first bet A loses £4; but on the second bet A gets back £4 plus a further £1, that is, wins £1. Once more A has an overall loss on the two bets of £3. The conclusion is that however the world turns out in respect of the arrival or non-arrival of buses, given A's two bets A must lose and cannot win. Losing regardless of how the world turns out is frustrating for any bettor, and a sign of incoherence in A's overall bets. In addition, there is a straightforward logical inconsistency in supposing that p can be both more and less probably than $\neg p$. How ought A to arrange the bets, and thus A's degrees of belief, so that A is not always a loser and can be in a position to win?

In the above, the word "ought" is important. It suggests a *normative* constraint, namely, that a person's degrees of belief in p, and in $\neg p$, always *ought* to add up to 1, whatever the value assigned to the person's degree of belief that p (or the value assigned to their degree of belief that $\neg p$). If A is not to be a loser, we require:

$$\text{Bel}_{A,t}(p) + \text{Bel}_{A,t}(\neg p) = 1$$

The constraint is that A's degree of belief ought to be in accordance with the rules of the probability calculus, in this case Theorem 2.

It is a well-known empirical discovery within the psychology of belief that people do not commonly reason in accordance with the rules of the probability calculus. Consider the result that flows from the logical consequence principle: a conjunction cannot be more probable than one of its conjuncts. Do people distribute their degrees of belief in accordance with this principle? Daniel Kahneman *et al.* (1982: esp. ch. 6) show empirically that this theorem is violated by many more than conform to it. From these and many other empirical studies, there are good reasons to conclude that, with varying degrees of frequency, people do not reason in accordance with the principles of probability. Our degrees of subjective belief are commonly not constrained by any norms of reasoning or method. But *ought A*, and the rest of us, be constrained by the principles of probability and logic? If so the principles (like the other principles of method of Chapter 3), are norms that we *ought* to follow. The same applies to our reasoning in science as well; so the rules of the probability calculus along with the rules of deductive inference can be included in a theory of the Level 2 norms of scientific method that govern our scientific beliefs at Level 1.

Let us say that a person's set of beliefs is *coherent* if and only if their assignment of values to degrees of belief is in accordance with the probability calculus. Then it is possible to regard all personal degrees of belief as probabilities. That is, $\text{Bel}_{A,t}(H)$ simply becomes *the probability that P*, for person A at that time, which we could write as "$P_{A,t}(H)$". If the context is clear, we drop the subscripts and write "$P(H)$" and mean by this *the probability of hypothesis* H *for* A *at* t, that is, *the coherent degree of belief that some person* A *has in* H *at a given time* t. The justification of the claim that coherent degrees of belief are probabilities is an important metamethodological result set out in the next section. The justification was provided by both Ramsey and de Finetti; so this important result is sometimes called the *Ramsey–de Finetti theorem* or the *Dutch book argument*.

8.6 Metamethodological justification and the Dutch book theorem

In §3.3 we briefly canvassed Descartes's idea that there are "rules for the direction of the mind" for any properly conducted enquiry, including science. In §3.4 Newton's "Rules of Reasoning in Philosophy" were intended to play a similar role in directing us in the proper conduct of science. Both sets of rules are incomplete, and to some extent they rival one another. But both Descartes and Newton thought their own rules ought to be part of any respectable theory of scientific method. Along with many others since Descartes and Newton, Bayesians have also thought that there were rules for "directing the mind"; but their rules are of a quite different character from Cartesian or Newtonian rules, and they are to be justified in a quite different way. In the case of Descartes, his strictures concerning certainty led him to admit only full belief, suspension of belief or total disbelief; but these turn out to be too coarse-grained. The view we are investigating here is broader and only requires the constraint that our degrees of belief be distributed in accordance with the probability calculus. (From this stance the Cartesian constraints are a special case.) To what extent do the rules of the probability calculus provide a theory for "directing the mind" and if so, how is this to be justified? This section provides an outline of some reasons for thinking that probability justifiably provides "rules for directing the mind".

In the previous section we showed that if A's degrees of belief about bus arrivals were not in accordance with a theorem of the probability calculus then A could not win and must lose in the bets placed on the beliefs. Something unfortunate happens; A's betting activities are frustrated because A is always a loser. Ramsey generalized this result to the probability calculus as a whole: "Any definite set of degrees of belief which broke them [the laws of probability] would be inconsistent .... He could have a book made against him by a cunning better and would then stand to lose in any event" (Ramsey 1990: 78). In place of Ramsey's talk of a "book" being made against A, it is now more common to talk of a "Dutch book" being made against A. A better term than "Dutch book" might be a "sure-to-lose" set of bets.[13] Also Ramsey's talk of inconsistency is now more commonly replaced by talk of incoherence. Since inconsistency is a well-defined notion within deductive logic, in probability the parallel notion should be given a different name, hence "incoherence".

There are two aspects to claims about (in)coherence that make up the Dutch book theorem. The first is a sufficient condition for a Dutch book to be made: if any of the axioms of the probability calculus (and thus any of the theorems and principles that flow from them) are violated in distributing values for a person's degrees of belief, then a Dutch book can be made against that person. The second is a sufficient condition for Dutch book avoidance: if all the axioms of the probability calculus (and thus any of the theorems and principles that flow from them) are satisfied in distributing values for a person's degrees of belief, then a Dutch book cannot be made against that person. (That is, one can live without fear of a Dutch book if one stays on the straight and narrow path of keeping one's degrees of belief in accordance with the probability calculus.) Establishing these claims is an important part of the metamethodological justification for distributing one's degrees of subjective belief in accordance with the probability calculus and for adopting its axioms and theorems as principles of scientific method.

There are several different, but not unrelated, arguments that suggest alternative ways of arriving at the same conclusion about the coherence requirement. Different metamethodologists have found some of these arguments more compelling than others; in particular some agree with the coherence requirement but reject the Dutch book considerations mentioned below as a way of arguing for coherence and offer other arguments instead. But that these different approaches do converge on the same result does tell us something significant about keeping one's degrees of belief coherent. What follows are some of the main considerations commonly given on behalf of the Dutch book theorem.[14]

These considerations turn on a "bettor" who offers odds of $m:n$ on the truth of some hypothesis H, and a "bookmaker" ("bookie") with whom the bets are placed. Suppose the bettor puts up m units of some currency (or other unit of utility) and a bookie puts up n units of the same currency so that there is a total stake of $m + n$ units. If H is true the bettor collects the total stake, getting the original m units back and profiting n units, while if H is false the bookie collects the total stake and the bettor loses the original m units. Odds can vary from 0 to infinity, with 1 as a point of indifference when the odds are $1:1$. However, it is more useful to introduce the idea of a betting quotient q associated with the odds $m:n$, where $q = m/(m + n)$ (i.e. the amount m the bettor puts up over the total stake $m + n$). This yields a scale over the interval $[0, 1]$, with equal odds being $1/2$. (Since $q = m/(m + n)$, it readily follows that the odds $m:n$ are $q:(1 - q)$.) As can be readily seen, betting quotients are just like probabilities.

The kind of betting situation commonly envisaged in the arguments given here is somewhat idealized and is not the normal situation under which people standardly bet. To begin with, here a bettor is asked to place bets on each of their beliefs, such as p, $\neg p$, q, $p \vee q$ and so on. (Here we assume that betting odds can be made on all these beliefs.) Once that has been done a bookie who takes these bets does all the rest. The bookie determines the total stake (which should not be so large as to frighten off the bettor, as in the example of a total stake of £1 below). The bookie also determines whether the bettor bets for or against any given belief. Not knowing how the bets are to be placed helps ensure that the bettor's bets do reflect his degrees of belief. If the bettor knows how they are to be placed then he might bet at a rate higher than his degree of belief if he thought he was going to win (to maximize gain), or at a lower rate if he thought he would not win (to minimize loss). If the bettor does not know which way his bets are in fact to be placed, then the odds he is willing to bet will more likely reflect his degrees of belief. This now leaves room for a clever bookie, if the bets on the various beliefs are made in a certain way, to ensure that the bookie wins and the bettor loses (see the bus example of the previous section). Thus a Dutch book is said to be made against the bettor by the bookie. The task of the bettor is to so arrange his bets that no Dutch book can be made against him. How is this to be done?

Betting arrangements can be illustrated in the "pay-off matrix" below. Suppose the bookie sets £S as the total stake in a bet on the truth of H. Then a bettor with betting quotient q will bet £Sq on H being true; and the bookie betting against the bettor will bet £$S(1 - q)$. Then the "pay-off matrix" below represents the various pay-offs for H being true and H being false (with positive pay-offs as gains, negative pay-offs as losses):

	Pay-off for bet on H	Pay-off for bet against H
H	+£$S(1 - q)$ $[1 - q]$	−£$S(1 - q)$ $[-(1 - q)]$
$\neg H$	−£Sq $[-q]$	+£Sq $[q]$

Thus if your betting quotient is q and the bookie sets the stake at £S then when the bet is placed on H being true, if H is true you get your £Sq back and gain +£$S(1 - q)$ while the bookie loses that amount; but if H is false you lose £Sq (i.e. gain −£Sq) while the bookie wins that amount. Similar considerations hold if you are to bet against H being true (see right-hand column). In what follows we shall, for simplicity, take £S to be £1, which we can reasonably suppose to be small in relation to the wealth of the bettor. This enables us to drop the currency sign; the simplified pay-offs are then as in the square brackets.

Already the following claim has been introduced: (a) personal degrees of belief can be represented as personal betting quotients. The next task is to show the following: (b) personal betting quotients *ought to be* coherent; and (c) the personal betting quotients are coherent if and only if they are in accordance with the probability calculus.

The following sets out some considerations on behalf of (b) and (c) with a focus on one aspect of the Dutch book theorem, namely, if any of the three axioms are violated then a Dutch book can be made in which the bettor is always a loser. To show this consider the three axioms of the probability calculus.

Axiom 1 says: $0 \leq P(H) \leq 1$. The desired result can be quickly seen as the betting quotient is defined to lie between $[0, 1]$. But it is useful to show what happens when the betting quotient is above 1 or below 0. First, suppose $q > 1$. Since the aim of betting is to win, then one can only lose if one advances more than a pound to win just a pound. When $q > 1$, $(1 - q)$ is negative while $-(1 - q)$ and q are positive. Given the pay-off matrix above, a clever bookie can make a Dutch book against a bettor by betting *against* H while the bettor is required (by stipulation of the bookie) to bet *for* H. Under the column "Pay-off for bet against H", both pay-offs would be positive.

Next, suppose $q < 0$. Then $-q > 0$ and $(1 - q) > 1$; so both are positive. It then follows from the above pay-off matrix under the column "Pay-off for bet for H", both pay-offs $1 - q$ and $-q$ are positive (regardless of whether H or ¬H obtains). Suppose a clever bookie requires the bettor to bet against H. Then the bookie can guarantee a gain by betting for H while the bettor's pay-offs are negative since he bets against H.

Concerning Axiom 2, a slightly more general version says that $P(\text{Certainty}) = 1$. We have already seen above that q must be in the interval $[0, 1]$; so to violate the axiom suppose that $q < 1$. In the pay-off matrix above, the bottom line will not arise since H is certain; so consider the top line only in which H is true. This results in a pay-off for H of $(1 - q)$ and a pay-off against H of $-(1 - q)$. On the assumption that $q < 1$, $(1 - q)$ is positive. If a bookie bets on H then a Dutch book can be made against the bettor. Since H is true and a certainty, the bettor gives away to the bookie an amount of $(1 - q)$. The only way a bettor can prevent this is to make the betting quotient $q = 1$ (i.e. odds are even).

Consider now Axiom 3: $P(H_1 \vee H_2) = P(H_1) + P(H_2)$ where H_1 and H_2 are mutually inconsistent. Suppose the betting quotient is p for H_1, q for H_2 and r for $(H_1 \vee H_2)$. There are several standard accounts of what happens when Axiom 3 is violated and $r \neq p + q$ (here we follow Hacking [2001: 166–7]). Suppose a bookie gets a bettor to make the following bets (where, as above, the stake is £1):

- Bet 1: Bet p on H_1 to win $(1 - p)$ if H_1 is true; lose p if H_1 is false.
- Bet 2: Bet q on H_2 to win $(1 - q)$ if H_2 is true; lose q if H_2 is false.
- Bet 3: Bet $(1 - r)$ against $(H_1 \vee H_2)$ to win r if $(H_1 \vee H_2)$ is false; but if one of $\{H_1, H_2\}$ is true then lose $(1 - r)$.

Now a pay-off matrix can be drawn up. Since the pair $\{H_1, H_2\}$ are mutually inconsistent there are only three rows of possibilities to consider; there is no top line in which both H_1 and H_2 are true.

H_1	H_2	Pay-off on Bet 1	Pay-off on Bet 2	Pay-off on Bet 3	Pay-off
T	F	$1 - p$	$-q$	$-(1 - r)$	$r - p - q$
F	T	$-p$	$1 - q$	$-(1 - r)$	$r - p - q$
F	F	$-p$	$-q$	r	$r - p - q$

If $r < p + q$, then $r - (p + q)$ is negative. So the bettor loses to the bookie the amount $r - (p + q)$, whatever happens. For the case in which $r > p + q$, the bettor bets in the opposite way, that is, $1 - p$ against H_1, $1 - q$ against H_2 and r on $(H_1 \vee H_2)$. Again the bettor's loss will be the amount $r - (p + q)$, whatever happens.

The above considerations show that if the bettor does not make his betting quotients conform to Axiom 3, then he will lose out to a clever bookie who is in the position to arrange bets once the betting quotients are known. The above considerations can also be used to show that if the betting quotients do conform to Axiom 3, then there is no way in which a Dutch book can be made against the bettor. This gives assurance in the use of Axiom 3.

Similar results can be obtained for the definition of conditional probability in terms of unconditional probabilities and the three axioms expressed for conditional probabilities.[15] The overall result of the important Ramsey–de Finetti Dutch book theorem is: one's degrees of belief are coherent if and only if they are distributed according to the probability calculus.

The kind of metamethodological justification for employing the probability calculus that arises from the Dutch book theorem crucially depends on the following two matters.

1. There is some way of linking degrees of belief to choices and/or actions by making bets (or following Ramsey's more general considerations based in utilities). In §8.5 some problems were raised about considering betting behaviour that need more discussion than can be given here. But to a large extent these can be set aside if we view the kind of account given as an ideal model of betting, which turns on a counterfactual about what would happen if the ideal conditions of the model were to obtain.[16]

2. There is a pay-off matrix in which one determines whether one is a winner or loser. In one sense this is an uncontroversial piece of mathematical reasoning about what happens when the probability calculus is violated. But that reasoning takes place within the context of the idealized model of betting behaviour.

Even though some agree that one's degrees of belief ought to be coherent, they do not accept the idealizations about betting that are presupposed (some of which were mentioned in §8.5).[17] Hilary Putnam also suggests that the model in which a cunning bookie arranges bets once he knows the bettor's betting quotients may not be a good model for how we are to place our bets against nature instead of a cunning bookie. He writes that the arguments for coherence based on this:

must be taken *cum grano salis*. ...For we are not playing against a malevolent opponent but against nature, and nature does not always exploit such "incoherencies"; and even if we *were* playing against a malevolent opponent, there are many ways to lose one's bets besides being "incoherent".   (Putnam 1975: 303)

Further related issues are also raised by Rosenkrantz.[18] In particular he asks whether, from the Dutch book theorem just established, one can draw the conclusion of what he calls the "Dutch Book Argument" about *rationality* (Rosenkrantz 1981: §2.1). This says that if one is not coherent in the distribution of one's beliefs in accordance with the probability calculus, then one is *irrational* (i.e. *rationality* implies *coherence*). On the face of it, unreasonableness about one's beliefs ought to lead to changes in one's beliefs; but irrationality is a much stronger charge. Even though the notion of rationality is broad and somewhat fuzzy, many do agree that the notion of coherence as defined here is an important part of rationality (see Salmon 2005: ch. 8). However, the question Rosenkrantz asks is whether the idealized assumptions of betting behaviour that go along with the Dutch book argument are adequate to the task of establishing such a strong conclusion about rationality or irrationality. In his view one can violate some of the idealized assumptions about betting and not thereby be irrational. So he is not satisfied that they are strong enough and, instead, argues for a different approach to the same conclusion. Rosenkrantz (1981: §2.2) considers ways in which being incoherent can be irrational in that it undermines other cognitive goals one also wishes to realize; for example, incoherence, in the defined sense of violating the rules of the probability calculus, undermines the assessment of the accuracy of the hypotheses under consideration. This interesting result is akin to the conclusion of the Dutch book argument, but it is not based on an inference from the Dutch book theorem (thereby avoiding some of its idealizations about betting that are open to question).

Let us set aside matters to do with the ideal model implicit in (1) and (2). Then there is an important metamethodological matter that arises from the kind of argument employed in the Dutch book theorem. Its arguments are all deductive, an important feature noted by Talbott (2006: §3). This is significant for the Level 3 metamethodological project envisaged here in which an attempt is made to justify adopting probabilistic rules as Level 2 principles of method in science. The Dutch book theorem makes no use of inductive reasoning and depends only on deductive reasoning. Of course some of its premises are based on considerations that turn on issues to do with (1). But here we are concerned with the nature of the argument and not its premises. In so far as the justificatory argument is concerned, the various forms of the arguments used do not beg questions of justification that go beyond what is needed for the justification of deductive logic. Importantly, a justification of inductive modes of reasoning is *not* required since no inductive modes of reasoning are used. As Talbott writes: "even if Bayesian epistemology only extended the laws of deductive logic to degrees of belief, that alone would represent an extremely important advance in epistemology" (*ibid.*). If we accept the Dutch book theorem, then we do have a Level 3 metamethodological justification for the adoption of the rules of the probability calculus as Level 2 principles of scientific method. This seems to be a considerable boon from the point of view of metamethodological considerations; only deductive reasoning is needed.

8.7 Bayesian conditionalization and pure subjective Bayesianism

How does one rationally change one's degrees of belief in a hypothesis when one acquires some new information or evidence? There are several ways of doing this. Consider how one might employ Bayes's theorem in the simple form of version 1:

$$P(H, E) = P(E, H)P(H)/P(E), \ \text{providing } P(E) \neq 0$$

Suppose one starts with a personal initial probability for one's scientific hypothesis $P_1(H)$, or alternatively one's prior probability in the absence of any evidence (but perhaps not in the absence of other background beliefs, which we set aside as not strictly relevant here). Where this comes from is not of immediate concern; but we require that $P_1(H) \neq 0$, otherwise we would not get started in revising our degrees of belief.

Now suppose a new piece of evidence E_1 is obtained. Our personal probability, $P_1(H, E_1)$, in the light of new evidence is:

$$P_1(H, E_1) = P_1(E_1, H) \ P_1(H)/P_1(E_1)$$

Since our personal probabilities are coherent in the sense of the previous section, then they will be in conformity with the rules of the probability calculus, and in particular Bayes's theorem. In taking E_1 into account we will have made adjustments to our probabilities all round.

What is our *second* (as opposed to the first $P_1(H)$) personal degree of belief in H, $P_2(H)$, once we have taken E_1 into account? We could adopt a rule as follows: $P_2(H) = P_1(H, E_1)$; that is, the new probability for H is the initial probability, but conditionalized on evidence E.

Now suppose new evidence E_2 comes along. Then there are two ways of proceeding. First we could use Bayes's theorem all over again, just as above and arrive at $P_1(H, E_1 \ \& \ E_2)$. Alternatively, if we adopt the suggested rule, we can begin from a new initial stating-point $P_2(H)$, take the new evidence, E_2, on board and conditionalize on it as in $P_2(H, E_2)$. Then our new personal degree of belief in H, $P_3(H)$, is given by a reapplication of the same rule, that is, $P_3(H)$ = $P_2(H, E_2)$.

Subjective Bayesians think of learning as a process in which we revise our beliefs not only when we acquire new evidence, but also when we revise our degrees of belief from what they initially were before learning E to a posterior or final degree of belief that is responsive to what we have learned. To this end they adopt the following rule:

Simple rule of conditionalization: $P_{final}(H) = P_{initial}(H, E)$

It is assumed that a learner, who may initially be uncertain of E (in that $0 < P_{initial}(E) < 1$), comes to learn E, and this has the effect of raising the learner's subjective probability to certainty so that $P_{initial}(E) = 1$. (All other hypotheses inconsistent with E then have probability zero.) No inference is involved at this stage; but in the second stage inference is involved as the learner conditionalizes on E according to the above rule.

A corollary of the rule, along with Bayes's theorem, has already been used in the above:

$$P_{final}(H) = P_{initial}(H, E) = P_{initial}(E, H)P_{initial}(H)/P_{initial}(E)$$

This is an expression for the final probability of H in terms of the initial likelihood of H in the light of E and the initial prior probabilities of H and E.

The factor on the right-hand side, $P_{initial}(E, H)/P_{initial}(E)$, is the *Bayesian multiplier*. Thus we may rewrite the rule as follows:

$$P_{final}(H) = P_{initial}(H) \times (\text{Bayesian multiplier})$$

The Bayesian multiplier is in fact the ratio of the degree of confirmation evidence E bestows on H to that H had before E turned up (see §8.3). As the confirmation goes up or down, so the Bayes multiplier goes up or down. And in the light of the rule, the ratio $P_{final}(H)/P_{initial}(H)$ goes up or down. So the rule can tell us what degree of confirmation $P_{final}(H)$ has once the stream of different bits of evidence has come in.

The above simple rule of conditionalization assumes that the evidence is certain; but this is often an unreal assumption. Scientists can learn about other matters that lead them to revise their degrees of belief in evidence. They learn that, say, the instruments used could have malfunctioned, or at the time they acquire the evidence they are aware that it is not fully certain, or the evidence came to them by way of reports yet unconfirmed or by rumour and so on. The classic example of the discussion of such cases is Jeffrey's account of the observation of a cloth by candlelight in which the three hypotheses under consideration are: "it is green", "it is blue" and "it is violet". These have initial probabilities that undergo revision when an observer gets the impression that the cloth is green but concedes that it could still be blue or more improbably violet.

Jeffrey proposes a new rule of conditionalization (or of probability kinematics [as in Jeffrey 1983: ch. 11]); this is given in the simple form for one hypothesis H (where subscripts "i" and "f" indicate initial and final probabilities, and where $0 < P_i(E) < 1$):

Rule of Jeffrey conditionalization: $P_f(H) = P_i(H, E)P_f(E) + P_i(H, \neg E)P_f(\neg E)$

This rule has the simple rule of conditionalization as a special case when the evidence is certain so that $P_i(E) = 1$ and $P_f(\neg E) = 0$.

Are there grounds for thinking that following either the simple rule of conditionalization or the Jeffrey rule is the coherent thing to do and that a Dutch book cannot be made against a person who adjusts their degrees of belief in accordance with either rule? We shall not discuss the matter here, although several argue that the answer is yes.[19]

We are now in a position to state some of the main tenets of what we shall call pure (subjective) Bayesianism. It starts from the point of view of an individual enquirer or scientist and their subjective or personal degrees of belief.

- *Tenet 1.* For all persons x and all propositions p about any subject matter into which they can enquire, x has a degree of belief that p, and this can be specified by a betting quotient.
  This tenet is not something that follows from the probability calculus. It is a philosophical doctrine that requires that all propositions (especially those of Level 1 sciences) are such that all persons have some degree of belief in them. As such it is a considerable idealization of actual persons and what they believe.

- *Tenet 2.* The personal degrees of belief are coherent iff they are in accordance with the rules of the probability calculus.
  This introduces a normative element on top of the purely descriptive character of Tenet 1. The Dutch book theorem plays a prominent role in establishing the normative character of Bayesianism. This highlights two further aspects of the subjectivity of pure subjective Bayesianism: (a) a person is permitted to have any degree of belief in any proposition they like; (b) the only constraint on (a) is that, given any set of propositions a person believes, the numerical values of the probabilities, which are degrees of belief, must be distributed in accordance with the probability calculus.

- *Tenet 3*. A person, on the receipt of new evidence, must update their degrees of belief according to the rule of conditionalization (in either of the two forms mentioned).
  Here once more Dutch book considerations play an important role in establishing the normative character of this tenet.

- *Tenet 4*. The above three tenets are all that are required for a person to be a "rational", or at least coherent, enquirer.
  This tenet says that all and only the first three tenets characterize pure subjective Bayesianism. Any further "additives" makes that kind of Bayesianism less than pure.

In Chapter 9 we explore some of the consequences of this position and some difficulties it might face. But one question we can address now is the following. Although Bayesians talk much of degrees of belief, do they ever believe anything in the sense of detaching a hypothesis *H* from its network of probabilistic relations and believe *H*, or at least accept *H*? In the discussion of detachment in §5.2, it would appear that many scientists do detach their hypotheses, and many methodologists propose rules of detachment about when it is appropriate to do this. Some Bayesians might follow suit and propose that hypotheses with sufficiently high degrees of confirmation can be detached. Yet other Bayesians see no role for detachment at all. Rather, a person has merely to keep track of how well their hypotheses are doing in the light of evidence using the rules of the probability calculus and the rule of conditionalization. If a person wishes to make a decision about their hypotheses then decision theory provides all the machinery to do this using whatever current probability each has and whatever preferences a person has. There is no need for detachment.[20]

9. Bayesianism: applications and problems

Chapter 8 set out some of the main principles of probability including Bayes's theorem and investigated the subjective interpretation of probability in terms of coherent degree of personal belief, ending with three core tenets of "pure (subjective) Bayesianism". It also considered the ways in which Bayesianism captures a number of important aspects of scientific method, including an account of confirmation and disconfirmation and the good aspects of the H-D method that survive within a probabilistic context, also providing it with a theory of confirmation. In this chapter we consider further successful applications of the probabilistic approach to methodology along with some problems for Bayesianism.

Section 9.1 considers the problem of priors that has often been thought to bedevil subjective Bayesianism. Is it sufficient for a theory of scientific method for one to simply adjust beliefs in accordance with the rules of the probability calculus? Section 9.2 considers whether subjective Bayesianism is incomplete and whether some additional principles are needed, even for those who adopt the subjectivist stance. Section 9.3 examines the account that Bayesianism can give of new evidence, and a problem it encounters with old evidence and how it might be overcome. Section 9.4 considers the successful account that Bayesianism can give of Kuhnian values. In §5.4 we outlined some accounts of inference to the best explanation (IBE). Since it is alleged that IBE is a rival to Bayesianism, §9.5 considers how well Bayesianism and IBE can accommodate one another. Chapters 5 and 6 explored the role of induction in science and the longstanding problem of its justification. In §9.6 we consider what account and justification Bayesianism can provide of simple enumerative induction. Already the Quine–Duhem thesis has loomed large as a problem for H-D confirmation. In §9.7 we see the extent to which Bayesianism can provide a solution to the problem of confirming hypotheses in isolation. Although much else can be said about Bayesianism, the above should indicate the power that it has to illuminate problems in methodology and some of the difficulties it faces.

9.1 The problem of priors

The simple version of Bayes's theorem gives the probability of a hypothesis on evidence: $P(H, E) = P(E, H)P(H)/P(E)$. Given the tenets of pure Bayesianism at the end of Chapter 8, the theorem tells us how to distribute the values of one's probabilities in such a way that they are coherent. As such the theorem can be viewed as a consistency condition for degrees of belief. Pure Bayesians often employ the following comparison. Deductive logic provides consistency conditions for the premises and conclusion of an argument (along with deducibility relations). But it does not provide the premises of arguments; they come from elsewhere. Similarly, the probability calculus provides consistency (i.e. coherence) conditions for the assignment of values to degrees of belief; it does not tell us what assignments of values to degrees of belief we ought to make, although once we have made them they ought to be coherent. Is this to give in to a rampant subjectivism in which "anything goes"? Not necessarily. This is a charge often brought against pure Bayesianism, especially when it comes to the topic of what values to assign to prior probabilities; but it cannot apply generally. Just as deductive arguments apply to any premises and conclusion, so one can choose any values for degrees of belief in probabilistic contexts. But in both there remains something quite objective, in the one case consistency of premises and conclusion, and in the other coherence.

Granted this, how free are Bayesian agents to assign degrees of belief in the range [0, 1]? Totally free, given the tenets of pure Bayesianism (but coherence must be observed). However, some constraints can enter in the case of the likelihood $P(E, H)$. When $H \vdash E$ then, on pain of incoherence, $P(E, H)$ must be 1; and when $H \vdash \neg E$ then $P(E, H) = 0$. Again there may be empirically determined frequencies or chances (see the principal principle in the next section) that constrain the value of $P(E, H)$ at values of 1 or less. There are similar proposals for ensuring that degrees of belief are, as is said, *well calibrated*,[1] that is, there is a match between degrees of belief and corresponding relative frequencies.

Even a supposed subjectivist such as Ramsey took a line akin to the above about when a person can be said to be reasonable (see §5 of his paper "Truth and Probability" [Ramsey 1990: 86–94]). In the ideal case we would like to have the truth and be certain of it. If this is not realisable, what is? Ramsey argues that we need correct habits of belief formation, as illustrated in the following case. Suppose we have "the habit of proceeding from the opinion that a toadstool is yellow to the opinion that it is unwholesome". Then what degree of belief ought one to have in the proposition that yellow toadstools are unwholesome? Ramsey answers: "it will in general be best for his degree of belief that a yellow toadstool is unwholesome to be equal to the proportion of yellow toadstools that are in fact unwholesome" (1990: 91). As his following remarks make clear, degrees of belief are not only to be coherent but are also to be constrained by objective frequencies. There is also an appeal to a reliabilist account of the warrant for induction in determining those frequencies.

So in some cases there are fixed points to take into account while also assuring that assignments of degrees of belief are coherent. Nor is the factor $P(E)$ open to free choice. Likelihoods can also partially constrain $P(E)$, since, by the total probability principle, $P(E) = P(H)P(E, H) + P(\neg H)P(E, \neg H)$, we have that $P(E)$ contains some likelihoods that may well be fixed.

What seems not to be constrained are prior probabilities such as $P(H)$. Pure Bayesianism appears to allow assignments anywhere in the closed interval [0, 1], including the endpoints. Thus the hypothesis that God exists and was created by the authors of this book could be assigned 1 and its rival hypotheses 0, providing that the tenets of pure Bayesianism are obeyed. Less extremely, the assignments of values could be restricted to the range (0, 1); thus the prior probability of the same hypothesis might be 0.9999 or 0.0001 for different people. Something like this proposal arises when restrictions are placed on admissible H, such as that logically contingent propositions must have values other than 1 or 0 (although tautologies and contradictions can still have these values).[2] Shimony proposes an even stronger restriction of "tempered personalism", which clearly goes beyond pure Bayesianism; this we discuss in the next section. Shimony also provides a note of caution; without such a tempering condition, the prospects of any later agreement about posterior probabilities based on evidence can be quite dim. Given two scientists who start with quite different prior probabilities for the same rival hypotheses, if there is no tempering the "swamping of the priors" (to use Harold Jeffreys's apt phrase) by evidence "would consequently not be achievable with a moderate amount of data, and consensus would be severely delayed" (Shimony 1993: 207).

This leads to the first consideration about the problem of priors. Independently of any tempering condition, some pure Bayesians have a relaxed attitude. They say that through its own internal resources, there is sufficient Bayesian machinery which leads to the "washing out of priors" that are markedly divergent. It is a fact of scientific and everyday life that different people will start off with different prior probabilities for the same hypothesis; this is something that pure Bayesianism correctly captures. The problem is whether, for different people with quite different subjective prior probabilities for H, there is something objective that determines how well H is doing as evidence comes in over time, regardless of the initially very different priors for H that each person adopted before any evidence. Such results have been established concerning the possibility of objectivity by a number of theorems to do with "convergence of opinion". Put simply, suppose persons A and B have the priors, $P_A(H)$ and $P_B(H)$, and these differ widely. Then there will be convergence if the following holds: for increasing evidence E_i (for $i = 1, 2, \ldots$, and assuming Bayes's theorem and similar values for likelihoods), there is convergence of both $P_A(H, E_i)$ and $P_B(H, E_i)$ on one another such that the difference between them becomes vanishingly small as i increases. The theorems show that in the long run the widely differing initial priors become irrelevant.

While the above is promising the problem of priors does not go away entirely; such convergence theorems apply under conditions that might be too limiting.[3] Shimony's worry is that if extra constraints are not placed on the extent to which the priors can diverge then convergence might be far too slow or there may not be any at all (as Keynes reportedly quipped in another context, "in the long run we are all dead"). The theorems say little about the rate of convergence (which might be very slow indeed); nor do they provide an estimate of it. Also the convergence theorems do not apply equally to all kinds of hypotheses; they will do well for observational hypotheses but much less well, and sometimes not apply at all, for theoretical hypotheses about unobservables. This last matter is disappointing and does lessen the utility of the convergence results in interesting highly theoretical contexts.

Given the limitations on the "convergence-of-opinion" theorems, it might have been too high a hope that, by itself, the machinery of the probability calculus in the context of pure Bayesianism would yield rapid convergence under any conditions and for any hypotheses. However, even in the absence of such a strong guarantee of convergence, it is a fact that some kinds of evidence do swing an entire community of scientists behind some theory despite their initial misgivings about it. And Bayesianism can still give an account of this in terms of, say, surprising or novel evidence. There was much doubt in the minds of many leading scientists at the turn of the twentieth century about the existence of atoms. But it was the combination of Einstein's 1905 paper on Brownian motion and Jean Perrin's subsequent experimental testing of a law Einstein had deduced relating time and displacement of Brownian particles, that converted many doubters such as the leading chemist Wilhelm Ostwald. Clearly there are different priors concerning Einstein's hypothesis H about Brownian motion, with Ostwald's being quite low. Yet one experimental outcome E (the testing of the law) was sufficiently striking to bring Ostwald (and others) into accord so that despite differing $P_{x,t}(H)$, there is much closer agreement over $P_{x,t^*}(H, E)$ (where x ranges over Einstein, Perrin and Ostwald and t and t^* are earlier and later times, respectively).

A second response to the problem of priors is to consider them as resulting from plausibility arguments. But first we must consider an issue that has bearing on this. Version 2 of Bayes's theorem is: $P(H, E \& B) = P(E, H \& B)P(H, B)/P(E, B)$, where B is any background information. The important factor here is $P(H, B)$, which corresponds to the prior probability $P(H)$ in the simpler version 1. In version 2 H is considered against background B of either evidence or other theories; it is a prior probability only in the sense of being prior to E. If we replace B by tautologies only, then version 2 becomes version 1. What this tells us is that prior probabilities are those in which there is no other information to draw on beyond tautologies that could constitute a background B against which the probability of H could be assessed. The problem that priors constitute can then be formulated as follows. If non-tautologous empirical information is drawn on to determine $P(H, B)$, then there needs to be a further application of Bayes's theorem that must make an appeal to a further prior in which that information is assessed against some new non-tautologous and empirical background information B^*. A regress then emerges of successive applications of Bayes's theorem with appeals to ever newer kinds of empirical background information. On the other hand if the regress does stop in a prior probability that requires no further information beyond tautologies, then we have no way of determining what the value of that prior is. The upshot is that the posterior probability on background information becomes the next prior probability, but there is no grounding in a prior that does not appeal to some background and that stops the regress. Either way the model of reasoning that is provided by Bayes's theorem is not sufficient to determine the value of prior probabilities.[4]

If this problem is to be overcome by the use of plausibility arguments, then they must be determined in ways that do not draw on either Bayes's theorem or further empirical information; drawing on tautologies would be fruitless since they are contentless and provide no way of yielding values for priors or of determining them differentially in order to discriminate between the priors of rival hypotheses. One person who has recommended an appeal to plausibility arguments is Salmon.[5] He distinguishes three kinds of plausibility arguments, only two of which are germane to our purposes. The first are formal arguments and concern logical relations between propositions. Thus, what prior probability ought we to assign to the hypothesis of telepathy that there can be instantaneous propagation of thought across space? Given what else we know from physics about the absence of instantaneous propagation of anything, this hypothesis is inconsistent with accepted hypotheses within physics; so it is implausible and ought to be accorded a very low prior or zero probability. But this determination does turn on the higher posterior probability that some current hypotheses in physics have obtained from evidence as opposed to the posterior probability of some earlier theories, which hold that there is no upper bound for the propagation of a signal and that propagation is instantaneous. (Descartes held this view.) Such earlier theories of physics would not be inconsistent with telepathy. In the plausibility argument against telepathy, much turns on what are the theories that now have the highest posterior probabilities; so background information is not entirely eschewed.

Salmon's other plausibility consideration he calls "material"; it turns on the content of the hypotheses themselves and gives rise to several further kinds of consideration. The first is that based on arguments from analogy. As an illustration, Darwin drew an analogy between the selection processes at work in the case of human intervention, which gives rise to domestic selection, and the selection processes in the case of the intervention of nature when it changes, which give rise to natural selection. These are inductive analogies in which inferences are made on the basis of certain similarities between human and natural interventions that lead to changes in characteristics. When based on an analogy with domestic selection, Darwinian natural selection theory can be accorded a reasonably high prior probability over some of its rivals. (Whether it gets higher or lower posterior probability is an entirely different matter.) Of course, there are dissimilarities as well. In the case of human intervention there is a certain amount of teleology involved in human selection for characteristics desired by human beings that is not present when nature selects, since nature desires no particular outcome. In natural selection it is the members of a species with sufficient advantageous variability in characteristics that survive. This provides a further plausibility consideration based on causal mechanisms. Since the physical sciences have been successful using causal models of explanation and have abandoned teleological models, then higher prior probability is to be accorded the theories that employ causal models over those that do not. So the Darwinian analogy is successful in only certain respects, something that is true of all analogical arguments.

Salmon also argues that "prior probabilities ... can be understood as our best estimates of the frequency with which certain kinds of hypotheses succeed" (2005: 102). This is not quite the same as the requirement, mentioned at the beginning of this section, that our degrees of belief ought to be well calibrated, that is, to be in accordance with long-run frequencies or objective chance. In fact this is something Salmon would endorse since he advocates a notion of probabilistic reasoning that is somewhat opposed to pure Bayesianism; it is frequency driven rather than degree-of-belief driven (and is of a piece with the principal principle discussed in the next section). Rather, Salmon's remark tells us something about the frequency with which certain kinds of hypotheses succeed in science. As such it adds to the claims by Shimony about tempered personalism (also discussed in the next section). Finally, Salmon places great store on the role of simplicity in determining prior probabilities. We have already met a view of this sort in §5.6 in Jeffreys's attempt to find an objective simplicity ordering for mathematical hypotheses that involves no empirical considerations; rather, the hypotheses themselves are inspected for the order, degree and number of parameters they possess to determine an ordering for their degree of prior probability.

A third and final approach takes its cue from the fact that in determining the priors for a set of hypotheses (which, we suppose, are exhaustive and exclusive of one another and may well include a catch-all), no empirical information is to be used to discriminate between them. That is, the distribution is to be made on the basis of maximum ignorance or the minimum of information. Bayes's own suggestion (and in this he was followed by Laplace) seems to have been that we should treat them equally and distribute the priors uniformly. Such a distribution is linked to a principle of indifference or of insufficient reason. It yields a way of distributing priors in which for n hypotheses the prior probability of each is $1/n$. Such an indifference principle faces well-known paradoxes, some of the more serious of which are attributed to Bertrand. (These are not discussed here; see e.g. van Fraassen 1989: ch. 12) In addition Jaynes shows that uniform distribution is not strictly information-less. He establishes an interesting result concerning a possible simple experiment (i.e. whether some unknown compounds are water soluble or not), some experimenters, the hypotheses they hold and their priors. From this he establishes the conclusion:

> It thus appears that the Bayes–Laplace choice will be the appropriate prior if the prior information assures us that it is physically possible for the experiment to yield either a success or a failure, while the distribution of complete ignorance describes a "pre-prior" state of knowledge in which we are not even sure of that. (Jaynes 1968: §VII)

That is, even with uniform distribution of the Bayes–Laplace variety, we have not reached a situation in which we have the least amount of information about a prior hypothesis or the maximum amount of uncertainty.

Jaynes is a Bayesian but not a pure Bayesian. He proposes a way for determining priors in many (but not all) cases through a principle of maximum entropy that is also said to be objective. In information theory the notion of entropy is used as a measure of the uncertainty of information. The higher the entropy the less the information, with maximum entropy yielding maximum uncertainty. This notion is employed by Jaynes as a way of representing any prior information, and is used to formulate a rule for determining priors: "the prior probability assignment should be the one with the maximum entropy consistent with prior knowledge" (*ibid.*: §II). This is clearly a way of determining priors that rivals that of the pure Bayesian. But it remains a controversial matter as to whether it is as objective as is claimed, a matter we shall not explore further here.[6]

9.2 Is Bayesianism complete?

The tenets of pure Bayesianism tell us that we ought to bring our personal degrees of belief into accordance with the rules of the probability calculus and the rule of conditionalization. But does this suffice for a theory of scientific method, or is something left out? On a classificatory system with eleven facets (and further sub-facets), the Bayesian I. J. Good (1983: ch. 3) argues that there is no unique Bayesian position but rather 46,656 different positions; there may be more Bayesian positions to occupy than Bayesians to fill them. Despite the varieties of pure Bayesianism we shall consider three claims to the effect that the tenets of pure Bayesianism need supplementing.

The first supplementation is due to Shimony and concerns what he calls "tempered personalism".[7] He argues for at least the elements of pure Bayesianism, but makes a significant addition of a "tempering" condition. It is tempered in the sense that it seeks the middle ground between two extremes: the objectivism of theories of logical probability (in his view there are no such objective probabilities) and rabid subjectivism. Despite the convergence of opinion theorems, Shimony fears that pure Bayesianism with its lack of restriction on admissible priors, allows people to set their prior degree of belief in some hypotheses at, or close to, the extremes of 0 and 1 so that convergence might not take place in their lifetime of evidence gathering, or take place at all. Although they might not be so extreme as to assign probability 1 to the claim that the authors of this book created God, they might give it 0.9999. In order to avoid excessive dogmatism or scepticism on the one hand and excessive credulity on the other, and to encourage a genuinely open-minded approach to all hypotheses that have been seriously proposed, including the catch-all hypothesis, Shimony proposes that pure Bayesianism be tempered by adding the following "tempering condition" (also suggested by others such as Jeffreys): "the prior probability ... of each seriously proposed hypothesis must be sufficiently high to allow the possibility that it will be preferred to all rival, seriously proposed hypotheses as a result of the envisaged observations" (Shimony 1993: 205).

This plea for "critical open-mindedness" prohibits choosing too high or too low a prior probability for any hypothesis, which is intended to treat all hypotheses equally and to correct any personal prejudice. It allows for considerable differences between priors but not differences so large that no stream of subsequent evidence will make a difference to the posterior probabilities. It also suggests that the catch-all hypothesis ought to be given sufficiently high prior probability compared with other hypotheses since it is unlikely that our current set of prized hypotheses contains the correct one (something amply illustrated by the history of science). Tempered personalism is also seen as contributing towards a "social theory of inductive logic", in contrast to the individualism of the untempered subjectivist interpretation, in that the tempering condition applies to all enquirers and all the hypotheses they entertain.

The tempering condition is a substantive methodological supplement to pure Bayesianism. Shimony recognizes that there is vagueness in what is meant by "seriously proposed hypothesis" and that, since there is no way of establishing the tempering condition using the axioms of probability, there is an issue about its status. Initially he thought that there might be an *a priori* justification for it. However, in a searching analysis of what the tempering condition might mean and the status it might have, Paul Teller (1975) shows that no *a priori* justification for it is available. Rather than pursue an *a priori* justification, Teller advocates an empirical approach in which "the process of subjecting a method of scientific inference to scientific investigation" (*ibid.*: 201) is to be set in the context of metamethodological investigations of the sort suggested by Goodman's reflective equilibrium or Quinean naturalism.

In his later paper "Reconsiderations", Shimony adopts this empirical stance in a retreat from his earlier *a priori* approach to the tempering condition. He proposes four further principles of methodology, "chosen to expedite the machinery of Bayesian probability" (1993: 286; for the principles see §V, §VI). The four principles are proposed as contingent claims that are not robust and fail in some possible worlds; but they are alleged to be true of our world and to have some empirical support. They also suggest substantive additional principles of method. We shall consider only the first two principles, both of which concern "understanding":

> *Principle 1*: The class of hypotheses which at a given time offer "understanding" is statistically more successful in predicting subsequent empirical data than the complement of this class, where the word "understanding" is to be interpreted primarily in terms of the prevalent scientific standards of the time ...

> *Principle 2*: A hypothesis that leads to strikingly successful empirical predictions is usually assimilable within a moderate time interval to the class of hypotheses that offer "understanding", possibly by an extension of the concept of understanding beyond earlier prevalent standards.
>
> (*Ibid.*: 286–7)

In so far as these principles are empirical, it is possible to test them by drawing on the history of science to determine the extent to which they have been adopted and, if so, whether they have led to successful science. This investigation is to be extended to the catch-all hypothesis since, quite often in science, the hypothesis that subsequently most advances science might not be among those that were envisaged at an earlier time.

Unfortunately, both principles are expressed as descriptive rather than normative claims, although their transformation into norms is fairly obvious. But both turn on the unanalysed notion of "understanding", criteria for which are open to change and are not fixed. As an example, Shimony has in mind the prediction of the Balmer series from Niels Bohr's early (1913) theory of the atom. Given this surprising prediction, on Principle 2 Bohr's theory ought to be assimilated in whatever way into the prized circle of hypotheses that offer "understanding". Clearly the two principles draw heavily on Bayesianism. The role of surprising predictions is something that can be well accommodated within Bayesianism, as can the notion of "understanding", which seems tantamount to explanation. What they add to Bayesianism is empirical information about the extent to which open-mindedness in the allocation of prior probabilities to hypotheses has promoted advances in "understanding". This is to be compared with any information about the extent to which a radical version of pure Bayesianism would have progressed "understanding" by eschewing such principles and permitting the allocation of extremely low or high prior probabilities. Shimony's supposition is that such an investigation would show that an open-mindedness that accords with the above principles would be more successful in advancing "understanding".

A second, different, supplementation of pure Bayesianism is suggested by van Fraassen; he calls it a principle of *reflection*. For a person A, and where t is an earlier time and $t + x$ is a later time:

Reflection: $P_t(H, [P_{t+x}(H) = r]) = r$

The expression "$P_{t+x}(H)$" is A's degree of belief in H at a future time $t + x$, while "$P_t(H)$" is A's degree of belief in H at earlier time t (which can be now). Reflection tells us that A's beliefs now ought to be constrained by those beliefs that A thinks A will have in the future. Reflection is an expression of A's optimism or self-confidence in that one's future beliefs are to be taken seriously, presumably because they have come about by a rational process involving the consideration of evidence and learning on the basis of such evidence. As an instance of reflection, given that next year A's subjective degree of belief that global warming increases (from the current year to next) is 75 per cent, then A's subjective degree of belief now that global warming increases (from the current year to next) should also be 75 per cent.

Whereas most of the principles we have considered so far are synchronic in that they concern the coherence of our beliefs at the same time, reflection, like the rule of conditionalization, is diachronic in that it applies to the coherence of beliefs over a period of time. It is a rule about how we ought to treat our beliefs over time spans and not merely at a given time. Its justification is to be found in certain Dutch book considerations on its behalf; but it is controversial, having both supporters and detractors.[8]

One of the difficulties commonly raised about reflection is evident in the global-warming example. A's judgement next year might have become clouded in various ways (A leads a more stressful life or has become a drug addict). Or there might have been other evidence but A is inadvertent in overlooking it. Or if one were to know now that before next year one will undergo a change in one's belief-forming habits that is not reliable (e.g. A puts total reliance interpreting omens), then one would not now give future belief much credence. And so on. These doubts arise because there are occasions when one ought not to defer to the beliefs of one's future self. There could be good reasons for this if one's future processes of belief-formation are not reliable for the truth and not due to genuine learning, something that reflection needs to take into account. Thus A might think now that at the end of the party when he has had many drinks he will not be safe to drive home, even if at the end of the party his drinking has made him confident that he can drive safely home (see Christensen 1991). However, the principle of reflection can also be generalized to the case in which the degree of belief that A has in H is brought into accordance not with A's future self but with the opinion of an expert in matters to do with H, or several experts concerning H (thereby adding a social dimension). Thus A's degree of belief about global warming next year ought to be in conformity with what experts believe (assuming that the experts are not divided). Overall, reflection is an attempt to add to pure Bayesianism a further diachronic dimension that some deem it lacks over and above diachronic considerations based on the rule of conditionalization.[9]

As has been noted, de Finetti's slogan "probability does not exist" emphasizes the subjectivism of pure Bayesianism and appears to rule out any objectivist account of probability. But if one thinks that there are objective frequencies or objective propensities or chances, how are they to be linked to pure Bayesianism? This suggests a third kind of supplementation of pure Bayesianism that is in accordance with both the notion of calibration and a suggestion by Ramsey mentioned in the previous section. Ramsey requires that our beliefs ought to meet the pure Bayesian constraint that they be coherent; this is an internalist constraint. But as well as being coherent in the strict sense defined, our beliefs ought also to be *reasonable*, in some broader and looser sense; they are to meet the externalist constraint of accuracy in that they reflect objective chances or objective frequencies. Thus to use Ramsey's example, to meet the constraint of reasonableness one should take a person's "degree of belief that a yellow toadstool is unwholesome to be equal to the proportion of yellow toadstools that are unwholesome" (Ramsey 1990: 91).

Let H be some hypothesis (say, that a coin tossed at time t lands heads), and suppose that the chance of H ($\mathrm{ch}(H)$) is 60 per cent. Then what ought to be A's subjective degree of belief that H? If one agrees that it ought also be 60 per cent, then this can be expressed more generally as an instance of the principal principle (announced in Lewis 1986: ch. 19):

Principal principle: $P(H, [\text{ch}(H) = r] \text{ \& } E) = r$

In the above "ch(H)" is "the chance that H is the case", and E is any other admissible total evidence. Rational believers who know what the chances are ought to adjust their beliefs in accordance with this. Thus of the several isotopes of plutonium, ^{239}Pu has a half-life of 24,100 years and ^{244}Pu has a half-life of about 80 million years. Both of these express objective chances; so one's degree of belief about their half-life ought to be determined according to the principal principle. The principle is intended as an additional constraint for coherent subjective beliefs beyond those of the probability calculus alone; importantly, it forges a link between chances and subjective belief. So not only do objective chances obey the probability calculus (not an uncontroversial matter), but also our rational subjective beliefs ought to track these chances. Although we shall not pursue this principle further, it has had much discussion and has undergone refinement by its initial proposer.[10]

9.3 New evidence and the problem of old evidence

Consider version 2 of Bayes's theorem, rewritten in the following form:

$$\frac{P(H, E \text{ \& } B)}{P(H, B)} = \frac{P(E, H \text{ \& } B)}{P(E, B)} \text{ , where } P(E, B) \neq 0$$

We can think of the background B as earlier evidence and E as new evidence. Then what we are interested in is the left-hand side, which tells us about the probability of H given evidence E over H's probability in the absence of E (but in the presence of B). That is, if the ratio is greater than 1, then E incrementally confirms H in the (presence of B); if the ratio is less than 1, then E incrementally disconfirms H in the (presence of B); and if the ratio is 1, there is neither confirmation nor disconfirmation.

This confirmation ratio is equal to the factors on the right-hand side. The expression in the numerator, $P(E, H \text{ \& } B)$, is a likelihood. This will be 1 when H entails E; or it will be close to 1 when E is highly probable given H (and B). Given this understanding of the numerator, if we fix it at 1 or close to 1, then the confirmation of H varies inversely with the denominator, $P(E, B)$. Clearly the lower this is, the higher is the confirmation of H.

The denominator is the expectedness of E against the background B of earlier evidence. Now this factor will be quite high if E is more of the same kind of evidence found in B; that is, where all the Es are the same kind of evidence then $P(E, E_1 \text{ \& } E_2 \text{ \& } \ldots \text{ \& } E_n) \approx 1$. But $P(E^*, E_1 \text{ \& } E_2 \text{ \& } \ldots \text{ \& } E_n) \ll 1$ if E^* is a quite different variety of evidence, or is surprising evidence, given E_1 & E_2 & ... & E_n. In the light of the form of Bayes's theorem we are considering, evidence E gives only a little confirmatory support to H whereas evidence E^* gives H a large confirmatory boost. In this way the common idea that variety of evidence, or the surprising character of evidence, boosts confirmation has a rationale within Bayesianism, as it should.

Consider now version 5 of Bayes's theorem; this can tell us something about the confirmation of one theory H_1 compared with another theory H_2 given E (relative to background B). This is what Salmon calls *the Bayesian algorithm for theory preference* (see next section):

$$\frac{P(H_1, E \& B)}{P(H_2, E \& B)} = \frac{P(E, H_1 \& B)}{P(E, H_2 \& B)} \times \frac{P(H_1, B)}{P(H_2, B)}$$

The factor on the right-hand side, $P(H_1, B)/P(H_2, B)$, concerns the prior probabilities of the two hypotheses (with respect to background B). We can assume that these are either the same or they are an unvarying constant fraction, since what we are considering is the difference evidence E makes. On this assumption, comparative confirmation is proportional to a likelihood ratio; the more likely H_1 makes E than H_2 does, the greater the confirmatory support E gives H_1 over H_2.

As an illustration, consider the general theory of relativity, H_1, with its prediction, E, that a ray of light from a distant star should bend by a given amount when it passes close to the sun; then compare it with a contemporary or historical rival theory H_2 that does not make that prediction. In this case we can set $P(E, H_1 \& B) = 1$. But on the basis of any theory H_2, $P(E, H_2 \& B)$ is low. So, evidence that is improbable against the background of theories that prevailed just before the introduction of the general theory of relativity will give a confirmatory boost to the general theory of relativity when it is introduced. In this case the comparative confirmation of H_1 with respect to H_2 given E varies inversely as the expectedness of E given H_2. Once again, that surprising evidence plays an important confirmatory role has a rationale in the Bayesian framework.

Although Popper is well known for being anti-inductivist, he should not always be understood to be anti-probabilistic because he does use probabilities to express many of his measures. (But Popper is opposed to the subjective interpretation of the probability calculus and Bayes's theorem). Popper's idea of "severity of test" can be given a setting within version 2 of Bayes's theorem. Popper (1963: 391) gives two definitions of severity of test, which he regards as topologically equivalent since they are order preserving. Popper takes "B" to be background knowledge in the sense of all those propositions that we tentatively accept as unproblematic in the course of testing H (this may range from initial conditions to other theories). The severity of test of H by E against background B, which Popper abbreviates as "$S(E, H, B)$", is proportional to either (a) $P(E, H \& B) - P(E, B)$ or (b) $P(E, H \& B)/P(E, B)$. Both of these are expressed in terms of likelihoods and compare the possibility of E when, against background B, H is or is not given. Consider (b) in the light of version 2 of Bayes's theorem. This is a likelihood ratio of the degree to which E is made probable in the presence of H, and then in the absence of H (relative to the background B). And this (by version 2) is the same as $P(H, E \& B)/P(H, B)$, a ratio that tells us about the confirmation E provides. Thus Popper's idea of severity of test is something that can find a place in the above Bayesian considerations as a likelihood ratio, since both Bayes's theorem and Popper's measure of severity compare likelihoods. The difference is that whereas Bayesianism contains a theory of confirmation, Popper adopts no such notion and instead adopts his theory of non-inductive corroboration.

Popper's notion of corroboration is in fact a function of probabilities that is expressed by him as a ratio of the severity of a test $S(E, H, B)$ over a normalizing factor that is chosen simply because it provides a convenient scale from −1 to +1 as a measure of degree of corroboration. Note that Popper emphasizes that the measure does not capture all there is to corroboration, which is, minimally, an account of the extent to which a theory passes or fails a severe test. More generally, corroboration is intended as a report on the extent to which a hypothesis H has withstood critical examination up to a given time t, but makes no claims about the performance of H after t. Important for Popper is the idea that corroboration has no inductive force, a feature of Popper's general anti-inductivism about methodology. For Popper we cannot infer inductively that if a highly corroborated hypothesis has passed a test then it will pass the next test. One might agree that the inference is shaky if it is a quite different kind of test that is to be next performed from those already performed in the past; but one need not agree if the next test to be performed is merely a repeat of some previously performed test that was corroborating.

Popper's measure of corroboration is of a hypothesis H by evidence E against a background B, $Cor(H, E, B)$, and is given by:

$$Cor(H, E, B) = [P(E, H \& B) - P(E, B)]/[P(E, H \& B) - P(E \& H, B) + P(E, B)]$$

When the test is severe, if E supports H then $Cor(H, E, B)$ is positive; if E undermines H then $Cor(H, E, B)$ is negative; if E neither supports nor undermines H then $Cor(H, E, B) = 0$. The maximum corroboration of 1 is achieved when the most severe test is passed; and it is at its minimum of −1 when the most severe test is failed. Even though the notion of a severe test does have a counterpart within Bayesian considerations, there is no obvious counterpart to his measure of corroboration, even though it is a function only of probabilities.[11] But Bayesianism equally has a way of determining the confirmation (or disconfirmation) hypothesis H receives when it passes (respectively fails) a severe test.

The above shows how Bayesianism can accommodate the idea of evidence that has novelty in the sense of being improbable either with respect to earlier evidence or the background of prevailing earlier theories. However, there is a problem with the way in which it accommodates old, well-known evidence raised by Clark Glymour (1980: 86). Consider Bayes's theorem in the simple form $P(H, E) = P(E, H)P(H)/P(E)$. Now, it was a well-known fact from the middle of the nineteenth century that Newtonian mechanics could not fully explain the anomalous behaviour of the precession of the perihelion of the planet Mercury; there was a missing 43 arc-seconds per century for which an account was needed. This was old evidence E; since E is a fact, then for many pure Bayesians $P(E) = 1$. In 1915 Einstein realized that his general theory of relativity, H, was the first to account for this fact in a non-*ad hoc* way by entailing it (with suitable background assumptions): so $P(E, H) = 1$. Apart from this example, we can argue more generally that since $P(E) = 1$ then $P(E, H)$ will also be 1. If we substitute these values in the simple form of Bayes's theorem above, then it reduces to $P(H, E) = P(H)$. On the difference measure of degree of confirmation, $d(H, E) = P(H, E) - P(H)$ reduces to 0 (see §8.3). So there is no confirmation of H by the old, but well-known, evidence E, even though H was the first theory to accommodate this E. Hence the problem of old evidence for Bayesianism.

The problem for Bayesianism is that it fails to account for a case such as that of Einstein's general theory of relativity, which gets confirmation from old, well-known evidence that it first entails. Stephen Brush (1989) provides much evidence to show that scientists themselves regarded the general theory of relativity as being more highly confirmed by its success in accounting for the old evidence concerning the precession of the perihelion of Mercury than by any of the other novel predictions that flowed from Einstein's theory; in their view old evidence weighs more than novel evidence (contrary to the assumptions of many philosophers). But Bayesianism seems not to be able to accommodate the common view of scientists that old evidence carries more confirmatory weight than novel evidence.

Some claim that the above is not a real problem but is due to an unsatisfactory representation of what happens in the case of confirmation by well-known evidence; moreover, Bayesianism has the resources to probe this issue further. This problem has had considerable discussion in the literature;[12] three ways of addressing the problem will be briefly mentioned here.

The first is to deny that $P(E) = 1$. If $P(E)$ is not treated as certain and is less than 1 but still high, then some confirmation can accrue; by Bayes's theorem there can still be confirmation if $P(E)$ is slightly less than 1, since $P(H, E) > P(H)$ (even in the case where $P(E, H) = 1$, such as in the example of the general theory of relativity above). Such an approach might be applauded by "tempered"

Bayesians who restrict prior probabilities to the range (0, 1) for non-tautologous propositions. A tempered subjective Bayesian could then replace the rule of strict conditionalization for learning by the rule of Jeffrey conditionalization, which can account for cases when $P(E) \neq 1$.

This response will not satisfy all pure Bayesians. It remains to say what value one ought to attach to $P(E)$ since it is less than 1; nor is it clear what measure of the degree of confirmation would result from considering the difference between $P(H, E)$ and $P(H)$. Pure Bayesians might view some old evidence in science as very well established indeed, too well established to claim that $P(E) \neq 1$ (like the missing 43 arc-seconds per century mentioned above). Finally, they also argue that even if $P(E)$ is close to but less than 1, this still has very weak confirming power, since the difference measure of confirmation, $d(H, E)$, can still be quite low.[13] The confirmation conferred on H by a high $P(E)$ is small and tends to zero as $P(E)$ tends to 1. So even though Bayesianism has the machinery to deal with cases of confirmation where evidence E is such that $P(E) \neq 1$, this need not solve the "old evidence" problem for some Bayesians when we are certain of the evidence E and do establish for the first time that H entails E (which on some accounts amounts to H giving the first explanation of E).

The second approach is to accept that $P(E) = 1$, but adopt some modified account of confirmation. Bayesianism is broad enough to cover a number of different approaches to the idea of confirmation, only one of which will be mentioned here. Even if E is an old, well-known fact, something new is learned when scientists come to think about a new theory H, namely, that hypothesis H entails E, that is $H \vdash E$. It is unrealistic to assume that Bayesian epistemic agents are "logically omniscient", as is said, in the sense that they know all the logical consequences of their beliefs and assign coherent degrees of belief to them. To be more realistic one needs to allow that scientists, like the rest of us, make logical discoveries; they discover not only facts such as E, but also the logical fact that $H \vdash E$. Evidence E may be old, but that H entails E may be new; and both old and new facts can be used as evidence for H. So in the case of old evidence it is not sufficient to say:

E confirms H iff $P(H, E \& B) > P(H, B)$

Rather, a new account of confirmation is required that allows:

E confirms H iff $P(H, [E \& B] \& [H \vdash E]) > P(H, E \& B)$

Or, put more simply, E confirms H iff $P(H, [H \vdash E]) > P(H)$.[14]

While the above modification to what counts as confirmation is useful to note, it might not solve the problem. We do speak of E confirming H; it is the fact that there is an unaccounted 43 arc-seconds per century that does the confirming, not the fact that Einstein discovers that his general theory of relativity (along with background B) entails this fact. So again, this approach within Bayesianism does not confront the problem fully.

A third approach has been suggested by David Christensen (1999) and James Joyce (2004). Given the definition of (incremental) confirmation, a measure for the degree of confirmation, either for or against, can be constructed in terms of a *difference measure $d(H, E)$* defined as $P(H, E) - P(H)$. This difference measure leads to the problem of old evidence since it tends to 0 as $P(E)$ tends to 1, and is zero when $P(E) = 1$. As this shows, E ceases less and less to function as evidence for H as the certainty about E approaches 1. This is simply another facet of the problem of old evidence in which it appears that increasing $P(E)$ undermines increasing confirmation for H.

To overcome this problem a closely related difference measure, d^*, is considered by Joyce and Christensen, which captures a different aspect of confirmation: $d^*(H, E) = P(H, E) - P(H, \neg E)$. What this invites a person to consider is the probability hypothesis H would get when they learn that E by adding it to what they already know, with the probability H would get when it is learned that E is false when similarly added to what they know. Importantly, this measure is independent of a person's degree of belief in E, that is, $P(E)$ can range from 0 to 1, the case of interest for the problem of old evidence being when $P(E) = 1$. Joyce and Christiansen show that the connection between the two measures d and d^* is: $d(H, E) = P(\neg E) \times d^*(H, E)$ (where $0 < P(E) < 1$). The two measures are not radically different and are close to one another. But the measure d^* is regarded as that component of the measure d that does not depend on the prior probability of E, while d explicitly depends on it. By using measure d^* for confirmation, the degree of belief in E, that is, $P(E)$, is independent of the extent to which E confirms or disconfirms H. If the measure of confirmation d^* is employed instead of d, then the problem of old evidence does not arise. Distinguishing different measures of confirmation is a promising approach to the problem of old evidence.[15]

9.4 Kuhnian values and Bayesianism

It is possible to apply Bayes's theorem to Kuhn's views about scientific theory choice. To see how this can be done, we need to consider Kuhn's post-1962 views after the publication of *The Structure of Scientific Revolutions* (see §2.4). On theory choice Kuhn writes:

> These five characteristics – accuracy, consistency, scope, simplicity, and fruitfulness – are all standard criteria for evaluating the adequacy of a

theory ... I agree entirely with the traditional view that they play a vital role when scientists must choose between an established theory and an upstart competitor. Together with others of much the same sort, they provide the shared basis for theory choice.   (Kuhn 1977: 322)

These five characteristics function as criteria for choosing among rival theories – but with a weighting that can differ from scientist to scientist.

For Kuhn it is the subjective weightings that undermine the idea of an algorithm for theory choice; granted the same values there can still be, for different scientists, different choices of theory due to their different weighting of values. For Kuhn this is an important feature of scientific method that is overlooked by those who claim that there is an objectivity and rationality to science; for example, supporters of the H-D method would reject Kuhn's claim that "paradigm choice can never be unequivocally settled by logic and experiment alone" (Kuhn 1970a: 94). What Kuhn resists is the idea that there can be a "logic-based algorithm" (like the H-D method) that, in a choice situation in which several theories are being considered, churns out one and only one theory as the right one to choose. Such a "logic-based algorithm" goes along with a strong account of the objectivity and "rationality" of methods of choice in science. The probability calculus, including Bayes's theorem, might seem to be such a "logic-based algorithm"; in this respect Bayesians differ from Kuhn. But in another respect they are close to Kuhn. The probabilities are to be understood as coherent degrees of personal belief, and there is a certain freedom in the choice of the values of the probabilities, subject to the usual coherence constraints. In such cases there can be sameness of algorithm but difference in choice of theories. But of course Bayesians can make use of their convergence of opinion theorems, which have no counterpart in the Kuhnian account of theory choice. This restores a certain objectivity, and even rationality, to the Bayesian position not found in Kuhn's.

Let us see how Kuhn's considerations can, or cannot, be incorporated into Bayesian methodology. Begin with the first point that theory choice is always a matter of comparing rival accounts about the same domain of phenomena. Salmon shows that this insight can be captured by the Bayesian methodology in the following way.[16] For simplicity, we shall assume that we are dealing with the same body of evidence E and only two rival theories or hypotheses, H_1 and H_2 (although as the various versions of Bayes's theorem show, this can be extended to a range of hypotheses and evidence).

Consider version 5 of Bayes's theorem, expressed in the following ratios:

$$\frac{P(H_1, E \& B)}{P(H_2, E \& B)} = \frac{P(E, H_1 \& B)}{P(E, H_2 \& B)} \times \frac{P(H_1, B)}{P(H_2, B)}$$

This enables us to compare two hypotheses for the purpose of choice on the basis of a confirmation ratio (see left-hand side); this is given (on the right-hand side) by two ratios, one of likelihoods and the other of prior probabilities. Before any evidence E is gathered, scientists should prefer H_1 over H_2, provided that the prior probability of H_1 is greater than that of H_2. What happens when E becomes available? Then scientists need to take into account the likelihood ratios, that is, the degree to which one theory gives a better explanation of E, or a better prediction of E, than the other. Since the ratio of prior probabilities is fixed, after sufficient evidence has come in the likelihood ratios can become the dominant factor "swamping" the fixed ratio of the priors. This can be seen from the equation above as it directly yields the relation:

$$P(H_2, E \& B) > P(H_1, E \& B) \text{ iff } P(E, H_2 \& B)/P(E, H_1 \& B) > P(H_1, B)/P(H_2, B)$$

Salmon calls this relation a *Bayesian algorithm for theory preference* (1990: §7; 1998a: §7). When evidence E becomes available, scientists should prefer H_2 over H_1 provided that the ratio of the likelihoods is greater than the reciprocal of the ratios of the prior probabilities. In this way Bayesian methodology can incorporate Kuhn's idea that theory choice is essentially a matter of comparing rival theories. But the swamping effect does provide stronger grounds for claiming objectivity and "rationality" in theory choice than Kuhn's weighted values model.

Turning to Kuhn's criteria, consider simplicity first. Scientists tend to prefer simpler theories over more complicated ones. A theory may be simpler than another because it postulates fewer entities or because it makes calculations simpler. But simplicity is also a factor for estimating the prior probability of a theory. The simpler a theory is (however this is measured), the greater its prior probability will be. In one sense of simplicity, Kuhnian simplicity is already a part of some versions of Bayesianism. However, considerations of simplicity are not always simple, as §5.6 and §5.7 show. Kuhn is aware of the fact that a pair of values such as simplicity and, say, accuracy can pull in different directions. But he often leaves the resolution of this problem to the idiosyncratic weightings that different scientists can give to such values. As we argue in §5.7, there is a principled way of trading off the virtue of accuracy against simplicity that does not depend on such a subjective feature.

Second is fruitfulness; given two theories, scientists prefer the one that is more fruitful. There are a number of different things that fruitfulness can mean. Here we focus on the sense in which a theory H_1 may be more fruitful if it discloses more new phenomena than H_2, thereby predicting novel facts that are quite unexpected with respect to background information. We have already discussed this in the previous section as an example of the confirmatory power of new evidence. Here is another bridge between Bayesian methodology and Kuhnian criteria.

A third criterion is consistency. If a theory or hypothesis is internally inconsistent in the sense that it is known to contain contradictions, then $P(H, E)$ will be zero no matter what the evidence is and what the other probabilities are, and this in turn will make $P(H, E \& B)$ zero. This means that no matter how much evidence is gathered, it does not increase the posterior probability of H. This is as it should be. For a contradictory theory or hypothesis entails every piece of evidence, so no evidence can really be new.

The fourth Kuhnian criterion is scope. This can again mean many different things. In one sense, a hypothesis H_1 has broader scope than H_2 if H_1 gives much more information about the world than H_2. To use Popperian language, it is more falsifiable, or, alternatively, has more empirical content, and therefore has a lower prior probability. As this last comment makes clear, width of scope can be expressed in probabilistic terms. However, informational scope cannot be handled so easily within Bayesian confirmation theory. As Salmon (1990: 197) points out, this is because having broad scope is an informational virtue, not a confirmational virtue like fruitfulness.

A second sense of scope is a confirmational virtue. Breadth of scope arises when a hypothesis predicts some facts other than those it was designed to accommodate. Some might argue that if some facts are used in the construction of a theory, then these facts cannot contribute to the confirmation of the theory. But this is not so within the Bayesian framework; such facts, even if used in the development of the theory, are still entailed by it and so contribute to its confirmation through Bayes's theorem. Somewhat different are predictions of facts already known but not used in the construction of a theory. This is closely akin to the confirmation that a theory gets from old, well-known facts. This is an issue addressed in the previous section; there it was shown that the confirmatory support by old evidence can be problematic on some understandings of what confirmation is, but not others. So Bayesianism does have the resources to accommodate scope of the second sort.

The final Kuhnian criterion that we need to consider is accuracy. Since Kuhn defines it as quantitative agreement between the consequences of a theory with the observational or experimental results, it may well be called *predictive accuracy*. Clearly, other things being equal, we prefer the theory that is predictively more accurate than its rival. And this is straightforwardly captured by the Bayesian approach because the posterior probability of H_1 will be much greater than that of H_2 if it has more correct predictions than its rival. In that case we should naturally prefer H_1 over H_2.

As the above considerations show, the Bayesian framework has the resources to deal with the thorny issue of theory choice understood as comparison between rival theories. These resources can be effectively mobilized to give an account of most of the theoretical virtues that Kuhn endorsed in his influential book *The Structure of Scientific Revolutions*, and much more explicitly in later writings.

9.5 Bayesianism and inference to the best explanation

In §5.4 we considered various forms of inference to the best explanation (IBE) and the different conclusions that can be drawn from it. IBE turns crucially on the idea that from premises concerning some facts and a hypothesis that explains those facts best, we can infer the conclusion that the hypothesis is (approximately) true. In this section we shall consider the way in which Bayes's theorem can accommodate many of these explanationist considerations.

Suppose that we are given some facts F, and a set of hypotheses; to keep matters simple consider the two rival hypotheses H_1 and H_2. If B is the background knowledge (or information) from science or common-sense belief, then one form of Bayes's theorem for each hypothesis is the following:

$$P(H_1, F \,\&\, B) = P(F, H_1 \,\&\, B) \times P(H_1, B)/P(F, B)$$

$$P(H_2, F \,\&\, B) = P(F, H_2 \,\&\, B) \times P(H_2, B)/P(F, B)$$

If we express these two equations as a ratio, then we can eliminate the common factor $P(F, B)$:

$$\frac{P(H_1, F \,\&\, B)}{P(H_2, F \,\&\, B)} = \frac{P(F, H_1 \,\&\, B)}{P(F, H_2 \,\&\, B)} \times \frac{P(H_1, B)}{P(H_2, B)}$$

How are we to understand these expressions? In §5.4 we met most of them. Consider the expressions $P(H_1, B)$ and $P(H_2, B)$ on the right-hand side. These indicate the initial plausibility of the two hypotheses when considered only against B, the background knowledge from science, and without considering facts F. An example was used to illustrate this. The fact to be explained is how Michelangelo painted the Sistine Chapel ceiling, which is high above the ground. The two rival hypotheses are that he used scaffolding to climb up and that he levitated. But the hypothesis of levitation has, given what else we know about levitation from science and ordinary life, a low probability (or, in Lipton's terms, likeliness), and so is implausible. And this militates against it counting as a minimally adequate explanation. The ratio on the right-hand side, $P(H_1, B)/P(H_2, B)$, indicates the relative initial plausibility of hypotheses H_1 and H_2 against the same background B.

Consider now the two expressions $P(F, H_1 \,\&\, B)$ and $P(F, H_2 \,\&\, B)$. These are likelihoods; they tell us the probability of F, given other kinds of varying information. What we are asked to consider is how likely are the facts F given the various explanations available. Since the background knowledge B is common to both, any difference is made by the two differing hypotheses H_1 and H_2. We can think of F as fixed and the hypotheses as variable and ask how probable F is made by the varying hypotheses. The ratio $P(F, H_1 \& B)/P(F, H_2 \& B)$ expresses this for a pair of hypotheses. In §6.3 we argued that the notion of likelihood did capture an important aspect of explanation; it tells us about the explanatory connection between the various hypotheses as *explanans* and the facts F as *explanandum*. A number of factors become important in assessing this. In §5.4 we also noted that issues to do with consilience of facts, and the importance of facts, have a role in determining how good an explanation is; and we also noted other contributing factors such as simplicity, scope and fertility of the explanatory hypotheses. All are factors in determining likelihoods.

These explanatory considerations, when taken together, provide an account of the overall credibility of an explanation. The right-hand side of the expression above captures these considerations and provides a comparative measure of just how good one hypothesis is at explaining F when compared with another. Such an iterated procedure applied to all the hypotheses available can lead to a uniquely best explanation. In this way one can provide a role for explanatory considerations in determining the values of the priors and likelihoods.

If we do arrive at a uniquely best explanation, say, H_1, then what can we infer from this? We cannot infer that H_1 is true, but rather the probability of H_1 given F and B, namely, $P(H_1, F \& B)$, is higher than for any other rival hypothesis H_2. And this is what the left-hand side of the equation tells us. This does not get us as far as many explanationists would want; and perhaps it goes further than some Bayesians might desire. But it does show how, when Bayes's theorem is applied to a pair of rival hypotheses, explanationists' considerations can enter into determining some of the probabilities involved in the theorem, thereby ultimately determining the more probable hypothesis.

The above is an approach that a Bayesian who takes on board explanationist considerations might adopt, or an explanationist who goes Bayesian. But not all Bayesians are obliged to follow this path. Their overall concern is to ensure that when they allocate probabilities to the various factors in Bayes's theorem they do it in a coherent way; and when new evidence comes in they conditionalize on it in the appropriate way. Apart from such considerations they are free to distribute the probabilities any way they wish. So what does the explanationist have to offer the strict Bayesian? There is one offer, based in an argument by van Fraassen (1989: ch. 7.4), that any Bayesian ought not to take up. Some might claim that explanationist considerations have an independent weight that ought to be taken into account. They claim that as evidence comes in, not only should the Bayesian adjust their probabilities in accordance with the probability calculus, but they should award extra "points" to those hypotheses that explain the evidence, and the most points to the hypothesis that explains the evidence best. But awarding extra points to the values of the probabilities is a strategy that leads any Bayesian into incoherence. If we do not allow explanationist considerations to award extra points then a strict Bayesian might argue that explanationist considerations have nothing to offer, and need not be countenanced. Looked at this way, considerations based on IBE are either incoherent, or they are not needed and are superfluous.

The incoherence charge is one that ought to be avoided. But are explanation-ist considerations always superfluous? If applied in the right way, internally, as described, rather than externally imposed as above, they are not. Awarding extra points on top of coherence considerations, is not the way to think of what the explanationist can offer the Bayesian. As mentioned, strict Bayesians can, pro-viding coherence is maintained, distribute probabilities to the priors in any way they please, and to likelihoods to a lesser extent. (Some constraints have been mentioned in §9.1 and §9.2.) An explanationist Bayesian may assign these values on grounds based in explanationist considerations, and then tailor the remain-der to ensure that overall coherence is achieved. In contrast the strict Bayesian (who might ignore explanationist concerns) is equally entitled to assign these greater or lesser values, again providing overall coherence is maintained. There is no conflict here between the strict and the explanationist Bayesian; each goes his or her own way. So does the latter have nothing to offer to the former?

Here we adopt a suggestion made by Lipton. Often, when we wish to assign values to prior probabilities and to likelihoods, we find that within subjective Bayesianism just about "anything goes" (apart from some special cases, and the overall constraint of coherence). We can feel all at sea with such liberal lack of constraint. In finding our way about, explanationist considerations can give us bearings. Even though they might not fix priors and likelihoods precisely, they can help fix them within certain bounds: "explanatory considerations provide a central heuristic we use to follow the process of conditionalisation, a heuristic we need because we are not very good at making the probabilistic calculations directly" (Lipton 2004: 107). Here explanatory considerations are a route, but not the only one, for reaching that hypothesis best supported by the evidence. For those who advocate a methodology that is permissive rather than manda-tory, using IBE is simply one of the routes along which we are permitted to travel.

9.6 Induction and Bayesianism

Does (pure) Bayesianism resolve the problem of induction (as set out in §6.2)? We have already seen that Bayes's theorem can represent the idea of induc-tive confirmation (see the end of §8.3). Ramsey regards Hume's argument that induction cannot be justified by a deductive argument as "final", and he adds, contrary to the view of Keynes, "that it can be got round by regarding induction as a form of probable inference cannot in my view be maintained" (Ramsey

1990: 93). This negative verdict is also the conclusion of many Bayesians. Other programmes within the theory of probabilistic reasoning, such as the logical theory of probability based on partial entailment championed by Carnap and others, did hold out the prospect of a theory of probabilistic inference in which we can work out, in an objective fashion, the degree of support that the premises of an inductive inference give to a conclusion. But that programme has run its course without realizing one of its goals, namely, to provide a theory of inductive inference that would resolve the sceptical problem at the heart of any attempt to justify induction. Pure Bayesians take a quite different approach.

The probability calculus does have a way of representing inductive inference. Suppose that one observes that drinking water quenches thirst on occasion 1 (dwqt_1), and similarly on up to n other occasions. We can express the rule of enumerative induction as an inference to the generalization that always drinking water quenches thirst, H, as a posterior probability: $P(H, \text{dwqt}_1 \& \text{dwqt}_2 \& \dots \& \text{dwqt}_n)$. Pure Bayesians also have a way of representing what goes on as evidence for the generalization that all water-drinking quenching thirst mounts up from each occasion of water-drinking quenching thirst. They require that each Bayesian agent update their beliefs in a way which accords with a rule of conditionalization. In its simplest form the rule says in this case:

$$P_{\text{final}}(H) = P_{\text{initial}}(H, \text{dwqt}_n)$$

If one accepts a Dutch book theorem in respect of the rule of conditionalization, then following the rule is coherent while not following it leads to incoherence. Here lies one kind of justification that Bayesians can find for a person updating their beliefs on the basis of evidence in accordance with the rule. But this is not yet a justification of induction.

We can pursue instances of the rule to earlier cases in which evidence dwqt_{n-1}, dwqt_{n-2} and so on is conditionalized on, down to the first bit of evidence dwqt_1 on which conditionalization took place: $P_{\text{final}}(H) = P_{\text{initial}}(H, \text{dwqt}_1)$. Using Bayes's theorem (see §8.7) this can be transformed as follows:

$$P_{\text{final}}(H) = P_{\text{initial}}(H) \times (\text{Bayesian multiplier})$$

This is an expression for the final probability of H in terms of the prior probability of that hypothesis, along with the multiplier factor (which is the likelihood of H in the light of the first bit of water-drinking evidence, $P(\text{dwqt}_1, H)$ over the probability of that evidence, $P(\text{dwqt}_1)$, which is non-zero). Each application of the rule will meet the norms of coherence; so the sequence of conditionalizations does have some justification.

Now one can ask about the prior probability $P_{\text{initial}}(H)$. If a person sets their prior belief in the hypothesis at zero then nothing can be learned from acquiring new bits of evidence by drinking water. However, if one adopts a somewhat "tempered" view and leaves oneself open to learning through experience, then the prior ought to be set at a number other than zero. But which non-zero number should be set for the prior? If one were to set a higher (or lower) non-zero prior than one in fact does, then one's final prior for the hypothesis after the n bits of evidence have been conditionalized on would be higher (respectively lower) than one's actual final prior (setting aside matters to do with possible convergence of opinion).

So, even though one has correctly conditionalized on the evidence and is thereby justified in doing so, there appears to be no unique final prior that is to be arrived at; all depends on one's initial choice of a prior before any evidence comes in. There appears to be no justification at hand for the choice of that prior; and any arbitrariness in its choice also comes to reside in the final prior, which the Bayesian agent arrives at after correctly conditionalizing on all the n bits of evidence. So a final justification remains elusive. Some Bayesians see in this a reflection of the very problem that sceptics find in all induction: "it is in the priors that the question-begging that Hume declared is present in all inductive argument is located" (Howson 2000: 237). In sum, even though one has been reasonable in adjusting one's degrees of belief as evidence comes in, there is no justification for any set of coherent degrees of belief as being uniquely correct.

There is one important way in which the problem of induction and Bayesian-ism are at odds with one another. In the case of simple enumerative induction, as with most forms of inductive inference, it is assumed that there is a rule that can be formulated that has the form: from n observed As that are B infer that all As are Bs (see §6.3). Just as formal rules of inference can be found in deductive logic, so it is assumed that these can serve as a model for the rules of inductive inference. It is also assumed that such rules of inductive inference are reliable and that we ought to follow them since they can be rationally justified, or that they are somehow constitutive of rationality.

Critics of this idea argue that no rules of inductive inference have ever been successfully formulated.[17] Although this might be of concern to inductive logicians, critics argue that there is no need to formulate any such rules. Rather, they propose that we go completely Bayesian and simply adjust our opinions in accordance with the rules of the probability calculus, and update them according to a rule of conditionalization. Of course, this does not mean that there are no rules that one ought to follow. One ought to ensure that one's degrees of belief are in accordance with the rules of the probability calculus to ensure coherence. But these rules are quite different and are not those that have been standardly proposed as part of a logic of inductive inference. They are embedded in a quite different perspective, which allows for a quite nuanced appreciation of differing degrees of belief, whereas many of the central rules proposed for an inductive logic are all-or-nothing, that is, either believe their conclusions or not.

This leads to a further difference. The rules of inductive inference are often accompanied by rules of detachment; we can detach the conclusion and believe it (or not, as the case may be). In contrast many pure Bayesians do not adopt rules of detachment; they see their task as one of keeping track of all the probabilities as evidence comes in, noting the changing distribution of their degrees of belief. If one needs to perform some action on the basis of such beliefs, then there is a Bayesian decision theory ready to accomplish that; there is no need to detach in an all-or-nothing fashion.

Bayesians can set aside the problem of justifying the rules of an inductive logic since in their view there are no such rules to justify. The only rules one needs are those of the probability calculus and a rule of conditionalization. The only kind of justification that is required is that one's degrees of belief are coherent if and only if they are in accordance with those rules. If this bypasses the problem of induction as traditionally understood, then all the better; there is no need to be embroiled in it. Although Popper and pure Bayesians have little in common, they do share one feature: they both recommend bypassing the problem of induction and seek what rationality there is in science by recommending other (quite different) principles of method. As Popper tells us about the rule of enumerative induction: "there is no such thing as induction by repetition in logic" (1972: 6). Although strange bedfellows, both Popper and many Bayesians disparage the idea that there are rules of inductive inference. But they propose quite different ways of getting by without them.

9.7 The Quine–Duhem problem and Bayesianism

We have already met what is commonly called the Quine–Duhem thesis in §2.6 and Chapter 7. It says that no constituent hypothesis H (which may be a single proposition or a conjunct in a conjunction of other hypotheses) can be sufficiently isolated from its context, including auxiliary assumptions A, so that it can be separately falsified. Suppose $\neg E$ is a consequence of $(H \& A)$ that can be compared with observation or experimentation, which is shown to be false by establishing that E is true; then since $(H \& A) \vdash \neg E$ but E, so either $\neg H$ or $\neg A$. So far this is a logical truism. But what makes the Quine–Duhem thesis a stronger claim is that we can never be in a position to sufficiently isolate H so as to subject it to direct falsification. For some, this has been taken to be a direct threat to the claim that falsification of constituent H is possible. Adolf Grünbaum's paper "Can We Ascertain the Falsity of a Scientific Hypothesis?" (1971) is one of several papers by him that show that there are counter-examples to the Quine–Duhem thesis and that it is not generally true. Within Bayesianism it has also been shown in a number of different ways that the thesis is false and that we can have good reason for saying which of H or A is the culprit. Here we shall report on Dorling (1979), only one of the early, and original, papers on the thesis in a Bayesian context; the reader is referred to the growing literature that investigates different Bayesian solutions to the alleged problem.[18] Although only an incomplete sketch will be given here, it should be enough to demonstrate that Bayesianism is successful in undermining the Quine–Duhem thesis, a common supposition of many theories of method

Suppose that $(H \& A) \vdash \neg E$, but E is true (i.e. $P(E) = 1$); then, by *modus tollens*, $\neg(H \& A)$. That is, $P(H \& A, E) = 0$, and $P(H \& A, \neg E) = 1$. But how does one proceed further to break open the conjunction and trace the effect of the adverse evidence E to one or both of the pair $\{H, A\}$? Here it will be useful to keep in mind Dorling's example drawn from the history of science concerning the secular (i.e. slow, long-term change in the) acceleration of the moon (i.e. the moon is slowly speeding up in its orbit). Laplace, using Newtonian mechanics (H), produced the first explanation of this phenomenon based only on gravitational effects largely due to the sun as the moon orbits the earth. The prediction of the amount of the secular motion accorded quite closely with what had been observationally known, namely, about 11 arc-seconds per century. This was regarded as a triumph for Newtonian theory. Laplace's mathematics was re-investigated by Adams later in the mid-nineteenth century. He detected an error in the calculations that when corrected trimmed off half the predicted value, thereby removing the accordance between observation and prediction. Both Adams and Laplace adopted the following auxiliary hypothesis, A: the effects of tidal friction on the earth are not sufficient by themselves to affect the secular motion of the moon. (The effects of tidal friction were not known and remained an obscure matter at that time.) The conjunction of H and A (along with other auxiliaries and revision of the mathematics) entails an amount for the secular acceleration that does not fit what is observed. Which is at fault, H or A?

In what follows we shall assume that the hypothesis under test H and the auxiliaries A are logically independent of one another, that is, $P(H, A) = P(H)$ and so on. This is not an unreasonable assumption to make about many cases drawn from the history of science, and in particular the one just outlined. The assumption also makes the following considerations easier to explore. (It is not necessary to make the assumption; but we will make it since the considerations below become clearer without anything essential being lost.) Given E falsifies $(H \& A)$, we are interested in how blame for falsification can be asymmetrically distributed between H and A; that is, we are interested in the differential (dis)confirmation the components H and A receive from observational evidence E, namely, $P(H, E)$ and $P(A, E)$. These probabilities are given by Bayes's theorem: $P(H, E) = P(E, H)P(H)/P(E)$ and $P(A, E) = P(E, A)P(A)/P(E)$. To work these out we need to know the values of two likelihoods, $P(E, H)$ and $P(E, A)$, which contribute to the value of $P(E)$. The following tells us how to do this.

Consider the case of the likelihood $P(E, H)$ first. By the total probability principle for conditional probabilities we have:

$$P(E, H) = P(E, H \& A)P(A, H) + P(E, H \& \neg A)P(\neg A, H) \qquad [1]$$

On the assumption of the independence of H and A (for example, $P(H, A) = P(A)$, $P(\neg A, H) = P(\neg A)$, and the like) this becomes:

$$P(E, H) = P(E, H \& A)P(A) + P(E, H \& \neg A)P(\neg A) \qquad [2]$$

Since $P(E, H \& A) = 0$, [2] simplifies to

$$P(E, H) = P(E, H \& \neg A)P(\neg A) \qquad [3]$$

A similar result can be found for $P(E, A)$ by swapping H and A around:

$$P(E, A) = P(E, A \& \neg H)P(\neg H) \qquad [4]$$

An equivalence based on the total probability principle can be given for $P(E, \neg H)$ using [2]:

$$P(E, \neg H) = P(E, \neg H \& A)P(A) + P(E, \neg H \& \neg A)P(\neg A) \qquad [5]$$

By the total probability principle we have, in the case of $P(E)$:

$$P(E) = P(E, H)P(H) + P(E, \neg H)P(\neg H) \qquad [6]$$

Since to apply Bayes's theorem we need to know the two likelihoods, $P(E, H)$ and $P(E, A)$, then by the above we also need to know further likelihoods $P(E, H \& \neg A)$, $P(E, A \& \neg H)$; and it turns out that we also need $P(E, \neg H \& \neg A)$. In addition we need the priors $P(H)$ and $P(A)$. Given these probabilities, we now have all the ingredients to fill in the probabilities to get, via Bayes's theorem, $P(H, E)$ and $P(A, E)$. In principle it is now possible to find a way to evaluate the contributions made by each of H and A, which in turn leads to their separate (dis)confirmation by evidence.

To complete this task, methodologists must now move in the direction of a historicist approach to methodology in which methodological principles are brought into contact with actual episodes in the history of science and the scientists who are the actors in these episodes (see §4.5). What is required at this point in the discussion of the Quine–Duhem thesis is an empirical investigation into the actual degrees of belief of various scientists (to be culled from their remarks in their papers, or their behaviour, etc.). Once these have been uncovered, they can be used in the various probabilities listed above. These probabilities are to be understood in the context of pure Bayesianism; they are nothing other than the coherent degrees of belief that each scientist has at a time about various propositions. This is a strategy that Dorling explicitly adopts. Although there is room for further research, Dorling is able to glean sufficient from the historical record to advance the investigation (and here we simply follow him).

Dorling proposes that for Newton's theory $P(H) = 0.9$ and for the auxiliaries $P(A) = 0.6$. What is not so important are the precise numbers. More important is that, in the prevailing nineteenth-century context, it would not have been contentious for scientists to claim that H is more probable than not, and is more probable than A, although both still have a probability greater than 0.5. So the range of probabilities is $0.5 < P(A) < P(H) < 1$. (Note also the values of the priors $P(H)$ and $P(A)$ are relative to their respective backgrounds and are not prior in any stricter sense).

Dorling also argues that there is no plausible rival to Newton's theory H that could predict E quantitatively rather than just qualitatively (although no rival even managed this adequately). In fact no plausible rival theory at the time was sufficiently adequate quantitatively so that it could capture the quantitative facts of the moon's secular motion. The secular motion of the moon has been noted since ancient times; but no adequate theory of it existed before Newtonian mechanics and its application by Laplace and others. So Laplace's prediction was explanatorily novel against the background of prevailing non-Newtonian theories, which would have had great difficulties in predicting the qualitative claim that there is secular acceleration of the moon. For this and other reasons, $P(E, \neg H \& A)$ could be set quite low; Dorling suggests $1/1000$. This reflects the probability of the quantitative value of the secular variation supposed by a non-Newtonian who also does not hold with the idea that tidal friction produces sufficient effect.

Now consider both of $P(E, H \& \neg A)$, and $P(E, \neg H \& \neg A)$. The common factor in both, $\neg A$, expresses, in a back-handed way, the idea that tidal friction does have sufficient effect to produce the moon's secular acceleration and to the right magnitude, an idea whose time was yet to come. These will be higher than the probability $P(E, \neg H \& A)$ discussed in the previous paragraph, and combined with further considerations Dorling assigns them a similar low-ish probability of $1/20$.

Putting these suggested probability values into the appropriate formula yields: $P(E, \neg H) = 0.0206$; $P(E, H) = 0.02$; $P(E, A) = 0.0001$; $P(E) = 0.02006$. Using these results in Bayes's theorem yields: $P(H, E) = 0.8976$ and $P(A, E) = 0.003$. This shows that the problem of the conflict between ($H \& A$) and acceptable evidence E is not with hypothesis H but rather with A (despite its high-ish prior probability).

Even if the precise numbers are replaced by a range of numbers in some interval, the same result in which $P(H, E) \gg P(A, E)$ still holds.[19] The upshot is that the Quine–Duhem thesis cannot be correct; in principle there are ways in which the blame for a failure of prediction from the conjunction $(H \& A)$ can be placed on one of H or A. The H-D method was rather powerless in the face of the problems raised for it by the Quine–Duhem thesis. Here is another reason for placing the H-D method in the context of Bayesian probability; it not only provides a theory of confirmation that the H-D method lacks but it also removes the Quine–Duhem problem, which plagues the method.

This completes our survey of some of the successes and some of the problems that face Bayesianism in its various forms. It is currently the leading area in which research into methodology is taking place. It is able to capture many methodological principles that have been proposed in the past, and to show that some are not viable constraints on method, such as the Quine–Duhem thesis. It deals with issues that we cannot cover here such as the ravens paradox and unification in the sciences;[20] and it provides important links to theories in statistics, something that is highly problematic for non-probabilistic theories of method. It is ambitious in that it attempts to provide an entire Bayesian epistemology for science. It does face problems, such as the problem of old evidence; but it has a research programme with sufficient resources to cope with them. However, it is not without theories that rival it to some extent, such as formal learning theory, also known as computational epistemology or logical reliability theory.[21] In a different vein is the rival theory of error statistics (Mayo 1996), which adopts a non-Bayesian stance. Assessing these rival contemporary theories involves matters that go beyond our purposes here.

IV. Popper and his rivals

10. Popper, Lakatos and scientific method

Both Popper and Lakatos are strong advocates of the idea of scientific method, although they differ in several crucial respects as to what this might be. They also give different metamethodological arguments on behalf of their differing conceptions of scientific method. In this chapter we shall focus on their conception of method and their attempts at a metamethodological justification of it. Much has been written on other aspects of their views, especially on Popper's anti-inductivism, his non-inductivist account of corroboration, his account of verisimilitude, and the like. These will enter into our discussion only in so far as it is necessary to develop Popper's rule-based conception of method and its justification. Popper's basic stance is that of a hypothetico-deductivist, but with several distinctive variations. Arising from this is a proposal for a criterion for the demarcation of science. This is itself a central rule of method that is intended to realize certain aims, and that needs to be accompanied by several other methodological rules if it is to be effectively applied. Taken together these rules and values constitute the principles of Popper's theory of scientific method, often called *critical rationalism*; they govern what he calls "the game of science", the many particular moves in theory change made by scientists in the many episodes within the history of science. There are a number of ways to evaluate Popper's rules for science, some of which will arise in §10.1.2. Popper himself gives two varieties of metamethodological justification employing his H-D stance as a metamethod; these are explored in §10.1.3.

Lakatos proposed a novel conception of the structure of a science. Rather than view a science as a static axiomatic structure, he recommended that we adopt the dynamic stance set out in what he calls *a scientific research programme* (SRP). However, there are also strong H-D elements in his characterization of how each phase of an SRP is to be developed. Accompanying this new structure is also a novel methodology for science, namely, *the methodology of* SRPs. He also uses the methodology of SRPs as a meta-level criterion for adjudicating between rival theories of method. Both Popper and Lakatos were early advocates of something like the three-tiered model in Figure 4.1 of Level 1 sciences, Level 2 principles of method and Level 3 metamethodology; their positions sit quite naturally with the version given here.

10.1 Popper's theory of scientific method: critical rationalism

10.1.1 Popper on demarcation

As we have already indicated in §2.5, the early Popper was impressed by the way in which, on the whole, science, unlike many other bodies of belief, is open to radical revision or replacement. The prime example of this is the overthrow, in the first quarter of the twentieth century, of the highly confirmed Newtonian mechanics by the special theory of relativity, and later the general theory of relativity, and by quantum mechanics. In contrast, Popper alleges that advocates of supposed sciences, such as Freudian and Adlerian psychology and Marxism, are defensive or evasive when it comes to dealing with difficulties for their theories; they shun openness to revision and adopt an uncritical approach to their subject. One of the overriding aims of Popper's account of the dynamics of theory change is its openness to critical revision using rationally based methods. For this reason we shall call Popper's theory of method *critical rationalism* rather than *falsificationism*, which is only a component of his overall methodological approach.

What is Popper's further analysis of the aim of being open to critical scrutiny? He sets this within the context of hypothetico-deductivism, which provides the framework for the testing of theories. In the case of a simple model, if B is some true observational information used as input into theory T, and C is an observational consequence (true or false) following from B and T as premises, then we can write this as: $T, B \vdash C$. By the deduction theorem (Church 1956: 88) this becomes: $T \vdash (B \supset C)$, where "$B \supset C$" is an *observational conditional* linking the observational claims B and C. For example, T can be a theory of thermodynamics, including the simple law-like generalization "for any metal x, if x is heated then x expands". If B is the particular claim "copper wire w is heated" and C is the particular claim "w expands" then the particular observational conditional says: "if copper wire w is heated then w expands". (Not made explicit are other matters such as the period of heating and operational tests for the heating and the expansion; these are inessential to the logical points being made and are set aside.) There is an indefinitely large number of such particular observational conditionals, all of which are, since they are consequences of T, part of the (infinite) set of logical consequences of T. Here we may speak of the *logical content* of T, $LCont(T)$, the set of T's (non-tautological) logical consequences. In analysing these and other notions of content further, Popper uses Alfred Tarski's theory of consequence classes. The set of observational conditions will be part of $LCont(T)$.

The logical content of a theory T is not the same as its *information content*, $ICont(T)$, but they are related. Popper was an early advocate of an intuitive idea concerning the information content of any statement, namely, the more a statement prohibits the more it says.[1] In its various guises this idea is now a cornerstone of information theory. Here there is a focus on what a theory prohibits rather than what it entails (i.e. its logical content, including the observational conditionals). One way of understanding the intuitive idea of information content and its link to logical content is as follows; for every statement p in $LCont(T)$ there will be a corresponding statement in $ICont(T)$, that is, not-p; and conversely. Thus if the observational conditional "if copper wire w is heated then w expands" belongs to $LCont(T)$, then its negation "copper wire w is heated but w does not expand" belongs to $ICont(T)$.

Popper was also interested in the class of statements that form the *empirical content* of a theory, $ECont(T)$. This is a *content* because it is a subset of the information content of a theory; that is, the statements in the empirical content are the negation of some statement in the logical content of the theory (such as the observational conditional given above). It is *empirical* content because it pertains to the statements that report what we can observe. We shall say more about the idea of empirical content when we turn to Popper's idea of a basic statement shortly.

One of the values we wish our theories to exemplify is that they be informative, that is, have high information content. Another is that they tell us much about the world we observe; that is, we wish them to have high empirical content. The above more technically expressed notions of $ICont(T)$ and $ECont(T)$ are one way of making more precise our understanding of what these values involve. Also important is the following, based on the logical consequence principle of the probability calculus, where one theory T entails another T^*:

If $T \vdash T^*$ then $P(T) \leq P(T^*)$

That is, the logically stronger theory T has less prior probability than the logically weaker theory T^*. If we also accept that the information content of T covaries (in some manner) with the logical strength of T, then it must vary in some inverse manner with the absolute probability of T. One way (but not the only one[2]) for capturing this is to say that the information content of T, $ICont(T)$, can be understood to bear some inverse relation to absolute probability. The following is one simple kind of inverse relation:

$$ICont(T) = 1 - P(T)$$

This is a view that Popper adopts (1963: 385–6; Schilpp 1974: 18–20); it captures the initially odd, but correct, claim that the greater the informational content of a theory the less is its prior probability.

How may we further characterize the statements that constitute the empirical content of a theory? To make matters simple, consider the particular observational conditional introduced above: "if copper wire w is heated then w expands". This observational conditional is, by the rule of universal instantiation (for quantified logic), an instance of a law-like generalization L: all metals expand when heated. Being an instance of L, the observational conditional is part of the logical content of the law. The observational conditional is to be distinguished from the conjunction of two particular claims that says: "w is heated and w expands". This is consistent with the observational conditional. But does it confirm it, and also the law from which it follows? One obstacle is Hempel's classic paradox of instance confirmation (§7.4). This shows that any unheated non-expanding object also confirms the observational conditional and the law from which it follows, and this is paradoxical.

An asymmetry emerges when we consider a second conjunction of two further claims: "w is heated and w *contracts*". This second conjunction, but not the first above, is part of the *empirical* content of the law, not its logical content. The conjunction contradicts the observational conditional "if w is heated then w expands"; and it also contradicts law L, of which the observational conditional is an instance. If we accept the second conjunction then we can refute the observational conditional and the law. (In setting out this asymmetry between confirmation and falsification, we set aside issues to do with the Quine–Duhem thesis that are said to undermine any such simple asymmetry for more complicated theories and their test.)

Popper makes much of the asymmetry between falsification and any alleged verification or confirmation of laws. In this he is supported by Quine, who writes in this context of "Popper's negative methodology" (Schilpp 1974: 218). For Quine, and for Popper, the asymmetry between confirmation and refutation lies in the fact that the first conjunction fails to offer confirmatory support to the law. In Quine's view the failure has not so much to do with Hume's point about the lack of justification for inductive inference generally (something that Popper would strongly urge); rather, the failure is due to Hempel's ravens paradox (a matter over which Popper and Quine are in agreement). In contrast the second conjunction does offer grounds for refuting the law. As Quine puts it concerning Popper's negative methodology: "Evidence does not serve to support a hypothesis, but only to refute it" (*ibid.*). We might, in a Pickwickian sense, speak of evidence supporting a law because it does not refute it. Quine's response is: "Very well; this is rather support than refutation, but it is negative support; the mere absence of refutation. Adverse evidence is the primary kind of evidence …" (*ibid.*).

Whether or not one can bypass or resolve Hempel's paradox remains an open question for some. But what Quine does capture in his talk of "Popper's negative methodology" is one rationale for Popper's otherwise counterintuitive claim that we search for refutations rather than supporting evidence. Popper's well-known stance is that supporting evidence for theories is allegedly unavailing on several grounds (such as the lack of justification for induction further compounded by Hempel's paradox). In contrast, refuting evidence can emerge. However, Popper's methodology is not entirely "negative". He does propose a positive theory of non-inductive support through his notions of the degree of severity of a test, and if a theory passes a severe test, the degree of (non-inductive) corroboration that it thereby obtains (see §9.3).

This brings us to Popper's idea of a *basic statement* and the role basic statements play in his methodology. First there is what Popper calls the *material* requirement on basic statements: that they be "observational" in some sense. Popper wishes to avoid any suggestion that the observable be restricted only to items of sensory experience, or reports of these. In fact, he leaves open what is to count as observable, saying of the word "observable", and cognates such as "observational", that it "should be introduced as an undefined term which becomes sufficiently precise in use: as a primitive concept whose use the episte-mologist has to learn" (Popper 1959: 103). Popper's suggestion is that the term "observable", and so what is to count as an observational statement, is to be implicitly defined in the context of its use in an epistemological theory. This is a common strategy for the implicit definition of theoretical terms by means of the contextual role they play in a scientific theory. Just as terms such as "force" or, to use Popper's suggestion of "mass-point", get their meaning through the role they play in a theory of dynamics, so the term "observable" will get its meaning in large part through its use, that is, through the role it plays in an epistemological theory. We find this "contextualist" account of what is to count as observable a useful one to adopt; it also makes clear that the observable need not be tied to what is given in sensory experience.

More important from our point of view is what Popper calls the *formal* requirements for basic statements (*ibid.*: §28). These are: (a) that no basic statement can be inferred from a universal statement alone; (b) a universal statement and a basic statement can contradict one another. Popper simply stipulates that such "basic statements have the form of singular existential statements" (*ibid.*); that is, they have the form "there is φ in the restricted region of space S at time t" (where φ stands for some object, property, event, etc.). Using the illustration above, examples of basic statements are: "there is a heated copper wire here now", "there is no expansion occurring around here over the next minute", "there is a contracting copper wire here, now" and so on. From requirements (a) and

(b) it can be readily seen that basic statements can be among those statements that belong to the empirical content of some theory *T*. They pertain to the "observable"; and they do not logically follow from *T* but can contradict it.

Using the above logical and epistemological notions, we are now in a position to introduce Popper's demarcation criterion for science. It turns on the idea that any scientific theory ought to yield some observational conditionals that can conflict with some basic statements. First he defines what it is for a theory to be called "empirical" or "falsifiable":

> [The theory] divides the class of all possible basic statements unam-biguously into the following two non-empty subclasses. First the class of all those basic statements with which it is inconsistent (or which it rules out, or prohibits): we call this the class of *potential falsifiers* of the theory; and secondly the class of those basic statements which it does not contradict (or which it "permits"). (*Ibid.*: 86)

That is, the theory makes a cut through the class of all possible basic statements forming two subclasses: (i) the subclass of basic statements with which it is consistent; (ii) the subclass of basic statements with which it is inconsistent, these being the potential falsifiers of the theory. The potential falsifiers may always remain potential if the theory gets everything right with respect to what can be observed; but the actual course of the observable may turn some potential falsifiers into actual falsifiers. (It should be noted that the presence of actual falsifiers is not, by itself, sufficient for falsification since there are further rules, yet to be elaborated, as to how many actual falsifiers falsify some hypothesis.)

There are two extremes to be considered. A theory will always have some logical content in that some logical consequences will always follow from it. But if this content contains no observational conditionals then there will be no corresponding empirical content; that is, the class of potential falsifiers of the theory remains empty because the theory makes no contact with what we can possibly observe. In this category will be found propositions that are math-ematical, definitional, analytic or metaphysical including influential metaphysi-cal theories that are proto-scientific in that there is at the time no known way of bringing them into relation with anything we could observe (such as ancient Greek atomism or aspects of Freudian psychology). But propositions of science are not to be found in this category if they are to tell us anything about what we can possibly observe about our world. In contrast an inconsistent theory will entail all propositions; so its empirical content will contain a host of actual falsifiers. Setting these two extremes aside, a theory will be empirical if and only if it lies between these two extremes and makes a cut through the class of possible basic statements in which the two subclasses are not empty. The definition also allows for there to be differing degrees to which theories can be empirical. Intuitively, this would appear to be a matter that depends on the size of the subclass of potential falsifiers. However, it turns out to be a difficult, technical matter to provide not only a satisfactory absolute measure of the degree to which any theory T is empirical, but also a comparative account of how any two theories can be compared for their degrees of empiricalness; these matters are not explored here.[3]

The above sets out a logico-epistemological definition of what it is for a theory T to be empirical (or falsifiable). Alternatively we can say that the theory is *testable*. Some have argued that the idea of testability has fallen on hard times; there is no clear notion of testability. However, following Sober (1999), we find this an odd position to adopt. It is unproblematic to take a theory, conjoin to it any required auxiliary statements, and draw from it a conclusion that can then be compared with observation or experiment; this is part of the H-D method, or its generalization in the form of Bayes's theorem. If an actual test can be carried out it must follow that it is *possible* to have a test, that is, that the theory is testable. The modality of "possible" might be taken to mean what is *logically* possible, or what is *nomically* possible (what the laws of nature permit us to do in the way of testing), or what is *technologically* possible (what our current techniques of experimentation permit us to test), or what is *epistemically* possible (what additional information the current state of our background knowledge in science provides us in the way of auxiliary theory in order to test some other theory), and so on. A statement will then be untestable in any of the above four ways if the requisite kind of possibility has been ruled out by the laws of logic, or by the laws of nature, or by current technology, or by limitations on what we currently know. From the actuality of testing, it follows that there is testability. We take it that the above account of what it means for a statement to be empirical at least sets out some of the logical conditions for such testability.[4]

What does it mean to say that a proposition is scientific in a way that demarcates science from mathematics, logic, metaphysics and, we might add, pseudo-sciences? This Popper sees as an issue that preoccupied Hume and Kant. As we have seen in §3.3 and §3.4, it was an issue for Descartes and Newton; and it was also an issue for Popper's contemporaries, the logical positivists and inductivists, who proposed demarcation criteria that he did not accept. Popper proceeds differently from these demarcationists; he takes the above logico-epistemological notions, and his definition of what it is for a theory to be empirical, and makes what he calls "*a proposal for an agreement or convention*". Why adopt the proposal? Notoriously he adds that this is "a matter of decision, going beyond rational argument" (Popper 1959: 37). This is one aspect of Popper's decisionism that for many seems to go against the grain of his rather hard-line critical rationalism; we shall see in the next section that there can be some argument for adopting the proposal that undercuts this aspect of decisionism.

Popper's *rule of demarcation* is not a reportive or analytic definition of "science" but a convention, or a proposal to adopt, for what is to count as scientific. A theory is *scientific* just in case it is empirical (as defined above). Importantly Popper makes it clear that he recognizes that others have made different proposals, or adopted different conventions, and that there is a need to adjudicate between the various rival proposals. The rivals can be assessed in much the same way rival hypotheses in science can be assessed. This is a metamethodological matter investigated in §10.1.3.

This is a quite broad criterion as to what is to count as scientific. It includes not only theories that we might currently accept because none of their potential falsifiers have, so far, become actual (in sufficient numbers for refutation); but also theories whose potential falsifiers are actual in sufficient numbers so that the theories are refuted. On Popper's definition falsified theories are scientific. For Popper great theories of the past that have been refuted, such as Newtonian dynamics, are supreme examples of scientific theories. Some might find this counterintuitive; but it is only so if one employs a different notion of science, such as "what is currently accepted as a scientific theory and is used in leading research", or some such.

In the 1930s positivist context in which Popper first set out his views on method, meaningful statements were either empirical or analytic; if neither, they were meaningless. For Popper the rules of scientific method are not to be construed as empirical regularities of some science; or, as he puts it, they are not to be taken naturalistically. Nor are they analytic, and nor do they have the same status as the rules of deductive logic. Not wanting to adopt the unpalatable positivist consequence that his methodological rules were meaningless, Popper adopted the view that they were meaningful conventions, like the rules that govern games:

> Methodological rules are here to be regarded as *conventions*. They might be described as the rules of the game of empirical science. They differ from the rules of pure logic rather as do the rules of chess, which few would regard as part of *pure* logic; seeing that the rules of pure logic govern transformations of linguistic formulae, the result of an inquiry into the rules of chess could perhaps be entitled "The Logic of Chess", but hardly "Logic" pure and simple. (Similarly, the result of an inquiry into the rules of the game of science – that is scientific discovery – may be entitled "The Logic of Scientific Discovery"). (*Ibid.*: 53)

For Popper the way out of the positivist impasse was to draw an analogy with the meaningful rules of chess, regarded as conventions governing the game of chess. Within methodology there are also meaningful rules that govern the game of science; they are rules concerning a "logic" of discovery. But here we are not to take "discovery" in the sense of inventing theories or laws; rather, given theories or laws, there are rules of method that assist in discovering the truth-value of theories, or discovering to what extent they can withstand tests, and the like.

But the chess analogy cannot be pushed too far since the rules of chess are constitutive of the game, while it is not obvious that Popper's rules are consti-tutive of the game of science. As noted, the early more liberal Popper of the 1934 *Logik Der Forschung* recognizes that for the same thing, science, there can be quite different Level 2 methodological rules such as those of inductiv-ism, conventionalism and his own critical rationalism; but the different sets of rules are to realize quite different aims. Although these different sets of rules and aims have the status of conventions (i.e. they are neither empirical nor analytic), Popper maintains that there is a metamethodology that provides a way of adjudicating between them (and in favour of his own methodology). This is touched on in §10.1.3.

Popper's rule of demarcation is the proposal that science be empirical (or falsifiable), that is, that it always be possible for there to be a confrontation between theory and what we observe, the greater the confrontation the better. The goal that the rule of demarcation is intended to realize is that of having theories open to revision, the more open the better. In Popper's view the rule of demarcation realizes this goal better than its methodological rivals, such as conventionalism, which, in his view, tends to close off revisions based on confrontation with observation. For Popper, the revisions are not made for the sake of revision, the need to "make it new" with a fashionable theory. Such might be the position of some postmodernists such as Lyotard, who advocate *paralogy*.[5] Rather, we revise our theories in order to solve what Popper calls the central problem in epistemology, namely, the problem of the growth of (scien-tific) knowledge. Although "the problem" is not fully specified, it is clear that it will involve discovering the methods that best help us realize the search for (interesting) truth (Popper 1959: 15). What needs to be shown is that Popper's central methodological proposal of the rule of demarcation is a reliable rule for the goal of increased knowledge, and thus truth. Clearly it is not unreliable as a rule. What is unclear is whether it is more reliable than any other rule.

The idea that principles of method are expressions of means for some epis-temic or cognitive end, that is, they are hypothetical imperatives, is implicit in the account Popper gives of methodology in *The Logic of Scientific Discovery* (see esp. §9, §10, §11, §20). It is more explicit in later works when he writes, in criticism of some doctrines of essentialism in science: "I am concerned here with a *problem of method* which is always a problem of the fitness of means to ends" (Popper 1963: 105 n.17). Later he emphasized that the "ought" of meth-odology is a "*hypothetical* imperative" (Schilpp 1974: 1036) with the growth in scientific knowledge as a major goal and its means the rules of critical rational-ism. These rules are set out next.

10.1.2 Popper's methodological rules for the game of science

In "Towards a Rational Theory of Tradition" (Popper 1963: ch. 4) Popper speaks of "first-order traditions", which contain stories, myths, theories or systems of hypotheses about the world and about ourselves as members of the world. Popper's talk of such first-order traditions is akin to our talk of Level 1 theories (or more generally systems of hypotheses). Since at least the time of the ancient Greeks, Popper argues that we have come to apply a second-order tradition to our various first-order traditions; this is the critical or argumentative attitude and is akin to our idea of Level 2 methodology applied to the theories, stories and so on at Level 1. Popper emphasizes that the theories within our first-order traditions do not come equipped with a second-order theory of method written on their face. Some of the propositions within these systems of thought might stand in logical relations, but this does not determine what further methodological principles ought to be applied to them. We could accept them dogmatically, or choose them on the basis of the toss of dice, or adopt them because we think they are pleasing to the gods, or reject them because we think they are displeasing to the gods, or whatever. Only if we are members of a Level 2 critical tradition does the issue of what methodology we ought to apply to the items at Level 1 come to the fore.

This underscores a second aspect of Popper's decisionism that concerns the adoption of any second-order critical tradition. First-order traditions need to have an "add-on", a second-order critical tradition; otherwise they simply remain uncritically adopted theories or systems of hypotheses. For Popper, adopting such a second-order critical tradition is an important part of the scientific attitude first developed by the ancient Greeks; and it is important for us as it is the core of what can be broadly described as the Enlightenment tradition. But it is a tradition that does not force itself ineluctably on us; we need to adopt it. As Popper proposes in a section entitled "Why Methodological Decisions are Indispensable": "empirical science should be characterised by its method: *by our manner of dealing with* scientific systems" (Popper 1959: 50, emphasis added). This indispensable aspect of Popper's decisionism about methods as a whole requires us to apply a methodology to our theories in order for them to be scientific in the first place; they do not come ready tailored by some theory of method. This is a broader aspect of Popper's decisionism than merely the decisionism involved in adopting the rule of demarcation as a proposal.

In this section we shall set out several rules that Popper proposes for the game of science; in the next section we consider one way in which we might assess them. We have already met the rule of demarcation and the values of openness to revision and to truth that go along with it. But there are a host of other rules as well.[6] As will be seen, some of the rules are almost trivial and can be readily accepted; others are controversial and not widely accepted.

Once the rule of demarcation has been proposed a number of other rules follow in its wake, several of which are to be found in a section entitled "Methodological Rules as Conventions" (Popper 1959: §11) Popper's first example (R1) is not even expressed in rule form: "The game of science is, in principle, without end. He who decides one day that scientific statements do not call for further test, and that they can be regarded as finally verified, retires from the game" (*Ibid*.: 53). Presumably Popper intends that we *ought* not to stop subjecting our scientific claims to test and regard them as verified. Given his fallibilist stance, one might stop testing and accept a false claim that would be revealed to be false if we had continued testing a little longer. This suggests that the value the rule realizes is that of avoiding the acceptance of false claims; clearly it would reliably realize this goal. However, such a rule, to be at all practicable, must be qualified by considerations of diminishing returns on repeats of the same test.

The next is a two-part rule (R2) of acceptance and rejection of hypotheses:

> Once a hypothesis has been proposed and tested, and has proved its mettle, it may not be dropped without "good reason". A good reason may be, for instance: replacement of the hypothesis by another which is better testable; or the falsification of one of the consequences of the hypothesis. (*Ibid*.: 53–4)

As Popper makes clear, a hypothesis proves its mettle when it has been subject to severe tests and passes them, that is, it has been corroborated. This is a rule for the (provisional) acceptance of corroborated hypotheses.[7] Falsification is not necessary for the rejection of a hypothesis; a less testable hypothesis can be replaced by a more testable hypothesis in the same domain. Nor is falsification sufficient for rejection. In later writings Popper recognized that the falsification of a hypothesis does not entail the rejection, abandonment or elimination of a hypothesis, these being methodological notions with intentional overtones.[8] One may continue to employ a falsified hypothesis for a number of reasons, such as: it is the only hypothesis available; to eliminate it would denude us of one of the best, albeit false, theories available; there may yet be novel truths to discover even though the hypothesis has been falsified. However, even though a falsified hypothesis can continue to be used, it will not be a candidate for the truth. Along with this rule, Popper also recognizes a version of the principle of tenacity in which we are not to give up on our theories too readily, even in the face of apparent falsification (Schilpp 1974: 984).

However, in R2 Popper misleadingly states his own account of the conditions for falsification of a hypothesis when he characterizes it as "the falsification of one of the consequences of the hypothesis". When we come to the rules governing falsification we will see that the falsification of a single consequence of a hypothesis (presumably applied in some circumstance) while necessary for falsification is not sufficient. The basic statement that falsifies the consequence cannot be stray, and must be repeatable (see Popper 1959: 86; also rules R9 and R10 below). But even this is not enough for falsification if one takes into account the Quine–Duhem problem.[9]

When Popper introduces the rule of demarcation, he recognizes that it is always possible to evade the rule by decreasing the degree of testability of a hypothesis by adopting various "saving" stratagems. To combat these stratagems he adds a necessary methodological supplement to the rule of demarcation in the form of a *supreme meta-rule* about all other rules of method:

> a supreme rule is laid down which serves as a kind of norm for decid-
> ing upon the remaining rules, and which is thus a rule of a higher type.
> It is the rule which says that all the other rules of scientific procedure
> must be designed in such a way that they do not protect any statement
> in science against falsification. (*Ibid.*: 54)

For Popper the ultimate goal of science is the growth of knowledge, not merely in the accumulation of facts but more importantly in the revision of our theories so that we obtain deeper and more informative theories. That goal is best realized, according to Popper, by adopting the rule of demarcation. But this rule by itself is not enough to guarantee its associated goals. It needs supplementing with a meta-rule, which says that all the other rules of science should be so expressed as to best realize the goal of the rule of demarcation. The justification of the meta-rule is based in simple means–ends considerations. The meta-rule ensures that the rule of demarcation is applicable; and the other rules that conform to the meta-rule are reliable for the values associated with the rule of demarcation. Although these various rules are not logically connected, they are at least systematically linked and can be said to form a theory of method.

The rather contentless meta-rule is fleshed out when Popper proposes a number of rules against making conventionalist and *ad hoc* moves within the dynamics of theory change, especially when theories that face problems are revised through the introduction of novel or auxiliary hypotheses. Here we need to distinguish between two senses in which Popper uses the term "conventionalism". The first gets Popper's approval: it is the one in which rules of method have the status of conventions. The second is "conventionalism" understood as a theory of scientific method that rivals critical rationalism and inductivism; Popper is an opponent of conventionalism as a method. What Popper takes conventionalist methodology to be can be gleaned from the rules he proposes to ban it. One of the main sins Popper discerns in conventionalist methodology is the way it rescues theories from criticism, especially from refutation by observations. As such conventionalism is a direct challenge to an immediate corollary of the rule of demarcation, which is that we ought to keep our theories open to criticism by means of observations. Popper has no argument against conventionalism; rather he simply makes "the decision not to apply its methods" (*ibid.*: 82). (In the next section we shall see that Popper need not have been so decisionist in rejecting conventionalism since he thinks there are ways of assessing methodologies as a whole.) This decision gives rise to the broad anti-conventionalist rule (R3): "We decide that if our system is threatened we will never save it by any kind of *conventionalist stratagem*" (*ibid.*) The rule is universal, but to make it more specific we need to be told what conventionalist stratagems to avoid, and there are many of these.

The next group of rules is designed to counter specific conventionalist stratagems. The first of this group (R4) governs the dynamics of theory change in which saving auxiliary hypotheses are introduced; its goal is to enhance the values embodied in the rule of demarcation when making such changes. Rule R4 says: "only those [auxiliary hypotheses] are acceptable whose introduction does not diminish the degree of falsifiability or testability of the system in question, but, on the contrary, increase it" (*ibid.*: 82–3). This rule has been roundly criticized on several grounds, two of which will be mentioned here. One of Feyerabend's main critical points against Popper is that even if we may agree with him that one of the values to be realized in science is growth in knowledge, many of Popper's proposed rules are quite unreliable to this end. If they were to be followed they would cripple the growth of science.

Feyerabend provides us with a number of case studies from the history of science in which *ad hoc* hypotheses are introduced that are themselves not testable at the time of their introduction, or for a long time after; yet to ban them according to R4 would have crippled the growth of science. The following are just two such examples. Copernicus introduced the saving hypothesis that the stars are at a great distance from us, in fact so great that the angular parallax that Aristotle argued we should observe cannot be observed with the naked eye (it was first observed in the 1830s using telescopes). Unless independent evidence can be found about the distance between the stars and the earth, such an assumption would appear to be gratuitous, and ought to be banned according to R4. Yet to do this would be to adopt an Aristotelian stance thereby crippling the growth of a Copernican-based theory of the structure of the solar system.

The second example that Feyerabend discusses at length is Galileo's argument about the tower experiment, in which a stone is (allegedly) observed to fall to the foot of the Tower of Pisa (Feyerabend 1975: chs 6–11). Does this support the idea of a rotating earth or not? Galileo made an independent, and at that time untestable, assumption about the earth's daily rotation. Feyerabend argues that Galileo made this *ad hoc* assumption in order to establish a new theory of dynamics to accompany the Copernican model of the solar system. This needed to be added to the Copernican theory, which was still mired in many aspects of Aristotle's theory of motion.

If R4 is not to be abandoned in the light of these objections, it is not clear how it is to be modified. Adding a time limit for the introduction of *ad hoc* hypotheses would not help as it remains unclear just how long one has to wait for the extra testability that Popper requires to emerge; in the case of Copernicus and Galileo this ran into several hundred years. A second possibility canvassed by Feyerabend, also to be found in Lakatos, is that even if the saving hypotheses themselves cannot be directly tested then their introduction is acceptable if the overall system in which they are introduced is itself progressive in that it yields extra testability somewhere (again assuming some unspecified time limit). But this requires a plausible account of extra testability, something that Grünbaum (1976) shows is not readily available. This leads to the second kind of criticism of R4.

Suppose that hypothesis H is modified to H^* by the introduction of saving hypotheses (and perhaps the dropping of some other hypotheses in H). R4 crucially employs the notion of degrees of testability or falsifiability of H and H^*, and it requires that the modification of H to H^* is acceptable only if the degree of testability of H^* is greater than, or at least equal to, the degree of testability of H. Expressed this way, crucial weight is placed on how we are to compare degrees of testability, even if we cannot provide measures of an absolute degree of testability based on some scale. If no comparison is available then the formulation of R4 is seriously flawed and unusable. This Grünbaum shows about Popper's notion of *ad hocness*.

As is evident from the previous section, Popper employs the intuitive ideas of the logical, information and empirical contents of a theory, and also the idea of the degree of testability (or falsifiability or empiricalness) of a theory. But often he sets the theory of these contents within Tarski's theory of consequence classes. What Grünbaum (1976) shows is that if we understand these notions in the way Popper recommends, then no modified H^* can stand in the relation of having greater testability than unmodified H; there are always overlaps and underlaps of the various contents to take into account that prevent H^* having greater content *simpliciter* than H. These are technical results that we shall not pursue further; but they do undermine the formulation of R4 since it is expressed using notions that are themselves faulty; and they cast doubt on the way Popper recommends that we understand the very idea of empirical content that arises from the rule of demarcation.

Popper introduces further rules to counter other conventionalist stratagems. Theories can be saved by stratagems directed not at the theory under test but at the observations or experiments that allegedly refute them (e.g. questioning the competence of the observers or experimenters). To combat this Popper proposes a further anti-conventionalist rule (R5): "Intersubjectively testable experiments are either to be accepted, or to be rejected in the light of counter-experiments" (Popper 1959: 84).

There are also two anti-conventionalist rules proposed to combat saving theories by altering the meanings of their constituent terms; the aim of the rules is to preserve the semantic stability of the terms in a theory while the theory undergoes tests. Popper allows for the implicit definition of the meaning of scientific terms within the context of a theory. But this should not undercut the empirical character of a theory thereby precluding its being open to test. Granted the view that a theory provides an implicit definition of (some of) its terms, Popper proposes R6: "changes in these definitions are permissible if useful; but they must be regarded as modifications of the system, which thereafter has to be re-examined as if it were new" (*ibid.*: 83). Similar semantic constraints are introduced for the terms at a lower level of a theory that might also be undefined but whose meaning is established by usage. For these terms Popper recommends the unexceptionable rule (R7): "we shall forbid surreptitious alterations of usage" (*ibid.*: 84). For R6 and R7 the aim is to ensure that, while testing continues, there is semantic stability; and if there is semantic change, new tests need to be carried out.

In opposition to conventionalism as a whole, and in line with the rule of demarcation, theories have some degree of testability, a measure of the extent to which they confront the observable. When it comes to testing theories Popper proposes the following rule (R8) about the order in which we are to test them: "those theories should be given preference which can be most severely tested ... [which is] equivalent to a rule favouring theories with the highest possible empirical content" (*ibid.*: 121). This supposes, of course, that there is a way of ordering theories according to their various contents. But this is only possible if one content is contained in another and there are no overlaps or underlaps of contents, which may be impossible to compare. For most interesting cases in science the latter is far more common than the former.

We now turn to rules concerning the acceptance or rejection of basic statements. It is a common matter in science that stray occurrences can arise in experimentation and observation that ought to be set aside; they can arise in conditions that have not been controlled for, or some unknown causal factors have produced an occurrence that in the normal course of events would not arise, and so on. Wilhelm Röntgen's observation of the bones in his hand in the conditions in which he first discovered X-rays is not one of these, since this occurrence turned out to be a reproducible effect. Popper attempts to capture some conditions that determine the relevance of basic statements in the following rules, beginning with R9: "we should not accept *stray basic statements* – i.e., logically disconnected ones – but that we should accept basic statements in the course of testing *theories*; of raising searching questions about these theories, to be answered by the acceptance of basic statements" (*ibid.*: 106).

In the course of testing a theory, accepting a basic statement that contradicts the theory is necessary for the refutation of the theory, but not sufficient. One reason for the insufficiency is the problem of stray basic statements. R10 sets out a further necessary condition for refutation:

> We shall take it [a theory] as falsified only if we discover a *reproducible effect* which refutes the theory. In other words, we only accept the falsification if a low-level empirical hypothesis which describes such an effect is proposed and corroborated. This kind of hypothesis may be called a *falsifying hypothesis.* (*Ibid.*: 86)

So, single basic statements while necessary for refutation are not sufficient. This is a much stronger condition on falsification than many often claim, including Popper himself in other contexts. On the basis of R10 refutation (or falsification) is a three-place relation between a higher level theory *T* under test, a set of accepted basic statements *B* that contradict *T*, and a falsifying hypothesis *F*, which is inconsistent with *T* but which the *B* corroborate. But not all refutations need be of the form prescribed by R10, as Popper recognizes when he discusses how a white raven here and now can refute the generalization "All ravens are black" (*ibid.*: 87 n.1).

Popper recognizes the seeds of a regress in his account of refutation. According to R10, to corroborate a falsifying hypothesis for theory *T* we need to accept some basic statements. There are two issues here that suggest a regress. The first is that *T* is to be knocked out on the basis of not basic statements but another hypothesis. But this falsifying hypothesis stands in need of test by the same methods; so a regress of tests threatens. The second concerns which basic statements we should accept, and on what grounds? R9, which bans stray basic statements, does not tell us which basic statements we should accept, only those we should reject. Popper in fact proposes no satisfactory rule for the acceptance of basic statements. He writes:

> the decision to accept a basic statement ... is causally connected with our experiences – especially with our *perceptual experiences*. But we do not attempt to *justify* basic statements by these experiences. Experiences can *motivate a decision*, but a basic statement cannot be justified by them ... (*Ibid.*: 105)

In part Popper is reacting to the logical point that, at best, only statements can stand in a relation of justification to one another; non-statement-like items such as experiences cannot stand in such a relation, but they might cause or motivate a decision to accept a basic statement. On the basis of this Popper concludes: "Basic statements are accepted as the result of a decision or agreement; and to that extent they are conventions. The decisions are reached in accordance with a procedure governed by rules" (*ibid.*: 106). Here is a third aspect of Popper's decisionism, which differs from the two already mentioned. The first two kinds of decisions are made with respect to the adoption of the methodological rule of demarcation or a whole methodology; this third kind of decision is made with respect to the acceptance of basic statements that are to be employed by a methodology to critically evaluate theories.

The rules Popper offers are hardly adequate to the task of telling us what basic statements to accept as opposed to reject (because they are stray), or to use in the contexts of testing theories. Popper rightly emphasizes that even basic statements such as "there is a glass of water here and now" are claims that can be used in the course of testing theories but that are themselves open to test. But, as even followers of Popper have noted, there is a need for stronger rules for the acceptance of basic statements than merely decisions to accept. Such decisionism is very weak in the epistemic warrant it gives to basic statements. It also threatens the critical rationalism that Popper espouses since theory accept-ance and rejection turn on basic statements that are accepted only on the basis of decisions.

There are several other kinds of rules that Popper advocates. In the positiv-istic climate in which the 1934 *Logik der Forschung* was written, Popper was able to find a role for suspect metaphysical principles as methodological rules. One is the "principle of causality", which is transformed into R11: "the simple rule that we are not to abandon the search for universal laws, nor ever give up our attempts to explain causally any kind of event we can describe. This rule guides the scientific investigator in his work" (Popper 1959: 61). For Popper this rule is to be understood in such a way that it is not undercut by explanations in quantum physics. Not to follow this rule is to give up on science, including quantum physics. Another rule of transformed metaphysics is that of scientific objectivity (R12): "only such statements may be introduced in science as are inter-subjectively testable" (*ibid.*: 56).

Popper proposes further methodological rules governing the dynamics of theory change. Rule R13 runs: "any new system of hypotheses should yield, or explain, the old corroborated, regularities" (*ibid.*: 253). While this initially seems to be a plausible rule to adopt, Laudan[10] gives us reasons to think that it ought not to be adopted since it does not reliably realize its associated goal (of truth or advancing knowledge). Popper also provides a set of rules for the falsification of probability statements (not discussed here). Finally, there are two rules of method that govern the process of criticism itself that any advocate of critical rationalism ought self-consciously to adopt: (R14) "we should always try to clarify and strengthen our opponent's position as much as possible before criticizing him, if we wish our criticism to be worthwhile" (*ibid.*: 260 n.); and (R15) "after having produced some criticism of a rival theory, we should always make a serious attempt to apply this or a similar criticism to our own theory" (*ibid.*: 85 n.).

Although there are more rules of Popperian methodology these will suffice. What the above makes clear is that Popper's methodology is not a simple combination of some principles of deductive logic with statements based in observation and experiment. Rather, these are surrounded by a network of rules and values for playing the game of science. Popper stands in the tradition at least as old as Descartes in which there are rules for directing the mind when it comes to science, but his rules are certainly not those of Descartes. We may now ask: is this what a theory of scientific method is like? If so, what is so great about it? Popper's response is rather disarming when he writes: "Admittedly the pronouncements of this theory [of method] are ... for the most part conventions of a fairly obvious kind. Profound truths are not to be expected of methodology" (*ibid.*: 54). This is surprising given the heat that methodological disputes have generated. In Popper's view what a theory of method can do is clarify the logic of the situation in epistemology and provide ways for eliminating contradictions and solving methodological problems. In the next section we consider Popper's grounds for accepting his conventions, which make up his theory of scientific method.

10.1.3 Popper's metamethodology

There are two broad ways of evaluating Popper's rules of method. The first we have already considered; it concerns the reliability of the rule in achieving some goal (e.g. Feyerabend's criticism of the anti-*ad hoc* R4), or logical criticisms of the sort adduced by Grünbaum on the viability of some of the concepts the rules employ (such as comparative degree of testability). A second, broad mode of evaluation is to be found in Popper's metamethodological justification of the rules he proposes. For Popper, the rules are akin to proposals that have the status of conventions. They are not to be treated as empirical claims of science; nor can they be shown to be *a priori* true, or analytically true. So how are they to be tested? The only way Popper can see of evaluating them "is to analyse their logical consequences: to point out their fertility – their power to elucidate problems in the theory of knowledge" (*ibid.*: 38). This suggests that the H-D method at the core of Popper's Level 2 methodology is to be employed at Level 3 as a metamethodology to evaluate the principles of method given by the rules of the previous section.

The same idea is reiterated when Popper tells us: "It is only from the consequences of my definition of empirical science, and from the methodological decisions which depend upon this definition, that the scientist will be able to see how far it conforms to his intuitive idea of the goal of his endeavours" (*ibid.*: 55). The theory to be tested is the conventionally adopted rule of demarcation, the supreme meta-rule and rules R1–R15, and other rules as well. These are the rules of Popper's methodology of *critical rationalism*. The method of test is, in large part, the H-D method. Here a benign form of rule-circularity will be involved, since the H-D method is both a central part of critical rationalism at Level 2 and a metamethodological principle used to test the rules of critical rationalism. What is the test basis against which the rules of critical rationalism and any of their consequences are to be compared? This is not clear since there are several aspects to it.

Like any system of hypotheses dealing with a domain of phenomena (in this case those connected with methodology), critical rationalism can be compared with any rival methodology M to discover which does best according to some set of values. A first ground of comparison invokes the value of internal consistency and the associated disvalue of internal inconsistency; we are to reject any internally inconsistent methodology. A second ground has to do with simplicity; if critical rationalism does equally well without a principle that M employs, and does so without falling into inconsistency, then other things being equal we are to prefer critical rationalism to M. Since Popper alleges that his critical rationalism can do without any principle of induction then it is to be preferred to any other methodology M that does employ induction (see *ibid.*: 52–3). Moreover, on Popper's diagnosis of the problems arising from Hempel's ravens paradox for inductive confirmation, critical rationalism avoids the paradox since Popperian "negative methodology" has no need to employ it; in contrast, methodologies employing inductive confirmation are saddled with the paradox. Whether Popperian methodology can get by without even a "whiff of inductivism" (Lakatos 1978: 159) and remain purely non-inductive is a highly contested point. In contrast, for those who see elements of induction as important to any theory of method, critical rationalism would fail on grounds of not being sufficiently general since it does not capture important aspects of methodology.

A third ground of comparison of critical rationalism with any rival M concerns their respective abilities to solve problems in epistemology. It might be hard to identify the problems in epistemology that need solving, and then weigh them according to their importance once they have been solved. But this needs to be done to get either a reasonable absolute measure of problem-solving power, or a comparative measure of when one methodology has greater problem-solving power than another. These three grounds can be broadly construed as aspects of the H-D method, in that matters of consistency, simplicity and generality do arise for hypotheses treated in H-D fashion. But issues to do with problem-solving power are more directly related to the H-D method in that the solutions arise from consequences drawn from the application of hypotheses in special circumstances.

Even more directly H-D in character is the comparison of the consequences of a theory of method with the scientists' "intuitive idea of the goal of his endeavours" (Popper 1959: 55). It remains quite unclear exactly what intuitions are being appealed to here. Are they intuitions that scientists might have about the rules of method themselves? Or are they intuitions about the application of the rules to some particular episode in science? In some places Popper suggests the former. For example, if scientists intuitively favour the exposure of a theory to test, especially where the test concerns novel test consequences, or they like the challenge opened by a falsification, then Popper says that they will favour his methodology of critical rationalism, which incorporates these intuitions over conventionalist methodology, which plays them down (*ibid.*: 80).

But sometimes the intuitions are about the worthiness of some move in the game of science, independently of what rule of method might sanction the move. It is a further matter to bring together particular intuitive judgements about moves in the game of science and a set of methodological rules that might best capture such moves. Such a procedure could be usefully understood in terms of the methodology of reflective equilibrium discussed in §4.4, in which intuitive judgements and rules of method are assayed in order to produce the best overall systematization of both. However, Popper's procedure is not an application of the metamethod of reflective equilibrium. Rather critical rationalism, and its consequences when applied in particular circumstances, are to be compared with a test basis somehow constructed out of scientist's intuitions about the goal of their endeavours. Has such a test ever been carried out? No Popperian to our knowledge has actually done the empirical hard work similar to that carried out by normative naturalists (see §12.2) to test their conjectured theory of method encapsulated in the rules of critical rationalism in this way. The endorsement that many scientists such as John Eccles, Herman Bondi and Peter Medawar have given Popper's methodology will not suffice. As unspecific as the test basis is, it is clear that Popper's approach is "quasi-empirical" (to use a useful term coined by Lakatos); the H-D method is employed to test the consequences of critical rationalism against the test basis. It is this idea that is further developed in slightly different form in the later Popper and more fully explored by Lakatos in the context of a more overtly empirical metamethodology.[11]

A more specific basis against which his methodology can be tested emerges in Popper's "Replies to my Critics" in a section entitled "The Problem of Demarcation" (Schilpp 1974: 976–87). Popper revisits his earlier definition of science in terms of his criterion of demarcation, as well as the definitions of others, and casts aspersions on them all, writing: "A discussion of the merits of such definitions can be pretty pointless" (*ibid.*: 981). His reasons have to do with a change in his metamethodological justifications for adopting a theory of scientific method, since he continues: "This is why I gave here first a description of great or heroic science and then a proposal for any criterion which allows us to demarcate – roughly – this kind of science". For Popper the paradigms of great or heroic science are the laws of Kepler and the theories of Newton and Einstein; instances of disreputable science are those of Marx, Freud and Alfred Adler.

On Popper's metamethodological criterion, any acceptable methodology must capture all those sciences on the great/heroic list and miss none (otherwise the methodology is too narrow); and it must capture none of the sciences on the disreputable list (on pain of refutation). Popper does not say how the two lists are drawn up; but given the lists they constitute a (fallible) foundation against which methodologies can be tested in much the same way that scientific observations are a (fallible) foundation against which scientific theories can be tested. Such a procedure is, once again, benignly rule-circular in that it uses the H-D method as a metamethodology to be applied to rules of method, many of which contain features of the H-D method themselves. Given such a fallible test basis, Popper's approach to the evaluation of methodologies including his own is empirical, or "quasi-empirical", rather than *a priori* or conventionalist.

Where do Popper's intuitions about great and disreputable science come from? They appear to be plucked out of the air and lack any basis at all. As such they are a flimsy test basis for any theory of method. In contrast Lakatos suggests a different way of drawing up the fallible foundation against which methodologies are to be tested. Appeal is made to the general community of scientists working in a given field, the scientific elite, and their judgement as to what is, and what is not, an acceptable move in the game of science. Such judgements are not informed by some theory of method. Rather, they arise out of the day-to-day workings of scientists independently of methodological or philosophical reflection on their scientific enterprise. While there is considerable dispute, even among scientists, over what is an acceptable theory of method, there is, alleges Lakatos, no comparable dispute over whether some move in "the game of science" is scientific or unscientific (Lakatos 1978: 124). How are the judgements of the scientific elite to be determined? This can only be done by employing the methodology of surveys used by sociologists to determine a spectrum of opinions on some matter. Here a little methodology must be drawn on independently if a test basis for other aspects of method is to be available. We shall return in §10.2.2 to Lakatos's use of the particular intuitive judgements of a scientific elite to assess methodologies. It is clearly a superior approach to that of Popper.

We noted in the previous section that Popper adopts a decisionist stance towards the adoption of the rule of demarcation. But given that Popper thinks that there are some metamethods that can be used to evaluate rival methodologies then, if the metamethods can be successfully applied, the decision to adopt critical rationalism with its central rule of demarcation, cannot remain, as Popper says, a "decision going beyond rational argument" (Popper 1959: 37); if successful, metamethodology provides grounds for accepting critical rationalism that are not decisionist. This leads to the third metamethodological attempt to justify critical rationalism. In his 1984 book, *The Retreat to Commitment*, William Bartley proposed a modified version of Popper's critical rationalism, which he called *comprehensively critical rationalism*, although he later changed this to "pancritical rationalism" (Bartley 1984: ch. 5). Bartley sought to show that critical rationalism might be applied to the adoption of the critical rationalist position itself, so that critical rationalism might be comprehensive (or "pancritical") rather than limited.

Popper had taken the contrary view. In *The Open Society and its Enemies*, he argued that rationalism rests on an "irrational *faith in reason* ... [it] is necessarily far from comprehensive or self-contained" (Popper 1962: 231). Rationalism, in this context, is the position that only claims supported by rational argument are to be accepted. But the position of rationalism itself cannot be established by rational argument. For no argument for the position of rationalism could persuade one to adopt the position unless one has already decided to accept the results of rational argument. Hence, the decision to abide by reason is a decision that is logically prior to the decision to adopt the position of rationalism. Because of such decisionist fideism, Popper took the view that a comprehensive rationalism based on a rational acceptance of the position of rationalism is logically impossible. For this reason, the rationalist position must make a "minimum concession to irrationalism" (*ibid.*: 232).

According to Bartley, it is possible to adopt a comprehensive rationalist position provided that rationalism is understood in critical rationalist terms. This involves rejection of the traditional idea that the rational adoption of a belief involves the rational justification of the belief. It is, Bartley claims, impossible rationally to adopt the position of rationalism if this requires rational justification. The requirement of rational justification has no force unless one has already decided to comply with the requirement to justify one's beliefs rationally. But if instead rationality is understood in terms of the critical attitude of holding beliefs open to critical scrutiny, then it may be possible to adopt rationalism on a rational basis. For the position that only beliefs that are open to criticism are held rationally may itself be held open to criticism. Hence, it is possible to adopt the critical rationalist position in a rational manner.

Bartley's proposal of comprehensively critical rationalism has been subjected to criticism by Popperians. One major line of criticism turns on the question of whether comprehensively critical rationalism may itself be genuinely held open to criticism. The question arises by considering whether it might be shown that position is unable to be criticized. This could happen in various ways. For example, it might be shown that some standard of criticism used by comprehensively critical rationalism must be taken to be exempt from criticism in order to avoid circularity or infinite regress. Or perhaps it might be shown that there is no circumstance in which it might be shown to be false. Because comprehensively critical rationalism rests on the claim that it may be held open to criticism, to show that it cannot be held open to criticism would be a fundamental objection to it. If such an objection were to succeed, it would have precisely the effect of demonstrating that comprehensively critical rationalism is open to criticism. So even if it were shown not to be open to criticism, that would just show it to be open to criticism, which suggests that it is impossible to criticize the position. This criticism and a number of similar objections were the subject of some considerable debate within the Popperian school of critical rationalists.[12]

10.2 Lakatos's methodology of scientific research programmes

10.2.1 SRPs and their methodology

Many theories within science are presented in axiomatic fashion, a prime example being Newton's display of his theory of motion in Book I of his *Principia*. Fundamental definitions and laws are set out, the laws being treated as axioms from which are derived theorems (commonly less fundamental laws) and applications of these under special conditions (as illustrated in the H-D schema). In contrast Lakatos proposes that we view each science dynamically as a sequence of "phases" of theory, some of which initially exhibit growth and later exhibit decline or stagnation. This sequence Lakatos calls a *scientific research programme* (SRP). SRPs can rival one another in the same domain in much the same way that Kuhn envisages that there could be rival paradigms, or Popper and others envisage that there are rival sets of hypotheses. Thus the Ptolemaic, Copernican and Newtonian SRPs rival one another in the domain of planetary phenomena; similarly Marxist, monetarist, Keynesian (and other) SRPs within economics rival one another concerning economic phenomena.

How are SRPs to be individuated? In §1.5 we have given an account of the positive and negative heuristics that govern the construction of the phases of a SRP. The heuristics, in combination with what Lakatos calls the "hard core" of an SRP, are the two items that, taken together, help individuate an SRP. The hard core of an SRP is a set of fundamental postulates that are held to be true for the life of the programme (even though they may be false). Thus for the Newtonian SRP its hard core contains at least the three laws of motion. For Prout's programme in early-nineteenth-century chemistry, the hard core is the basic assumption that the atomic weights of all pure chemical substances are whole number multiples of the basic building block, hydrogen (which has unit weight 1). (The positive heuristic of Prout's SRP is "to overthrow, and replace, the contemporary false observational theories applied in measuring atomic weights" (Lakatos 1978: 118–19).) The idea of a hard core in fact carries more weight in individuating an SRP than does its heuristic since, on some occasions, the same heuristic can accompany different hard cores. Thus the Copernican and Ptolemaic SRPs, on Lakatos's reconstruction of them, both contain the same guiding heuristic, namely, that of explaining the wayward motions of the planets using Plato's directive that all such motions are to be shown to be combinations of circular uniform motions about a centre. Where they differ is in their hard cores: the Ptolemaic hard core contains the assumption that the earth is stationary while the Copernican hard core contains the assumption that the sun retains a fixed position with respect to the stars while the earth moves.

Given the above we can now express the idea of an SRP schematically as follows. Let "HC" stand for hard core, which remains constant for the life of the SRP. Let "$^{+}H_{\_}$" be the positive and negative heuristics of the programme, which gets applied to the HC to develop each phase of the SRP. $^{+}H_{\_}$ will generate a sequence of auxiliary assumptions A_i that act as a "protective belt" to prevent refutation of HC (this is part of the negative heuristic, $H_{\_}$, of $^{+}H_{\_}$). But each A_i will also be a creative development of the SRP; the positive heuristic of $^{+}H_{\_}$ guides the construction of a sequence of models to which HC is applied (see §1.5 on the model-building capacities of $^{+}H_{\_}$). Each application of $^{+}H_{\_}$ generates each theoretical phase of the SRP, T_i, where each T_i ($i = 1, ..., n$) represents the elements of the sequence that constitute the n distinct theoretical phases of growth and decay of the programme. An SRP can now be represented as follows:

$$\text{SRP} = T_1, T_2, T_3, ..., T_n, \text{ where each } T_i = \{[\text{HC}] \,\&\, [A_i]\} \ (i = 1, ..., n)$$

SRPs are not as immediately apparent in the history of science as individual hypotheses might be, although these individual hypotheses will play a role either in the hard core or in some of the T_i of the SRP. Rather, Lakatos treats SRPs as "rational reconstructions" of episodes in the history of science made by some philosophically minded historian of science acquainted with Lakatos's methodology of SRP. Nor are the hard cores necessarily objects of belief on the part of scientists working on the programme. This Lakatos makes clear when he says, somewhat paradoxically, "Prout never articulated the 'Proutian programme': the Proutian programme is not Prout's programme" (*ibid.*: 119). Lakatos's point is that perhaps many of the scientists who can be taken to have been working on what Lakatos identifies as the Proutian SRP did not articulate to themselves their theoretical beliefs and the scientific practices and experimentation in the way Lakatos does. It may rarely be the case that scientists are so self-aware of their scientific activities and framework of thought that they can express their theory in any philosophically recommended form, whether it is in axiomatic form or as a Lakatosian SRP. An important matter for Lakatos is how one takes the seemingly inchoate activities that make up episodes in the history of science and gives them some overall "form", such as that of an appropriate hard core and heuristics, which then constitutes an SRP. Lakatos's own advice here is to (a) give a rational reconstruction, and then (b) compare the reconstruction with actual history in order to criticize both (*ibid.*: 52–3). The two-way comparison is essential because, according to Lakatos's quip, "philosophy of science without history of science is empty; history of science without philosophy of science [and its rational reconstructing activities] is blind" (*ibid.*: 102).

One important aspect of an SRP is its ability to grow in the face of an "ocean of anomalies", that is, unsolved problems that are deemed relevant to the programme, or well-known facts that contradict it. These can be set aside for the time being if the SRP has enough internal impetus through the application of the positive heuristics to the hard core to generate growth in the sense of posing new problems and solving them. What is this internally generated growth? One way to characterize it is in terms of the growth in the empirical content of one phase of the SRP over its immediate predecessor phase. That is, T_{i+1} has more empirical content than its immediate predecessor T_i. But as we have seen in §10.1.1, satisfactory and unproblematic measures of the degree of empirical content that some T_{i+1} possesses over its immediate predecessor T_i are hard to come by; it is even hard to obtain comparisons of degrees of content let alone absolute measures. We could also express this growth in terms of T_{i+1} having excess corroboration over predecessor T_i. But there is no reason why this growth should be characterized in terms of Popper's controversial non-inductive corroboration rather than ordinary confirmation.

Instead, let us talk more neutrally of novel consequences of theories (including novel predictions) and novel facts. Here novelty is not always to be understood in terms of being previously unknown; there are several kinds of novelty to note. The first kind we can call *logical novelty*: p is a *logically novel* consequence of T_{i+1} with respect to its immediate predecessor T_i in some SRP if and only if p is a logical consequence of T_{i+1} but not its immediate predecessor T_i, or any other predecessor in the SRP. (If we are to consider conditions for positive growth in the SRP then we need also to add to the idea of a novel consequence the condition that T_i has no logical consequences that T_{i+1} does not also have; otherwise T_{i+1} and T_i could overlap so that both T_{i+1} and T_i have consequences that the other does not have.) Logical novelty captures the idea that T_{i+1} entails something, namely, p, that T_i does not. Is the novel consequence true or false? We have p is a *novel fact* if and only if (a) p is a consequence of T_{i+1} but not T_i and (b) p is true. This notion of novel evidence is very close to the Bayesian notion of new evidence discussed in §9.3.

Logical novelty says nothing about the time at which its novel consequences are discovered. We should not assume that all the novel consequences of T_{i+1} are immediately available. As is common in mathematics and the sciences, consequences are not immediately evident and much time and hard work are required to deduce p from some axioms or premises. Here an epistemic issue arises about our access to p as a consequence of T_{i+1}. This gives rise to a second kind of novelty, which we can dub *epistemic novelty*: p is epistemically novel in that there is epistemic access to p as a consequence of T_{i+1} at a time later than the time at which T_{i+1} is first mooted. The time at which we acquire our first knowledge that p as a consequence of T_{i+1} marks the difference between logical and epistemic novelty.

There are yet other kinds of novelty. Often a theory is developed to account for some known facts. Call the facts they are specifically designed to accommodate "designer facts". Such facts, of course, fit the theory designed to accommodate them since they must be consequences of theory (when applied). But does it follow that they give support to the theory? Some would say that they give no, or negligible, support. To claim that they do give some positive support is to add something to a purely logical theory of confirmation. Not only must one take into account the support that consequences give to a theory, but other matters such as whether the facts were involved in the construction of theory must also be considered. From a purely logical point of view this is deemed to be irrelevant to any logic of confirmatory support; either the consequences support the theory or they do not. But some wish to build into the account of confirmation elements of the history of the way in which theory and facts have evolved together. There is a tradition in the theory of confirmation, supported by many such as Mill, Keynes and Carnap, which insists that confirmatory relations ought to be considered only as logical relations; these theorists adopt an *ahistorical* account of confirmation. In contrast others, such as Whewell, Popper and Lakatos, argue that historical relations between theory and fact ought to be taken into account in assessing confirmatory support; they adopt a *historical* account of confirmation.[13] On the ahistorical view, it does not matter which comes first, hypothesis or evidence; nor does it matter if some fact was used in the construction of the theory. All that matters is the logical, confirmatory relation between evidential facts and theory. On the historical view the evolutionary order of facts and theory is an important matter to consider in working out the degree of support evidence gives to some hypothesis. This is also a crucial matter in what follows.

Consider now the case in which a theory does not use certain well-known facts in the course of its construction, but once it is constructed it is shown to entail these known facts. Call these *non-designer facts* since they are not used in the design of the theory. Do these give an additional boost to the degree of confirmatory support? Those who adopt an ahistorical account of confirmation would say no, while those who support an historical account do see "non-designer", known facts as adding to confirmatory support. Whether a fact is a designer or a non-designer fact with respect to a given theory depends on whether the fact is or is not employed in the construction of the theory; so a fact's status as designer or non-designer can vary from theory to theory. In addition, non-designer facts can be well known. Such facts become relevant to theories of confirmation when a known non-designer fact is shown to be a consequence of the theory. That is, a theory predicts something well known that it was not designed to accommodate. Let us call a known non-designer fact *explanatorily* novel when it is incorporated into a theory for the first time. Those who adopt a historical view of confirmation claim that such novel facts ought to give greater support to a theory than purely designer or non-designer facts. Ahistorical theories of confirmation do not take this into account.

A commonly cited example of the above kind of explanatory novelty is the case of the missing 43 arc-seconds per century in the precession of the perihelion of Mercury (see §9.3). This fact, well known from the middle of the nineteenth century, remained unexplained for some time until it received its first generally acceptable explanation in late 1915 when Einstein introduced his general theory of relativity. Various other attempts to explain this well known fact used *ad hoc* theories that were, in the long run, unacceptable. Does such explanatory novelty give added confirmation to the general theory of relativity? As we mentioned in §9.3, Brush (1989, 1994) discusses this example and others, claiming that many scientists do not put much weight on such novelty for confirmatory purposes (although a few do). Rather, he adds, it contributes to the publicity value of the theory instead of its confirmatory support. If Brush is right, such scientists have an ahistorical view of confirmation in which what matters is the mere logical relation of a theory to evidence, and not anything to do with the history of the evolution of theories and facts. Are we to treat Brush's report about the negative views of most scientists concerning novel confirmation as an interesting historical fact, or one with normative force about what is not acceptable in a theory of confirmation (i.e. the ahistorical view ought to be adopted but not the historical view)? It remains unclear which. A response of those who support a historical view of confirmation might be that scientists are not taking epistemic advantage of something that is an important feature of confirmation.

Finally, we need to consider the facts that could not be either designer or non-designer facts because they were simply not known by the scientific community at the time a theory is proposed. Rather, it was by examining the consequences of the theory after it has been proposed that some novel fact is uncovered and not before. We may call this *anticipatory* novelty in that a theory anticipates some true proposition p by entailing it, but no one knows at the time the consequence is drawn whether it is true or false; ultimately, however, it turns out to be true. Even a sceptic about the historical account of confirmation such as Brush admits that there are some examples of anticipatory novelty. Mendeleev predicted from his table of elements that certain elements ought to exist, and subsequently gallium, scandium and germanium were discovered. Again, the discoveries of some subatomic particles were anticipatorily novel, such as the positrons anticipated by Dirac's theory or the mesons anticipated by Yukawa's theory. These three cases concern novel facts about what exists. However, those who join Brush in the ahistorical camp would say that even if these novel existence facts were anticipated by theory, this adds little to the confirmatory boost of the theory that anticipated them. In contrast those in the historical camp do see this as a big confirmatory boost, of which scientists ought to take epistemic advantage if they do not. It would be up to those who support the historical viewpoint to show how such epistemic advantage is to be incorporated into a theory of confirmation.

There is a commonly cited case of anticipatory novelty that raises problems for the historical theory of confirmation. In 1818 the members of the French Académie des Sciences were considering Fresnel's recently proposed theory of light diffraction. The theory had been applied to variously shaped opaque objects placed between a light source and a screen, and the theory's consequences had been checked by observations of the shadow cast on the screen. Fresnel had not applied his theory to opaque discs (or a sphere), but Poisson did. He derived the surprising conclusion that a spot would appear on the screen in the centre of the shadow it cast, and the spot would be as bright as if the opaque disc were not there. This is both a logically novel, and an epistemically novel, consequence of an application of Fresnel's theory. To Poisson it is also anticipatorily novel in that it was not something of which he had prior knowledge before the consequence was deduced. Poisson also thought that the novel consequence would be false, and so be an important test case for Fresnel's theory. Consequently he asked Dominique François Arago, a fellow member of the Académie des Sciences, to perform the experiment. The novel consequence became a novel fact for members of the academy. The positive outcome was instrumental in giving Fresnel's theory of diffraction wide acceptance even by doubters such as Poisson, Laplace and Biot.

But such anticipatory novelty can harbour certain undesirable relativities to what a group of people knows at a given time. In 1723 Jacques Maraldi had published in Paris the results of observing the bright spot when performing a similar experiment (see Feather 1964: 225). But these results had fallen into oblivion and were unknown by the members of the Académie des Sciences in 1818. Had they known their literature the example would not have been one of anticipatory novelty but, at best, explanatory novelty. This raises a difficulty for a historical theory of confirmation based on notions of novelty. The degree of confirmation depends on the wayward contingencies of what is and is not known by groups of people at given times. For those members of the Académie des Sciences who do not know their scientific literature, the anticipatory novelty of the experimental outcome can give a large boost to the degree of confirmation to the theory of Fresnel that they might already accept. For those who do know their literature, anticipatory novelty does not arise; so for them Fresnel's theory does not get any extra confirmatory boost. For those who hold the ahistorical view, the degree of confirmatory support of a theory by evidence ought not to depend on such contingencies of who knows what and when.

The above sets out some of the different ways in which facts can be said to be novel. What is disputed is whether such novel facts do give an extra boost to the degree of confirmation in virtue of their novelty. In contrast to those who adopt an ahistorical account of confirmation, Lakatos adopts a strong version of the historical view and uses novelty in its several senses to characterize SRPs as progressive or degenerate.

What does Lakatos mean by a *progressive problem-shift*, or *theoretical* and *empirical progress*? T_{i+1} is *theoretically* progressive with respect to T_i just when T_{i+1} has some novel consequence p that T_i does not have and p is open to test (and may be either true or false). T_{i+1} is *empirically* progressive with respect to T_i just when T_{i+1} has some novel consequence p that T_i does not have and p is open to test and passes the test. We are now in a position to set out Lakatos's criterion for the demarcation of SRPs as scientific. Given the sequence T_i ($i = 1$, 2, ..., $k-1$, k, ..., n) that make up the SRP, the SRP is scientific if and only if there is at least one theoretical phase, T_k, such that it is empirically progressive with respect to it predecessor T_{k-1}. Of course, SRPs may exhibit many theoretical phases that are empirically progressive with respect to their predecessors, and so would make a large contribution to the growth of science, and thus the degree to which the SRP is scientific. The minimum requirement for an SRP to be scientific is that it has at least one empirically progressive phase. It makes it scientific in the strong sense that the SRP produces at least one novel fact during its lifetime. If it has no such phase at any point in its development, the SRP can be deemed to be unscientific. In such a case Lakatos talks of *empirical stagnation* in that the SRP produces no novel fact during its lifetime (even though it might have exhibited some theoretical progress).

Given the above we can now characterize a number of different kinds of what Lakatos calls *degenerating problem shifts*, which involve either stagnation or genuine degeneration. An example has just been mentioned, that of empirical stagnation. But *theoretical stagnation* can also arise when, in the move from T_i to T_{i+1}, there has not been any theoretical progression; both T_i and T_{i+1} have the same empirical content. *Theoretical degeneration* sets in when T_{i+1} has even less empirical content than its predecessor T_i (that is, T_i has some consequences that T_{i+1} does not have).

The final, and most serious, kind of degenerating problem shift arises when there are two rival SRPs, but only one of them is strongly empirically progressive in the sense that it uncovers many novel facts relevant to both SRPs. The other programme is not empirically progressive at all, and may even be stagnating or degenerating in the senses indicated above. It may be in this state because its heuristic has run out of steam and can no longer suggest new ways in which the SRP can be developed so that it is empirically progressive. However, the novel facts uncovered in its rival are importantly relevant to it. So adjustments are made to its positive heuristic so that the SRP can accommodate these facts, but in an *ad hoc* way. There is no rationale to the adjustments made to the heuristic to accommodate novel facts emerging from elsewhere other than that such adjustments make it possible to incorporate novel facts into the SRP. Such a phase of an SRP is said to be *empirically degenerate*.

Consider now the dynamic lifetime of an SRP with many theoretical phases making up the entire sequence. A sub-sequence at the beginning will commonly exhibit much theoretical and empirical progress. Its progress may be consistent over the sub-sequence, or it might be intermittent; however, at some point in the sub-sequence there should be some empirical progress. But later phases may slow down and exhibit only theoretical progress, or even theoretical stagnation (which again might be intermittent or consistent). Then the remainder of the SRP exhibits the decline characteristic of consistent stagnation or degeneration. A significant part of Lakatos's methodology of the appraisal of SRPs is to keep the record straight as to whether, at a given time, the SRP is progressive or degenerate.

The methodology of the appraisal of an SRP should be kept separate from more pragmatic matters such as the SRP a budding scientist should choose to work on in order to make progress in their research. Should young scientists only join SRPs that are exhibiting consistent empirical growth? Or should they join SRPs that, while not currently exhibiting growth, are expected to do so (for example, the situation for geologists in the 1950s with tectonic plate theory, which had yet to reveal its progressive character)? Or should they keep away from programmes that have signs of various kinds of degeneration? Perhaps what the programme needs is new blood with a creative flair for developing possibilities that might lie unrealized in its positive heuristic. Lakatos makes it clear that his methodology of SRPs does not claim to offer such pragmatic advice. Rather, it offers a novel way to assess the status of the programmes themselves. It assesses, for example, the progressive character of the SRP of the general theory of relativity after 1915 compared with the degenerating character of the Newtonian SRP, especially in respect of matters to do with the motion of the planet Mercury. How scientists might react to this assessment is another matter; but their reaction relies on an assessment of the status of the programme from a purely methodological point of view.

10.2.2 The metamethodology of SRPs

Like Popper, Lakatos recognized that there are theories of scientific method that rival his own methodology of SRPs; these include the rivals Popper recognized such as inductivism and conventionalism; but it also includes Popper's own critical rationalism, and sometimes the views of people such as Michael Polanyi, who deny that there is any explicit theory of method. How are such rival methodologies to be assessed? In some respects Lakatos's procedure resembles

Popper's procedure of §10.1.3. The methodology of SRPs is elevated to a Level 3 metamethodology to assess the rival theories of method at level 2, including his own. In proceeding in this way Lakatos would have to endorse a benign form of rule-circularity in using a version of the methodology of SRPs to assess all methodologies, including his own. But Lakatos makes some novel proposals that make his metemethodological approach distinct from Popper's. As already noted at the end of §10.1.3 Lakatos does not accept Popper's "quasi-empirical" test basis founded in some list of great science and disreputable science. Rather, his test basis is much better founded in the empirically discovered judgements, made by a scientific elite, about what are good and not so good moves in the game of science.

Lakatos proposes as his metamethodology a version of the methodology of SRPs but applied to the historiography of science. According to Lakatos many histories of science are written with some implicit theory of scientific method in mind. Each methodology will render episodes in the history of science rational by its own lights, thus providing an internalist explanation of why some episode occurred in the history of science. However, it will not be able to explain all aspects of all episodes, even some of those judged to be acceptable moves by the scientific elite. These will be relegated to an externalist approach to history of science in which the "irrational" leftovers are available for social or psychological explanation. The task of an SRP applied to the historiography of science will be to discover which of the various scientific methodologies yields the maximum number of episodes in the history of science that it makes rational by its own lights, that is, maximizes the internalist explanations of scientific change.

Just as an SRP requires that there be some empirical progress, that is, that it uncovers novel facts, in order for it to be dubbed "scientific", so a successful historiographical SRP will uncover some novel historiographical facts. The notion of novelty need not be confined to the discovery of previously unknown facts; it will also include the facts that were known but that get their first explanation within some new progressive SRP while rival SRPs of longer standing fail to explain them. The same applies to judgements made by the scientific elite; these can be novel in the sense that they get their first internalist explanation in terms of some scientific methodology while up to that time all other methodologies treated them as irrational leftovers available for psychosocial explanation. In terms of his own criteria for competing SRPs, Lakatos tells us to accept the SRP that is progressive with respect to its rivals. In the case of historiographical SRPs, we are to accept the SRP that is progressive in the sense that it renders rational (by its own lights) judgements of the scientific elite that no other historiographical SRP was able to render rational (by their own lights). As Lakatos puts it: "*progress in the theory of scientific rationality is marked by discoveries of novel historical facts, by the reconstruction of a growing bulk of value-impregnated history as rational*" (1978: 133).

Lakatos's procedure is to elevate his own Level 2 theory of method to Level 3 as a metamethodology and then assess all Level 2 methodologies according to whether or not they show empirical progress by rendering rational more of the historical changes in science. Here an important role is played by the basic value-judgements of the scientific elite about scientific change. Lakatos recognizes that no methodology will capture all such value-judgements. He argues that this raises a problem for Popper's critical rationalism when elevated to a metamethodology to adjudicate between rival methodologies; he argues that it gets falsified by its own meta-criterion. But he considers that this is not a problem for his own methodology of SRPs elevated to metamethodology (since it allows for progress in an ocean of anomalies): "*rational reconstructions remain for ever submerged in an ocean of anomalies. These anomalies will eventually have to be explained either by some better rational reconstruction or by some 'external' empirical theory*" (*ibid.*: 134).

The role played by the basic value-judgements of the scientific elite explains why Lakatos's metamethod is "quasi-empirical" and not *a priori* or conventionalist. The history of such judgements provides an empirical basis against which scientific methodologies are to be tested, using whatever meta-criterion of test. It has been assumed that such judgements are unproblematic and readily available. But are they? Lakatos cannot relegate all sociological considerations in science to external factors; some sociology is needed to survey the scientific elite to discover what are their judgements about particular moves in the game of science. Nor should it be assumed that there would be unanimity among the elite; a sociological survey might show that the views of scientists ranged from strong consensus to equal division for and against. Nor is it clear what the lowest threshold for agreement might be; if there is less than, say, 80 per cent agreement then some of the value-judgements might not be usable to decide important methodological matters. In addition allowance might have to be made if the scientific community were to change its views about some episode over time.

Finally, how is the scientific elite to be determined? We should not admit that all scientists can make value-judgements about all moves in all the sciences, including the many sciences with which they are not acquainted. Nor should we allow the elite to be chosen by the fact that they are *good* scientists, for what counts as good could well turn on whether they are appropriate users of some scientific methodology, the very matter over which the judgements of a scientific elite have been invoked in order to make adjudications. Nor should any methodology be invoked by the elite as the grounds on which their judgements are made on pain of similar circularity. Presumably philosophers are to be excluded from the ranks of the scientific elite since most of them are untutored in the ways of science; if this is the case then Popper's own list of heroic and disreputable science is hardly to be given the significance he gives it as a test basis.

The earlier Laudan of *Progress and Its Problems* also assumed that we have *"our preferred pre-analytic intuitions about scientific rationality"* (1977: 160) based on episodes in the history of science that are much more firm than any intuitions we have about the theories of scientific method that embody such rationality. But he later abandoned any such role for pre-analytic intuitions for some of the reasons given above, and others such as the following. The methodologies being judged are deprived of any substantive critical role; this is to be played by the intuitions, which no methodology should overturn. Nor is it clear that the intuitions will single out some preferred methodology above all others; it might well be the case that, given all the widely acceptable intuitions, methodologies as disparate as those advocated by Bayesians, Popperians, Lakatosians and Kuhnians might fit them equally as well. That is, in Quinean fashion our intuitions, which play a role similar to that of observations in science, might underdetermine methodologies in that two or more of them are tied for best fit with the intuitions (Laudan 1986).

In §12.2 we shall look at normative naturalism, the view developed by the later Laudan, in which an empirical approach is taken to the assessment of principles of method, but it does not depend on any judgements of a scientific elite so central to the "quasi-empirical" approaches of Popper and Lakatos. It also bypasses the need for particular judgements of the sort required by the metamethodology of reflective equilibrium (see §4.4). In this respect normative naturalism is superior in its metamethodological approach to the approaches of Popper, Lakatos and reflective equilibrium, mired as they are in the need to provide intuitions of some scientific elite about moves in the game of science. None may be found; and if they are they may have less than decisive weight when pitted against methodologies.

11. Kuhn and Feyerabend

In this chapter we discuss the methodological views of Thomas Kuhn and Paul Feyerabend, two philosophers of science who have had considerable impact on recent work on methodology. While both Kuhn and Feyerabend have a reputation as anti-methodologists and advocates of epistemological relativism, this is not an entirely accurate assessment of their views. Both oppose the idea that there is some single, invariant and binding method that provides scientists with an "algorithm" of theory-appraisal. Nevertheless, both continue to uphold a role for method in the pursuit of science. In the case of Kuhn we distinguish several phases of development of his account of method; and in the case of Feyerabend we argue that he is not the advocate of "anything goes", as is commonly thought.

11.1 Kuhn and methodology

11.1.1 Kuhn's theory of method in The Structure of Scientific Revolutions

Kuhn is best known for his model of scientific theory-change proposed in his influential and controversial book, *The Structure of Scientific Revolutions*, first published in 1962. This model has been interpreted by some commentators as containing the seeds of an anti-methodological view of science. It has also been widely understood as leading to a relativistic account of science. But, as we shall argue, Kuhn had a sustained interest in the methodology of science, even if his view of the nature of scientific method broke with traditional thinking on the subject. Moreover, despite the evident relativistic leanings of his position, he sought to distance his views from those of the thoroughgoing relativist. At both the levels of methodology and metamethodology, Kuhn continued to revise and develop his views throughout his career.

According to the model of science advanced by Kuhn in *The Structure of Scientific Revolutions*, research in any field of science is ordinarily conducted under the auspices of a single overarching theoretical framework, a so-called "paradigm", which reigns supreme in that field for a period of time. A paradigm is not simply a theory; it is the source of an agenda of research problems, of exemplars used to solve problems, of experimental techniques and evaluative standards. It provides scientists with a conceptual framework, as well as a way of perceiving the world. Scientists within a given scientific field typically pursue what Kuhn calls "normal science". This is research devoted to the solution of "puzzles", which arise in the course of applying the paradigm to the natural world. Normal scientific research is characterized by the regular and successful resolution of a broad range of research puzzles within the context of the accepted paradigm. However, over the course of time, problems arise in the attempt to apply the paradigm to nature, which resists solution within the framework of the paradigm. These constitute "anomalies", which, if they are particularly important or persist or mount up in number, may give rise to a "crisis" within the paradigm. As is not ordinarily the case during normal science, in a period of crisis scientists subject the paradigm to critical scrutiny and propose a number of alternatives so that there is no longer any dominant paradigm. A "scientific revolution" occurs when the community of scientists rejects the older paradigm, choosing instead to adopt an alternative theoretical framework as the new paradigm on which to base future normal scientific research. So far this model attempts to be descriptive of what happens in science; just how well it fits science is not a question we need answer here (see Hoyningen-Huene 1993: pt III).

Kuhn's conception of the basis of the deliberations that take place in a period of crisis and throughout a scientific revolution is of most immediate relevance to the methodology of science. Kuhn suggests in some places that standards of scientific theory appraisal depend on a paradigm. When one paradigm prevails, as it does in normal science, then there are common standards of theory appraisal; but standards undergo change in the transition from one paradigm to the next. As a result, paradigms are "methodologically incommensurable"; there are no shared standards from paradigm to paradigm. Kuhn also includes perceptual, conceptual and semantic variation in his characterization of the incommensurability that he claims to obtain between competing paradigms (Kuhn 1970a: 148–50), although we shall not go into these matters here.[1] Because of the incommensurability of competing paradigms, Kuhn describes the decision that scientists make between paradigms as more akin to a religious conversion or gestalt switch, suggesting that the decision is not one that may be made entirely on rational grounds: "The transfer of allegiance from paradigm to paradigm is a conversion experience that cannot be forced" (*ibid.*: 151).

There are a number of passages in *The Structure of Scientific Revolutions* that support anti-methodological, relativistic or even irrationalist readings of

Kuhn. In one passage, Kuhn employs a political metaphor to describe scientific revolutions. Writing of scientists who work in different paradigms, he says that "because they acknowledge no supra-institutional framework for the adjudication of revolutionary difference, the parties to a revolutionary conflict must finally resort to the techniques of mass persuasion, often including force" (*ibid.*: 93). Continuing the metaphor, Kuhn also suggests that the methods of evaluation in normal science do not carry over to the evaluation of rival paradigms:

> Like the choice between competing political institutions, that between competing paradigms proves to be a choice between incompatible modes of community life. Because it has that character, the choice is not and cannot be determined merely by the evaluative procedures characteristic of normal science, for these depend in part upon a particular paradigm, and that paradigm is at issue. When paradigms enter, as they must, into a debate about paradigm choice, their role is necessarily circular. Each group uses its own paradigm to argue in that paradigm's defence. (*Ibid.*: 94)

Later Kuhn describes paradigms "as the source of the methods ... for a scientific community" (*ibid.*: 103). These and other passages tell us that methodological principles might hold within a paradigm but that there are no paradigm-transcendent principles available. In light of such comments by Kuhn, it would appear that Lakatos was right to say of paradigm change that "*in Kuhn's view scientific revolution is irrational, a matter for mob psychology*" (Lakatos 1978: 91).

Not only does Kuhn seem to suggest that there are no principles of theory appraisal other than those internal to paradigm, he also seems to endorse a sociological account of the basis of principles of method, as well as a rhetorician's view of argumentation:

> As in political revolutions, so in paradigm choice – there is no standard higher than the assent of the relevant community. To discover how scientific revolutions are affected, we shall therefore have to examine not only the impact of nature and of logic, but also the techniques of persuasive argumentation effective within the quite special groups that constitute the community of scientists. (1970a: 94)

While this passage allows a role for "nature and logic", it suggests that the ultimate rationale for principles of method is social acceptance rather than rational justification. He also suggests that such acceptance can be brought about by rhetorical techniques of persuasion, rather than the objective, rational justifications commonly advocated by methodologists. Here Kuhn is right to emphasize the role that rhetoric can play on some occasions in bringing about theory accept-ance. But this is not necessarily inconsistent with, and can be complemented by, more objective and rational grounds advocated by methodologists, especially for those outside the rhetorical context in which rival views are contested.

In his book Kuhn does not always play down the role of methodology when he importantly tells us:

> there is another set of commitments without which no man is a scien-tist. The scientist must, for example, be concerned to understand the world and to extend the precision and scope with which it has been ordered. That commitment must, in turn, lead him to scrutinize ... some aspect of nature in great empirical detail. And, if that scrutiny displays pockets of apparent disorder, then these must challenge him to a new refinement of his observational techniques or to further articula-tion of theories. Undoubtedly there are still other rules like these, ones which have held for scientists at all times.   (*Ibid.*: 42)

Here Kuhn endorses the idea that there are some rules of method that hold at all times and for all scientists, and are not paradigm relative. Although not very specific, they concern understanding, observational precision (Kuhn always set great store on observational accuracy as a value), scope and the degree of order that our theories tell us prevails in the world. There is also a strong hint about the way in which observational precision can challenge our theories, but it is not entirely clear how this is to be done.

Following remarks already cited above Kuhn writes: "the issue of paradigm choice can never be unequivocally settled by logic and experiment alone" (*ibid.*: 94). While logic and experiment by themselves can play an important role in the growth of normal science the claim is that these by themselves are not sufficient for paradigm choice. There is a missing extra ingredient that is an important part of scientific rationality. So far the extra ingredient can involve persuasive argument and rhetoric or patterns of communal assent or dissent. But also important are the idiosyncratic weightings that each scientist gives to the values they endorse (see section 2.4). This is an important issue that we will take up in the next section.

In light of the passages quoted above, it is possible to extract from Kuhn's early work a view on which methods are relative to paradigms, and their justi-fication resides in factors that are subjective or "non-rational". This has formed the basis of an influential interpretation of Kuhn as a relativist in which there is no meta-justification for methodology beyond social acceptance. This inter-pretation has been widespread both among philosophers critical of such rela-tivism and sociologists who derive inspiration from it. But this is not always Kuhn's position even in his 1962 book. In the following sections we turn to

Kuhn's later work in which he further clarified his position in the light of these misunderstandings. We distinguish two further phases in which other views on method emerge.

11.1.2 Middle-period Kuhn: paradigm-independent values

By the time Kuhn came to write the "Postscript" for the 1970 edition of *The Structure of Scientific Revolutions*, he had effectively abandoned talk of paradigms in favour of talk of exemplars and disciplinary matrices. Values are one of the elements of a disciplinary matrix. Contrary to the impression given above, they are "widely shared among different communities" (1970a: 184). That is, scientists in different communities, who thereby work in different "paradigms", value theories because of such features as the following: they yield predictions (which should be accurate and quantitative rather than qualitative); they permit puzzle-formation and solution; they are simple; they are self-consistent; they are plausible (i.e. are compatible with other theories currently deployed); they are socially useful. These quite traditional notions turn out to be Kuhn's paradigm-transcendent criteria of theory choice. And later he added scope and fruitfulness. In middle-period Kuhn there is a strong endorsement of the idea of paradigm-independent values to be used in theory and paradigm choice, a position we have already set out in §2.4.

Kuhn's list of values does not include several important values that have been endorsed by other methodologists. Thus, Kuhn does not mention high degree of support of hypotheses by evidence on which inductivism and Bayesian confirmation theory place much emphasis. It has been suggested by Worrall (2000: 135–6) that this omission can be reconciled with Kuhn's views. Values such as accuracy, scope and fruitfulness can only be adequately understood in a context that takes into account confirmatory values. On the alethic value of truth, Kuhn gives it a role when it comes to the further values of predictive and observational accuracy. But he does not endorse it in connection with our theories and whether they tell us something about unobservable reality. These are matters we have spelled out in §2.4.

In §2.4 we also considered Kuhn's idea that scientists can have different understandings of what these values are; but it is a relatively simple matter to disambiguate these different understandings in a full account of the values one ought to endorse. More important is Kuhn's idea that each scientist can give each value an idiosyncratic weighting; this is something that allegedly undercuts the idea that there can be an algorithm for theory choice. This gives rise to the problem for Kuhn's theory of weighted values of how an individual is to aggregate the different values each endorses. And it also gives rise to the problem of how individual outcomes are to be aggregated for a community of scientists leading to either consensus or dissensus. Finally, we have argued in

§9.4 that many of the values that Kuhn endorses can be captured in a Bayesian framework.

We can now return to Kuhn's important claim, mentioned in the previous section, that "paradigm choice can never be unequivocally settled by logic and experiment alone" (1970a: 94). What is the extra ingredient in scientific method that goes beyond logic and experimentation? One extra ingredient is the weighting found in Kuhn's theory of idiosyncratically weighted values. The extra ingredient is the weighting. Since this can differ from scientist to scientist there is no one "algorithm" that they all use in making theory choices. As a result there may well be different choices that arise on Kuhn's model. Even though there is a rational procedure for the application of the model, it has an inescapable subjective element that undermines any stronger sense of scientific rationality.

Kuhn's criticism of many standard theories of method is that they suppose that there is just one "algorithm", which leads to the same choice of theory for all scientists, and this underpins an over-strong sense of objectivity and rationality in science. In supporting this view much depends on what one takes logic to be. Logic could be understood narrowly to be the rules of deductive or inductive logic. More broadly it could encompass the H-D method (see Chapter 7). Perhaps Kuhn's objection can best be seen as a critique of those who would see scientific method as being the H-D method alone. But as we have seen, even that method needs much supplementation by principles of confirmation and the like.

Perhaps Kuhn's target could be something like Carnap's theory of confirmation based on a theory of partial entailment. As we have noted in §1.6, Carnap's theory attempts to develop an account of c-functions that tell us, for given H and E, that there is some r such that $c(H, E) = r$ ($0 \leq r \leq 1$). But as we have also seen, there is much more to Carnap's theory of confirmation than this; he also develops a theory of method that tells us how to apply Carnapian probabilistic logic to particular hypotheses and evidence. For Carnap the extra ingredient to add to logic and experiment is a set of methodological principles for the application of his c-functions. These are akin to what we called M-principles in §3.1.

That scientific methods might be just logic and observation becomes something of a straw-man position when one considers the account of Popper's theory of method given in §10.1.2 (despite what Popper himself might have said at various times in giving too simple an account of his theory of method). In Popper's methodology of critical rationalism there are the two Kuhnian ingredients of experimental observations and logic, understood as rules of deduction (but not induction). But these must be supplemented by a host of rules of method that are proposed to realize Popperian aims of science and that govern the game of science. Without them there can be logic and observation but no scientific method. For Popper these extra methodological ingredients are objective and have a "rational" basis. Once again Popperian M-principles are the extra ingredient to be added to logic and observation.

Finally Kuhn's use of the term "logic" might also be taken to refer to the probability calculus. But as we have seen for subjective Bayesianism, the probability calculus by itself is not enough. To have any normative force probability needs to be understood as degrees of belief, and this must be supplemented by a theory of degrees of *coherent* belief based on considerations due to Dutch book arguments. Only then can the probability calculus provide a theory of method. In sum, few would hold that scientific method is just logic and experiment (or observation); there is a third ingredient that is an important part of any theory of scientific rationality, but there are differing views as to what this is.

Kuhn's target is the view that there is just one algorithm of theory choice, which leads to a unique choice of theory for all. His view is that there is no single algorithm that scientists use in theory choice and this leads to difference in choices. In contrast, Bayesians will maintain that there is a single algorithm, but this can still lead to different theory choices. Their single algorithm is the probability calculus, including Bayes's theorem. But there can be differences in the theoretical choices that scientists make, since each is free to assign whatever probabilities they like to hypotheses and evidence (providing they distribute them according to the probability calculus). In this sense Bayesians and Kuhn share the view that there is something ineradicably subjective in science, but they differ over what this is. For Bayesians it is the subjective, personal understanding of probability; for Kuhn it is idiosyncratic weightings of values. But Bayesians part company with Kuhn in that their kind of subjectivity does not always imply lack of objectivity. For Bayesians there is the possibility of "swamping priors" through a convergence of opinion for all scientists as evidence comes in; for Kuhn there is no such account of convergence available. While many can accept Kuhn's point that theory choice may not be just a matter of experiment and logic (however this is to be understood), the extra ingredient he offers of weightings is too subjective; this leads to the claim that Kuhn's account of scientific method leaves too much room for disagreement, subjectivity and irrationality.

Whether scientists do or do not make theory choices according to Kuhn's model of weighted values is a factual question to answer. But what does the model say about what we ought to do? And what is the normative, rational basis of the model? In particular why, if $T1$ exemplifies some Kuhnian value(s) while $T2$ does not, should we adopt $T1$ rather than $T2$? Kuhn's answer to the last metamethodological question is often disappointingly social or perhaps "intuitionistic" in character. In his 1977 paper Kuhn refers us to his earlier book, writing: "In the absence of criteria able to dictate the choice of each individual, I argued, we do well to trust the collective judgements of scientists trained in this way. 'What better criterion could there be', I asked rhetorically, 'than the decision of the scientific group …'" (1977: 320–21). As to why we ought to follow the model, Kuhn makes a convenient is–ought leap when he writes, in reply to a query from Feyerabend:

> scientists behave in the following ways; those modes of behaviour have (here theory enters) the following essential functions; in the absence of an alternative mode that would serve similar functions, scientists should behave essentially as they do if their concern is to improve scientific knowledge. (1970a: 237)

The argument is not entirely clear, but it appears to be inductive: in the past certain modes of behaviour (e.g. adopting Kuhn's model of theory choice) have improved scientific knowledge; so in the future one ought to adopt the same modes of behaviour if one wants to improve scientific knowledge. It would appear that Kuhn is offering a meta-inductive argument to justify his model; but as we shall see this was not his final view on metamethodological justification. These matters become important when we consider Kuhn's role in the historical turn in the philosophy of science in which the history of science is used to adjudicate between methodologies (see §4.5). It turns out that even though Kuhn puts great store on considerations based on the history of science, as for any other methodologist there is an issue for him of how his theory of weighted values is to be brought into relation with history of science.

The methodology proposed by Kuhn in his middle period is less prone to relativistic interpretation than the position originally suggested in *The Structure of Scientific Revolutions*. Because there is a set of core values shared throughout the sciences, rationality is no longer relative to variant paradigm-dependent standards. However, Kuhn did not entirely exorcise the spectre of relativism. For, according to Kuhn, the choice between conflicting theories is governed by a number of different values, each of which can be given a different weighting. On this account, the rationality of theory-acceptance is relative to the weighting and interpretation of the shared scientific values. Such weightings and interpretations can vary with respect to theory, social context, or even the personal idiosyncrasies of individual scientists. Thus, while Kuhn avoids relativism due to paradigm-dependent standards of evaluation, the problem of relativism reappears in the form of relativism due to variance of value-weighting and interpretation. There are no considerations available for Kuhn to show that, despite idiosyncratic weightings, there can be a prospect of convergence of opinion.

While the idea that scientific theory appraisal is multi-criterial has found favour among methodologists, the suggestion of an inevitable relativism continues to attract criticism. Some have sought to avoid the impression of relativism by embracing a notion of rational disagreement, which allows that scientists may have rational grounds for conflicting viewpoints. Some have proposed a theory of non-algorithmic judgement in which a significant role is played by scientists' capacity to reason in a manner that is not determined by algorithmic rules (see Brown 1988: ch. 4; Sankey 1997: ch. 8). Others have objected to the seemingly inescapable subjectivity implied by the variant weightings and interpretations of scientific values described by Kuhn. One influential approach has been that proposed by Laudan (1984: chs 3, 4), in which he attempts to show that it is possible to subject scientific values to rational evaluation within the context of a reticulated model of scientific rationality.

However, Kuhn did come to think that a justification was required for the values used in his model of theory choice; to this we now turn.

11.1.3 Late-period Kuhn and a metamethodology of values

Kuhn's views on the function of values in theory choice did not shift significantly in the later stages of his career. However, his metamethodological views about the justification of method did continue to evolve and emerged in a 1983 symposium paper "Rationality and Theory Choice" (reprinted in Kuhn 2000: ch. 9). In it Kuhn tells us that he is "venturing into what is for me new territory" (*ibid*.: 211).

A problem for Kuhn is in the shift from the use of his model of weighted values as an explanation of how scientists do in fact behave when they choose theories (this is a matter to be investigated empirically), to its use as a norm that justifies their behaviour. Consider the value of "puzzle-solving", which Kuhn takes to be the matching of a theory's predictions with experiment and observation; the number of matches and their closeness of fit yields a measure that enables us to say when one theory realizes this value better than another, that is, one theory solves more puzzles than the other. Why *ought* one to adopt puzzle-solving as a value? As a first step in an argument Kuhn writes:

> Clearly, a scientist who subscribed to this goal would be behaving irrationally if he sincerely said, "Replacing traditional theory X with new theory Y reduces the accuracy of puzzle solutions but has no effect with respect to the other criteria by which I judge theories; nevertheless, I shall select theory Y, setting X aside". Given the goal and the evaluation, that choice is obviously self-defeating.   (*ibid*.: 209)

And the same verdict of being self-defeating, and so irrational, can be reached in the case of other values such as simplicity, accuracy and so on. But all this shows so far is that there is a conflict between the choice one makes and the goal one professes. What one needs is a further argument as to why one ought to adopt such values in the first place; only then does one have grounds for the normative force of the value adopted, and so grounds for making theory choices in the light of that normatively sanctioned value. To make this argument Kuhn appeals to the local holism, or analyticity, of the word "science". But as we shall see, the meaning of the word "science", as specified in its holistic context, is a very thin gruel out of which to squeeze anything substantive about the normative force of the values he recommends.

The notion of local holism arises out of Kuhn's longstanding conception of theories in which theoretical terms are interlinked with one another to form a network of semantic connections. (Kuhn calls this a "lexicon", with its accompanying "lexical structure".) Also included in the network are the laws into which the terms enter. For Kuhn this is not only a doctrine about the meaning of the terms of a theory but also an account of how we learn a theory. To use Kuhn's example of Newtonian mechanics, the terms "force", and "mass" (and perhaps "acceleration", "space" and so on) form, within Newton's theory, a network of meaning connections. Also included in this network are laws, such as "$F = ma$", which further constrain the relations into which the terms can enter. It is a consequence of Kuhn's view that if the laws change sufficiently while the same terms are retained (as in the change from Newtonian to relativistic laws), then the network of interconnections of meanings (and even the referents of the terms) will alter. In this respect the holism is local to the theoretical context in which it occurs and does not hold globally for all terms and times of use.

Kuhn's holism is not so extensive that all the terms of a theory are so interlinked with one another; not all laws will enter into this network of interdefinitions of terms. Kuhn envisages (*ibid*.: 212) that we are to treat the law of universal gravitation as a contingent law whose terms will separately enter into the semantic networks mentioned, but this law itself is not part of the network. Which terms and which laws enter into the interconnections that characterize local holism, is an important issue, but not one we need explore further here. The main point is that, in Kuhn's view, for any theory some of its terms and some of their law-like relationships are central in specifying a local holism. What is of interest is the way in which Kuhn extends the notion of local holism for theories to the contexts in which the very word "science" occurs, thereby specifying its meaning holistically.

The term "science", says Kuhn, enters into a disciplinary cluster that is to be contrasted with other disciplinary clusters labelled "art", "engineering", "medicine", "law", "philosophy", "theology" and so on. Each cluster will bear similarities to and differences with other clusters. Importantly, none of these terms can be defined explicitly using some set of necessary and sufficient conditions; rather, each is defined by means of other terms in their respective clusters in the interdependent manner characteristic of local holism. And they have to be learned together, just like the terms of Newtonian mechanics. To learn the term "science", and to know what it means, one has to learn "its position within the acquired semantic field that also contains these other disciplines" (*ibid*.: 213). If these conjunctions and contrasts were to differ, the very meaning of a term such as "science" will be different because of the different holistic contexts in which it can occur. Kuhn then feels able to write that "in Greece before the death of Aristotle there was no entity quite classifiable as philosophy or as science" (*ibid*.).

It may be seriously doubted that the term "science" does have the local holism that Kuhn attributes to it with its alleged connections to, and contrasts with, a number of other disciplines that can vary over time producing new holistic connections. Whatever connections there may be between "science", "law" and so on, they are far too loose and weak to generate a locally holistic meaning for each term. Setting these objections aside, suppose we grant such holism for the term "science"; then there is one further step that Kuhn needs to make to justify his values:

> a speaker of the relevant disciplinary language may not, on pain of self-contradiction, utter statements like the following: "the science X is less accurate than the non-science Y" otherwise the two [i.e. X and Y] occupy the same position with respect to all disciplinary characteristics". Statements of that sort place the person who makes them outside of his or her language community. (*Ibid.*: 214)

In the previous example concerning puzzle-solving, X and Y were both a science; but, all other things being equal, X solved fewer puzzles than Y. If X is chosen then there is a contradiction between the goal one professes (increased puzzle-solving) and the theory choice one makes that goes against the professed goal. But is there such a clear contradiction in the case just mentioned? It is said that the less accurate X is a science while the more accurate Y is a non-science. If one were to make the same choice of X over Y, then, according to Kuhn, there is a semantic violation, and one "simply opts out of the scientific language game" (*ibid.*: 215). But are the alleged semantic rules robust enough to show that there is something odd in this case? It is hard to see what such rules might be like unless built into the very idea of a non-science is that it cannot be the kind of thing to which accuracy of any degree can apply; in contrast built into the idea of science is that it is something that admits of degrees of accuracy.

Kuhn alleges that there is no breach of a convention; nor is a tautology negated. Rather, "what is being set aside is the empirically derived taxonomy of disciplines" (*ibid.*: 214) that are associated with terms such as "science". Like many claims based, in the long run, on an appeal to a broad notion of analyticity (although Kuhn does not call it that[2]), or an appeal to meaning or to taxonomic principles, one might feel that Kuhn has indulged in theft over honest toil in reaching for such a metamethodological justification of the values he endorses. The metamethodological role that Kuhn gives to analyticity has close affinities to the appeal to analyticity that can be found in Strawson (1952: ch. 9, pt II) for the justification of induction. Finally there is also a further matter of a possible is–ought violation. It remains unclear in Kuhn's account of the local holism of "science" whether or not there is a normative element to be found. On the face of it there is none. But from the non-normative local holism of "science" we are meant to derive something about the justifiability of Kuhnian virtues, and this is norm-laden.

In one of his final papers, published in response to critics in 1993, Kuhn reiterates much the same position. He re-endorses the idea that there can be no science that does not involve at least some of the values he had long advocated. This makes such values a permanent fixture of all science that would be abandoned if science were to be abandoned. The basis of this claim turns once more on the analytic link of the values to the local holism of "science" that provides its definition:

> Accuracy, precision, scope, simplicity, fruitfulness, consistency, and so on, simply are the criteria which puzzle solvers must weigh in deciding whether or not a given puzzle about the match between phenomena and belief has been solved. Except that they need not all be satisfied at once, they are the "defining" characteristics of the solved puzzle. ... To select a law or theory which exemplified them less fully than an existing competitor would be self-defeating, and self-defeating action is the surest index of irrationality. Deployed by trained practitioners, these criteria, whose rejection would be irrational, are the basis for the evaluation of work done during periods of lexical stability, and they are basic also to the response mechanisms that, at times of stress, produce speciation and lexical change. As the developmental process continues, the examples from which practitioners learn to recognise accuracy, scope, simplicity, and so on, change both within and between fields. But the criteria that these examples illustrate are themselves necessarily permanent, for abandoning them would be abandoning science together with the knowledge which scientific development brings. (Kuhn 2000: 251–2)

His later claims about overarching scientific rationality are far removed from the earlier Kuhn, in which these values were paradigm-relative. Kuhn's views of paradigms and theory choice underwent a "paradigm change" in the course of Kuhn's exploration of these issues.

In sum, Kuhn's attempt to establish the rationality of his values through an attempted metamethodological justification fails on a number of counts. The first is the weak analogy between the local holism of the terms of Newtonian mechanics and the local holism of terms with which "science" is to be networked. Secondly, there is no clear contradiction in claiming that a non-science can be more accurate than a science. Theological claims are alleged by some to be accurate; but on Kuhn's taxonomy of disciplines this is not a science. Thirdly, the normativity of values such as accuracy, puzzle-solving and the like cannot be established on the basis of the descriptive character of the local holistic links of the word "science", unless that normativity is built into the very notion of science in the first place. However, Kuhn's (failed) attempt at a metamethodological justification, along with the values he endorses, does place his later work firmly within traditional philosophical concerns about scientific method.

11.1.4 Kuhn's rejection of the sociology of scientific knowledge

The early Kuhn has been inspirational for many sociologists of scientific knowledge but, as should already be evident, they have not followed the later Kuhn; and nor has Kuhn returned the compliment of endorsing their views on methodology. In a 1990 paper entitled "The Road Since *Structure*", Kuhn gave notice of a (still) forthcoming book that would reconcile his account of incommensurability with notions such as that of the rational evaluation of truth in a way that would not accommodate the views of sociologists of knowledge about theory choice:

> incommensurability is far from being the threat to rational evaluation of truth claims that it has frequently seemed. Rather, it's what is needed, within a developmental perspective, to restore some badly needed bite to the whole notion of cognitive evaluation. It is needed, that is, to defend notions like truth and knowledge from, for example, the excesses of post-modernist movements like the strong program.
>
> (Kuhn 2000: 91)

And in a 1991 address Kuhn distanced himself from "people who often call themselves Kuhnians" (*ibid.*: 106), and added: "I am among those who have found the claims of the strong program absurd: an example of deconstruction gone mad" (*ibid.*: 110). Kuhn's view here is even endorsed by Feyerabend (1993: 271). What Kuhn objects to is the way in which the theses of the strong programme are applied to all aspects of science:

> Interest, politics, power and authority undoubtedly do play a significant role in scientific life and its development. But the form taken by studies of "negotiation" has, as I've indicated, made it hard to see what else may play a role as well. Indeed, the most extreme form of the movement, called by its proponents "the strong program", has been widely understood as claiming that power and interest are all there are. Nature itself, whatever that may be, has seemed to have no part in the development of beliefs about it. Talk of evidence, of the rationality of claims drawn from it, and of the truth or probability of those claims has been seen as simply the rhetoric behind which the victorious party cloaks its power. What passes for scientific knowledge becomes, then, simply the belief of the winners. (*Ibid.*: 110)

Kuhn employs a version of the distinction between internal and external influences on science. Few would disagree with the claim that sociopolitical matters have an external effect on science. But are they also the only causes at work on internal aspects of science bringing about such effects as theory choice? If so, they would come into conflict with Kuhn's own model of weighted values for theory choice. In the above Kuhn invokes more than his usual list of weighted values; he also lists matters not explicitly mentioned before such as evidence, and the rationality of claims based on it, which lead to the truth or high probability of some hypothesis. Kuhn's and the sociologists' positions are merely presented as opposing viewpoints, with no argument in favour of one over the other. It is possible to reject both positions. We agree with Kuhn's criticisims of the strong programme and postmodernism; and as we have suggested in §9.4, the good points of the Kuhnian model can be captured within an overall Bayesian position.

11.2 Feyerabend: the methodological anarchist?

Given that Feyerabend is famous for alleging that the only universal principle of rationality is "anything goes", and for giving his books titles such as *Against Method*, or *Farewell to Reason*, it might come as a surprise to find that, in his autobiography completed just before his death in 1994, he makes the following claim on behalf of rationality: "I never 'denigrated reason', whatever that is, only some petrified and tyrannical version of it" (1995: 134). Or:

> science is not "irrational"; every single step can be accounted for (and is now being accounted for by historians ...). These steps, however, taken together, rarely form an overarching pattern that agrees with universal principles, and the cases that do support such principles are no more fundamental than the rest. *(Ibid.: 91)*

From Feyerabend's point of view, some think of a theory of method as fixed once and for all with universal principles applicable at all times and in all circumstances to all theories. Call this "Rationalism" with a capital R. (Perhaps Descartes's *Rules for the Direction of the Mind* (§3.3), Newton's "Rules of Reasoning in Philosophy" (§3.4) and Popper's rules (§10.1.2) are to be understood in this way.) Are there any such principles of method? Only one, Feyerabend notoriously tells us: "there is only *one* principle that can be defended under *all* circumstances and in *all* stages of human development. It is the principle: *anything goes*" (Feyerabend 1975: 28). But it turns out that this is not a principle of method he endorses. Rather, he says it is his Rationalist opponents who crave for such general principles of method; "anything goes" is the only principle that survives critical evaluation.

> But "anything goes" does not express any conviction of mine, it is a jocular summary of the predicament of the rationalist.
> (1978: 188; also 32, 39–40)

> As for the slogan "anything goes", which certain critics have attributed to me and then attacked: the slogan is not mine and it was not meant to summarise the case studies of *Against Method* ... (1987: 283)

> ... "anything goes" is not a "principle" I defend, it is a "principle" forced upon a rationalist who loves principles but who also takes science seriously. (*Ibid.*: 284)

> ... "anything goes" is not a "principle" I hold ... (1993: vii)

The joke has backfired, and has been costly in misleading many about Feyerabend's real position. If Rationalists want universal rules of method then, given that, according to Feyerabend, all such rules have counter-examples to be culled from the study of historical episodes, the only universal rule left "will be empty, useless and pretty ridiculous — but it will be a 'principle'. It will be the 'principle' 'anything goes'" (1978: 188).

But this is hardly convincing since Rationalists need not take up Feyerabend's invitation to adopt "anything goes". From "anything goes" Rationalists can infer (by instantiation) that every universal rule of method also "goes"; but if Rationalists also accept Feyerabend's claim that these have counter-examples and are to be rejected as universally applicable then, by *modus tollens*, Rationalists can infer that "anything goes" cannot be an acceptable rule of Rationalist method, even if jocularly imposed by Feyerabend on serious universalizing Rationalists. "Anything goes" does not mean what it appears to say; it is not even a principle of method that Feyerabend endorses. So it can be set aside.

Feyerabend's position can be captured by the following argument.

(1) If an episode in the history of science is rationally explicable then it must be in accordance with the principles of a Rationalist conception of method;

(2) most episodes in the history of science are not in accordance with Rationalist principles of method; so,

(3) much of science is irrational.

This is the valid argument of *modus tollens*; but is it sound? Feyerabend rejects conclusion (3), that much of science is irrational. But he accepts (2), the results of his historical investigations into science. So he must reject (1), the claim that Rationalist conceptions of method really do capture what counts as rational in science (and elsewhere). This leaves room for Feyerabend to express his position in a seemingly paradoxical way: there is rationality in science but no Rationality.

If Rationalist methods (whatever these may be) are to be rejected, then what are Feyerabend's views concerning rationalist methods? We shall claim that Feyerabend did endorse various scientific values, did accept rules of method (on a certain understanding of what these are) and did attempt to justify them using a metamethodology somewhat akin to a principle of reflective equilibrium. Our case will be largely based on the third edition of *Against Method*, which he tells us "merges part of *Against Method* [first edition of 1975] with excerpts from *Science in a Free Society* [Feyerabend 1978]" (1993: vii). Given Feyerabend's intellectual trajectory, there is a consistency in his views between the 1978 and 1993 books that should not be overlooked, but often is.

11.2.1 Feyerabend on values and methodological principles

One value that Feyerabend often endorses is growth in scientific knowledge (GSK). But this is not a value to be endorsed at all times and places. Feyerabend is often sceptical of the value of science and questions whether GSK is always a good thing and asks whether we might be better off without it, or with less of it, or with no GSK in particular domains. But granting GSK as a value, what rule(s), r, best realize it? That is, what hypothetical imperative of the form "if you want to realize value GSK, then follow rule r" should we adopt? According to Feyerabend there is no way of completing the schema so that there is some rule (or rules) r that we should always follow to realize GSK. If some rule r is not 100 per cent reliable in realizing GSK, then what degree of reliability does it have? It might have low reliability; or we might not know what reliability it has. Moreover, Feyerabend argues that the application of r may itself have conditions that we cannot always specify in advance, or even be aware of. In other words the rules, and the principles, of Feyerabendian method are not universal but are *defeasible* (see §3.1). Defeasibility is not a notion that Feyerabend discusses; but it is one that fits quite well with his conception of the role of rules and principles within scientific methodologies.

Reason, with its rules and values (whatever these might be for Feyerabend), is also something we can value. However, in the first edition of *Against Method*, Feyerabend thought that during the 1970s reason in the context of those times, was a value to be given a low weighting on his idiosyncratic scale (understanding this along the lines of Kuhn's model). But he warns: "There may, of course, come a time when it will be necessary to give reason a temporary advantage and when it will be wise to defend its rules to the exclusion of everything else". That time had come, according to the 1993 third edition, owing to the prevalence of, among other things, postmodernism (1993: 13 n.12). For Feyerabend, reason (with its rules) is a value, but only a weighted value, the weighting varying with person, time and circumstance; there is nothing about reason that is absolutely binding in some Kantian, or other, sense.

Feyerabend's Kuhn-like weighted-values approach can be found in both his earlier and later writings. According to Farrell (2003: §8.5.1) there are a number of values the later Feyerabend endorsed, but not always under their traditional names. Thus he values comprehensiveness, with which are associated values such as simplicity, generality and explanatory power. He views the empirical tradition as something, on the whole, to be valued; associated with this is the alethic value of empirical accuracy. He values tenacity in science because it may realize the Kuhnian value of fruitfulness. And finally, he values proliferation of theories, which is to realize the value of increasing the testability of the theories. Understood this way, Feyerabend's position is not all that radical and is close to Kuhn's. It turns on the idea of a set of weighted values, which gives one an orientation in a field of evaluative possibilities for theories. This is unlike rules understood as exceptionless directives that determine a single course of action. Values have a flexibility of application that rules, understood along the lines of the Ten Commandments, do not have. But if rules are not understood in this way but as defeasible then they, too, are flexible and give one a similar orientation in a field of evaluation possibilities for theories.

As an illustration of Feyerabend's commitment to the idea of principles of method in science, consider the principle of proliferation, which he seems to have endorsed at most times in his career.[3] This is a principle that Feyerabend thought had very wide application in social as well as scientific contexts; it is one of the themes of Mill's view on liberty and freedom of speech that he always endorsed (Feyerabend 1981: 139). The aim or value associated with the principle of proliferation is: "maximum testability of our knowledge". He gives no reason for adopting this value but does footnote a reference to Popper for a justification for it. Its associated rule is: "*Invent, and elaborate theories which are inconsistent with the accepted point of view, even if the latter should happen to be highly confirmed and generally accepted*" (*ibid.*: 105). And he adds: "Any methodology which adopts the principle will be called a *pluralistic methodology*" (*ibid.*: 106).

The challenge that Feyerabend's pluralism presents to more traditional conceptions of methodology is the idea that the value of maximizing testability cannot be realized by considering one theory at a time but only by several together. It might appear that the principle of proliferation is inconsistent with the value of conservatism. This might be so for fainthearted conservatives who remain content with their current theories. But activist conservatives could adopt a principle like the principle of proliferation; in ensuring that their current theory is epistemically worthy they might also wish actively to explore alternatives to ensure that their theory is not to fall too easily to a rival. However, it is not clear how the principle of proliferation is to be justified; the justification cannot be *a priori* unless there is a proof that following the rule will in fact lead to the specified value, or that it is the only way to realize it.

Should we adopt Feyerabend's rule? Note first that there is a rival rule: Newton's Rule 4 (§3.4), which bans imagining and employing rival hypotheses and tells us to stay with the method of induction from the phenomena. In fact in each of his four rules Newton recommends a kind of parsimony of hypothesis formation. So here we have rival rules to achieve the same valued end of maximum testability. In contrast Bayes's theorem (version 4; §8.2) requires that a set of exhaustive and exclusive hypotheses needs to be considered in assessing the evidential support, or lack of it, that any hypothesis gets. Although Feyerabend appears to make no mention of Bayes's theorem, much of what he says about the principle of proliferation and its role in evidential testing can be set in a Bayesian context.

Consider a more specific formulation of the principle of proliferation. As expressed, it applies to some theory T that is already highly confirmed. One might well ask how it got highly confirmed in the first place. To get highly confirmed, either the principle of proliferation had already been invoked or it was not. If not, then it would appear that we do not need the principle of proliferation. There is the quite traditional H-D method, which can provide tests of theories, one theory at a time; no rivals to T are required to provide this test of T. So T might have been highly confirmed in H-D fashion without the need to invoke other rival theories as required by the principle of proliferation. Since the H-D method can be subsumed under Bayes's theorem, then the same considerations can also apply to a Bayesian approach. However, Bayesianism is a quite general approach, which can encompass the point just made as well as Feyerabend's more general considerations about the principle of proliferation.

The principle of proliferation requires us to maximally test T. What it says is that the only way to do this is by inventing and elaborating rivals to T (a very Bayesian point). Call the set of these "$\{T\}^*$". Now, talk of inventing and elaborating is hardly enough; we have to propose all of the $\{T\}^*$, draw out all their logical consequences (presumably when applied in some circumstances), and compare these with one another, and particularly with those of T. What the principle of proliferation says is that *only* when we do all of this will we be able to maximally test T; there is no other way of maximally testing T. Now it is true that in some cases there may be some empirical fact F that is evidence relevant for the testing of T. (Here we can note the Feyerabendian point that in some cases we may even know of fact F but do not realize that it is evidence relevant to T.) But it is possible that F only comes to our notice as relevant evidence when the rivals in $\{T\}^*$ are examined and yield F as a consequence. Importantly, T plays no role in disclosing that F is relevant to T. On further developing T, either F

becomes supporting evidence for T or T is refuted by F. On several occasions Feyerabend cites an example of this that arose within thermodynamics concerning the theory of the motion of Brownian particles. These particles give rise to the possibility of a "perpetual motion machine" and this provides grounds for testing, and thereby refuting, the second law of a phenomenological version of thermodynamics, something that could not have been uncovered by the phenomenological theory alone but needed the development of a rival statistical theory of thermodynamics to be realized.[4]

Now we do not deny that the above can occur. What is denied is that this is the *only* way of increasing the degree of testability of T. There are alternatives. One alternative is the use of H-D methods for the test of T; in this case no rival to T is invoked. Or if other theories are invoked they can be consistent with T and need not be rivals as the principle of proliferation requires. One example of this is the following. The test of one of the consequences of Einstein's general theory of relativity, namely, the bending of electromagnetic waves as they pass through gravitational fields, was originally done in 1919 using the bending of light waves around an eclipsed sun; but it contained unacceptably high experimental errors. Much later, with the development of not just theory, as Feyerabend mentions, but experimental techniques as well, further testing became possible. The scientific developments involved a combination of radio astronomy, the theory of radio waves, the development of radio interferometry and the discovery of quasars as sources of waves. All of these developments were consistent with Einstein's general theory; together they enabled much more accurate observations of the deflection of electromagnetic waves in a gravitational field, and thereby an increase in the testability of the general theory.[5] Here the goal of the principle of proliferation is realized but not by the means of its rule of proliferation. (This example can fit with Bayes's theorem by including information about background theories, as in version 2; §8.2.)

In sum, increasing or maximizing the testability of theory T can be done without invoking rival theories. Or if other theories are invoked to realize the value, as in the Einstein example, they need not be rivals that are inconsistent with T. And there are cases in which examining inconsistent rivals does increase the testability of T, and even might maximize it. But these possibilities should not be restricted by proposing a rule that requires, as a necessary condition for the (maximal) testing T, the presence of inconsistent rivals to T. As has been pointed out, contemporary methodologies that Feyerabend does not consider, such as Bayesianism, can encompass all of these cases. For these theories it is routine that rivals to T, along with considerations about background theories, are involved in any evidential test of T, and not just for maximizing testability. Since employing rivals to T is simply part of such methods of Bayesian testing, there is no need to invoke distinct principles such as the principle of proliferation.

11.2.2 Feyerabend on principles of method and their defeasibility

We have seen that for Feyerabend values do play a central role in his conception of scientific method. He is much more critical of the idea that there are principles of method, either categorical imperatives or hypothetical imperatives, in which rules are proposed as means to the realization of values. In what follows we shall focus on rules that are hypothetical imperatives or means–ends principles of method; but what is said here of rules can be extended to all principles of method. As noted, Feyerabend is opposed to the following idea of Rationality:

> (I) There is a universal rule (or small, unified set of rules) of scientific method/rationality, *R*, such that for all moves in the game of science as it has historically been played out in all the sciences, the move is an instance of *R*, and *R* rationally justifies the move.

His opposing position can be easily expressed by shifting the order of the quantifiers in (I) from "there exists – all" to "all – there exists", and then adding a qualification about the nature of the principles. Call this doctrine "rationalism" with a lower-case "*r*".

> (IIa) For each move in the game of science as it has been historically played out in all the sciences, there is some distinct rule (or set of rules) contained in the principles of scientific method/rationality, *r*, such that the move is an instance of *r*, and *r* rationally justifies the move.[6]

It is assumed in (IIa) that there are distinct rules, $r_1, r_2, r_3, \ldots$ only one (or a few) of which is (are) employed in any episode in the history of science; it is not intended that they be conjoined, in which case (IIa) would hardly differ from (I). (IIa) leaves open two extreme possibilities: that a different rule is needed for each of the moves, or the remote possibility that there is still one universal rule that covers all the moves. Feyerabend's position is more particularist and closer to the first alternative. There might be principles that cover a few moves, but the principles are so contextually limited that they will not apply to a great number of other moves and other rules will have to be invoked. Feyerabend also has an account of the nature of these rules:

> (IIb) Rules of method are highly sensitive to their context of use and outside these contexts have no application; each rule has a quite restricted domain of application and is defeasible, so that other rules (similarly restricted to their own domain and equally defeasible) will have to apply outside that rule's domain. (Feyerabend often refers to these as "rules of thumb".)

Direct support for claims (IIa) and (IIb) comes from Feyerabend's response to critics of the 1975 *Against Method,* and in his restatement of his position in part I of his 1978 *Science in a Free Society,* which was incorporated into the 1993 third edition of *Against Method.* Feyerabend contrasts two methodological positions: *naive anarchism,* with which his own position should not be confused (presumably Feyerabend is a sophisticated anarchist); and another version of Rationalism, which he dubs *idealism,* in which there are absolute rules, but they are conditional with complex antecedents that spell out the conditions of their application within the context of some universal Rationalist methodology. Of naive anarchism he writes:

> A naive anarchist says (a) that both absolute rules and context depend-ent rules have their limits and infers (b) that all rules and standards are worthless and should be given up. Most reviewers regarded me as a naive anarchist in this sense overlooking the many passages where I show how certain procedures *aided* scientists in their research. For in my studies of Galileo, of Brownian motion, of the Presocratics I not only try to show the *failures* of familiar standards, I also try to show what not so familiar procedures did actually *succeed.* I agree with (a) but I do not agree with (b). I argue that all rules have their limits and that there is no comprehensive "rationality", I do not argue that we should proceed without rules and standards. I also argue for a contextual account but again the contextual rules are not to *replace* the absolute rules, they are to *supplement* them.   (1978: 32; 1993: 231)

Thesis (b) marks the crucial difference between naive anarchism and Feyerabend's own position; moreover, the denial of (b) shows that Feyerabend cannot be an arch irrationalist. There *are* rules worth adopting, but not those commonly advocated. Oddly enough, universal rules are not to be replaced but are to be supplemented. What this means is unclear; but it might be understood in the following way. Consider as an example of a universal rule Popper's "do not adopt *ad hoc* hypotheses" (which is to realise the value of advancing knowl-edge). For Feyerabend this is not to be understood as a universal ban that applies to all sciences and in all circumstances come what may. Sometimes adopting *ad hoc* hypotheses will realize our values (advancing knowledge) better than not adopting them. Feyerabend seems to suggest that alongside this universal rule are other rules (supposedly equally open to supplementation) about its appli-cation. The task of these other rules will be to specify the occasions when we should, or should not, adopt this Popperian rule. What Feyerabend needs is the notion of a defeasible rule, but defeasibility is not something he ever discusses. If rules are defeasible, then Rationalists with universalizing tendencies will not be able to apply their rules regardless of their situation. Viewed in this light the passage cited above supports the position outlined in (IIa) and (IIb), as do other similar passages in his writings.[7] The passage does not support the view that Feyerabend rejects scientific method; rather, he proposes a revised view of it in which methodological principles are not universal but defeasible.

In the passages surrounding the long quotation above, Feyerabend distinguishes between a modified rationalism that he calls "idealism", in which universal rules are said to be conditional and have antecedents that specify the conditions of their application, and his own view, in which rules are contextual and defeasible. Presumably the difference is that for Rationalist "idealists" the conditions of application of the rules are fully spelled out in the very specific antecedents of conditional rules. But in Feyerabend's view such conditions cannot be fully set out in some antecedent in advance of all possible applications of the hypothetical rule; at best such conditions are open-ended and never fully specifiable. So Feyerabend opts for a notion of a rule that is not conditional in form but categorical, and is best understood as contextual and defeasible. So even if rules appear to be universal, as in "do not adopt *ad hoc* hypotheses", there will always be vagueness and imprecision concerning their application. There is also no mention of the conditions under which they can be employed or a time limit imposed on their application; presumably this task is to be left to supplementary rules.

11.2.3 Feyerabend's attempted justification of principles of method

Given that one can adopt defeasible principles and remain a rationalist about method (but not a Rationalist), Feyerabend does not appear to be the opponent of theories of scientific method that he is often made out to be, or says that he is. Granted such Feyerabendian principles, what does he say about their justification? There are two approaches. The first would be to take some principle that Feyerabend advocates (such as the principle of proliferation or rules of counter-induction) or some principle he criticizes (such as the alleged principle of consistency or Popper's anti-*ad hoc* rule) and attempt to evaluate them either on logico-epistemological grounds or on the historical record of the decision context of various scientists. But the latter would take us into a long excursion through episodes in the history of science, and the former has to some extent been carried out.[8] Instead we shall look at Feyerabend's metamethodological considerations in justification of his views on scientific methodologies.

If we are to attribute to Feyerabend a metamethodology concerning his defeasible rules, then it veers between that of a Protagorean relativist and that of a dialectical interactionist, in which principles and practice inform one another. In setting out his position he adopts the Popperian notion of a rational tradition[9] that can be applied to mythical and scientific systems of belief. But he also uses the term "tradition" more broadly to include religion, the theatre, music, poetry and so on. In speaking of the rational tradition he does not, unlike Popper, privilege it by claiming some special privileged "higher-order" status for it. For Feyerabend, all traditions, including the critical or rational tradition, are on an equal par. In resisting the idea that there is a special status to be conferred on the rules that constitute the tradition, Feyerabend adopts a Protagorean relativism about traditions. He makes three claims about traditions:

(i) *Traditions are neither good nor bad, they simply are.* ... rationality is not an arbiter of traditions, it is itself a tradition or an aspect of a tradition. ...

(ii) *A tradition assumes desirable or undesirable properties only when compared with some tradition.* ...

(iii) *(i) and (ii) imply a relativism of precisely the kind that seems to have been defended by Protagoras.* (1978: 27–8; 1993: 225–6)

For Feyerabend there still remains a rational tradition with its contextual defeasible rules, which can be used to evaluate claims in other traditions (which in this context we can take to include not only the principles of any scientific methodology but also any metamethodology that attempts to justify any such principles). But given his Protagorean relativism about traditions, all such evaluations are from *within* some tradition and are directed at some other tradition. There is no absolute tradition, encapsulated in some metamethodology, that stands *outside* all other traditions and from which we can evaluate them. In this sense no tradition is an absolute arbiter of any other. Putting it another way, there is no privileged or *a priori* story to be told about the justification of our principles of method.

What does this mean for the contextual and defeasible rules of method that Feyerabend endorses? Perhaps it means that such rules of method have no further justification other than that they are what we have simply adopted as part of *our* critical tradition. Their truth, validity or correctness is at best relative to our tradition; there is no further metamethodological account of their status to be given by appealing to some absolute or privileged tradition of Rationality. It is this relativism that has led some to claim that Feyerabend, even if he admits there are defeasible rules of method, is at heart an irrationalist. But this is too strong a claim. Rather Feyerabend is akin to Wittgenstein in this respect in claiming that these are our practices, and there is nothing behind them that could act as a justification of them.

Although there is a strong streak of relativism in Feyerabend, there is also a pluralist streak, which is not to be confused with relativism. A pluralism about rules and the traditions they embody need not entail any relativism. But what pluralism still excludes is any attempt to invoke metamethodology to give an *a priori*, or even an empirical, justification of defeasible rules of method. Also pluralism does make possible the critical "rubbing together" of different traditions, something that Feyerabend would endorse given his principle of proliferation (but applied to rival methodologies). It does make possible a more dialectical view of the interaction between traditions, rules and practices. It is this critical "rubbing together" of different traditions through their "dialectical interaction" that allows us to say that there remains a whiff of metamethodological evaluation for Feyerabend.

How does Feyerabend's dialectical interactionism differ from the above kind of relativism commonly attributed to him? There are remnants of the positions of the later Popper and Lakatos, with their appeal to the intuitions of a scientific elite, in Feyerabend's talk of the interaction between reason and practice, of which he distinguishes three aspects. First, he acknowledges that reason can be an independent authority that guides our practices in science, a position he dubs "idealistic". But also "reason receives both its content and its authority from practice" (1978: 24; 1993: 222), a position he dubs "naturalism". Although he does not say how reason gets its authority, his position is one in which a strong role is given to intuitions about good practice. This is reminiscent of the later Popper, Lakatos, and even the metamethod of reflective equilibrium advocated by Goodman. But both naturalism and idealism have their difficulties, says Feyerabend. Idealists have a problem in that too ideal a view of rationality might cease to have any application in our world. And naturalists have a problem in that their practices can decline because they fail to be responsive to new situations and need critically to re-evaluate their practice. He then canvasses the suggestion "that reason and practice are not two different kinds of entity but *parts of a single dialectical process*" (1978: 25; 1993: 223).

But Feyerabend finds that the talk of reason and practice being separate "parts" of a single process draws a misleading distinction; so he concludes: "*What is called 'reason' and 'practice' are therefore two different types of practice*" (1978: 26; 1993: 224). The difference between the two *types* of "practice" is that one is formal, abstract and simple, while the other is non-formal, particular and submerged in complexity. Feyerabend claims that the conflict between these two types of practices recapitulates "all the 'problems of rationality' that have provided philosophers with intellectual … nourishment ever since the 'Rise of Rationalism in the West'" (1978: 26–7; 1993: 225). As true as this may be at some level of abstraction, Feyerabend's shift to a position of dialectical interactionism with its additional plea for a principle of proliferation with respect to interacting traditions (including traditions about theories of method), does have the characteristics of an appeal to some metamethodological theory.

For Feyerabend there is always the dialectical task of bringing our practices (in science and elsewhere) into line with our theories of those practices (i.e. our theories of method); and, conversely, of bringing our theories into line with our practices. In this respect he can be viewed as an advocate of the methodology of reflective equilibrium in which an attempt is made to bring particular practices and general principles into accordance with one another (see §4.4 on this meta-method). But he would not claim that there is a fixed, permanent equilibrium point; rather, any achieved or near equilibrium point would be temporary and would shift as the history of scientific practices and proposals about new principles evolve alongside our evolving sciences. Looked at this way, we can resist the temptation to go relativist by viewing the activity of bringing the rules of "reason" and the particularity of "practice" into accordance with one another as yet just one more activity on a par with any other activity. Rather, this activity is a substantive one that is part of assessing the principles of our second-order critical tradition. In this respect Feyerabend adopts a somewhat different position from that of Wittgenstein (as suggested above) in that our practices do admit criticism through "dialectical interactionism" and are not beyond criticism (although it is clear that even this is just one more practice, although a meta-practice). In adopting this approach one needs to be both a methodologist and a historian of science in bringing together, in "dialectical interaction" or "reflective equilibrium", both methodology and practice.

In conclusion, can Kuhn and Feyerabend be viewed as philosophers of science who stand outside the methodological tradition and attempt to overturn it? No. Both have recast in some ways our conception of what that methodology ought to be like by correcting over-simple accounts of the role of rationality in the growth of scientific knowledge. As different as their views might be from others within the tradition, there is no strong case for claiming that they have abandoned methodology or rationality altogether. In the case of Kuhn this is quite clear in his later writings. The case of Feyerabend is harder to determine. But on one interpretation he does say that there are defeasible principles of method, and there is always the task of bringing practice and principles together to prevent both the decline of practice through lack of criticism, and our principles becoming too abstract and irrelevant. And these two aspects of his work, despite its other maverick aspects, are common to those who do view themselves as members of the methodological tradition.

V. Naturalism, pragmatism, realism and methodology

12. Naturalism, pragmatism and method

The broad philosophical project of naturalism can be extended to theories of scientific methodology. Initially it might seem implausible that normative matters, whether of rationality and principles of method or of morality, should find a place within any kind of philosophical naturalism, which, on the face of it, is non-normative in character. So, what is naturalism and how does it resolve this *prima facie* problem? Naturalism comes in two broad varieties, metaphysical (or ontological) and methodological. The metaphysical doctrine can be expressed in various ways. The first way is that the only entities that exist are those that have a location within the spacetime system; there are no entities outside it. A second way is that what exists is whatever is postulated in the various sciences such as electromagnetic waves, DNA, pulsars or the sociologist's anomie. Some argue that numbers and sets are ineliminable postulates of mathematics used in science, and then they point out that numbers and sets are abstract objects and are not locatable within the spacetime framework; so the second kind of naturalism must be broader than the first and contains abstract items outside the spatiotemporal. Here we need not enter into disputes about the more precise characterization of metaphysical naturalism.

The other variety of naturalism is methodological; this is the view that our methods of enquiry are just those of the sciences. Some take the view that there are no methods worthy of the name outside those of science. Others claim that there is a seamless connection between our ordinary methods of enquiry and scientific methods, and the latter are just an extension of the former. Some also wish to add that there are no substantive non-empirical or *a priori* methods; all methods are to have some kind of empirical basis. Some pragmatists adopt this view. But other pragmatists reject any kind of distinction between the empirical and the *a priori*; so there are no broad categories into which principles of method can be placed. There is a seamless fabric of belief encompassing the sciences and their methods.

The problem mentioned at the beginning now emerges in reconciling methodological naturalism with the all-encompassing metaphysical naturalism. What grounds the norms of scientific method? Is there a realm of *sui generis* normative fact to which our norms are answerable? If so, then it would appear that there is an autonomous Platonic realm of normative fact beyond metaphysical naturalism. This is a quite strong version of the unbridgeable "is–ought" gap that is intolerable to metaphysical naturalists. They are conscious of the need to give some account of the normativity and justification of principles of method within the metaphysical naturalist framework of science itself; these are not to be understood as lying outside that framework. There are broadly two approaches to resolving this issue: locate or eliminate.

The first of these approaches locates normative principles of method within the metaphysical naturalistic framework of science without ontological addition. Various ways have been proposed for doing this, the details of which will emerge subsequently. Eliminative tendencies prevail when there seems to be no way of locating the problematic items within a naturalist framework. This is especially the case for sociology of scientific knowledge. Their doctrines move between two positions. The first is a nihilism about principles of method; there are really no such principles because the actual practices of scientists, as they understand them, do not reveal any such principles. The second is that if there are such principles, they have to be stripped of their normative force and treated as locatable items within the naturalistic framework of science. This is because the sociologists (wrongly) understand the norms of reason to be an intrusion on the natural order. Such norms are banned by one of the central "symmetry" tenets of Bloor's strong programme: "The symmetry requirement is meant to stop the intrusion of a non-naturalistic notion of reason into the causal story. It is not designed to exclude an appropriately naturalistic construal of reason, whether this be psychological or sociological" (Bloor 1991: 177). For such naturalistically inclined sociologists of scientific knowledge, all thinkers are to be treated as natural reasoners, even in the case of scientists. But for some this is a quite severe way of locating normative principles of method within the natural; the baby of normative rules of method has been thrown out with the bathwater muddied by non-naturalistic items.

Many philosophers of science see themselves as pursuing a broadly naturalistic agenda. Quine developed what has become known as "naturalized epistemology", which is to be accompanied by a naturalized account of the methods of science. We shall discuss Quine's account of scientific method in the next section. Quine says little that is novel about methodological principles. His main contribution is metamethodological in placing methodology and epistemology within the framework of naturalism. Just how successful he has been in this metamethodological task remains unclear. Other naturalists take on board not just the results of empirical science but also the actual practices of scientists themselves. They draw extensively on the history of science to determine what these practices are. An influential approach along these lines is the normative naturalism of Laudan. It also addresses the question of how the normativity of method can be reconciled with the empirically determined actual practice of science (see §12.2). In the final section we shall consider the closely related methodological pragmatism of Rescher.

12.1 Quine and naturalized methodology

Quine adopts a rather traditional account of the principles of method. Often he assumes something like the H-D method accompanied by standard views of confirmation and disconfirmation. In respect of falsification his views are quite close to those of Popper. Although he does not spell it out in any detail, he supposes, contrary to Popper, that there is some theory of positive support from evidence. But observational evidence alone cannot justify theories even though it can refute them. In a section of *Pursuit of Truth* called "Test and Refutation", Quine tells us:

> It is clearly true, moreover, that one continually reasons not only in refutation of hypotheses but in support of them. This, however, is a matter of arguing logically or probabilistically from beliefs already held. It is where the technology of probability and mathematical statistics is brought to bear. Some of those supporting beliefs may be observational, but they contribute support only in the company with others that are theoretical. Pure observation lends only negative evidence, by refuting an observational categorical that a proposed theory implies.
>
> (1992: 13, §1.5)

From the above, Quine's account of how observation bears on theory can be set out as follows. Let T be a theory, O_1 be observational input and O_2 be observational output such that $(T \& O_1) \vdash O_2$ (i.e. O_2 is a logical consequence of $(T \& O_1)$). This is equivalent to $T \vdash (O_1 \supset O_2)$, where "$(O_1 \supset O_2)$" is what Quine calls an *observational categorical* if O_1 then O_2. Any theory will have as logical consequences a large number of observational categoricals. If the observational categorical is false, $O_1 \& \neg O_2$, T is deductively shown to be false. But in Quine's view, in arguing from the truth of an observational categorical to the support of a theory, matters are not so simple; observational reports are not enough. Here the metaphor of the "technology" of probability and statistics is invoked without saying more about how observational conditionals provide positive support for hypothesis T. We shall return to this metaphor since Quine puts it to crucial work elsewhere.

Quine also champions a number of non-evidential virtues (some of which were discussed in §2.3). In *Word and Object* he crisply tells us: "Scientific method was vaguely seen ... as a matter of being guided by sensory stimuli, a taste for simplicity in some sense, and a taste for old things" (1960: 23). The taste for old things is an aspect of his virtue of conservatism in which the old and familiar are employed as far as possible and used to construct our explanations and predictions.

In Quine's overall philosophy method is given a crucial role: "scientific method, whatever its details, produces theory whose connection with all possible surface irritations consists solely in scientific method itself, unsupported by ulterior controls. This is the sense in which it is the last arbiter of truth" (*ibid.*). Here is a quite clear statement that what gets us from the surface irritations of stimuli to the verbal output of theory is nothing but scientific method, whatever it is. A large burden is placed on the notion of scientific method not only to come up with theory, but also to come up with theory that is true. A requirement placed on our scientific methods is that they are to be reliable for the truth; presumably if not, and we discover this, we are to discard them for some other principles of method. In part this is the story of our developing technology, whatever it is, of probability and statistics; these, along with methods of support and refutation accompanied by non-evidential values give us a theory of scientific method.

Even though Quine has little to contribute at the level of methodology that is novel, what is of interest is the naturalistic stance that he adopts towards epistemology, and thus the conception of metamethodology that it entails. This will be our main focus.

Quine's methods have much to do with the dynamics of theory revision. He advocates a form of epistemological holism often expressed in his repeated use of the metaphor of Neurath's boat (e.g. Quine 1969: 84, 127), which we must renovate while we remain afloat at sea; there is no dry dock to externally secure the boat during renovation. In light of such all-encompassing holism, not only the sciences but also its principles of method along with logic are all part of a seamless web of belief, like the planks of a boat. Any of these are open to revision if lack of fit arises between the system of beliefs and our experiences (more strictly our reports of experience). If we pursue the boat analogy we might want to distinguish the superstructure of a boat, which is easily modified, from its hull, which is much harder to modify, and both of these from its keel, which is very difficult to modify. Analogously there can be different degrees of entrenchment of different kinds of belief within the system of beliefs. In principle none are immune to revision but keel-like beliefs are to be preserved as far as possible. Are our methodological principles akin to keel-like beliefs in that we revise them only as a last resort? Or do we keep them come what may and not revise them at all? Making them immune to revision need not be tantamount to treating them as *a priori*. If revisions elsewhere do not restore overall "fit" between our systems of beliefs (including methodology), then we might resort to revising our principles of logic, as Quine suggests we could do. But can this be extended to even our principles of method?

Any revisions we make in methodology could only be piecemeal and not wholesale if the overall "Neurath's boat" metaphor is to be maintained. Even with piecemeal change some methodological principles might be exempt from revision. If revisions are needed due to the lack of "fit" between our system of beliefs and experience, then presumably some methodological principle of conservatism about change, or a maxim of minimum mutilation, or of reflective equilibrium, will play an important role in determining how we are to remove lack of fit. If these principles were not exempt from revision then it might be hard to see how important elements of the holistic picture could still be maintained. Without methodological guidance there would simply be a lurching from one system of belief to another with no apparent rationale. Even the requirement of "fit" or overall coherence takes us into the province of meta-methodology in which there is at least some meta-principle (or a meta-value) of overall consistency and/or degree of coherence across our total web of belief. So it would appear that some stable principles of metamethodology must always be available for any rationale for change.

Accompanying Quine's holism is the radical view that there is no first philosophy on the basis of which we can make a metamethodological stand in, say, analyticity, or *a priori* knowledge, or whatever (although the requirements of consistency and coherence, along with a H-D model of testing, are necessary if the holistic picture is to be preserved). As Quine puts it elsewhere:

> I see philosophy not as an *a priori* propaedeutic or groundwork for science but as continuous with science. I see philosophy and science as in the same boat – a boat which, to revert to Neurath's figure as I often do, we can rebuild only at sea while staying afloat in it. There is no external vantage point, no first philosophy.   (1969: 126–7)

If we take methodology to be included in philosophy then it, too, is continuous with science, and like science must be open to revision, although the extent of its revisability remains problematic.

The naturalistic approach tends to deflate epistemological and methodological pretensions; this is well expressed by Quine in a number of places. Consider, first, his "Five Milestones of Empiricism", the fifth being: "naturalism: the abandonment of the goal of first philosophy. It sees natural science as an inquiry into reality, fallible and corrigible but not answerable to any supra-scientific tribunal, and not in need of any justification beyond observation and the hypothetico-deductive method" (1981: 72). This is a weaker characterization of naturalism than the one to follow. Pride of place has been given to the H-D method, supplemented with some principles of confirmation and disconfirmation. But given the problems that face the H-D method mentioned in Chapter 7, it can be doubted whether it can fulfil the role of a "supra-scientific tribunal ... not in need of any justification".

A stronger version of naturalism occurs in an oft-cited passage from Quine's "Epistemology Naturalized":

> Epistemology ... simply falls into place as a chapter of psychology and hence of natural science. It studies a natural phenomenon, viz., a physical human subject. This human subject is accorded a certain experimentally controlled input ... and in the fullness of time the subject delivers as output a description of the three-dimensional world and its history. The relation between meagre input and the torrential output is a relation that we are prompted to study for somewhat the same reasons that always prompted epistemology; namely, in order to see how evidence related to theory, and in what ways one's theory of nature transcends any available evidence. (1969: 82–3)

Quine appeals only to the science of psychology. But if we extend an invitation to all the sciences to join in an investigation into epistemology as a natural phenomenon, then we must allow sociologists their say as well. Broadly construed to include all the sciences, there is nothing so far in Quine's account of naturalism that a supporter of the strong programme in the sociology of science could not endorse.

Central to Quine's account of science and its methods is the relationship between the meagre input of surface irritations and the torrential verbal output of either observation sentences or of theory. Is this relationship normative or naturalistic? If we are to take the theory of this to be a science, such as psychology, then it would appear that the connection can only be a natural one involving causal or law-like links. Within the human subject there is a causal or law-like connection between the surface irritations and/or sensory experience in seeing a tiger in the grass and the verbal output of the English sentence "There is a tiger in the grass". Quine sometimes calls this relationship evidential. But calling it an *evidential relation* is a questionable description for two reasons. First, the evidence relation can only hold between sentences (or beliefs or propositions as some might prefer to say); it cannot hold between a sentence and a non-sentence such as surface irritations or sensory experience. So it is not possible for it to be an evidential relation since the relata are of the wrong sorts. Considered this way, the relationship between surface irritations and the output of sentences can only be causal (or law-like). If it is causal then the second objection is that this cannot be a normative relation of the sort determined by principles of scientific method. Normativity has been eliminated in favour of naturalistic items only.

Elsewhere Quine tells us: "Naturalism does not repudiate epistemology, but it assimilates it to empirical psychology" (1981: 72). But talk of "assimilation" still leaves us with our quandary about the connection between the normative and the natural. Quine goes on to say that science itself tells us that the only informational access we have to the world is due to our surface irritations. But science does something else as well:

> The epistemological question is in turn a question within science: the question of how we human animals can have managed to arrive at science from such limited information. Our scientific epistemologist pursues this inquiry and comes out with an account that has a good deal to do with the learning of language and with the neurology of perception.
>
> (*Ibid.*)

Now, a naturalizer will have an interest in these scientific matters that concern learning and perception, and other scientific matters that Quine goes on to mention such as evolution. But the story of *how* we have managed to arrive at our theories will be two-part. The first part is descriptive and not normative; it is a scientific story (but to arrive at any scientific theory, principles of scientific method will have had to have been applied). The second part is one in which we, as learners, might have also applied some principles of method (although not all learning need be by the application of principles of method). This brings out the still unresolved problem in Quine's position, namely, the lack of assimilation of the second part of learning, in which we apply methods, to the first part, which is a scientific account of what actually goes on in us when we learn (and in which scientists would have had to have used methods to come up with their theories about our learning).

Let us focus on methodology, and in particular the evidence relation. This is a partly normative or evaluative notion in that we speak of good, less good or bad evidential connections between observation and theory. But it appears to have been replaced by a descriptive account, perhaps containing causal or law-like claims within several sciences from theory of perception to linguistics, about the chain of links from sensory input to linguistic outputs. Our unresolved problems are these. Is Quine's position eliminativist in that the norms of evidential reasoning are deemed to be non-existent in much the same way as we now deem phlogiston or Zeus's thunderbolts to be non-existent? Or are the norms still there but they lead a life in heavy disguise through definition in terms of the predicates of the biological, psychological and linguistic sciences? Or are they supervenient in some way on the properties denoted by such predicates? In the case of supervenience we lack an account (if there is one) of the special features of those causal links between sensory input and linguistic output that characterize justified or warranted or rational belief in theory, and the special features that produce unjustified, unwarranted or irrational belief in theory. Moreover, which human subjects should be chosen for study: the good or the bad reasoners?

In his later *Pursuit of Truth*, Quine changes tack and emphasizes the distinction between the normative and the descriptive, writing:

> Within this baffling tangle of relations between our sensory stimulation and our scientific theory of the world, there is a segment that we can gratefully separate out and clarify without pursuing neurology, psychology, psycho-linguistics, genetics and history. It is the part where theory is tested by prediction. It is the relationship of evidential support.
>
> (1992: 1)

This appears to suggest that the evidential relation is outside the scope of the naturalists' programme. This becomes clearer when Quine goes on to make the following distinction about what is to be naturalized to what, in a section entitled "Norms and Aims": "Insofar as theoretical epistemology gets naturalized into a chapter of theoretical science, so normative epistemology gets naturalized into a chapter of engineering: the technology of anticipating sensory stimulation" (*ibid.*: 19). In the second kind of naturalization, normative epistemology is alive and well. But it is not a chapter of the sciences we have envisaged; it is still metaphorically described as "a chapter of engineering" or a piece of technology. If these are also normative then the old worry about the normative disappearing into the natural goes by the board. But are they normative and in what way?

This more modulated position occurs in his replies to some critics:

> A word now about the status, for me, of epistemic values. Naturalism in epistemology does not jettison the normative and settle for indiscriminate description of the on-going process. For me normative epistemology is a branch of engineering. It is the technology of truth seeking, or, in more cautiously epistemic terms, prediction. Like any technology it makes free use of whatever scientific findings may suit its purpose. It draws upon mathematics in computing standards of deviation and probable error in scouting the gambler's fallacy. It draws upon experimental psychology in scouting wishful thinking. It draws upon neurology and physics in a general way in discounting testimony from occult or parapsychological sources. There is no question here of ultimate values, as in morals; it is a matter of efficacy for an ulterior end, truth or prediction. The normative here, as elsewhere in engineering, becomes descriptive when the terminal parameter has been expressed.   (1986: 664–5)

Here the epistemic value to be realized is truth; this includes true predictions and truths of theory. Granted these values, what means are we to use to achieve them? Here the technology of mathematical statistics or probability can be employed. But we are not to employ wishful thinking (psychological investigations warn us against this); nor are we to employ the gambler's fallacy (probability warns us against this); we are not to employ unblinded clinical trials; and so on for other warnings that other scientific investigations give us. Why should we be so warned? These methods are not reliable realizers of their associated goals of truth, or just predictive truths. In contrast the methods, or technologies, that statistics and probability have given us are highly reliable for their goal of truth, or predictive success.

We can formulate Quine's views expressed here in terms of principles of method that are hypothetical imperatives of the sort set out in §3.1. If v is the value we are to realize (such as truth or predictive success) and r is some rule we are to follow such as a rule that arises from the application of principles of statistics and probability, then the principle of method will be of the form: if you wish to realize v then follow r. These can be viewed as principles of Quinean methodological technology, or as instrumental means–ends rules.

Quine appears to restrict the rules to those that arise from the sciences; but this is too narrow. We claimed in §3.1 that there are distinctive M-rules that do not arise from any science such as mathematics or probability but are part of our *sui generis* principles of method. It is these that are distinctive of scientific method and are not reducible in the way Quine suggests. Not all the norms of science, especially the M-rules, are to be naturalized into a part of a science, such as psychology, that delivers principles of engineering technology. In the next section we shall consider the account given by Laudan of how the hypothetical imperatives of method including M-rules are to be naturalized and what that science might be. Laudan appeals to a not yet well-developed science of means–ends strategies that people have employed to realize their epistemic goals throughout the history of science. If such a science is to be employed as their basis then there are reasonable prospects that the normative principles of science can retain their autonomy as principles of method.

There are some points concerning the final few sentences of Quine's above remarks that need clarification. He claims that there is no ultimate value, but there are ulterior ends such as truth or predictive truth. Perhaps one can view this as expressing the claim that there is a range of values that can be substituted for the variable v in the hypothetical imperative "if you want v follow r". Although it would appear that truth has a prominent place, if one adopts a pragmatic view of method then value-pluralism is to be admitted. However, what is meant by the claim that the normative becomes descriptive when the terminal parameter has been expressed? Does this mean that once we specify v as, say, predictive truth, it is a purely empirical matter to determine what rule r best realizes this? A more fully worked out account of this emerges from Laudan's normative naturalism, to which we now turn.

12.2 Laudan's normative naturalism

For Laudan methodology is a large part of a general theory of enquiry and one that, in the case of scientific method, has an historical dimension in that it has evolved with the growth of science itself. Laudan has highlighted a number of aspects of methodology from his earlier view of methodology as problem-solving to his later views on normative naturalism; here our focus will be on his later metamethodology of normative naturalism. His initial question about scientific method is one we have already adopted. Since each science exhibits a sequence of changing theories, how come this change? As we have already noted, there is a long history during which methodologists have proposed principles of method that they believe have, on the whole, guided the changes they and others have made in scientific theory. The rules and values the principles embody were followed either individually or collectively (the collective practices in turn being arrived at by consensus or by what prevailed for a majority).

With the post-positivist historical turn in the philosophy of science from the 1960s, methodologists have delved into the history of science and have proposed models of these changes, some aspects of these models involving historically evolving methodology. Their historical investigations play an important role in establishing an empirical basis for the naturalizing of methodology. This is an important aspect of Laudan's normative naturalism, which is to promote a research programme to determine what methodologists have actually claimed. (See Laudan *et al.* [1986] for a report of over two hundred claims made by a handful of contemporary methodologists.) Once the claims have been assembled, the next task is to test them. The process of test is important in our account of the metamethodology of normative naturalism.

Laudan's account of the form taken by principles of method is one we have already employed in §3.1. Methodological rules are all instrumental means–ends hypothetical ought-imperatives that can be applied to any theory and have the following form (where r is a rule and v any value that is to be realised in some theory under consideration):

(*P*) If one's cognitive goal is v then one ought to follow r.

Such principles combine axiology with rules for proceeding. The cognitive value v that T will hopefully realize need not always be truth; for pragmatists a range of different values can serve as their aims for their various theories, from the aims of realists to those of non-realists. Also, r need not be the one and only rule that realizes v; it may be one of several that will serve equally well.

That all principles of method are hypothetical is a substantive thesis that rules out categorical imperatives that fail to specify any value v. Either there is a value that is implicitly understood by those who use the categorical form; or the value is so widely shared that there is no reason to explicitly mention it; or the principle P is elliptically expressed and a value can be readily supplied. Using an example of Laudan (1996: 133), Popper's categorical rule "avoid *ad hoc* hypotheses" (i.e. changes in theory that do not increase its testability) becomes the hypothetical "if one wants to develop theories that are very risky, then one ought to avoid *ad hoc* hypotheses". What is important here is the aim that is introduced from other parts of a theory of method in which the rule has a role; in Popper's case this is the aim of proposing risky theories rather than safe theories that are less open to criticism. Examples like this support the view that values can be introduced to support the thesis that principles of method are instrumental in linking means to ends. But this does not constitute a proof that all such principles must be non-categorical.

Granted that there are many principles of method with the form of P, how are they to be warranted? Here Laudan appeals to descriptive hypotheses of the form:

(H) If anyone follows r then they realize v.

There is in fact a range of descriptive hypotheses H that can be envisaged. Some might be statistical rather than universal and claim that following r realizes v in n per cent of cases (where n is reasonably high). Others might be comparative and claim that following r rather than r^* leads to v (more often or always). It is hypotheses like H that need to be established in some way. Some hypotheses might be shown to be true on *a priori* grounds (because some particular H is necessarily true or analytic). But on the whole they are contingent claims to be shown true using empirical methods. Lurking in the background is now a paradox that, in order to establish any principle of method, some principles of method need to be employed; we shall return to this shortly.

To what science do the large numbers of descriptive hypotheses H belong? It appears to be none of the sciences of the kind Quine mentions, such as psychology, theories of learning, evolution and so on. They belong to a special science, currently under investigation by methodological naturalists, that deals with strategies in epistemic contexts to achieve certain ends. Such a science would not investigate the behaviour of scientists as to what they judge are the acceptable moves in science; this is the view of Popper and Lakatos. Rather, it would consider the actual moves the scientists did make and the goals they wished to realize and whether or not the moves they made were successful or not in realizing their goals. This involves historical, psychological and socio-logical investigations, along with some theory of games. The investigators of this science would explore a range of historical episodes to establish particular cases of a scientist adopting certain strategies to achieve certain ends in some given theoretical context. The history of science is in fact a vast repository of successful and unsuccessful means–ends strategies adopted in the construction of the historical sequence of theories within each science.

To illustrate using the case of the *ad hoc* rule of Popper mentioned above, an investigator would begin with a range of relevant historical episodes. In inves-tigating each they would come up with a number of particular claims about means–ends strategies. For example, consider the episode in which the astrono-mer Simon Newcomb attempted to solve the problem of the missing 43 arc-seconds per century in the precession of the perihelion of the planet Mercury. Newcomb proposed the following move: change the power of the distance in Newton's inverse square gravitational law from 2 to 2.0000001574, and the problem disappears! Does this seemingly *ad hoc* change make Newton's law more or less risky, that is, more or less testable (assuming that this is a goal that Newcomb also had)? This is a matter to be determined by an investigator who explores the actual goals that Newcomb had and the strategy he adopted to realize them. If the above story does capture Newcomb's procedures, then a particular case of a successful means–ends strategy has been established; if not, then a case has been uncovered in which a certain means–end strategy was a failure.

The development of such case studies provides a test basis for hypotheses such as H. They will reveal a large amount of data that can be used to confirm, disconfirm or determine the statistical probability of any proposed H; and the data can be used to adjudicate between rival hypotheses H and H^*. The standard methods of hypothesis testing that prevail in all the sciences would also apply to this means–ends science. As already noted, this gives rise to the paradox in which methods of science are used to establish those very methods. It would appear that if the justification of any H employs P then this is circular, but hope-fully a case of benign rule-circularity.

This conclusion would only follow if there is a close connection between the hypothetical ought-imperative P and the descriptive H. There is a close connec-tion; we can view hypothesis H as the naturalized version of principle P. Within normative naturalism a necessary condition for the correctness of a principle of method P is the truth of the corresponding descriptive claim H. Without H being true or having a high frequency if understood as a statistical hypothesis of the means–ends science, then there would not be much point in adopting the associ-ated principle of method P; it would have an unreliable past track record.

The matters raised here come together in Laudan's proposal for a meta-methodological inductive rule (MIR) of the following sort, which links what we can know about the evidence for some H with a principle of method P:

If actions of a particular sort, *m*, have consistently promoted certain cognitive ends, *e*, in the past, and rival actions, *n*, have failed to do so, then assume that future actions following the rule "if your aim is *e*, you ought to do *m*" are more likely to promote those ends than actions based on the rule "if your aim is *e*, you ought to do *n*".   (Laudan 1996: 135)

The premises of MIR concern empirical evidence of two kinds: E = (it has been empirically determined in a number of cases that) following some rule *r* has realized *v* always or with high frequency; and E^* = (it has been empirically determined in a number of cases that) following some other rule r^* has realized the same value *v* with a less than high, or a low, frequency. How is this evidence to be obtained? Merely investigating some case histories would not be enough. One would have to follow rules of statistical investigation and show that in a randomly selected number of relevant cases we obtain evidence E and E^*. Once that evidence has been obtained then one can inductively infer to the two empirical hypotheses H and H^* (where H = *n* per cent of cases of following *r* realize *v*, where *n* is high or 1, and H^* = *m* per cent of cases of following r^* realize *v*, where *m* is less than optimal or 0, that is, r^* is a bad realizer of *v*).

Now MIR does not mention hypotheses H or H^* in its premises, but only evidence E and E^*; the step via H and H^* is omitted. Instead the conclusions arrived at are principles of method, the hypothetical ought-imperatives P and P^* (where P = if you want to arrive at *v* with a high degree of reliability then you ought to follow *r*, and P^* = if you want to arrive at *v* with a high degree of reliability then do not follow r^*). MIR not only links the evidence E for the success of H to the success of an associated principle P, but also bridges the is–ought gap between the evidence E for H and the normative force of P. There are no "ought" claims in the premises but there are ought-claims in the principles arrived at in the conclusion. In this respect MIR is a Level 3 metamethodological principle that sets out the conditions of warrant for P, a Level 2 principle of method.

Sometimes MIR is regarded as an instance of the straight rule of enumerative induction. But the premises should more accurately be regarded as involving the frequency of the link between means *r* and ends *v*, and then a statistical inference is made based on those frequencies. Laudan endorses this, writing: "empirical information about the relative frequencies with which various epistemic means are likely to promote sundry epistemic ends is a crucial desideratum for deciding on the correctness of epistemic rules" (*ibid.*: 156). So the metamethodology of normative naturalism cannot merely be akin to the straight rule of induction; it must involve the full theory of statistical methodology for the estimation of frequencies and inferences from them.

For normative naturalism, the theory of statistical inference will appear at Level 2; it provides a number of principles of scientific method to be applied to scientific theories at Level 1. Among these theories will be the special science of means–ends strategies employed throughout the history of science. How does one get from the hypotheses of this means–ends science, once they have been established, to principles of method as normative naturalism envisages? This will be via MIR, which, properly understood as a metamethodological principle, will itself involve a statistical inference from hypotheses to principles of method. But it is more than just a statistical inference; the principles derived in the conclusions are normative in character and not only descriptive. In so far as the inference is statistical does this mean that circularity or infinite regress is involved in the justification of our norms of method? Not necessarily, as one can view the argument as involving a version of rule-circularity that is not a vicious form of circularity; the Level 3 meta-inference is itself an instance of a rule of method that applies widely at Level 2.

If normative naturalism encapsulates a quasi-statistical metamethodology of the kind just envisaged, it must have a quite broad sweep across all the sciences and their history. Suitably prepared investigations into a sufficient number of randomly selected episodes in the history of science are needed in the first place. The task of normative naturalism is not to generate from this historical base a set of means–ends hypotheses, or principles of method. Rather, it is assumed that they are given and can be culled from the writings of philosophers of science and scientists themselves. The task of normative naturalism is to bring proposed principles of method into some relation with researched episodes in the history of science. In this respect the approach of normative naturalism has elements of the H-D method for testing hypotheses. But it departs somewhat from the standard version in that the evidential base concerns the frequency with which, in a number of cases, some means has realized some end; and the principles to be tested have associated with them hypotheses that, if correctly expressed, are also statistical in character (they are also normative). Understood in this way, the research project of normative naturalism is a vast undertaking that so far can only be said to be partially advanced.

Instead a number of case studies in support of normative naturalism are used in a different manner. Some methodological principle is proposed and some episode in the history of science is investigated to see whether or not the principle was followed in this case. Here the metamethodology is that of instance confirmation and disconfirmation. The outcome is that some relevant principle of method has, or has not, been followed in some case. This method might serve to refute a principle but it will hardly confirm it or tell us anything about the frequency of success, or lack of it, of the principle. Moreover, as is well known, instance confirmation and disconfirmation is faced with the serious problem raised by Hempel's ravens paradox. It might be expecting too much of normative naturalism that it propose a solution to this paradox. But it does show that in relying on a theory of instance confirmation or disconfirmation the scope of the metamethodology of normative naturalism will be quite restricted in the range of problems in methodology that it can solve; there are problems it is powerless to solve.

It would appear from the above that there is no one metamethod that normative naturalism must employ; it could use one of several such as fully fledged statistical methods, the H-D method, or instance confirmation and disconfirmation.[1] But given some metamethod it does at least provide a procedure for investigating our claims about principles of method and their relationship to actual practice in science, and this is important. So what can be said about some of the results obtained so far with normative naturalism? If one were to adopt a simple meta-inductive rule of MIR then if some principle P were to pass its tests, a theory of method could be built up that includes not only induction but also P. These two principles can in turn be used to test further principles; the test need not be based on MIR alone and can employ only P. However, MIR would be the cornerstone of the programme of normative naturalism and the principles of method it uncovers would be derivative.

What principles have been found inadequate? Laudan lists some failures such as the commonly advocated "if you want true theories, then reject proposed theories unless they can explain everything explained by their predecessors", or "if you want theories with high predictive reliability, then reject *ad hoc* hypotheses".[2] We consider here only the first principle. This is often understood to be an important part of the correspondence principle, which in its general form says: when a successor theory T^* replaces its predecessor theory T, then T^* ought to explain all the phenomena that T explained, perhaps under limiting conditions in which certain parameters in T^* but not in T are ignored (this being the "correspondence limit"). There are some instances of such limiting correspondences holding, such as Einstein's special theory of relativity and Newtonian laws of motion; certain factors in Einstein's equations can be ignored, or tend to zero, such as the ratio v^2/c^2 in which the velocity v of a body is quite low when compared with the speed of light c. Laudan's claim is that the correspondence principle, even though there might be instances of it, is not a requirement that ought to be imposed on the way in which successor and predecessor theories are to be related. T^* can replace T yet not repeat all its explanatory successes. The correspondence principle can be understood to be a principle of permission in methodology but not a principle of obligation. Even if there are some counter-examples to the correspondence principle, there is yet to be an empirically determined frequency with which following the rule r (e.g. a successor theory ought to explain the successes of its predecessor theory) will realize the associated value v (truth); and it is yet to be determined whether that frequency is high enough to warrant adopting the correspondence principle as part of one's methodology.

Finally, there are three features of normative naturalism we wish to highlight. Normative naturalism goes about its task in a manner free from the difficulties that faced the metamethodologies of the later Popper and Lakatos, and the metamethodology of Feyerabend with its appeal to a reflective equilibrium principle. These three methodologists appeal to intuitions about what is good and bad science or what are the good and bad moves in each episode of science. Normative naturalism makes no appeal to such intuitions. Instead, episodes from the historical record of the sciences are investigated to uncover the strategies that best realize values.

The second issue is that Laudan maintains that all principles of method are hypothetical (or categorical with suppressed antecedents); however, this conflicts with the claim that the meta-rule MIR is categorical. The advocate of normative naturalism has a way of resolving this problem. Any inference pattern ought to be reliable in that it is guaranteed to take us from premises that are true to a conclusion that is true. If reliability for the truth is what we value in inductive inference, then we can take MIR to have a suppressed antecedent; it recommends that we follow a certain pattern of inference to arrive at a conclusion that realizes the value of truth. So MIR is not really a categorical rule; its use generally presupposes that one uses inductive rules to arrive at truths. In the case of MIR the value is the truth of its conclusions. And its conclusions are all principles of method. That is, MIR generates methodological truths.

The final issue concerns the testing of particular means–ends hypotheses. Consider a principle of the form: if person X wants v then X ought to follow r. How are we to test this? One needs to have good evidence that person X follows r (or intends to do so and does so successfully); and one needs to have good evidence that value v has been realized. In both cases, what is good evidence? Good evidence would be available if these were properties that could be detected by direct observation. This Laudan suggests when he proposes a naturalized version of the principle that "turns out to be a conditional declarative statement, asserting a contingent relationship between two presumably *'observable' properties*, namely, 'following r' and 'realizing v'" (1996: 134, emphasis added).[3] The assumption that these are observational properties is a strongly empiricist requirement. This can be relaxed somewhat if the properties are operationally detectable rather than directly observable; and it can be relaxed even further by broadening the requirement further so that there be only good evidence for each.

This becomes important for Laudan's view that our aims not be transcendent so that we are never in a position to tell when they have been realized. If we cannot tell, then reasons emerge for not pursuing them.

> Of course, if one has adopted a transcendental aim, or one which otherwise has the character that one can never tell when the aim has been realized and when it has not, then we would no longer be able to say that methodological rule asserts connections between detectable or observable properties. I believe that such aims are entirely inappropriate for science, since there can never be evidence that such aims are being

realized, and thus we can never be warranted in a position to certify that science is making progress with respect to them. In what follows, I will assume that we are dealing with aims which are such that we can ascertain when they have and when they have not been realized.

(*Ibid.*: 261 n.19)

Let us grant that we can have good evidence for person X following a rule r (although this may not be without its problems if X's behaviour fits two or more rules equally well, as in the case of the problems raised for rule-following by Wittgenstein). Can we have good evidence for X's realizing value v? If v were to be the value of a theory having excess true predictions over its rivals, then this does seem to be readily operationally detectable; so we can have good evidence for when this value has been realized. And the same might be said for values such as having greater empirical strength or excess empirical content or being consistent; all of these are readily detectable when realized. And if the values of simplicity and unity can be made sufficiently precise then we might have clear evidence when they have been realized. But some values might fail to ever be realized. One of these is certainty (of the strong Cartesian variety). We can have a clear definition of such certainty but also know that nothing will ever meet its requirements. Cartesian certainty is an unrealistically utopian value because we now know in advance that for any theory T it is not possible for it to realize the value of certainty; all our theories are fallible. So any principle of method involving a value such as certainty can be rejected. Another such value is actual verification for unrestrictedly general claims. Since these can never be shown to be true then any principle with actual verification as a value is to be rejected.

The value that Laudan challenges is that of theoretical truth. The value of obtaining observational truths is readily detectable, but not so theoretical truths. He claims against the realist who pursues the value of theoretical truth: "although he can define what it means for a theory to be true, he has no idea whatever how to determine whether any theory actually has the property of being true. Under such circumstances, such a value could not be operationalised" (1984: 53; see also ch. 5). And if the realist cannot tell when the value of theoretical truth has been realized he is adopting principles of method that are less than optimally rational since they involve end-states of value realization that, even if they were accidentally hit on, could not be operationally known.

Here the realist can be placed in an awkward position if they also embrace the programme of normative naturalism; the methodological naturalism they espouse undercuts their metaphysical naturalism to which their realism might be wedded. The realist might respond in two ways. The first might be to give way on normative naturalism since its project rules out some of their quite crucial principles of method designed to get at theoretical truth; they could then look for other ways of grounding their principles of method. The second might be to question the strong empiricism that normative naturalism is wedded to, especially its claim that the property of truth cannot be operationalized. There might be other ways of providing good evidence that the value of truth has been realized. Thus they might argue that we have good grounds for believing that theory *T* has hit on some theoretical truth when *T* entails striking novel predictions that turn out to be true. Here is a property, that of having novel true predictions, that realists argue is operationally detectable. And we can argue from this operationally detectable property to the truth of the *T*, or at least its increasing verisimilitude, using some standard method of providing evidential support. One such form of argument is inference to the best explanation. None of this is direct operational detection of theoretical truth but it is good evidence for theoretical truth. Methodologists such as Laudan who are not realists are fully aware of this response of the realist. What they attack is the adequacy of the claim that inference to the best explanation can help us here; it is a rule of method that fails its test, and so should not be used (*ibid.*: ch. 5). Controversies over the role of inference to the best explanation have been addressed in §5.4 and §9.5. The upshot is that we can avoid restrictive empiricist constraints on determining when a rule has been followed or when a value has been realized that make the project of normative naturalism committed to a quite empiricist view of science.

12.3 Rescher's methodological pragmatism

One philosopher who emphasizes the role of practice in metamethodological considerations is Rescher. Unlike the classical pragmatists, who construed the truth of individual claims in terms of practical utility, Rescher develops a methodological variant of pragmatism according to which methodological rules are justified by their success in practical application. Rescher accepts a correspondence theory of truth and rejects the pragmatist theory applied at the level of individual theses, that is, propositions such as those of scientific theories at Level 1. This he calls *thesis* pragmatism, in contrast with *methodological* pragmatism, which places the locus of justification on Level 2 methodological principles. For Rescher, propositional theses about the world are correspondence true or false. They are justified, not pragmatically, but on the basis of methodological principles. However, it is these principles, and not the propositional theses about the world that they help generate, that are to be justified by successful practical application of the theories they select.

Rescher's methodological pragmatism is a naturalistic account of the justification of method that treats methodological principles as, in part, subject to empirical evaluation. He recognizes a fundamental problem concerning the justification of principles of method, which he expresses in terms of the Pyrrhonian sceptic's problem of the *criterion* or *diallelus*, that is, circle or wheel (see Rescher 1977: ch. II, §2). This is a problem we have met previously (§4.2). Either we use principle M in justifying M, in which case M presupposes its own correctness and its justification is circular; or we use another principle M', in which case there is an infinite regress of principles. We need to see in what way the pragmatist's appeal to practice might overcome the problem of circularity or regress.

Rescher conceives of methodological principles as instruments, as tools for the realization of some end. So understood they are in conformity with the account of principles, and the values that the principles are supposed to realize, given in §3.1 and by Quine and Laudan. Rescher requires that principles be evaluated in the same way that instruments are evaluated, namely, pragmatically. Instruments are evaluated by determining whether they "work" in the sense that they produce some desired end. However, it is not sufficient for a principle of method to produce its end once, or a few times. Rescher requires that principles regularly realize their ends: "the instrumental justification of method is inevitably general and, as it were, statistical in its bearing" (*ibid.*: 5). This brings Rescher's account of principles of method and their justification close to Quine's position, and even closer to that of Laudan. Like Laudan's meta-inductive principle MIR, Rescher recognizes that a theory of statistics is needed to establish our principles of method. But unlike Laudan's programme of normative naturalism, Rescher does not engage in the task of testing principles of method; his, and so our, main focus is mainly metamethodological.

Although there are similarities between Rescher's and Laudan's metamethodological stances, there are also important differences. Rescher employs an argument of a kind that Laudan finds inadequate on the grounds of normative naturalism's own test procedures, that is, a modified version of inference to the best explanation (IBE) that links the success of science produced by the application of methodological principles to the truth-indicativeness of the principles themselves. Again unlike Laudan, in order to connect practical success with truth Rescher makes a number of metaphysical presuppositions that we can refine or abandon in the course of enquiry but that, at the moment, we hold of ourselves and the world in which we act as agents (*ibid.*: ch. IV). They are as follows.

(a) Activism: we must act in order to survive, hence beliefs have practical relevance since they lead to actions which have consequences.
(b) Reasonableness: we act on the basis of our beliefs so that there is a systematic coordination of beliefs, needs and action.
(c) Interactionism: human beings actively intervene in the natural world and are responsive to feedback from this intervention in both cases of satisfaction and frustration.
(d) Uniformity of nature: continued use of a method presupposes some constancy in the world.

(e) Non-conspiratorial nature of reality: the world is indifferent in the sense that it is neither set to conform to, nor set to conflict with, our actions.

On the overall metaphysical picture that emerges, the practical success of our belief-based actions and the theoretical success of our beliefs both turn on the correctness of assumptions such as (a)–(e). They set out general, but contingent, presuppositions about the sort of agents we are and the sort of world in which we act and believe (both individually and communally) and the fact that we have achieved a wide degree of success in action and belief.

In this light, consider principles of method that govern enquiry. They are not merely locally applicable but apply across the broad front of enquiry into diverse matters. They have a large measure of success in that they regularly deliver beliefs that instantiate our desired practical goals and theoretical values. Roughly, the idea is that our methods might mislead us some of the time, but it is utterly implausible to hold that most of the time they systematically lead us astray, given our success in the world and the way the world is as presupposed in the general metaphysical picture above. On the basis of this success, what particular epistemic property might we attribute to our methodological principles? Rescher sometimes describes this as the "legitimation problem" for our methods (*ibid.*: 14). A number of terms could be used to name the property possessed by our methods that leads to their success, such as "valid", "true" and "adequate"; Rescher uses these terms in various contexts along with "truth-correlative" and "truth-indicative" (*ibid.*: ch. 6, esp. 81, 83). We shall settle on the last of these and characterize Rescher's justification of his methodological pragmatism as one that attempts to show that the success of our methods is evidence that our methods are truth-indicative.

His justificatory argument has much in common with the use of IBE to establish the truth of some hypothesis. At one point, Rescher refers to it as a "'deduction' (in Kant's sense)" (*ibid.*: 92), although the argument is not strictly deductive (as the problematizing quotes allow). Rather, it is an inductive plausibility argument similar to IBE. But it is to be distinguished from certain forms of IBE that Rescher wishes to reject. He is critical of IBE on a number of grounds that we have already met in §5.4 on IBE. He argues that the set of available hypotheses from which we have to select may be defective on two grounds: the hypotheses in the set do not meet the minimum threshold for being good explanations; and even if they did the set may still not contain the true hypothesis. What we select as the best can either be no good as an explanation or not be the true explanation. More importantly for our purposes he argues that the values we use to determine which the best explanation is can be in tension or conflict with each other. Two or more explanatory hypotheses can emerge as the best hypothesis depending on the way in which one resolves the conflict (Rescher 2001: 128–33). Depending on how we aggregate the values used in selecting the best hypothesis, there will be an outcome. But it will not be a unique outcome since, given the problem of the aggregation of values, there is no unique aggregation. There may be several "best" explanatory hypotheses, each relative to the different ways of aggregating values.

If we grant these objections then Rescher's response is to appeal to a virtue of systems of belief that, as a pragmatist, he has long advocated, namely, *systematization*. He argues that while the notion of best explanation falls victim to the problem of aggregation, the notion of best systematization does not. What is the virtue of systematization and does it escape this objection? It is important to note that the notion of systematization applies not only to systems of belief such as those of science at Level 1, but also to methodological principles at Level 2, and it will encompass a number of general metaphysical presuppositions of the sort we have listed above, as well as others. To highlight the breadth of the application of systematization, we shall talk instead of *cognitive systems* (CS). These will contain at least the three elements just mentioned: Level 1 scientific beliefs; Level 2 methodologies; and metaphysical presuppositions (along with some other elements that need not concern us).

For epistemological coherentists such as Rescher, systematization applies to CSs as a whole. Systematization will involve several virtues we have already met, such as unity, coherence, simplicity, consistency, inferential interrelatedness and so on (Rescher 2005: 15–17). Explanatory power is also a virtue, as are the following. CSs are to be *comprehensive* in the sense that they are *complete* and leave out nothing relevant. They are to be *cohesive wholes* in that there is a unity and integrity with each constituent part having a significant role. They are intended to be *coherent*, this being a virtue that pragmatists advocate for all systems of belief. They are intended to be *efficient* and *economical* in that they are to perform their tasks effectively without superfluous effort being required. This is an important Darwinian consideration in that we have evolved as users of CSs; inefficient and uneconomical CSs are not conducive to our survival. Importantly, all of these virtues, and so systematization, can come in degrees, although it is unclear how comparative judgements are to be made, and even more unclear whether any scale or measure can be constructed.

Does the problem of aggregation arise for systematization in that the virtues that constitute it can come into conflict? If it does, then systematization would be subject to the same objection that Rescher raises for the notion of best explanation. Rescher is equivocal on this. He does recognize that trade-offs will have to be made when some of the virtues pull in opposite directions and one will be sacrificed for the other; for example, the degree of connectiveness may be lowered in order to accommodate disparate elements that contribute to comprehensiveness (*ibid*.: 26).

To illustrate, consider Rescher's worry (2001: 135) that there may be two systems of belief, S1 and S2, that have maximum explanatory coherence in that they are best explainers, yet are inconsistent with one another. If this is possible, as Lehrer (1974: 181) argues it is, then for some proposition p, p is best explained by $S1$, and not-p is best explained by $S2$. Now if we do not conjoin the two systems and leave them unconnected with one another, there is a deficit in systematicity in respect of lack of connectivity between systems of belief. If we conjoin the two systems of belief, there is a deficit in systematicity in that the conjunction is inconsistent. If we restore consistency but remain indecisive as to which of p or not-p to adopt and retain neither, then there is another deficit in systematicity in respect of comprehensiveness.

It would appear that systematicity is subject to the problem of aggregation when it comes to deciding between the virtues of consistency and comprehensiveness. Here we draw on our discussion of the problem of aggregation for Kuhn in §2.4. In making successful aggregations we need two further items that are hard to come by. One is a measure of the degree to which each virtue is realized. The other concerns weighting, where the weighting applies to each virtue according to the significance attached to it, or where the weighting is due to the degree to which it is realized (virtues that are fully realized might get a high weighting but if not well realized they could get a low weighting). Since the prospect of obtaining any measure, or getting a measure to any degree of satisfactoriness, is slim, then the problem of aggregation appears to be difficult to solve. Perhaps for this reason in a later work Rescher (2005: 17, 26) recognizes the problem of the aggregation of multiple virtues and settles for something less than maximum systematization in appealing to yet other virtues, for example the satisficing virtues of harmonization and balance. But on other occasions Rescher argues that what is distinctive about cognitive systematization is "overall efficacy and economy of intellectual effort … [that] provides for an across the board basis of comparison" (2001: 135–6). There is an overall cost–benefit analysis of gains and losses of virtues in which an economy of cognitive operation is meant to resolve any problem concerning the aggregation of conflicting virtues. But this is rather hopeful since the aggregation problem does not appear to have gone away.

Our view is that the notions of systematization and best cognitive systematization fall victim to the same problem of aggregation as Rescher claims besets best explanation, and also besets Kuhn's model of weighted values (as we claim in §2.4). However, we can set this aside and explore the notion of best systematization independently and see in what ways it is an improvement over the notion of best explanation (which it can incorporate).

What advantages, if any, does best systematization have over best explanation? Instead of IBE, inference to the truth of the best explanatory hypotheses, Rescher prefers to employ what we might call "IBS", inference to the *acceptability* of the hypothesis that is the best overall cognitive systematization. Sometimes the use of IBE might be the same as IBS, but the latter is much more general and, while sometimes exploiting IBE, IBS need not always be like IBE. So how is IBS to be characterized?

Rescher tells us that "we do not infer a system from the data but construct it on that basis" (*ibid.*: 135). The notion of data can be quite broad and can include not just the theories that have been proposed at any time in the history of science but also the principles of method that have been used to accept or reject any of these, the metaphysical assumptions (mentioned above) that might be made about enquiry in general, and so on. Let us lump all of these together as data D. In the context of evolving science, methods and metaphysical assumptions, we attempt to construct cognitive systematizations, CSs, of D. There may be several CSs, which we can label CS_1, CS_2, CS_3, …, for however many CSs we construct. Let us suppose that we can eliminate some of these as bad cognitive systematizations because they do not meet a minimum threshold criterion for counting as a satisfactory CS. Let us also assume that we can overcome the aggregation problem, perhaps by applying a cost–benefit analysis to each CS. (But now note that any methodological principles used in working out any such cost–benefit analysis are going to be a component of data D that is to be systematized.) Suppose at the end of this process we arrive at a unique best cognitive systematization CS^*. What can we infer from the existence of CS^*?

Rescher tells us that there is a conclusion we can draw: "What we can infer … is acceptability as such. That is to say we have good reason for accepting the best overall account we can provide as thereby true – or at any rate as affording us the best estimate of the truth that is available in the circumstances" (*Ibid.*: 135). That is, we can infer not that CS^* is true, but that CS^* is the best estimate of the truth we have, or that CS^* is acceptable (in the circumstances). Or as we have suggested earlier, CS^* is truth-indicative, including its component principles of method. This suggests an argument of the kind advanced by Peirce or Musgrave for IBE, which we can set out as follows:

> It is reasonable to accept as true the best available cognitive systematiza-
> tion of any set of facts;
> D is a set of data;
> CS^* systematizes D (to a satisfactory degree);
> No competing hypothesis systematizes D as well as CS^* does;
> ∴ It is reasonable to accept CS^* as true (or CS^* as truth-indicative).

This argument, we maintain, provides a satisfactory interpretation of what Rescher claims. It has the same form as an IBE argument, but it does not concern what we can infer from the best explainer; rather, it concerns what we can infer from the existence of the best cognitive systematization of all the "data", that is, all the components constituting a cognitive system.

Granted that we have some idea of what cognitive systematization is, we can then ask: what counts as best cognitive systematization? What can be inferred from this? To what use can these considerations be put as far as methodology is concerned? The main use for our purposes is to employ the notion of best cognitive systematization as a methodological principle to justify principles of method. Hopefully this can be done in a non-question-begging manner that avoids the problem of the *diallelus*, in which we are caught up in either circular justifications or a regress of justifications. For Rescher one form of his problem is this. We use what we take to be legitimate principles of scientific method to choose between rival scientific theories; and these theories are in turn legitimized because they have been chosen by legitimized principles while their rivals have been rejected by the same principles. So the path of legitimization is top-down from legitimizing Level 2 principles of method to legitimized Level 1 scientific theories.

We can now ask: why do we think that the principles of method are legitimate? We might argue that the best explanation of their legitimization is that in their application they have produced a sequence of scientific theories at Level 1 that are highly successful, and increasingly so, in their predictions and applications. Here the pragmatists' notion of success in practice plays a crucial role. The argument used is a form of IBE; and the path of legitimization is bottom-up. It goes from legitimizing scientific theories (made legitimate through their success in prediction and application) to the legitimized principles of method that produced the sequence of theories. Not only does Rescher regard this as a circular set of considerations, but also the form of argument used is one that itself stands in need of legitimization since it is an instance of some principles of method.

Rescher's way of overcoming these problems is to approach matters, as any coherence theorist will, through the idea of systematization. The problem is with the levels picture in which it has been couched. Justifications proceed from Level 1 to Level 2, and back down again, with the apparent linear character of this being really the two sides of a large circle. On top of this is the illusion of a neutral metamethodological stance. In contrast, Rescher claims: "the argumentation is *comprehensively systematic*, placing its several elements into a coordinative framework which unites them within one over-all nexus of mutual substantiation" (Rescher 1977: 103). While this is not crystal clear one can get the gist of the idea of systematization that lies behind this. The kind of linear picture of justification that gives rise to the *dialellus* gets replaced by the coherentists' justification based on the interconnectedness of the various components of the overall cognitive system. We propose the following rendition of Rescher's considerations.

What we need to look for is the best systematization of the data D. As we have indicated, this data is rather complex and contains the following elements: (a) theories which have been accepted or rejected; (b) principles of method employed in (a); (c) argumentative connections linking particular principles of method to the particular theories they legitimize; (d) argumentative connections linking particular successful theories used to legitimize the methods that were used to produce the successful theories; (e) any general metaphysical presuppositions or theories about ourselves as users of cognitive systems. As indicated there can be various ways in which all of this (and perhaps much else) can get systematized; some systematizations will be better than others, and hopefully one will emerge that is uniquely best. If there are problems with this (as we think there are) then one could at least look for systematizations that are quite good even though none can be determined as optimal. Once we have located the best systematization CS* of all of D, then we can infer, using the argument schema given above, that it is reasonable to accept that CS* is true, or correct, or right. CS* is truth-indicative. And from this we can infer the truth-indicativeness of the principles of method since they are part of an overall system of scientific theory and of principles of method that is the best systematized.

Some such version of IBS, we submit, lies at the core of the metamethodology of Rescher's methodological pragmatism. What justificatory basis is there for IBS as a form of argument? Rescher's response to the question is to see the re-emergence of the *diallelus*, or great circle or wheel of justifications. Characteristically for a pragmatist, there is no independent standpoint from which a justification can be given for IBS, or any other rock-bottom metamethodological principle. Rather the same form of argument is used at several points to: (a) validate scientific theories in terms of their success in practical and theoretical application; (b) validate principles of enquiry in terms of their success in yielding the successful science of (a); (c) validate the metaphysical picture of the world that sets out the presuppositions we must make about the sort of world in which we live and the sort of agents we are that makes such success in (a) and (b) possible. Some such pragmatist picture closes the circle without making it necessarily vicious.

But the pragmatic picture depends on some version of IBS, which is used at different levels and which closes the circle. And in doing so the idea of non-vicious rule-circularity becomes important since the form of IBS occurs not only within (a)–(c) above, but also, as indicated, in the overall structure of the argument for best cognitive systematization that lies at the heart of methodological pragmatism. If the above account of Rescher's argument is correct, it is one that would be contested by fellow naturalists such as Laudan, who restricts his metamethodology to induction and explicitly rejects the use of any form of IBE or IBS (Laudan 1984: ch. 5). For those who find that some form of IBE can be satisfactorily used, this helps draw another distinction between the kinds of pragmatism that Laudan and Rescher espouse.[4]

13. Scientific realism and methodology

Principles of scientific method play a considerable role in arguments for scientific realism and for rival positions. Scientific realists maintain not only that the aim of science is truth, but that pursuit of science does in fact give rise to truth about observable and unobservable dimensions of reality. Such a realist view has evident implications for the methodology of science. For if the pursuit of science gives rise to truth, it is presumably the methods employed by scientists that are responsible for this achievement. But in this case the use of scientific methods must lead to truth, that is, they are truth-conducive. Questions of an epistemological nature therefore arise about whether the methods of science are indeed genuinely truth-conducive methods for enquiry.

In this chapter, we first present the position of scientific realism before exploring methodological aspects of the position. In §13.1, we outline a number of different aspects of realism: axiological, metaphysical, semantic and epistemic. In §13.2, we consider the best-known argument for scientific realism. This is the so-called success argument that realism is the best explanation of the success of science. We also briefly discuss objections that have been raised against the success argument. In §13.3, we consider a problem that arises with respect to realization of the realist aim of truth. We then examine the metamethodological application of the success argument as an argument for the truth-conducive character of the methods of science.

13.1 Aspects of scientific realism

Scientific realism is not a simple thesis; it combines a number of distinct theses about the aim and content of science, the nature of the world investigated by science and our epistemological relation to the world. There are four main aspects to scientific realism arising from axiology, semantics, epistemology and metaphysics.[1] The founding principle of scientific realism is perhaps the epistemological claim that scientific enquiry produces genuine knowledge of the world. But spelling out this claim leads to further aspects of the realist position.

Axiology concerns the values we ought to adopt for science. For realists their axiology is centred on the alethic value of truth (see §2.2). The realist aim for science is to discover the truth, or the approximate truth, or truth with some associated degree of error, about not only the observable aspects of the world but also its unobservable aspects. Associated with this is the elimination of error or its minimization, while truth is maximized. While the pursuit of science may increase our ability to control the environment, or to predict observable phenomena, these are secondary pursuits compared with the realists' aim of acquiring (approximately) true theories. Science is also an epistemological enterprise leading to the discovery of evidence for and against some claim, and this, in the long run has as its aim the production of knowledge of which truth is a necessary condition. Although there can be failures, or a short-fall in truth seeking, realists remain epistemically optimistic.

The claim that the aim of science is truth has an immediate consequence with respect to the nature of scientific progress. If the aim of science is to obtain the truth, progress in science must consist in progress toward this aim. Progress toward truth can be understood in a number of different ways. One involves the idea of an accumulation of truth; the advance of science results in an increasing build-up of truths known about the world. Another way to understand the idea is to say that later theories have a higher degree of verisimilitude than earlier theories. However the notion is analysed in detail,[2] the idea that scientific progress is to be understood in terms of progress toward truth captures a basic aspect of the axiology of scientific realism.

There is also an ontological, or metaphysical, dimension to realism. Common-sense realists about the world hold that there exist ordinary everyday objects, such as trees, water, rocks and cats, with properties such as hardness, wetness, impenetrability and furriness; and these also stand in relations to one another (e.g. the cat is in the tree). All of these objects, properties and relations exist mind-independently of human beings; that is, if we were not to perceive any of these items, or think about them, or form theories of them or use language to refer to them, then they would still exist.

Scientific realists extend this conception of realism to the unobservable items postulated in science. These items also have an existence that is mind-independent in the sense expressed by the following counterfactual: if we were not to think about them, have theories about them or use language to refer to them or use models to represent (aspects of) them, then they would still exist.

Such mind-independence applies to unobservable objects such as atoms, DNA molecules or pulsars; this is the view of *entity realism*, in which such unobservable objects are said to exist mind-independently.[3] But we need not confine realism to just the category of unobservable objects. We can be realists about the unobservable properties these objects possess such as inertial mass, gravitational mass, electric charge and the like. We can be realists about unobservables that do not seem to be substantial objects such as entropy or the curvature of spacetime. Finally, we can be realists about the unobservable relations or structures in which these items stand (the helical structure of a DNA molecule), and be realists about events and processes (such as chemical catalytic processes at the molecular level).

There is a dispute between realists about the extent of realism. Some confine their realism to only a nominalistic version of entity realism. Others extend it to the full range of particulars, including events and processes, to properties, to kinds and to dispositional properties. More radical realists extend their doctrine further to include realism about properties and relations understood as universals. And then there are varieties of mathematical realism in which realism is extended to sets, numbers and other mathematical entities. There is no need for our purposes in characterizing realism to enter into these areas of debate as the core idea of scientific realism does not depend on whether there are universals or mathematical abstracta.

The core idea of realism is that there is a mind-independent world made up of items that have properties, enter into processes and stand in structural relations. But not everything in the world has a mind-independent existence. There are many things that the social sciences, including economics, investigate that are mind-dependent in the sense that their existence depends on our beliefs about them. Such is the case for social items such as money, private property, being married, being employed or scoring a goal (in sports games) and the like. Science can make objective claims about the mind-dependent items investigated in the social sciences as well as the mind-independent items investigated in the natural and life sciences. They are objective claims in that their truth-value is ascertainable by methods of everyday and scientific investigation as are other claims in any science. Although these social items do have an existence dependent on our cognitive attitudes, their existence is independent of any theories we may form about them. Thus that there is money might well depend on some of the beliefs we hold about bits of round metal, or bits of paper, inscribed in a certain way, namely, that they are money. But it does not follow that money is dependent on other beliefs we might hold, such as the beliefs that economists might hold in the economic theories they propose about money, such as Keynesian or monetarist theories.[4] From a methodological point of view we think that, as far as theory choice and hypothesis-testing are concerned, there are no great differences between the social and the natural sciences (although we do not argue the case here). The only significant differences in methodology pertain to the kinds of hypotheses that are to be investigated; and many different kinds of hypotheses are to be found in both the social and the non-social sciences.

Turn now to semantic aspects of realism. These all make essential reference to the theories we propose and the language we use to express our theories. Thus one semantic thesis of realism is that our theories take one of the two truth-values {true, false}; they do not lack truth-values. This stands in marked contrast to one non-realist understanding of theories, namely, instrumentalism. On most understandings of instrumentalism the sentences of theories are not taken to be propositions that can be true or false; rather, they are taken to be rules of inference, which do not possess truth-values.[5]

The kind of realism that Putnam attributes to Richard Boyd is also semantic in character and not purely ontological. In formulating its doctrine of realism it explicitly mentions that the terms of our scientific language refer, and that our theories are approximately true:

> Boyd tries to spell out realism as an over-arching empirical hypothesis by means of two principles:
> (1) Terms in a mature science typically refer.
> (2) The laws of a theory belonging to a mature science are typically approximately true. (Putnam 1978: 20)

Ontological aspects of realism have precedence over semantic aspects. Consider an example arising from clause (1), namely, if the term "electron" refers, then electrons do exist (an ontological existence claim). But the ontological realist claim about the existence of electrons does not require that there be a language with the term "electron" in it. Clearly electrons have always had a language-independent existence; moreover, they were investigated in physics from 1857 to the late 1890s when the term "electron" was first coined to refer to them. However, that the existence claims of a theory are true and that its law-like claims are also (approximately) true, captures an important aspect of realism that enters into arguments for realism, as will be seen.

Note that axiological realism, as formulated above, also depends on a semantic formulation of realism in that it makes essential reference to the (approximate) truth of our theories as the leading aim for science.

Finally, there are epistemic versions of theses about realism. These all use epistemic operators such as "it is reasonable to believe that p", or "it is known that p", or "there is good evidence that p" and so on, where p ranges over theses that pertain to other forms of realism. Thus we might say "it is known that some theoretical sentences have the truth-value true", "it is reasonable to believe that the theoretical sentences of current electron theory are approximately true to a high degree", "it is reasonable to believe that the term 'electron' denotes and is not a non-denoting term", "it is overwhelmingly far more reasonable to think that electrons exist than that they do not", "there is no evidence to think that the theory of Lamarckian evolution has greater verisimilitude than Darwinian evolutionary theory" and so on.

This will be sufficient to distinguish between the four broad varieties of realism: axiological, ontological, semantic and epistemic. Given these varieties it is possible to set out some non-realist rivals. The axiology of realism is that the aim of science is to obtain (approximately) true theories, and the epistemic stance of the realist in accepting a theory is the belief that it is (approximately) true. The rival axiology for constructive empiricists is to obtain theories that are only empirically adequate; and the epistemic stance of the constructive empiricist in accepting a theory is merely the belief that it is empirically adequate (van Fraassen 1980: 8, 12). We have also seen that the contrast between realists and instrumentalists is really a semantic difference in that realists claim that theories have truth-values while instrumentalists do not. Also, realists commonly claim that the two values are those of classical logic; in contrast some (such as Dummett) wish to replace classical logic by intuitionistic logic thereby generating a different kind of non-realist stance.

Given the rival realist and non-realist positions, and the different aspects under which they can be taken, which is correct? Here we move from constitutive issues about the definition of realism to arguments for and against one or other of the many different positions. We cannot survey them all here. Rather, we shall focus on some of the special methodological principles that are used in arguments for realism in one or other of the varieties distinguished.

13.2 The success argument for scientific realism

There are several related arguments in support of scientific realism, which are variously known as the "success argument", the "no miracles argument" or the "ultimate argument for realism".[6] We shall focus on one of the typical arguments in this group advanced by Putnam:

> [T]he modern positivist has to leave it without explanation (the realist charges) that "electron calculi" and "space-time calculi" and "DNA calculi" correctly predict observable phenomena if, in reality, there are no electrons, no curved space-time, and no DNA molecules. If there are such things, then a natural explanation of the success of these theories is that they are partially true accounts of how they behave. And a natural account of the way in which scientific theories succeed each other – say,

341

the way in which Einstein's Relativity succeeded Newton's Universal Gravitation – is that a partially correct/partially incorrect account of a theoretical object – say, the gravitational field, or the metric structure of space-time, or both – is replaced by a better account of the same object or objects. But if these objects don't really exist at all, then it is a miracle that a theory which speaks of gravitational action at a distance successfully predicts phenomena; it is a miracle that a theory which speaks of curved space-time successfully predicts phenomena.

(Putnam 1978: 18–19)

Here Putnam makes suggestive comments when he sets out what has become known as the "no miracles argument"; but it is not clear what the nature of the argument is. There are a number of interpretations of how it is to be understood; we shall adopt the one in which it is best understood as an argument that has the form of the non-deductive inference to the best explanation (IBE).

The item to be explained is that theory T is successful; call this "S_T". There are a number of things that T's success could be. First, T makes a large number of novel predictions that turn out to be true. Secondly, a more inclusive kind of success is simply having a large number of true observational consequences, as Putnam seems to suggest, and not just novel true predictions. Thirdly, the success might be pragmatic in the sense that T underpins a large number of technological applications that gives rise to conditionals of the form; if you want W (e.g. to construct a building that can withstand an earthquake of up to 7 on the Richter scale) then do Y. Theory T underpins the truth of conditionals of the following form: in conditions Y, W will obtain. We can take the claim that T is successful, S_T, to be that (most of) the consequences of T are true novel predictions, true observational claims or correct technological applications.

What could explain why T has so many successes? An obvious answer to which the realist appeals is that T itself is true. The realist explanation can be set out simply as follows:

Theory T is true;
T has logical consequences that are novel predictions, observational claims or technological applications;
Therefore, all the novel predictions, observational claims or technological applications are true.

The conclusion expresses the proposition that T is successful in that certain classes of its consequences are true. The *explanans* appeals to the notions of truth and logical consequence; and it deductively leads to the conclusion. It is hard to see in what way this is not an explanation of T's successes, that is, why certain propositions are true.

Putnam talks not only of the truth of T but also the partial truth of T as the explanation of success. This is a more complex consideration, which has a quite technical side that we shall not set out here (see Niiniluoto 1999: ch. 6); but it can be briefly motivated as follows. The idea here is that aspects of T are true while other aspects are not, but the explanation of the successes of T is due to the truths that T contains and not its falsities. The inadequacies of T might not have been uncovered at the time its successes were noted; or if they were, the successes of T are such that they still need to be explained because they are significant successes such as making a range of quite novel, true predictions. In this latter case realists still feel the need for an explanation of the successes of T even if it proves to be inadequate in other areas. So, the principles of T need only be a partially true account of how the entities T postulates behave. We do not need a full account of their behaviour, and have some of that behaviour wrongly characterized in theory T. What is important is that the partial truth of T underpins the truths of S_T that T (when applied) entails.

To advance this argument the realist understands theory T realistically; call this T_R. At least two things are involved in this:

1. The existential assumptions of T are largely correct; that is, T_R commits us to true claims about the existence of entities postulated by the theory T. And since these existence claims are (largely) correct, this semantic version of realism holds only if entity realism, a version of ontological realism, also holds. Ontological realism can also be extended to the properties the entities possess and the relations in which they stand.

2. T has laws and principles that are (a) either true or approximately true, and (b) when they are applied in particular circumstances, enable us to deduce novel predictions, observational claims and technological applications, which constitute the success of T, S_T. This is a semantic thesis of realism.

What is it to understand T non-realistically, T_N? For many non-realists, especially instrumentalists and the positivists Putnam mentions, (2b) holds, since the requisite deductions need to be made; but (1) and (2a) need not hold. Either the entities postulated in (1) do not exist, or the truth claims of (2a) are reconstrued some way, for example by treating the laws of T as rules of inference, which cannot be true or false. This does not capture the stance of constructive empiricism, which needs to be considered separately.

Within his account of the no-miracles argument Putnam makes two central claims:

(M) (Miracle) For T_N, since its existential presuppositions are false (from which it follows that its laws are also false or truth-valueless), it is quite surprising that T_N leads to any of the truths in S_T. One can say that T_N offers no adequate explanation of S_T; alternatively one can say that the probability of S_T given T_N, $P(S_T, T_R)$, is low.

343

(N) (No miracle) For T_R, since (most of) the central entities it postulates do exist, and the laws that govern these entities are at least partially true, then it is not surprising that T_R leads to the truths in S_T. One can say that T_R is a very good explanation of S_T; alternatively one can say that the probability of S_T given T_R, $P(S_T, T_R)$, is high.

But (M) and (N), and the above characterizations of T_R, T_N and S_T, are premises, or components in premises, in an argument yet to be made clear. Is an argument form available using (M) and (N) as premises? At this point some invoke the (highly contested) rule of IBE (see §5.4 and §9.5). Here we can understand this to be an inductive inference that says that given some (satisfactory) rival explanations of some facts (such as S_T) the best *explanans* is the correct or true *explanans*. In (M) and (N) the two rival *explanans* of the successes of T are T_R and T_N. Given (M) and (N), T_R is clearly the winner in the "best explainer" stakes. That is, the realist understanding of T explains best its successes (as defined above). On this construal the no-miracles argument is nothing other than a form of IBE.

A similar argument against the interpretation of T by the constructive empiricist (T_{CE}) is not readily available. The constructive empiricist claim that T is empirically adequate is tantamount to saying that all of T's observational claims, past, present and future, are true. But unlike the non-realist instrumentalists considered above, constructive empiricists insist that the theoretical claims of T have a truth-value. They do not go along with the realists' understanding of T as T_R; rather, they invoke the claim that T is empirically adequate, that is, T_{CE}. In general, whatever one can do with T_R one can also do with T_{CE}.

What now of the rival explanations of the success of T, S_T, by T_R and by T_{CE}? A constructive empiricist's explanation of T's successes modelled on that for the realist would be:

Theory T is empirically adequate;
T has logical consequences that are novel predictions, observational claims or technological applications;
Therefore, all the novel predictions, observational claims or technological applications are true.

For T to be empirically adequate is for T to have all its observational consequences true; so the explanation above simply tells us that some of these observational consequences are to be found in the empirical adequacy conditions of T. But this is hardly an explanation at all. Musgrave, whom we follow here, puts the matter thus: "This is like explaining why some crows are black by saying that they all are" (1988: 242; 1999: 63). The realist claims that it is not that T_{CE} offers an inadequate explanation; it really offers no explanation at all.

By default T_R offers the best available explanation. In this way of expressing the argument there is no premise claiming that success is a miracle given T_{CE}; rather, T_{CE} simply fails to offer any adequate explanation at all.

Overall, the realist's claim is that the realist understanding of T, which invokes the truth or approximate truth of T, offers the best explanation of the successes of T while the instrumentalist or positivist offers a much worse explanation, and the constructive empiricist fails to offer any kind of explanation at all. As Musgrave also argues, the same considerations about explanatory failure can be mounted against other kinds of non-realists who see the aim of science to be restricted to problem-solving, or who adopt the surrealist position that it is *as if T were true*. According to the realist, scientific theories tell us something about the unobservable entities and their properties and relations that make up the structure of the world. Also, scientific theories are true or approximately true descriptions of those entities. Given that our theories have latched on to a part of how the world works, it is not a surprise that a great deal of success (of the sort specified) can be attributed to them. Other non-realist interpretations that downplay a realism of this sort cannot appeal to it to explain success. Here methodological principles vindicate realist axiology and ontology.

There are some responses that can be made to these considerations. One is to deny the premises like (M) and (N); another would be to deny claims about one explanation being better than another, or lacking any explanatory power at all. Another would be to challenge the whole idea of the explanation of success. Finally the rule of IBE has been questioned on a number of different grounds; if there is anything to the no-miracles argument then it should not be understood as a form of IBE. Musgrave makes a radical departure in rejecting the non-deductive rule IBE and replacing it by a deductive argument supplemented with an epistemic premise about what it is rational to believe (see §5.4):

> It is reasonable to accept a satisfactory explanation of any fact, which is also the best available explanation of that fact, as true.
> F is a fact.
> Hypothesis H explains F.
> Hypothesis H satisfactorily explains F.
> No available competing hypothesis explains F as well as H does.
> Therefore, it is reasonable to accept H as true.
> (1988: 239; 1999: 283–6)

This is a deductively valid argument which replaces the non-deductive IBE rendition of the no-miracles argument. This deductivist stance puts a quite different complexion on its character. However, many of its premises are the same as for its IBE rendition. Consider the premises, taking the second premise first. The fact F to be explained is the same as above, namely, T's successes, S_T. Musgrave appeals to the strongest kind of success, namely, success in yielding true novel predictions. This is a startling fact that does stand in need of explanation. Concerning the third premise, the hypotheses are the realist and the non-realist understandings of theory T such as T_R, T_N and T_{CE}. The fourth premise also sets out minimally satisfactory requirements on any explanation, thereby avoiding the charge that the best explainer is the best of a bad lot. And it also uses the considerations given above, which show that the realist interpretation of T is a much better explainer of T's successes than any of its non-realist rivals.

Importantly the conclusion drawn is not an ontological thesis of realism or a semantic version of realism, that is, that realism is true; rather, it is the weaker epistemic version of realism, namely, *that it is reasonable to accept realism as true*. The novelty in the argument lies in the first premise: this is an epistemic principle about what it is *reasonable to believe* to be true in the given situation. Note that it does not tell us what is true, but the weaker *what is reasonable* to believe is true. Thus the argument is not one to the truth of scientific realism, but to the epistemic thesis of reasonable belief in scientific realism.

The first premise is crucial in getting us to the conclusion. In the ongoing dialectic between realist and non-realist, it is open to the non-realist to reject it. So why should one accept such an epistemic principle? First, it allows that our best available explanation might be false. But this in no way impugns the claim that it is reasonable to believe it; p may ultimately be false but it may not be unreasonable to believe that p, and this is so of best explainers. The grounds for the principle's acceptance cannot be that the best available explanation is probably true rather than true *simpliciter*. The overall deductivist and anti-justificationist stance that Musgrave adopts rules out the use of any probabilistic logic that would underpin this claim. Rather, we are to take the epistemic principle at face value. There may be no conclusive reasons that would give a *justification* of the epistemic principle; but this, in itself, is not a reason not to believe it. And as already noted it may be reasonable to accept that p while p is false.

Understood this way, the epistemically qualified realism of the conclusion is not a strong realist claim; it is much weaker than an ontological realist would want. They want realism to be true whereas the above argument only tells one that it is reasonable to believe scientific realism, albeit it is something more reasonable to believe than its rivals on the grounds of its superior explanation of success. That is, the ontological realist cannot conclude that the entities postulated in theory T do exist. But given that it is reasonable to accept that theory T is true, and given the further epistemic principle that if it is reasonable to believe that p, then it is reasonable to believe any consequence of p, then the realist can infer at least this much: it is reasonable to believe the existence claims of T. That is, the realist can infer a version of epistemic realism, namely, that it is reasonable to believe that the postulated entities of T exist; but this does not get us to ontological realism *simpliciter*.

The epistemic import of the success argument is of relevance to considerations in the methodology of science. The fact that the conclusion of the success argument is an epistemic claim that it is reasonable to accept scientific theories as true is of clear relevance to the methodology of science. For, on the assumption that such theories are the product of the methods of science, the success argument implies that a realist interpretation of scientific method is in order. In particular, it implies that the methods of science are to be understood as truth-conducive methods of enquiry that reliably lead to the truth. As we shall see in the next section, it is possible to apply the success argument at the metamethodological level as an argument specifically relating to the reliability of the methods of science.[7]

13.3 Realist axiology and the meta-level success argument

As we saw in §13.1, scientific realism takes the aim of science to be to discover the truth about the world. This axiological aspect of realism has been subjected to criticism by Laudan, who argues that the aim of truth is utopian. In this section, we consider Laudan's critique of realist axiology, before considering how it may be rebutted on the basis of a meta-level application of the success argument.

Laudan's criticism of realism derives from what he regards as the transcendent character of truth. He contrasts the aim of truth with an "immanent" goal such as "problem-solving effectiveness", which "(unlike truth) is not intrinsically transcendent and hence closed to epistemic access" (1996: 78). Immanent aims are ones whose realization may be empirically detected whereas transcendent aims cannot be shown to obtain. As he explains, "knowledge of a theory's truth is radically transcendent", since "the most we can hope to 'know' about [a theory...] is that [it is] false" and "we are never in a position to be reasonably confident that a theory is true" (ibid.: 194–5). Similar strictures apply to approximate truth. Since the truth of a theory transcends our capacity for knowledge, we can be in no position to judge how closely an actual theory approximates the truth (ibid.: 78).

Laudan's critique of realist axiology occurs in the context of a discussion of rational goals in his book *Science and Values*. He argues that in order to pursue an aim rationally there must be reason to believe that the aim may be realized (1984: 51). He rejects unrealizable aims as "utopian", distinguishing between "demonstrably utopian" goals, which can be shown to be unrealizable, vague or "semantically utopian" goals, and "epistemically utopian" aims, which cannot be shown to obtain. He takes truth to be an example of the latter. Laudan supposes that we have "no idea whatever how to determine whether any theory actually has the property of being true" (*ibid.*: 51). Hence, the realist places value on an unrecognizable property that "could evidently not be operationalized" (*ibid.*: 53). He concludes that:

> if we cannot ascertain when a proposed goal state has been achieved and when it has not, then we cannot possibly embark on a rationally grounded set of actions to achieve or promote that goal. In the absence of a criterion for detecting when a goal has been realized, or is coming closer to realization, the goal cannot be rationally propounded even if the goal itself is both clearly defined and otherwise highly desirable.
>
> (*Ibid.*)

Since Laudan understands truth and approximate truth to be transcendent, his argument against the realist aim of truth appears to be as follows: it is not rational to pursue an aim that may neither be recognized to obtain nor be close to obtaining; the goal of true theories may neither be recognized to obtain nor be close to obtaining; therefore it is not rational to pursue the goal of true theories.

Laudan's critique of realist axiology raises important issues to be addressed by the scientific realist. In particular, it raises the question of whether rational pursuit of goals requires that such goals be realizable, as well as the question of whether there is any means of detecting an advance towards the realist goal of truth. As for the first question, it seems clear that realizability of a goal cannot be an absolute desideratum; unrealizable goals may serve as regulative ideals, which guide or inspire conduct. Perfection may be humanly impossible, and yet the attempt to achieve perfection may lead to improvement in various areas of achievement. Moreover, it may be possible to achieve subordinate goals that subserve higher-order goals that either fail to be achieved, or that turn out in fact not to be achievable.

The second question relates to epistemological aspects of the realist aim of truth. Laudan regards the aim of truth or approximately true scientific theories as a transcendent aim whose achievement, or progress towards achievement, cannot be empirically detected to obtain. The problem with this, though, is that there may in fact be grounds on which to base judgements of progress towards truth. As we shall now argue, the satisfaction by scientific theories of various norms or criteria of scientific methodology may serve as evidence that a theory is either true or that it is closer to the truth than previous theories.

Laudan is right to insist that, in the case of a scientific theory, it is not possible to use direct observation to ascertain that the theoretical claims about unobservable entities are true. But to assume that this establishes that there is no means of gauging an advance on truth at the theoretical level is to overlook the fact that there exist methodological principles of scientific theory appraisal that can assist with this task. Such principles may be employed to assess the degree to which later theories are closer to the truth than earlier theories. For example, a theory that successfully predicts numerous novel facts not predicted by a rival theory, and that also performs better with respect to other criteria (e.g. simplicity, breadth, etc.), is likely to be closer to the truth than its rival. Such assessment of truth or approximate truth is not, to be sure, infallible. Nor is it based on direct observational verification of theoretical claims about unobservable entities. It is based on principles of theory appraisal rather than on immediate empirical inspection. But this is not, by any means, a reason to regard such appraisal as illegitimate. Nor is it a reason to lack confidence in judgements of a theoretical advance on truth.

The point that principles of scientific theory appraisal may be employed to evaluate the truth of theories, or progress towards truth, brings us back to the relation between the success argument and a realist interpretation of the methodology of science. As remarked earlier, the success argument has an indirect implication with respect to the truth-conducive character of the methods of science. For, on the assumption that the methods of science are responsible for the success of science (this success being best explained by scientific realism), then the realist is entitled to conclude that the methods of science are indeed a means of discovery of the truth about the world.

This is the basis of the metamethodological application of the success argument to the methods of science. We shall now make this argument explicit. In the first place, it needs to be made explicit that the methods of science play a significant role in the selection of successful scientific theories. The principles of scientific method perform a "quality-assurance" function, since they are employed to eliminate unsatisfactory theories and to certify theories that perform satisfactorily. Given that the methods of science serve this function, they have principal responsibility for the selection of theories that are successful.

But, given that the best explanation of the success of science is that scientific theories are either true, or approximately true, and given the role played by the methods of science in the selection of successful theories, it seems clear that the methods of science are a means towards the realization of such success. In particular, the methods of science constitute a reliable means of eliminating false theories, while enabling the retention of true or approximately true theories. The best explanation of the role played by methods in the success of science is, therefore, that the methods of science are a reliable, truth-conducive means of enquiry into the world investigated by science.

This application of the success argument to the methods of science is, in effect, an argument at the meta-level about the methods of science. It is a metamethodological argument about the reliability of methods. It is independent of the standard success argument, which is applied to theories, and leads to the conclusion that theories are true or approximately true. But it is nevertheless an application of the success argument at the meta-level to the methods of science.

The fact to be explained is the sequence of ever-increasingly successful scientific theories (successful in the senses mentioned in the previous section). There is a range of alternative explanations that could be offered of this success, including the explanations of the sociologists of science that it is the scientists' sociopolitical interests that have been efficacious, or it is the training and insight of scientists that have been efficacious; and there is a range of methods that could have been employed, such as coin-tossing, prayer, consulting entrails and, finally, using the principles of scientific methods of the kind we have been discussing. Most of these explanations are themselves implausible and they do not make the facts mentioned probable, except for the principles of scientific method themselves, which offer not just the best explanation but a high-grade explanation. The conclusion to be drawn is that there is something right, or correct, reliable or truth-indicative about our principles of scientific method.[8]

The argument is closely related to a similar argument that has been developed by Richard Boyd (e.g. 1981, 1996; also Psillos 1999: 78–81). Boyd also argues that the best explanation of what he terms the instrumental success of science is the fact that the methods employed by scientists are in fact reliable methods of scientific enquiry. Where Boyd's argument differs from ours lies in his emphasis on the "theory-dependence" of such methods. Boyd understands scientific methodology to include principles governing experimental design, choice of research problem, assessment of evidence and explanation, theory choice and use of theoretical language (1996: 222). So understood, methodology is theory-dependent in the sense that the methods scientists employ derive from the theories that they accept. Given this, Boyd argues that the only plausible explanation that can be given of the instrumental reliability of theories that result from the use of theory-dependent methods is that the theories on which the methods are based are approximately true. Such methods are themselves reliable in the sense that they give rise to successful theories, but this reliability can only be explained on the basis of the approximate truth of their underlying theories.

Our reply to Laudan's critique of realist axiology turns on an argument that is similar in form to this argument of Boyd's for a realist treatment of method. But we differ from Boyd on a few points of detail that turn on the issue of the theory-dependence of methods. While it may well be the case that low-level methodological principles (e.g. of experimental design) are theory-dependent, it is not clear to us that the more general principles of scientific theory appraisal (concerning, say, predictive accuracy, breadth, simplicity) are so dependent. Nor is it clear that inductive inference, or Bayesian conditionalization, are theory-dependent. But the main point remains about the connection between realism and the reliability of scientific methods.

Epilogue

It has become fashionable in some quarters to dismiss scientific method as an outmoded topic of little relevance to contemporary studies of science. Some see the theory of scientific method as a futile exercise in philosophical abstraction that has been shown by historical and sociological studies to have little relevance to the actual practice of science. For them, the work of Kuhn, Feyerabend or the strong programme and other sociologically based approaches spells the end of the theory of method.

As indicated at the outset, we beg to differ with this negative assessment of the methodology of science. It may be true that some simple-minded accounts of method have been shown to be unsustainable by historical studies of theory change or sociological studies of scientific practice. But the wholesale dismissal of the project of the methodology of science is premature to say the least. In fact, some of the studies that deny a role for methodology employ principles of method in making their claims. As we have sought to show in this book, the study of the methodology of science and the development of sophisticated and realistic theories of method is very much alive and well. The area is the focus of much vigorous and productive research.

While we have not nailed our flag to the mast on behalf of any particular theory of method, it is clear, we think, that there is a very great deal to be said on behalf of theories of method. Whether it is the epistemic import of novel prediction, the nature of confirmation, the role of simplicity, the problem of demarcation, Bayesianism, the Quine–Duhem thesis, methodologically based arguments for realism, or other issues, methodologists have made bold strides in developing theories of method and resolving some of the problems that these theories face. Contemporary theories of method have moved far beyond the naive conceptions of method that were thrown into question by the historical turn. Moreover, the historical turn itself, as we argue, is mired in methodological issues.

But while method is the focus of much productive discussion, it is also the case that there remain topics of dispute. There is broad agreement on many, but not all, aspects of method. Thus, there continues to be division on whether novel prediction actually provides confirmation for theories that lead to such predictions. Bayesians and many other methodologists (e.g. Popper, Lakatos and Kuhn) agree on the significance of novel prediction, although they might not all use the inductivist term "confirmation" to express the significance of such predictions. But there continues to be disagreement on this front, as we have seen in our discussion of Lakatos. Such differences at the level of the theory of method may also give rise to differences at the metamethodological level about how best to resolve differences of opinion at the level of method.

It is tempting, we think, to address this issue in a Lakatosian vein, in terms of the progressiveness of research programmes in the methodology of science. In the same way that a progressive SRP gathers the support of scientists by making headway with its problem agenda, so, too, in the methodology of science, a progressive research programme may gather the support of methodologists, which may in time lead to a convergence of opinion. We are particularly impressed by the way in which the Bayesian approach to method is able to resolve a number of difficult problems in the methodology of science, and is able to accommodate many of the insights of other theories of method within its scope. As a result of this performance, the Bayesian research programme, in one or other of its various forms, has gained very considerable support among methodologists of science.

Despite the fact that we have not endorsed a particular theory of method, we do have our preferences and predilections, as may be seen from some of the approaches and issues on which we have placed emphasis. As realists, we favour an approach to method that will reveal the epistemic basis for belief in the (approximate) truth of well-confirmed theories as well as supporting commitment to the reality of theoretical entities. This is likely to involve appeal to explanatory considerations, although we do not discount other possible lines of realist methodological argument, such as an appeal to novel-predictive success or arguments that come directly from Bayesianism. As naturalists, we tend to favour those approaches to method that emphasize epistemic reliability, and we have shown this in our examination of the reliabilist response to the sceptical problems of induction.

The methodologies of Popper, Kuhn, Lakatos and Feyerabend have been very influential, so much so that David Stove was reputed to have referred to them collectively as "Popkuhnlakabend" as a way of characterizing their core anti-inductivism. At the same time, we think that there are numerous insights about the nature of method found in these thinkers that should be incorporated into any mature and fully developed theory of method. Indeed, we have sought to do just this in our various discussions of the methodological views of these thinkers throughout this book.

In our view the Bayesian programme has made impressive progress in resolving problems of method. It also holds considerable promise as a unifying framework for the methodology of science. As such, it displays a number of theoretical virtues that methodologists have highlighted in discussing the method of science. The Bayesian theory of method is based on a central idea that is both simple and coherent. It draws a large variety of methodological ideas together in a systematic way. It can be used to account for Kuhn's scientific values. It deals with the issue of predictive novelty. It explains increase in confirmation by new evidence. It resolves the Quine–Duhem thesis. It reveals the strengths and weakness of the H-D method. It can accommodate inductive methodologies. It makes important links to theories of statistics that many other theories of method do not. Indeed, Bayesianism appears to us to be the most comprehensive current theory of method. It is hard to see what more one could ask of a theory of method.

Still, limitations of time and space prevent us from casting our net as widely as we would have liked over the full range of theories of method. There remain a number of alternative methodological research programmes to which we have been unable to devote attention in this book, for example, attempts to derive methodological insights from the study of artificial intelligence, theories of computation, cognitive science and formal learning theory (also known under other names such as formal epistemology, or reliable enquiry). Thus, while the Bayesian theory of method is certainly an important and highly impressive contemporary research programme in methodology, before issuing a final verdict it would be necessary to compare its range of application and degree of progressiveness with alternative programmes in the area.

Notes

Introduction

1. See R. Nola, *Rescuing Reason* (Dordrecht: Kluwer, 2003), pts II and III, and R. Nola & G. Irzik, *Philosophy, Science, Education and Culture* (Dordrecht: Springer, 2005), chs 5, 11, 12 and 13.
2. For a further discussion of some of the ways in which the alleged hegemony of science has been challenged see Nola & Irzik, *Philosophy, Science, Education and Culture*, pts III and IV.

1. What is this thing called scientific method?

1. The Bayesian approach is usefully compared with the traditional approach in: C. Howson & P. Urbach, *Scientific Reasoning: The Bayesian Approach*, 2nd edn (La Salle, IL: Open Court, [1989] 1993), chs 11 and 14; J. Kadane (ed.), *Bayesian Methods and Ethics in a Clinical Trial Design* (Chichester: Wiley, 1996), esp. ch. 1,"Introduction", J. Kadane, 3–18, and ch. 2, "Ethically Optimizing Clinical Trials", K. Schaffner, 19–64; and D. Spiegelhalter, K. Abrams & J. Myles, *Bayesian Approaches to Clinical Trials and Health-Care Evaluation* (Chichester: Wiley, 2004), esp. ch. 4. Howson & Urbach, *Scientific Reasoning*, 3rd edn (La Salle, IL: Open Court, 2006), ch. 6, provides a more technical account of clinic trials than that given here.
2. The authors discuss various BACON programs named after Francis Bacon, who championed the idea of discovering hypotheses from data; P. Langley, H. Simon, G. Bradshaw & J. Zytkov, *Scientific Discovery: Computational Explorations of the Creative Process* (Cambridge, MA: MIT Press, 1987), 25. Other programs are named after other scientists, such as GLAUBER, STAHL, DALTON and so on, who also advocated methods in science that were either data driven or theory driven.

2. Values in science

1. For an account of the work of Molina and Rowland, the discovery of ozone depletion and industry resistance to this, see M. Christie, *The Ozone Layer: A Philosophy of Science Persepective* (Cambridge: Cambridge University Press, 2000), pt I, esp. chs 5 & 6.
2. For more on the role of inconsistency in science and its place, or lack of it, in methodology see the papers collected in J. Meheus, *Inconsistency in Science* (Dordrecht: Kluwer, 2002).

3. For an excellent discussion of simplicity and parsimony, on which some of the above draws, see A. Baker, "Simplicity", in *Stanford Encyclopedia of Philosophy* (winter 2004 edition), E. N. Zalta (ed.), http://plato.stanford.edu/archives/win2004/entries/simplicity/ (accessed June 2007). For the role that simplicity and parsimony can play in actual science see H. Gauch, *Scientific Method in Practice* (Cambridge: Cambridge University Press, 2003), ch. 8.

4. The above is based on a procedure suggested in L. Bergström, "Scientific Value", *International Studies in the Philosophy of Science* **10**(3) (1996): 189–202, esp. §4, in which difficulties are also raised through the problem of aggregation.

5. For further recent discussions of theoretical values, see N. Maxwell, *The Comprehensibility of the Universe: A New Conception of Science* (Oxford: Clarendon Press, 1998).

3. Rules and principles of method

1. See P. Duhem, *The Aim and Structure of Physical Theory* (Princeton, NJ: Princeton University Press, 1954), ch. VI, §5, for his account of Ampère's alleged use of Newton's theory of method. Feyerabend is also an important critic of the use of methodologies, such as Newton's, as part of an official philosophy of science that is not, and often cannot be, adopted in actual practice. In a different vein would be William Whewell's development of Newton's theory of method in his writings.

2. The rules are cited from J. Cottingham, R. Stoothoff & D. Murdoch, *The Philosophical Writings of Descartes, Volume I* (Cambridge: Cambridge University Press, 1985), 9–78. There is a useful account in P. Achinstein (ed.), *Science Rules: A Historical Introduction to Scientific Methods* (Baltimore, MD: Johns Hopkins University Press, 2004), pt I, and a critical evaluation in D. Garber, *Descartes' Metaphysical Physics* (Chicago, IL: University of Chicago Press, 1992), ch. 2.

3. The formulation of Newton's "Rules of Reasoning in Philosophy" is taken from I. Newton, *The Principia*, I. B. Cohen & A. Whitman (trans.) (Berkeley, CA: University of California Press, 1999).

4. This is suggested in the useful account of the role of Newton's rules found in W. Harper, "Newton's Argument for Universal Gravitation", in *The Cambridge Companion to Newton*, I. B. Cohen & G. E. Smith (eds), 174–201 (Cambridge: Cambridge University Press, 2002); also see G. Smith, "The Methodology of the *Principia*", in *The Cambridge Companion to Newton*, 138–73.

5. For more on the methodological differences between Newton and Descartes, see A. Koyré, *Newtonian Studies* (Chicago, IL: University of Chicago Press, 1965), esp. chs III and VI.

6. Harper, "Newton's Argument for Universal Gravitation", sets out an excellent account of how we are to understand Newton's methodological approach using assumptions about models and parameters that are also common in much thinking elsewhere in physics. In so doing he undermines the claims of Duhem, Popper and Lakatos directed against Newton's procedure. See also D. Gillies, *Philosophy of Science in the Twentieth Century: Four Central Themes* (Oxford: Blackwell, 1993), ch. 3.

7. For an account of this see Duhem, *The Aim and Structure of Physical Theory*, pt II, ch. 6, §3; and C. Hempel, *Philosophy of Natural Science* (Englewood Cliffs, NJ: Prentice-Hall, 1966), 25–8.

8. Gillies, *Philosophy of Science*, 64, in making some biographical comments on Duhem, shows that in adopting oppositional stances to what has now become accepted physics, Duhem might not have exercised "*bon sens*". This includes his opposition to the statistical mechanics of Ludwig Boltzmann and Josiah Gibbs in favour of the failed energeticism of Ernst Mach and Wilhelm Oswald, his opposition to atoms in physics and a polemic against Einstein's theory of relativity, among other somewhat equally unsuccessful stances towards physical theories in his own time.

4. Metamethodology

1. Aristotle's theory has aspects that accord with quite recent accounts of the function that dreams might play in our physiology: see D. Gallop, *Aristotle on Sleep and Dreams* (Peterborough, ON: Broadview, 1990).
2. Accounts of the history of theories of method outside the survey period adopted here can be found, for example, in R. Blake, C. Ducasse & E. Madden, *Theories of Scientific Method: The Renaissance Through the Nineteenth Century* (Seattle, WA: University of Washington Press, 1960); L. Laudan, *Science and Hypothesis: Historical Essays on Scientific Method* (Dordrecht: D. Reidel, 1981); D. Oldroyd, *The Arch of Knowledge: An Introductory Study of the History of the Philosophy and Methodology of Science* (London: Methuen, 1986); J. Losee, *An Historical Introduction to the Philosophy of Science*, 3rd edn (Oxford: Oxford University Press, 1993); B. Gower, *Scientific Method: An Historical and Philosophical Introduction* (London: Routledge, 1997); and Achinstein, *Science Rules*.
3. See A. Gibbard, *Wise Choices, Apt Feelings* (Cambridge, MA: Harvard University Press, 1990) and H. Field, *Truth and the Absence of Fact* (Oxford: Oxford University Press, 2001), ch. 8, esp. §3, §4.
4. Field, *Truth and the Absence of Fact*, 382–4, recognizes the problem but accepts a limited kind of relativism. For a criticism of this position see P. Boghossian, "How are Objective Epistemic Reasons Possible?", in *Reason and Nature: Essays in the Theory of Rationality*, J. Bermúdez & A. Millar (eds), 15–48 (Oxford: Clarendon Press, 2002), 28–34.
5. The idea that the normative in ethics supervenes on a naturalistic base is argued in F. Jackson, *From Metaphysics to Ethics: A Defence of Conceptual Analysis* (Oxford: Clarendon, 1998), esp. ch. 5. The extension of this to the normativity of principles of method is argued in Nola, *Rescuing Reason*, ch. 3.
6. There are many systems of deductive logic such as classical, relevance, intuitionistic, many-valued, dialethic and so on for which Goodman's criterion is inadequate. Even for classical logic we do not agree that its justification is to be found by bringing it into accordance with our practice. Rather, the justification for any system is to be found in that system's notion of validity, which in turn is based in proof-theoretic and model-theoretic considerations.
7. The clearest account of the issues involved here can be found in S. Stich, *The Fragmentation of Reason* (Cambridge, MA: MIT Press, 1990), ch. 4, esp. 78–9.
8. For a detailed discussion of Kuhn's model of theory change, see P. Hoyningen-Huene, *Reconstructing Scientific Revolutions: Thomas, S. Kuhn's Philosophy of Science* (Chicago, IL: University of Chicago Press, 1993), pt III.

5. Induction in science

1. As well as R. Carnap, *The Logical Foundations of Probability*, 2nd edn (Chicago, IL: University of Chicago Press, [1950] 1962), there are useful expositions and criticisms in several books such as W. Salmon, *The Foundations of Scientific Inference* (Pittsburgh, PA: University of Pittsburgh Press, 1966), 68–79.
2. See C. Hempel, *The Philosophy of Carl G. Hempel: Studies in Science, Explanation and Rationality*, J. Fetzer (ed.) (Oxford: Oxford University Press, 2001), 126. The symbolization of Hempel's rule has been altered to conform to the symbols already used in the text. The tentative character of the rule reflects some of Hempel's qualms about the matter not raised here, such as the epistemic utility of accepting H as a member of one's current body of scientific claims.
3. This is an interesting, but different, conception of method that we do not discuss in this book; see R. Jeffrey, *The Logic of Decision*, 2nd edn (Chicago, IL: University of Chicago Press, [1965] 1983).

4. The data is taken from J. Hobson, *The Dreaming Brain* (New York: Basic, 1998), 142, who actually writes that the correlation is between 90 per cent and 95 per cent of the cases originally investigated in one of the first papers on rapid-eye-movement sleep. Fuller data are given later in the section.

5. For a discussion of the use of IBE in artificial intelligence and theories of computation, and its wide application as a mode of inference, see J. Josephson & S. Josephson, *Abductive Inference: Computation, Philosophy, Technology* (Cambridge: Cambridge University Press, 1994).

6. See P. Thagard, "The Best Explanation: Criteria for Theory Choice", *Journal of Philosophy* 75(2) (1978), 76–92, for the case of Darwin mentioned, as well as the oxygen theory of combustion and various wave theories of light. For all of these theories Paul Thagard finds that IBE is used as a form of argument for the correctness of the theory.

7. The points made above about range of facts to be explained, consilience and importance of facts are drawn from the excellent paper by Thagard, "The Best Explanation".

8. N. Rescher, *Cognitive Pragmatism; The Theory of Knowledge in Pragmatic Perspective* (Pittsburgh, PA: University of Pittsburgh Press, 2001), ch. 7.5, gives multiple criteria as to what is to count as the optimal explanation, and then gives a probability-based argument to show that some of these are in tension or conflict. Thagard, "The Best Explanation", 92, makes a similar point about problems in aggregating different values in theory choice that also carry over into selection the best explanatory hypothesis.

9. Goodman's own account of projection and entrenchment is to be found in N. Goodman, *Fact, Fiction and Forecast*, 2nd edn (Indianapolis, IN: Bobbs-Merrill, 1965), ch. IV. His solution has excited much commentary; see D. Stalker (ed.), *Grue! The New Riddle of Induction* (La Salle, IL: Open Court, 1994).

10. The data can be very accurate or within some degree of error; the problem to be raised does not depend on data accuracy, although this is an additional issue.

11. In his *Theory of Probability*, 3rd edn (Oxford: Clarendon Press, [1939] 1961), 47, Jeffreys writes of "absolute values of coefficients" (but with a procedure for removing fractions and common factors first); in contrast, in *Scientific Inference*, 2nd rev. edn (Cambridge: Cambridge University Press, 1957), 39, he writes of "the number of adjustable parameters". These can give different orderings of simplicity. Although all is not clear in Jeffreys' procedure, its general thrust is clear. A useful account of it can be found in A. Zellner, "Keep it Sophisticatedly Simple", in *Simplicity, Inference and Modelling*, A. Zellner, A. Keuzenkamp & M. McAleer (eds), 242–62 (Cambridge: Cambridge University Press, 2001), 245–50. It should be noted that many of Jeffreys's ideas about simplicity and his simplicity postulate altered over time from his first work in the area from the early 1920s and that no one account of his developing views can be found.

12. A useful account of more real situations can be found in Gauch, *Scientific Method in Practice*, ch. 8.

13. On a deeper analysis of the statistical theories involved, there are a number of other assumptions that lead to these results that need to be taken into account; but these will be set aside as not germane to the simple exposition proposed here. In the above we are indebted to M. Forster, "The New Science of Simplicity", in *Simplicity, Inference and Modelling*, Zellner *et al.* (eds), 83–119, and "Predictive Accuracy as an Achievable Goal in Science", *Philosophy of Science* 69(3) (2002), S124–S134, where a fuller account can be found.

6. Some justifications of induction

1. For an overview see Salmon, *The Foundations of Scientific Inference*, ch. II, and J. Earman, & M. Salmon, "The Confirmation of Scientific Hypotheses", in *Introduction to the Philosophy of Science*, M. Salmon, J. Earman, C. Glymour *et al.* (eds), 42–103 (Englewood Cliffs, NJ:

Prentice Hall 1992), §2.5, §2.6. For a more recent survey that includes the positions of Donald Williams and the statistician L. J. Savage, both of whom employ arguments based on the law of large numbers, see R. Weintraub, "Scepticism about Induction", in *The Oxford Handbook of Scepticism*, J. Greco (ed.) (Oxford: Oxford University Press, forthcoming).

2. See R. Braithwaite, *Scientific Explanation* (New York: Harper Torchbooks, 1960), 276ff., who draws a distinction between two kinds of circularity (but not under these names). The distinction is also used in J. Van Cleve, "Reliability, Justification and the Problem of Induction", in *Causation and Causal Theories*, P. French, T. Uehling and H. Wettstein (eds), *Midwest Studies in Philosophy* 9 (1984), 555–67. But Salmon, *The Foundations of Scientific Inference*, 12–17, finds both kinds question-begging. There is also a criticism of the use of rule-circularity in C. Howson, *Hume's Problem: Induction and the Justification of Belief* (Oxford: Clarendon Press, 2000), 25–9.

3. Hume's sceptical metamethodological argument is set out first in his 1739 *A Treatise of Human Nature* (pt III), and more pithily in his 1748 *An Enquiry Concerning Human Understanding* (§IV, pt II). It appears that Hume does not use the term "induction" at all, but often refers to "reasoning about causes and effects" or "reasoning about matters of fact", and even "moral reasoning".

4. We do not argue against its *a priori* status here; for a good argument see Salmon, *The Foundations of Scientific Inference*, ch. II.

5. For this approach see, among others, M. Black, *Problems of Analysis* (London: Routledge & Kegan Paul, 1954), ch. 11; for its further development, along with problems it faces, see B. Skyrms, *Choice and Chance*, 4th edn (Belmont, CA: Wadsworth/Thomson Learning, 2000).

6. Such a position can be found in B. van Fraassen, *Laws and Symmetry* (Oxford: Clarendon Press, 1989), ch. 7, esp. §5, and S. Okasha, "What did Hume Really Show About Induction?", *Philosophical Quarterly* 51(204) (2001), 307–27.

7. Such a hierarchy of inductive justifications is set out in Skyrms, *Choice and Chance*, 4th edn, 35–44.

8. See Skyrms, *Choice and Chance*, 4th edn, 42–4, for the hierarchy of counter-inductive rules and the need to discover a further condition that distinguishes the hierarchy, which provides a justification for induction from the hierarchy, which attempts to justify counter-induction.

9. Reichenbach's position is set out in his *The Theory of Probability* (Berkeley, CA: University of Califorinia Press, 1949), 470–82; it has been extensively examined by W. Salmon, *The Foundations of Scientific Inference* and "The Pragmatic Justification of Induction", in *The Justification of Induction*, R. Swinburne (ed.), 85–97 (Oxford: Oxford University Press, 1974); we largely follow Salmon here.

10. The factors k and w arise within the framework of languages in which Carnap constructs his inductive logic. In the case of width we can say informally that the two properties black, B, and small, S, are each wider than the conjunction of the properties, $S \& B$, but narrower than the disjunction $S \vee B$. In Carnap's view, neglect of factors k and w has caused many problems in the construction of an inductive logic. Needless to say, Carnap's procedure is not without its critics.

11. For a recent reply to some externalists concerning issue (a), especially matters to do with rule-circular justifications of rules of inference, see Howson, *Hume's Problem*, ch. 2.

7. The hypothetico-deductive method

1. There is a discussion of the Duhem thesis in §3.5 and §9.7. Some argue for a difference between Duhem's thesis and Quine's thesis and that the "Quine–Duhem" thesis is something of a misnomer; see Gillies, *Philosophy of Science in the Twentieth Century*, ch. 5, reprinted

in M. Curd & J. Cover (eds), *Philosophy of Science: The Central Issues* (New York: Norton, 1998), 302–19.

2. See the problem of alternative hypotheses and the useful discussion of the H-D method and some of its problems in Earman & Salmon, "The Confirmation of Scientific Hypotheses", §2.2.

3. Carnap, who reviews Hempel's four conditions of adequacy, actually shows that neither the consequence condition nor the converse consequence condition is correct (Carnap, *The Logical Foundations of Probability*, §87). So a seemingly plausible adequacy condition needs to be dropped.

4. See C. Hempel, *Aspects of Scientific Explanation* (New York: Free Press, 1965), ch. 1, §9. For two critiques of this see Carnap, *The Logical Foundations of Probability*, §88, and Earman & Salmon, "The Confirmation of Scientific Hypotheses", §2.4.

5. This and other related fallacies concerning inferences involving confirmation are discussed in M. Hesse, *The Structure of Scientific Inference* (London: Macmillan, 1974), 141–50.

8. Probability, Bayesianism and methodology

1. The diagram and the reasons for the definition can also be found in M. Curd & J. Cover's "Commentary" to "Part 5: Confirmation and Relevance: Bayesian Approaches", in *Philosophy of Science*, Curd and Cover (eds), 626–74, esp. 629–30. This commentary is an excellent introduction to issues to do with probability and Bayesianism in scientific method.

2. Throughout the standard logical symbols linking propositions are used. Thus "&" is the symbol for conjunction, "∨" stands for disjunction, "¬" for negation, "⊃" for the conditional "if ... then ...", and "≡" for equivalence. The turnstile "⊢" is used to indicate logical consequence.

3. In the following a number of theorems and principles are stated, largely without proofs from the axioms. Such proofs can be found in many standard treatments of the probability calculus.

4. Thus for the right-hand-side factor, $P(E \,\&\, \neg H)$, one can readily show, using the definition of conditional probabilities in terms of unconditional probabilities, that it is the same as $P(\neg H)P(E, \neg H)$. Alternatively there is a proof of the total probability principle from the axioms starting with the equivalence: $E \equiv [(E \,\&\, H) \vee (E \,\&\, \neg H)]$. The principle follows using Axiom 3 and the definition of unconditional probabilities in terms of conditional probabilities.

5. Other views consider logarithmic functions such as the logarithm of the ratio $[P(H, E)/(P(E)]$; log-likelihood functions are also considered.

6. Aspects of these matters are the topic of a debate in C. Hitchcock (ed.), *Contemporary Debates in Philosophy of Science* (Oxford: Blackwell, 2004) 67–114, in answer to the question "Does probability capture the logic of scientific confirmation or justification?", between P. Maher, "Probability Captures the Logic of Scientific Confirmation", 69–93 and C. Glymour & K. Kelly, "Why Probability does not Capture the Logic of Scientific Confirmation", 94–114.

7. Further discussions of problems for the H-D method and the "tacking problem" occur in Curd & Cover, "Commentary", 638–40 and J. Earman, *Bayes or Bust? A Critical Examination of Bayesian Confirmation Theory* (Cambridge, MA: MIT Press, 1992), 63–5. B. Fitelson, "Putting the Irrelevance Back into the Problem of Irrelevant Conjunction", *Philosophy of Science* **69** (2002), 611–22, contains a novel discussion of issues surrounding the problem.

8. H. Kyburg, *Probability and Inductive Logic* (New York: Macmillan, 1970), ch. 5 ("Degree-of-Entailment Interpretations of Probability"), has a useful account of the "logical" approach to interpreting probability. The classic work in this field is Carnap, *The Logical Foundations of Probability*.

9. For those who claim that probability also applies to the world as a frequency, or as objective chance, as well as to subjective belief, de Finetti's claim is extreme. As will be seen in §9.2, some make attempts to link subjective degree of belief to objective chance.

10. See R. Carnap, "Replies and Systematic Expositions", in *The Philosophy of Rudolf Carnap*, P. Schilpp (ed.), 859–1013 (La Salle, IL: Open Court, 1963), §25, 966–73.

11. Some philosophers adopt the radical position that there is no such thing as knowledge at the top of the scale [0, 1]. What goes there is just full belief. See for example R. Jeffrey, *Probability and the Art of Judgement* (Cambridge: Cambridge University Press, 1992), esp. ch. 3, in which the idea of probable knowledge is eschewed in favour of full belief.

12. For some of this literature see F. Ramsey, *Philosophical Papers*, D. H. Mellor (ed.) (Cambridge: Cambridge University Press, 1990), ch. 4; Jeffrey, *Probability and the Art of Judgement*, and *Subjective Probability: The Real Thing* (Cambridge: Cambridge University Press, 2004), ch. 1.1; and Howson & Urbach, *Scientific Reasoning*, ch. 5, §c.

13. This follows a suggestion by I. Hacking, *An Introduction to Probability and Inductive Logic* (Cambridge: Cambridge University Press, 2001), 169, who prefers to talk of "*sure-loss* contracts". His chapters 13–15 give some considerations about such contracts, aspects of which we follow here.

14. The following considerations can be found in many other places such as: B. Skyrms, *Choice and Chance*, 2nd edn (Belmont, CA: Dickenson, 1975), ch. V; Earman, *Bayes or Bust?*, ch. 2; Howson and Urbach, *Scientific Reasoning*, 2nd edn, ch. 5; Hacking, *An Introduction to Probability and Inductive Logic*, ch. 14; Jeffrey, *Subjective Probability*, §1.2. M. Kaplan, *Decision Theory as Philosophy* (Cambridge: Cambridge University Press, 1996), ch. 5, leads to the same results but via considerations based in utility theory. Earman, *Bayes or Bust?*, chs 2.4, 2.5, also considers different considerations in establishing the theorem.

15. The references in note 14 contain Dutch book theorem considerations for the definition of conditional probabilities, not considered here, in particular Hacking, *An Introduction to Probability and Inductive Logic*, 167–8, and Jeffrey, *Subjective Probability*, 12–13.

16. On this see D. H. Mellor, *Probability: A Philosophical Introduction* (London: Routledge, 2005), ch. 5.II; also Howson & Urbach, *Scientific Reasoning*, ch. 5 (at the bottom of p. 77 they also suggest an ideal model approach). See also R. Rosenkrantz, *Foundations and Applications of Inductive Probability* (Atascadero, CA: Ridgeview, 1981), ch. 2.1.

17. For a further account of some of the problems here see P. Baillie, "Confirmation and the Dutch Book Argument", *British Journal for the Philosophy of Science* 24 (1973), 393–7.

18. Rosencrantz's position in *Foundations and Applications of Inductive Probability* is in fact a more nuanced one than can be indicated here. See also A. Hájek, "Scotching Dutch Books?", *Philosophical Perspectives* 19 (2005), 139–51, for different considerations based on "fair-or-favourable" bets as opposed to just "fair" bets.

19. A Teller–Lewis proof can be found in P. Teller, "Conditionalization and Observation", *Synthese* 26 (1973), 218–58; also see Skyrms, *Choice and Chance*, 2nd edn, §IV.7, 190–93, or Earman, *Bayes or Bust?*, ch. 2.6. There are some voices of dissent, as in P. Maher, *Betting on Theories* (Cambridge: Cambridge University Press, 1993), ch. 5.2.

20. See Jeffrey, *Probability and the Art of Judgement*, ch. 1, for an account of why there is no need to detach, and his discussion of those who think one needs to detach.

9. Bayesianism: applications and problems

1. See van Fraassen, *Laws and Symmetry*, 157–8, who discusses calibration; also Jeffrey, *Subjective Probability*, 65–6, who also tells us that the jargon "calibration" comes from weather forecasting. See also A. Shimony, *Search for a Naturalistic World View: Volume I: Scientific Method and Epistemology* (Cambridge: Cambridge University Press, 1993), ch. 7, who argues

that "the epistemic probability statement, [i.e. reasonable degree of belief] $P(h, e) = r$ can reasonably be construed as stating an estimate of the relative frequency of individuals with the property M in the collection" (*ibid.*: 153).

2. See the discussion of the difference between coherence and strict coherence in W. Salmon, *Reality and Rationality* (Oxford: Oxford University Press, 2005), 128–33, which draws on discussions to be found in Shimony, *Search for a Naturalistic World View*, ch. 9, "Scientific Inference", esp. §III.

3. For a wide-ranging assessment of the strengths and weakness of the convergence of opinion results see Earman, *Bayes or Bust?*, ch. 6. For a simpler discussion see Curd & Cover, "Commentary", 646–50.

4. A version of this argument can be found in A. Burks, *Chance, Cause and Reason* (Chicago, IL: University of Chicago Press, 1977), 91.

5. See earlier essays now collected in Salmon, *Reality and Rationality*, ch. 4, "Plausibility Arguments in Science", and ch. 6, §4, "Prior Probabilities". The three broad categories of plausibility arguments he considers are formal, pragmatic and material.

6. For a sympathetic account see R. Rosenkranz, *Inference, Method and Decision* (Dordrecht: Reidel, 1977), esp. ch. 3. For alternative views see: Howson & Urbach, *Scientific Reasoning*, 2nd edn, 413–17, who also raise a query about the claimed objectivity; Shimony, *Search for a Naturalistic World View*, ch. 8; and van Fraassen, *Laws and Symmetry*, ch. 12.

7. The tempering condition is set out in a paper "Scientific Inference", which first appeared in a collection in 1970. Reference to the paper is made to its reprinted version in Shimony, *Search for a Naturalistic World View*, ch. 9; the reprint is followed by a reassessment of his views in ch. 10, "Reconsiderations on Inductive Inference".

8. B. van Fraassen, "Belief and the Will", *Journal of Philosophy* 81 (1984), 235–56, offers a Dutch book defence of reflection. For a critic see Maher, *Betting on Theories*, ch. 5.

9. Diachronic aspects of belief change are part of probability kinematics. However attempts to link reflection to the rule of conditionalization remain controversial.

10. For discussion see Earman, *Bayes or Bust?*, ch. 2.7. For refinement see D. Lewis, *Papers in Metaphysics and Epistemology* (Cambridge: Cambridge University Press, 1999), ch. 15.

11. For the account of corroboration discussed above, see K. Popper, *Realism and the Aim of Science* (Totowa, NJ: Rowman & Littlefield, 1983), §31. For an evaluation see H. Keuth, *The Philosophy of Karl Popper* (Cambridge: Cambridge University Press, 2005), §5.4

12. For example, see Curd & Cover, "Commentary", 656–9; a very full treatment of the problem is in Earman, *Bayes or Bust?*, ch. 5.

13. This is argued in Earman, *Bayes or Bust?*, 121; so an equivalent problem of old evidence arises even when $P(E)$ is slightly less than 1.

14. This approach is proposed by D. Garber, "Old Evidence and Logical Omniscience in Bayesian Confirmation Theory", in *Testing Scientific Theories: Minnesota Studies in the Philosophy of Science Volume X*, J. Earman (ed.), 99–131 (Minneapolis, MN: University of Minnesota Press, 1983), 115. Other papers in pt II of the same volume also discuss the problem of old evidence.

15. See D. Christensen, "Measuring Confirmation", *Journal of Philosophy* XCVI (1999), 437–61, and J. Joyce, *The Foundations of Causal Decision Theory* (Cambridge: Cambridge University Press, 1999), 200–215, and "Bayesianism", in *The Oxford Handbook of Rationality*, A. Mele & P. Rawling (eds), 132–55 (Oxford: Oxford University Press, 2004) for a fuller discussion of this approach to the problem of old evidence using d^* as a measure of confirmation.

16. In the rest of this section we shall follow the suggestion made by W. Salmon, "Rationality and Objectivity in Science, *or* Tom Bayes meets Tom Kuhn", in *Scientific Theories: Minnesota Studies in the Philosophy of Science volume XIV*, C. Wade Savage (ed.), 175–204 (Minneapolis, MN: University of Minnesota Press, 1990), reprinted in Curd & Cover (eds), *Philosophy of Science*,

551–83. John Earman, a pure subjectivist Bayesian, has some reservations about this sort of reconciliation between Kuhn's views about theory choice and the Bayesian methodology, if by "theory choice" is meant "accepting it as true". He argues that according to Bayesianism theories are never "chosen" in this sense, but only given some degree of probability. But if "theory choice" is taken to mean "decision to pursue the theory in question", "to put one's time and energy into it", then this is acceptable to the Bayesian. The issue raised by Earman is one we have already encountered; it turns on whether one adopts some rules of detachment and accepts a hypothesis for whatever reason, or one eschews the idea of detachment altogether. For Earman's own version of reconciliation see Earman, *Bayes or Bust?*, ch. 8.

17. Such critics include van Fraassen, *Laws and Symmetry*, ch. 7, esp. §5, and Okasha, "What did Hume Really Show About Induction?".

18. This section draws heavily on Dorling's work as do others, as a panacea for Quine–Duhem problems. Even though Bayesians accept that the Quine–Duhem thesis is unacceptable, not all are agreed about how Bayesianism is to be put to work to show this. For some of these differences, and further illustrations of Bayesianism at work in science, see: Earman, *Bayes or Bust?*, 83–6; Howson & Urbach, *Scientific Reasoning*, 2nd edn, 136–42 (which applies Bayesian considerations to Prout's programme in chemistry); M. Strevens, "The Bayesian Treatment of Auxiliary Hypotheses", *British Journal for the Philosophy of Science* 52 (2001), 515–37; and Jeffrey, *Subjective Probability*, 35–44 (which draws on published and unpublished work of Dorling).

19. See M. Redhead, "A Bayesian Reconstruction of the Methodology of Scientific Research Programmes", *Studies in the History and Philosophy of Science* 11 (1980), 341–7, for a reworking of aspects of Dorling's example in a more algebraic fashion, rather than using numerical values, which gives a better sense of the range of values that need to hold for (dis)confirmation to take place.

20. On the ravens paradox see Earman, *Bayes or Bust?*, 69–73, and Howson & Urbach, *Scientific Reasoning*, 99–103. On unification see W. Myrvold, "A Bayesian Account of Unification", *Philosophy of Science* 70 (2003), 399–423.

21. See K. Kelly, *The Logic of Reliable Inquiry* (Oxford: Oxford University Press, 1996) and Earman, *Bayes or Bust?*, ch. 9.

10. Popper, Lakatos and scientific method

1. Popper writes that "the amount of positive information about the world which is conveyed by a scientific statement is the greater the more likely it is to clash, because of its logical character, with possible singular statements.... The more they prohibit the more they say" (*The Logic of Scientific Discovery* [London: Hutchinson, 1959], 41).

2. Other suggestions about content can be found in I. Niiniluoto, *Critical Scientific Realism* (Oxford: Clarendon Press, 1999), §4.5.

3. Popper explores these intuitive ideas in an attempt to give a more formal account of them in various sections of *The Logic of Scientific Discovery*, esp. ch. VI, and in later works. However no simple, problem-free measures are readily available. For some of the serious problems confronting the comparison of contents along the lines Popper suggested, see A. Grünbaum, "Ad Hoc Auxiliary Hypotheses and Falsificationism", *British Journal for the Philosophy of Science* 27 (1976), 329–62.

4. There are logical problems to face in any notion of testability, such as the "tacking" paradox mentioned in §7.2. But this is more in the way of a problem to be solved by theories of confirmation rather than a knock-down argument against testability of any kind at all. One resolution of this problem can be found within Bayesianism; see §8.4.

5. This is an obscure but popular notion proposed in J.-F. Lyotard, *The Postmodern Condition:*

A Report on Knowledge (Minneapolis, MN: University of Minnesota Press, 1984), §14; a criticism of it can be found in R. Nola & G. Irzik, "Incredulity Toward Lyotard: A Critique of a Postmodernist Account of Science and Knowledge", *Studies in History and Philosophy of Science* 34(2) (2003), 391–421, esp. §8.

6. The task of sorting out the various rules in Popper's writings was begun in N. Maxwell, "A Critique of Popper's Views on Scientific Method", *Philosophy of Science* 39(2) (1972), 131–52, and I. Johansonn, *A Critique of Karl Popper's Methodology* (Stockholm: Akademiförlarget, 1975), and continued in Keuth, *The Philosophy of Karl Popper*, ch. 3. Our account draws on their work; they discuss some rules that we pass over.

7. Much has been said about the anti-inductivist aspect of Popper's notion of corroboration. See one of the more useful accounts of it in Keuth, *The Philosophy of Karl Popper*, ch. 5. We discuss corroboration in §9.3.

8. For Popper's distinction between falsification on the one hand and elimination, rejection, abandonment and so on, see "Karl Popper: Replies to my Critics", in *The Philosophy of Rudolf Carnap*, P. Schilpp (ed.), 961–1197, esp. 1009.

9. Although we shall not discuss it, Popper does have an early reply to problems for falsification raised by the Quine–Duhem problem that is commonly overlooked; see K. Popper, *The Poverty of Historicism* (London: Routledge & Kegan Paul, 1957), 132 n. There is an evaluation of Popper's response in C. Glymour, *Theory and Evidence* (Princeton, NJ: Princeton University Press, 1980), 34.

10. See L. Laudan, *Science and Values: The Aims of Science and Their Role in Scientific Debate* (Berkeley, CA: University of California Press, 1984), ch. 5, and *Beyond Positivism and Relativism: Theory, Method and Evidence* (Boulder, CO: Westview, 1996), 136.

11. For a fuller account of Popper's early encounters with conventionalism and his, and Lakatos's, more empirical approach to metamethodological matters (discussed in the next section) see R. Nola, "The Status of Popper's Theory of Scientific Method", *British Journal for the Philosophy of Science* 38 (1987), 441–80. C. Hempel, "Valuation and Objectivity in Science", in *The Philosophy of Carl. G. Hempel*, ch. 20, §5, also discusses the status of Popper's metamethodology, saying that despite appearances it is not merely decisionist but has justificatory aspects that are empirical in character.

12. The original objection is due to John Watkins, "Comprehensively Critical Rationalism", *Philosophy* 44 (1969), 57–62. A useful overview of the debate about comprehensively critical rationalism may be found in G. Radnitzky & W. Bartley, *Evolutionary Epistemology, Rationality, and the Sociology of Knowledge* (La Salle, IL: Open Court, 1987), pt II, 203–341.

13. The differences between historical and ahistorical theories of confirmation are discussed well in A. Musgrave, *Essays on Realism and Rationalism* (Amsterdam: Rodopi, 1999), ch. 12.

11. Kuhn and Feyerabend

1. See H. Sankey, *The Incommensurability Thesis* (Aldershot: Avebury, 1994), 16–30, for discussion of these matters.

2. T. Kuhn, *The Road Since Structure*, J. Conant & J. Haugeland (eds) (Chicago, IL: University of Chicago Press, 2000), 212, seems to reject use of the notion of analyticity in this context. But it is difficult to see how else to describe the situation, since the considerations he presents turn on the meaning of the word "science" and its semantic relations to other words.

3. A list of methodological principles that Feyerabend at one time endorsed is given in J. Preston, *Feyerabend: Philosophy, Science and Society* (Cambridge: Polity, 1997), §7.5. The principle of proliferation is criticized in Laudan, *Beyond Positivism and Relativism*, 105–10, and in Achinstein, *Science Rules*, ch. 22 "A Critique of Feyerabend's Anarchism. Proliferation: Is it a Good Thing?".

4. For a fuller discussion see Preston, *Feyerabend*, ch. 7, esp. §§7.3–7.4.

5. See C. Will, *Was Einstein Right?*, 2nd edn (Oxford: Oxford University Press, 1993), ch. 4, for the story of the increasing accuracy of tests of Einstein's theory with increasing developments in theory and experiment and observation.

6. Feyerabend often talks of "rules" or "standards" rather than "principles", the terminology adopted in this book. The difference in terminology between that adopted here and by other writers should cause no problems.

7. See, for example, P. Feyerabend, *Against Method* (London: New Left Books, 1975), 32 & ch. 15, and *Science in a Free Society* (London: New Left Books, 1978), 98–9, 163–4.

8. Earlier criticisms of Feyerabend's position appeared in reviews of *Against Method* to which Feyerabend replied; many of the replies are collected in Feyerabend, *Science in a Free Society*, pt 3. For two recent evaluations of Feyerabend's views on particular principles see Laudan, *Beyond Positivism and Relativism*, ch. 5, and Preston, *Feyerabend*, ch. 7.

9. See K. Popper, *Conjectures and Refutations* (London: Routledge & Kegan Paul, 1963), ch. 4, "Towards a Rational Theory of Tradition".

12. Naturalism, pragmatism and method

1. In an introduction to a collection of papers that test particular principles of method, Laudan and his co-researchers recognize problems with their test strategy, writing:

> Some have asked why we choose to test theoretical claims in the literature rather than to inspect the past of science in an attempt to generate some inductive inferences. After all, the hypothetico-deductive method is not the only scientific method and it is not without serious problems. But our reading of the history of methodology suggests that hypothetical methods have been more successful than inductive ones. Add to that … that we see no immediate prospect of inductive generalisations emerging from the historical scholarship of the last couple of decades and it will be clear why we have decided on this as the best course of action. Many of the theorists' claims can be couched as universals and hence even single case studies … can bear decisively on them. Further, given enough cases, evidence bearing on even statistical claims can be compounded.
> (R. Laudan, L. Laudan & A. Donovan, "Testing Theories of Scientific Change", in *Scrutinizing Science: Empirical Studies in Scientific Change*, 2nd edn, A. Donovan, L. Laudan & R. Laudan [eds], 3–44 [Baltimore, MD: Johns Hopkins University Press, 1992], 12–13)

What this passage shows is that those carrying out research in the light of normative naturalism can, and do, abandon Laudan's original meta-inductive rule MIR, or its statistical version, and replace it by H-D methods of test. However, this must be provisional since these methods employed at the meta-level must themselves be open to test using meta-principles that are generally acceptable, such as MIR. The H-D method has not achieved comparable acceptance among methodologists. Moreover, the authors recognize that whatever successes the H-D method has, it cannot be used without some peril (*ibid.*: xiv ff.).

2. These and others are mentioned in Laudan, *Beyond Positivism and Relativism*, 136–7. But see also Donovan *et al.*, *Scrutinizing Science*, for the results of case studies testing various methodological claims against episodes in the history of science.

3. Laudan uses different abbreviations for following a rule and realizing a value. In the quotation these have been altered to conform to the abbreviations used in the text.

4. For an extended and sympathetic account of Rescher's pragmatism with respect to science, see C. Hooker, *Reason, Regulation and Realism* (Albany, NY: SUNY Press, 1995), ch. 4. Hooker also considers Popper, Piaget and naturalism in the same context of his "systems theory" of reason and knowledge in science.

13. Scientific realism and methodology

1. Several of these four aspects of realism are discussed in G. Hellman, "Realist Principles", *Philosophy of Science* 50 (1983), 227–49.

2. We do not discuss the complexities surrounding the analysis of verisimilitude; See Niiniluoto, *Critical Scientific Realism*, chs 3 & 4, for a survey of the issues.

3. In general we follow the account of scientific realism set out in M. Devitt, *Realism and Truth*, 2nd edn (Princeton, NJ: Princeton University Press, 1997), pt I, esp. ch. 2. But we do depart from his implicit nominalist version of realism.

4. Much more that we endorse is in J. Searle, *The Construction of Social Reality* (Harmondsworth: Penguin, 1995), esp. chs 1 & 2, about the mind-dependent nature of money versus the objectivity of claims we make about money. Searle's account of social objects and facts is also set within the general framework of scientific realism.

5. For a thorough critique of this position see Musgrave, *Essays on Realism and Rationalism*, ch. 4.

6. A fuller discussion of the range of arguments falling under these headings can be found in S. Psillos, *Scientific Realism: How Science Tracks Truth* (London: Routledge, 1999), ch. 4, and Niiniluoto, *Critical Scientific Realism*, ch. 6.

7. A quite different kind of argument for scientific realism based on purely Bayesian considerations can be found in J. Dorling, "Bayesian Conditionalization Resolves Positivist/Realist Disputes", *Journal of Philosophy* 89 (1992), 362–82, and developed in Howson, *Hume's Problem*, 198–201.

8. The argument here has the character of IBE. But it is close to one that Laudan mentions in *Science and Relativism* (Chicago, IL: University of Chicago Press, 1990), 102–3, and to which he might well give some credence even though it expresses the view of a "pragmatist" in a dialogue.

Bibliography

Achinstein, P. (ed.) 2004. *Science Rules: A Historical Introduction to Scientific Methods*. Baltimore, MD: Johns Hopkins University Press.

Bacon, F. [1620] 1994. *Novum Organum*, P. Urbach & J. Gibson (trans. and ed.). La Salle, IL: Open Court.

Baillie, P. 1973. "Confirmation and the Dutch Book Argument". *British Journal for the Philosophy of Science* 24: 393–7.

Baker, A. 2004. "Simplicity". In *Stanford Encyclopedia of Philosophy* (winter 2004 edition), Edward N. Zalta (ed.), http://plato.stanford.edu/archives/win2004/entries/simplicity/ (accessed June 2007).

Bartley, W. 1984. *The Retreat to Commitment*. Chicago, IL: Open Court.

Benson, H., A. Dusek, J. Sherwood *et al.* 2006. "Study of the Therapeutic Effects of Intercessory Prayer (STEP) in Cardiac Bypass Patients: A Multicenter Randomized Trial of Uncertainty and Certainty of Receiving Intercessory Prayer". *American Heart Journal* 151(4): 934–42.

Bergström, L. 1996. "Scientific Value". *International Studies in the Philosophy of Science* 10(3): 189–202.

Black, M. 1954. *Problems of Analysis*. London: Routledge & Kegan Paul.

Blake, R., C. Ducasse & E. Madden 1960. *Theories of Scientific Method: The Renaissance Through the Nineteenth Century*. Seattle, WA: University of Washington Press.

Bloor, D. 1983. *Wittgenstein: A Social Theory of Knowledge*. London: Macmillan.

Bloor, D. [1976] 1991. *Knowledge and Social Imagery*, 2nd edn. Chicago, IL: University of Chicago Press.

Boghossian, P. 2002. "How are Objective Epistemic Reasons Possible?". In *Reason and Nature: Essays in the Theory of Rationality*, J. Bermúdez & A. Millar (eds), 15–48. Oxford: Clarendon Press.

Bonevac, D. 2004. "Reflection without Equilibrium". *Journal of Philosophy* 101(7): 363–88.

Boyd, R. 1981. "Scientific Realism and Naturalistic Epistemology". In *PSA 1980 Volume 2*, P. Asquith & R. Giere (eds), 613–62. East Lansing, MI: Philosophy of Science Association.

Boyd, R. 1996. "Realism, Approximate Truth, and Philosophical Method". In *Philosophy of Science*, D. Papineau (ed.), 215–55. Oxford: Oxford University Press.

Braithwaite, R. 1960. *Scientific Explanation*. New York: Harper Torchbooks.

Brown, H. 1988. *Rationality*. London: Routledge.

Brush, S. 1989. "Prediction and Theory Evaluation: The Case of Light Bending". *Science* 246: 1124–9.

Brush, S. 1994. "Dynamics of Theory Change: The Role of Predictions". In *PSA 1994, Volume 2*, D. Hull, M. Forbes & R Burian (eds), 133–45. East Lansing, MI: Philosophy of Science Association.

Burks, A. 1977. *Chance, Cause and Reason*. Chicago, IL: University of Chicago Press.

Carnap, R. [1950] 1962. *The Logical Foundations of Probability*, 2nd edn. Chicago, IL: University of Chicago Press.

Carnap, R. 1963. "Replies and Systematic Expositions". In *The Philosophy of Rudolf Carnap*, P. Schilpp (ed.), 859–1013. La Salle, IL: Open Court.

Christensen, D. 1991. "Clever Bookies and Coherent Beliefs". *Philosophical Review* **100**: 229–47.

Christensen, D. 1999. "Measuring Confirmation". *Journal of Philosophy* **XCVI**: 437–61.

Christie, M. 2000. *The Ozone Layer: A Philosophy of Science Perspective*. Cambridge: Cambridge University Press.

Church, A. 1956. *Introduction to Mathematical Logic*, Volume 1. Princeton, NJ: Princeton University Press.

Cohen, I. B. & G. E. Smith (eds) 2002. *The Cambridge Companion to Newton*. Cambridge: Cambridge University Press.

Cottingham, J., R. Stoothoff & D. Murdoch 1985. *The Philosophical Writings of Descartes, Volume I*. Cambridge: Cambridge University Press.

Curd, M. & J. Cover (eds) 1998. *Philosophy of Science: The Central Issues*. New York: Norton.

de Finetti, B. 1974. *Theory of Probability: A Critical Introductory Treatment, Volume 1*. London: Wiley.

Devitt, M. 1997. *Realism and Truth*, 2nd edn. Princeton, NJ: Princeton University Press.

Darwin, C. [1872] 1962. *The Origin of Species by Means of Natural Selection*, 6th edn. New York: Collier.

Donovan, A., L. Laudan & R. Laudan (eds) 1992. *Scrutinizing Science: Empirical Studies in Scientific Change*, 2nd edn. Baltimore, MD: Johns Hopkins University Press.

Dorling, J. 1979. "Bayesian Personalism, the Methodology of Scientific Research Programmes, and Duhem's Problem". *Studies in History and Philosophy of Science* **10**(3): 177–87.

Dorling, J. 1992. "Bayesian Conditionalization Resolves Positivist/Realist Disputes". *Journal of Philosophy* **89**: 362–82.

Duhem, P. 1954. *The Aim and Structure of Physical Theory*. Princeton, NJ: Princeton University Press.

Earman, J. (ed.) 1983. *Testing Scientific Theories: Minnesota Studies in the Philosophy of Science Volume X*, Minneapolis, MN: University of Minnesota Press.

Earman, J. 1992. *Bayes or Bust? A Critical Examination of Bayesian Confirmation Theory*. Cambridge, MA: MIT Press.

Earman, J. & M. Salmon 1992. "The Confirmation of Scientific Hypotheses". In *Introduction to the Philosophy of Science*, M. Salmon, J. Earman, C. Glymour *et al.* (eds), 42–103. Englewood Cliffs, NJ: Prentice Hall.

Einstein, A. 1959. "III: Einstein's Replies to Criticism". In *Albert Einstein: Philosopher-Scientist*, P. A. Schilpp (ed.), 663–88. New York: Harper Torchbooks.

Farrell, R. 2003. *Feyerabend and Scientific Values: Tightrope-Walking Rationality*. Dordrecht: Kluwer.

Feather, N. 1964. *Vibrations and Waves*. Harmondsworth: Penguin.

Feyerabend, P. 1975. *Against Method*. London: New Left Books.

Feyerabend, P. 1978. *Science in a Free Society*. London: New Left Books.

Feyerabend, P. 1981. *Realism, Rationalism and Method: Philosophical Papers Volume I*. Cambridge: Cambridge University Press.

Feyerabend, P. 1987. *Farewell to Reason*, London: Verso.

Feyerabend, P. 1993. *Against Method*, 3rd edn. London: Verso.

Feyerabend, P. 1995. *Killing Time*. Chicago, IL: University of Chicago Press.

Feynman, R. 1998. *The Meaning of It All*. Harmondsworth: Penguin.

Field, H. 2001. *Truth and the Absence of Fact*. Oxford: Oxford University Press.

Fitelson, B. 2002. "Putting the Irrelevance Back into the Problem of Irrelevant Conjunction". *Philosophy of Science* **69**: 611–22.

Forster, M. 1995. "Bayes and Bust: Simplicity as a Problem for a Probabilist's Approach to Confirmation". *British Journal for the Philosophy of Science* **46**: 399–424.

Forster, M. 2001. "The New Science of Simplicity". See Zellner *et al.* (2001), 83–119.

Forster, M. 2002. "Predictive Accuracy as an Achievable Goal in Science". *Philosophy of Science* **69**(3): S124–S134.

Forster, M. & E. Sober 1994. "How to Tell when Simpler, More Unified, or Less *ad hoc* Theories will Provide More Accurate Predictions". *British Journal for the Philosophy of Science* **45**: 1–35.

Franklin, A. 2001. *Are There Really Neutrinos? An Evidential History*. Cambridge, MA: Perseus.

Friedman, L. M., C. D. Furberg & D. L. DeMets 1998. *Fundamentals of Clinical Trials*, 3rd edn. New York: Springer.

Gallop, D. 1990. *Aristotle on Sleep and Dreams*. Peterborough, ON: Broadview.

Garber, D. 1983. "Old Evidence and Logical Omniscience in Bayesian Confirmation Theory". In *Testing Scientific Theories: Minnesota Studies in the Philosophy of Science Volume X*, J. Earman (ed.), 99–131. Minneapolis, MN: University of Minnesota Press.

Garber, D. 1992. *Descartes' Metaphysical Physics*. Chicago, IL: University of Chicago Press.

Gauch, H. 2003. *Scientific Method in Practice*. Cambridge: Cambridge University Press.

Gibbard, A. 1990. *Wise Choices, Apt Feelings*. Cambridge, MA: Harvard University Press.

Gillies, D. 1993. *Philosophy of Science in the Twentieth Century: Four Central Themes*. Oxford: Blackwell.

Glymour, C. 1980. *Theory and Evidence*. Princeton, NJ: Princeton University Press.

Glymour, C. & K. Kelly 2004. "Why Probability does not Capture the Logic of Scientific Confirmation". See Hitchcock (2004), 94–114.

Goldman, A. 1999. *Knowledge in a Social World*. Oxford: Oxford University Press.

Good, I. J. 1983. *Good Thinking: The Foundations of Probability and its Applications*. Minneapolis, MN: University of Minnesota Press.

Goodall, J. 1986. *The Chimpanzees of Gombe: Patterns of Behaviour*. Cambridge, MA: Harvard University Press.

Goodman, N. 1965. *Fact, Fiction and Forecast*, 2nd edn. Indianapolis, IN: Bobbs-Merrill.

Gower, B. 1997. *Scientific Method: An Historical and Philosophical Introduction*. London: Routledge.

Grünbaum A. 1971. "Can We Ascertain the Falsity of a Scientific Hypothesis?". In *Observation and Theory in Science*, E. Nagel, S. Bromberger & A. Grünbaum (eds), 69–129. Baltimore, MD: Johns Hopkins University Press.

Grünbaum A. 1976. "Ad Hoc Auxiliary Hypotheses and Falsificationism". *British Journal for the Philosophy of Science* **27**: 329–62.

Haack, S. 1996. *Deviant Logic, Fuzzy Logic: Beyond the Formalism*. Chicago, IL: University of Chicago Press.

Hacking, I. 2001. *An Introduction to Probability and Inductive Logic*. Cambridge: Cambridge University Press.

Hájek, A. 2005. "Scotching Dutch Books?" *Philosophical Perspectives* **19**: 139–51.

Harman, G. 1965. "The Inference to the Best Explanation". *Philosophical Review* **74**: 88–95.

Harper, W. 2002. "Newton's Argument for Universal Gravitation". In *The Cambridge Companion to Newton*, I. B. Cohen & G. E. Smith (eds), 174–201. Cambridge: Cambridge University Press.

Hellman, G. 1983. "Realist Principles". *Philosophy of Science* **50**: 227–49.

Hempel, C. 1965. *Aspects of Scientific Explanation*. New York: Free Press.

369

Hempel, C. 1966. *Philosophy of Natural Science*. Englewood Cliffs, NJ: Prentice-Hall.

Hempel, C. 2001. *The Philosophy of Carl G. Hempel: Studies in Science, Explanation and Rationality*, J. Fetzer (ed.). Oxford: Oxford University Press.

Hesse, M. 1974. *The Structure of Scientific Inference*. London: Macmillan.

Hitchcock, C. (ed.) 2004. *Contemporary Debates in Philosophy of Science*. Oxford: Blackwell.

Hobson, J. 1988. *The Dreaming Brain*. New York: Basic.

Holton, G. 1993. *Science and Anti-Science*. Cambridge, MA: Harvard University Press.

Hooker, C. 1994. *Reason, Regulation and Realism*. Albany, NY: SUNY Press.

Howson, C. 2000. *Hume's Problem: Induction and the Justification of Belief*. Oxford: Clarendon Press.

Howson, C. & P. Urbach [1989] 1993. *Scientific Reasoning: The Bayesian Approach*, 2nd edn. La Salle, IL: Open Court.

Howson, C. & P. Urbach 2006. *Scientific Reasoning: The Bayesian Approach*, 3rd edn. La Salle, IL: Open Court.

Hoyningen-Huene, P. 1993. *Reconstructing Scientific Revolutions: Thomas S. Kuhn's Philosophy of Science*. Chicago, IL: University of Chicago Press.

Hume, D. 1978. *A Treatise of Human Nature*, P. H. Nidditch (ed.). Oxford: Clarendon Press.

Huygens, C. [1690] 1962. *Treatise on Light*. New York: Dover.

Jackson, F. 1998. *From Metaphysics to Ethics: A Defence of Conceptual Analysis*. Oxford: Clarendon Press.

Jaynes, E. T. 1968. "Prior Probabilities". *IEEE Transactions on Systems Science and Cybernetics* 4(3): 227–41.

Jeffrey, R. [1965] 1983. *The Logic of Decision*, 2nd edn. Chicago, IL: University of Chicago Press.

Jeffrey, R. 1992. *Probability and the Art of Judgement*. Cambridge: Cambridge University Press.

Jeffrey, R. 2004. *Subjective Probability: The Real Thing*. Cambridge: Cambridge University Press.

Jeffreys, H. 1957. *Scientific Inference*, 2nd rev. edn. Cambridge: Cambridge University Press.

Jeffreys, H. [1939] 1961. *Theory of Probability*, 3rd edn. Oxford: Clarendon Press.

Johansonn, I. 1975. *A Critique of Karl Popper's Methodology*. Stockholm: Akademiförlarget.

Josephson, J. & S. Josephson 1994. *Abductive Inference: Computation, Philosophy, Technology*. Cambridge: Cambridge University Press.

Joyce, J. 1999. *The Foundations of Causal Decision Theory*. Cambridge: Cambridge University Press.

Joyce, J. 2004. "Bayesianism". In *The Oxford Handbook of Rationality*, A. Mele & P. Rawling (eds), 132–55. Oxford: Oxford University Press.

Kadane, J. (ed.) 1996. *Bayesian Methods and Ethics in a Clinical Trial Design*. Chichester: Wiley.

Kahneman, D., P. Slovic & A. Tversky 1982. *Judgment Under Uncertainty: Heuristics and Biases*. Cambridge: Cambridge University Press.

Kaplan, M. 1996. *Decision Theory as Philosophy*. Cambridge: Cambridge University Press.

Kelly, K. 1996. *The Logic of Reliable Inquiry*. Oxford: Oxford University Press.

Keuth, H. 2005. *The Philosophy of Karl Popper*. Cambridge: Cambridge University Press.

Koertge, N. (ed.) 1998. *A House Built on Sand: Exposing Postmodernist Myths About Science*. Oxford: Oxford University Press.

Kornblith, H. (ed.) 1994. *Naturalizing Epistemology*. Cambridge, MA: MIT Press.

Koyré, A. 1965. *Newtonian Studies*. Chicago, IL: University of Chicago Press.

Kuhn, T. [1962] 1970a. *The Structure of Scientific Revolutions*, 2nd edn with "Postscript". Chicago, IL: University of Chicago Press.

Kuhn, T. 1970b. "Reflections on My Critics". In *Criticism and the Growth of Knowledge*, I. Lakatos & A. Musgrave (eds), 231–78. Cambridge: Cambridge University Press.

Kuhn, T. 1977. *The Essential Tension*. Chicago, IL: University of Chicago Press.

Kuhn, T. 2000. *The Road Since Structure*, J. Conant & J. Haugeland (eds). Chicago, IL: University of Chicago Press.

Kyburg, H. 1970. *Probability and Inductive Logic*. New York: Macmillan.

Lakatos, I. 1978. *The Methodology of Scientific Research Programmes: Philosophical Papers Volume I*. Cambridge: Cambridge University Press.

Lakatos, I. & A. Musgrave (eds) 1970. *Criticism and the Growth of Knowledge*. Cambridge: Cambridge University Press.

Langley, P., H. Simon, G. Bradshaw & J. Zytkov 1987. *Scientific Discovery: Computational Explorations of the Creative Process*. Cambridge, MA: MIT Press.

Laudan, L. 1977. *Progress and Its Problems*. London: Routledge & Kegan Paul.

Laudan, L. 1981. *Science and Hypothesis: Historical Essays on Scientific Method*. Dordrecht: Reidel.

Laudan, L. 1984. *Science and Values: The Aims of Science and Their Role in Scientific Debate*. Berkeley, CA: University of California Press.

Laudan, L. 1986. "Some Problems Facing Intuitionist Meta-Methodologies". *Synthese* **67**: 115–29.

Laudan, L. 1990. *Science and Relativism*. Chicago, IL: University of Chicago Press.

Laudan, L. 1996. *Beyond Positivism and Relativism: Theory, Method and Evidence*. Boulder, CO: Westview.

Laudan, L., A. Donovan, R. Laudan *et al.* 1986. "Scientific Change: Philosophical Models and Historical Research". *Synthese* **69**: 141–223.

Laudan, R., L. Laudan & A. Donovan 1992. "Testing Theories of Scientific Change". In *Scrutinizing Science: Empirical Studies in Scientific Change*, 2nd edn, A. Donovan, L. Laudan & R. Laudan (eds), 3–44. Baltimore, MD: Johns Hopkins University Press.

Lehrer, K. 1974. *Knowledge*. Oxford: Oxford University Press.

Lewis, D. 1986. *Philosophical Papers Volume II*. Oxford: Oxford University Press.

Lewis, D. 1999. *Papers in Metaphysics and Epistemology*. Cambridge: Cambridge University Press.

Lindgren, B. 1976. *Statistical Theory*, 3rd edn. New York: Macmillan.

Lipton, P. 2004. *Inference to the Best Explanation*, 2nd edn. London: Routledge.

Losee, J. 1993. *An Historical Introduction to the Philosophy of Science*, 3rd edn. Oxford: Oxford University Press.

Lycan, W. 1988. *Judgement and Justification*. Cambridge: Cambridge University Press.

Lyotard, J-F. 1984. *The Postmodern Condition: A Report on Knowledge*. Minneapolis, MN: University of Minnesota Press.

Maher, P. 1993. *Betting on Theories*. Cambridge: Cambridge University Press.

Maher, P. 2004. "Does Probability Capture the Logic of Scientific Confirmation?". See Hitchcock (2004), 69–93.

Maxwell, N. 1972. "A Critique of Popper's Views on Scientific Method". *Philosophy of Science* **39**(2): 131–52.

Maxwell, N. 1998. *The Comprehensibility of the Universe: A New Conception of Science*. Oxford: Clarendon Press.

Mayo, D. 1996. *Error and the Growth of Experimental Knowledge*. Chicago, IL: University of Chicago Press.

Medawar, P. 1984. *Pluto's Republic*. Oxford: Oxford University Press.

Meheus, J. 2002. *Inconsistency in Science*. Dordrecht: Kluwer.

Mellor, D. H. 1991. "The Warrant of Induction". In his *Matters of Metaphysics*, 254–68. Cambridge: Cambridge University Press.

Mellor, D. H. 2005. *Probability: A Philosophical Introduction*. London: Routledge.

Musgrave, A. 1988. "The Ultimate Argument for Scientific Realism". In *Relativism and Realism in Science*, R. Nola (ed.), 229–52. Dordrecht: Kluwer.

Musgrave, A. 1999. *Essays on Realism and Rationalism*. Amsterdam: Rodopi.

Myrvold, W. 2003. "A Bayesian Account of Unification". *Philosophy of Science* **70**: 399–423.

Newton, I. 1999. *The Principia*, I. B. Cohen & A. Whitman (trans.). Berkeley, CA: University of California Press.

Niiniluoto, I. 1999. *Critical Scientific Realism*. Oxford: Clarendon Press.

Nola, R. 1987. "The Status of Popper's Theory of Scientific Method". *British Journal for the Philosophy of Science* **38** (1987): 441–80.

Nola, R. 2003. *Rescuing Reason*. Dordrecht: Kluwer.

Nola, R. & H. Sankey (eds) 2000. *After Popper, Kuhn and Feyerabend: Recent Issues in Theories of Scientific Method*. Dordrecht: Kluwer.

Nola, R. & G. Irzik 2003. "Incredulity Toward Lyotard: A Critique of a Postmodernist Account of Science and Knowledge". *Studies in History and Philosophy of Science* **34**(2): 391–421.

Nola, R. & G. Irzik 2005. *Philosophy, Science, Education and Culture*. Dordrecht: Springer.

Okasha, S. 2001. "What did Hume Really Show About Induction?". *Philosophical Quarterly* **51**(204): 307–27.

Oldroyd, D. 1986. *The Arch of Knowledge: An Introductory Study of the History of the Philosophy and Methodology of Science*. London: Methuen.

Passmore, J. 1978. *Science and its Critics*. London: Duckworth.

Passmore, J. 1983. "Why Philosophy of Science?". In *Science Under Scrutiny: The Place of History and Philosophy of Science*, R. Home (ed.), 5–29. Dordrecht: D. Reidel.

Peirce, C. [1901] 1955. "Abduction and Induction". In *Philosophical Writings of Peirce*, J. Buchler (ed.), 150–56. New York: Dover.

Pocock, S. 1983. *Clinical Trials: A Practical Approach*. Chichester: Wiley.

Polanyi, M. 1958. *Personal Knowledge*. London: Routledge & Kegan Paul.

Polanyi, M. 1966. *The Tacit Dimension*. London: Routledge & Kegan Paul.

Popper, K. 1957. *The Poverty of Historicism*. London: Routledge & Kegan Paul.

Popper, K. 1959. *The Logic of Scientific Discovery*. London: Hutchinson.

Popper, K. 1962. *The Open Society and its Enemies, Volume 2: Hegel and Marx*, 4th rev. edn. London: Routledge & Kegan Paul.

Popper, K. 1963. *Conjectures and Refutations*. London: Routledge & Kegan Paul.

Popper, K. 1972. *Objective Knowledge: An Evolutionary Approach*. Oxford: Clarendon Press.

Popper, K. 1983. *Realism and the Aim of Science*. Totowa, NJ: Rowman & Littlefield.

Preston, J. 1997. *Feyerabend: Philosophy, Science and Society*. Cambridge: Polity.

Psillos, S. 1999. *Scientific Realism: How Science Tracks Truth*. London: Routledge.

Putnam, H. 1975. *Mathematics, Matter and Method: Philosophical Papers Volume 1*. Cambridge: Cambridge University Press.

Putnam, H. 1978. *Meaning and the Moral Sciences*. London: Routledge & Kegan Paul.

Quine, W. 1960. *Word and Object*. Cambridge, MA: MIT Press.

Quine, W. 1969. *Ontological Relativity and Other Essays*. New York: Columbia University Press.

Quine, W. 1974. "On Popper's Negative Methodology". In *The Philosophy of Karl Popper*, vol. 1, P. Schilpp (ed.), 218–20. La Salle, IL: Open Court.

Quine, W. 1981. *Theories and Things*. Cambridge, MA: Harvard University Press.

Quine, W. 1986. "Reply to Morton White". In *The Philosophy of W. V. Quine*, L. Hahn & P. Schilpp (eds), 663–5. La Salle, IL: Open Court.

Quine, W. 1992. *Pursuit of Truth*, rev. edn. Cambridge, MA: Harvard University Press.

Quine, W. 1995. *From Stimulus to Science*. Cambridge, MA: Harvard University Press.

Quine, W. & J. Ullian 1978. *The Web of Belief*, 2nd edn. New York: Random House.

Radnitzky, G. & W. Bartley 1987. *Evolutionary Epistemology, Rationality, and the Sociology of Knowledge*. La Salle, IL: Open Court.

Ramsey, F. 1990. *Philosophical Papers*, D. H. Mellor (ed.). Cambridge: Cambridge University Press.

Redhead, M. 1980. "A Bayesian Reconstruction of the Methodology of Scientific Research Programmes". *Studies in the History and Philosophy of Science* 11: 341–7.

Reichenbach, H. 1949. *The Theory of Probability*. Berkeley, CA: University of Califorinia Press.

Rescher, N. 1977. *Methodological Pragmatism*. Oxford: Blackwell.

Rescher, N. 1987. *Scientific Realism*. Dordrecht: D. Reidel.

Rescher, N. 2001. *Cognitive Pragmatism; The Theory of Knowledge in Pragmatic Perspective*. Pittsburgh, PA: University of Pittsburgh Press.

Rescher, N. 2005. *Cognitive Harmony*. Pittsburgh, PA: University of Pittsburgh Press.

Rosenkranz, R. 1977. *Inference, Method and Decision*. Dordrecht: D. Reidel.

Rosenkrantz, R. 1981. *Foundations and Applications of Inductive Probability*. Atascadero, CA: Ridgeview.

Russell, B. [1912] 1959. *The Problems of Philosophy*. Oxford: Oxford University Press.

Salmon, M., J. Earman, C. Glymour *et al.* (eds) 1992. *Introduction to the Philosophy of Science*. Englewood Cliffs, NJ: Prentice Hall.

Salmon, W. 1967. *The Foundations of Scientific Inference*. Pittsburgh, PA: University of Pittsburgh Press.

Salmon, W. 1974. "The Pragmatic Justification of Induction". In *The Justification of Induction*, R. Swinburne (ed.), 85–97. Oxford: Oxford University Press.

Salmon, W. 1990. "Rationality and Objectivity in Science, *or* Tom Bayes meets Tom Kuhn". In *Scientific Theories: Minnesota Studies in the Philosophy of Science volume XIV*, C. Wade Savage (ed.), 175–204. Minneapolis, MN: University of Minnesota Press. Reprinted in his *Reality and Rationality*, ch. 6 (Oxford: Oxford University Press, 2005).

Salmon, W. 1998a. "Rationality and Objectivity in Science, *or* Tom Bayes meets Tom Kuhn". Reprinted in *Philosophy of Science: The Central Issues*, M. Curd & J. Cover (eds), 551–83 (New York: Norton, 1998).

Salmon, W. 1998b. *Causality and Explanation*. Oxford: Oxford University Press.

Salmon, W. 2005. *Reality and Rationality*. Oxford: Oxford University Press.

Sankey, H. 1994. *The Incommensurability Thesis*. Aldershot: Avebury.

Sankey, H. 1997. *Rationality, Relativism and Incommensurability*. Aldershot: Ashgate.

Schilpp, P. (ed.) 1963. *The Philosophy of Rudolf Carnap*. La Salle, IL: Open Court.

Schilpp, P. (ed.) 1974. *The Philosophy of Karl Popper, Volumes I & II*. La Salle, IL: Open Court.

Searle, J. 1995. *The Construction of Social Reality*. Harmondsworth: Penguin.

Shimony, A. 1993. *Search for a Naturalistic World View: Volume I: Scientific Method and Epistemology*. Cambridge: Cambridge University Press.

Siegel, H. 1992. "Justification by Balance". *Philosophy and Phenomenological Research* 52: 27–46.

Simon, H. 1992. "Scientific Discovery as Problem Solving: Reply to Critics". *International Studies in the Philosophy of Science* 6(1): 69–88.

Skyrms, B. 1975. *Choice and Chance: An Introduction to Inductive Logic*, 2nd edn. Belmont, CA: Dickenson.

Skyrms, B. 2000. *Choice and Chance: An Introduction to Inductive Logic*, 4th edn. Belmont, CA: Wadsworth.

Smith, G. 2002. "The Methodology of the *Principia*". In *The Cambridge Companion to Newton*, I. B. Cohen & G. E. Smith (eds), 138–73. Cambridge: Cambridge University Press.

Sober, E. 1993. *Philosophy of Biology*. Boulder, CO: Westview.

Sober, E. 1999 "Testability". *Proceedings and Addresses of the APA* 73(2) (May): 47–76.

Sober, E. 2001. "What is the Problem of Simplicity?". See Zellner *et al.* (2001), 13–31.

Sokal, A. & J. Bricmont 1998. *Intellectual Impostures: Postmodernist Philosophers' Abuse of Science*. London: Profile.

Spiegelhalter, D., K. Abrams & J. Myles 2004. *Bayesian Approaches to Clinical Trials and Health-Care Evaluation*. Chichester: Wiley.

Stalker, D. (ed.) 1994. *Grue! The New Riddle of Deduction*. La Salle, IL: Open Court.

Stich, S. 1990. *The Fragmentation of Reason*. Cambridge, MA: MIT Press.

Strawson, P. 1952. *Introduction to Logical Theory*. London: Methuen.

Strevens, M. 2001. "The Bayesian Treatment of Auxiliary Hypotheses". *British Journal for the Philosophy of Science* 52: 515–37.

Swinburne, R. (ed.) 1974. *The Justification of Induction*. Oxford: Oxford University Press.

Talbott, W. 2006. "Bayesian Epistemology". In The Stanford Encyclopedia of Philosophy (fall 2006 edition), Edward N. Zalta (ed.), http://plato.stanford.edu/archives/fall2006/entries/epistemology-bayesian/ (accessed June 2007).

Teller, P. 1973. "Conditionalization and Observation". *Synthese* 26: 218–58.

Teller, P. 1975. "Shimony's *A Priori* Arguments for Tempered Personalism". In *Induction, Probability and Confirmation, Minnesota Studies in the Philosophy of Science Volume VI*, G. Maxwell & R. Anderson (eds), 166–203. Minneapolis, MN: University of Minnesota Press.

Thagard, P. 1978. "The Best Explanation: Criteria for Theory Choice". *Journal of Philosophy* 75(2): 76–92.

Van Cleve, J. 1984. "Reliability, Justification and the Problem of Induction". In *Causation and Causal Theories*, P. French, T. Uehling and H. Wettstein (eds). *Midwest Studies in Philosophy* 9: 555–67.

van Fraassen, B. 1980. *The Scientific Image*. Oxford: Oxford University Press.

van Fraassen, B. 1984. "Belief and the Will". *Journal of Philosophy* 81: 235–56.

van Fraassen, B. 1989. *Laws and Symmetry*. Oxford: Clarendon Press.

Watkins, J. 1969. "Comprehensively Critical Rationalism". *Philosophy* 44: 57–62.

Weinberg, S. 1993. *Dreams of a Final Theory*. London: Hutchinson.

Weintraub, R. forthcoming. "Scepticism about Induction". In *The Oxford Handbook of Scepticism*, J. Greco (ed.). Oxford: Oxford University Press.

Will, C. 1993. *Was Einstein Right?*, 2nd edn. Oxford: Oxford University Press.

Worrall, J. 2000. "Kuhn, Bayes and 'Theory Choice': How Revolutionary is Kuhn's Account of Theory Change?". In *After Popper, Kuhn and Feyerabend: Recent Issues in Theories of Scientific Method*, R. Nola & H. Sankey (eds), 125–51. Dordrecht: Kluwer.

Zellner, A. 2001. "Keeping it Sophisticatedly Simple". See Zellner *et al.* (2001), 242–62.

Zellner, A., A. Keuzenkamp & M. McAleer (eds) 2001. *Simplicity, Inference and Modelling*. Cambridge: Cambridge University Press.

Index

abduction 119–22
acceptance, rule of 112, 262, 266, 267, 268
accuracy
    as a value 46
    and trade-off with simplicity 141
    degrees of 46
Achinstein, P. 355, 356, 357, 364
ad hoc 263, 264, 265, 305, 322, 323, 326
aggregation, problem of value 48–9, 332–4
aim
    immanent 347
    of explanatoriness 37–8, 50–55
    of science 34, 38, 51, 53, 65–6, 337, 338,
        341, 345, 347
    of scientists 33–4
    transcendent(al) 327, 347, 348
algorithm (of theory choice) 76, 198, 232,
        237–8, 290–91
Ampère, A. 75, 365
anarchism 5, 298, 305, 365
anti-realism 55, 74, 77, 79
Aristotle 7, 34, 81, 82, 264, 357
axiology 35, 321, 338, 341, 345, 347–8, 350

Bacon, F. 8, 81, 114
BACON programmes 23–5
Baker, A. 355
Bartley, W. 272–3, 364
basic statements 256–7, 263, 266–8
Bayesian
    algorithm for theory preference 198, 232,
        238

multiplier 196, 200, 217, 243
Bayesian conditionalization 216–19, 229–30,
        235, 243–5, 350, 366
    Jeffery conditionalization 217–18, 235
Bayesianism 186–216, 220–49
    and confirmation 199–202
    and H-D method 202–4, 249
    and inference to the best explanation
        240–42
    and induction 202, 242–5
    and methodology 28–9, 86–7
    and plausibility 224–5
    and Quine–Duhem thesis 245–9
    pure subjective 218–19
Bayes, T. 186, 195
Bayes's theorem 194–8
belief
    degree of 103, 186, 204–10, 212, 216–18,
        222, 229–31
    revision of 40, 94–6
Bergström, L. 355
Black, M. 156, 359
Bloor, D. 6, 313
bon sens 76, 356
Boyd, R. 340, 350
Bricmont, J. 6
Brush, S. 234, 278
Burks, A. 361

Carnap. R. 28, 29–31, 86–7, 100, 110, 116,
        148–9, 163, 196, 204, 205, 243, 277, 290,
        357, 359, 360, 361, 364

catch-all hypothesis 130, 191, 197, 198, 226, 227, 228
cause, common 69
certainty 46
  Cartesian 58, 65–8, 74, 206, 210, 328
  Bayesian 189, 213, 217, 256
Christensen, D. 236
Christie, M. 354
circularity 80, 84, 88, 323, 330, 335–6
  premise 145–6
  rule 85, 145–8, 154–7, 168, 270, 272, 282, 323, 325
cognitive systems/systematization (CS) 332–6
coherence/coherentism 92, 103, 156, 186, 208–10, 211, 214–19, 221–2, 229–31, 241–5, 316, 332, 335, 362
comprehensive rationalism 273–4
confirmation 47, 56, 93, 109–12, 163, 171, 175–83, 203–5, 231–6, 277–80, 302, 325–6
  Bayesian 199–202, 217, 219, 239
  and consequence condition 180
  degree of 29–30
  and entailment condition 180
  historical theories of 277–9
  paradoxes of 181–3, 255
conservatism (as a theoretical virtue) 37, 38–41, 43, 94, 301, 315, 316
consistency (as a theoretical virtue) 36, 38–40, 46, 48, 55, 56, 77–9, 92–4, 208–10, 221, 238, 270, 306, 316, 332, 333
constructive empiricism 55–6, 341, 343–5
content
  empirical 111, 137–8, 191, 254–5, 257, 265, 276, 280
  information 254–5
  logical 111, 254–5, 257
convergence of opinion 223, 227, 237, 291, 292, 352, 362
correspondence principle see principle, correspondence
corroboration 233, 262, 267, 276, 362, 364
crucial experiment 75–6, 178, 198–9, 203
critical rationalism 51, 253–61, 263, 268, 269–74, 283, 290
  tradition of 306–9
  comprehensively 273–4, 364, 375

Darwin, C. 114, 119–20, 225

deduction 53, 73, 74, 77, 86, 107, 108, 125, 144–8, 170, 173, 175
  justification of 144–8
defeasible/defeasibility 61–2, 95, 300, 304–7
degeneration 26, 280–81
degrees
  of belief 99, 103, 186, 204–19, 221, 225, 229–31, 235–7, 244–5, 247, 291
  of confirmation 29–30, 196–7, 200–201, 234–7, 277, 279–80
  of simplicity 135–6
  of support 36, 47–9, 109–10, 112–14, 149, 149, 277, 289
  of testability 263, 265, 269, 303
demarcation 28–9, 51–2, 58, 66–7, 72, 253, 257–62, 263–6, 271–2, 280
  Popper's rule for 29, 51–2
Descartes, R. 8, 58, 65–8, 81, 210, 298, 336
  rules for directing the mind 65–8
detachment, rules of 112, 243
diallelus 330, 335, 336
dialectical interactionism 306, 308–9
discovery
  context of 19–21, 24
  methods for 22–5
  no method for 20, 21
Dorling, J. 245, 248, 363, 366
disunity 77–9
Duhem, P. 52–5, 74–9
Dummett, M. 341
Dutch book theorem 210–16, 218, 243
Dutch book argument 210, 215–18, 291

Earman, J. 28–30, 358, 359, 360, 361, 362, 363
economy of thought 53, 54, 79, 134
Einstein, A. 4–5, 139, 199, 223, 234, 278, 303, 326
empirical adequacy 55–6, 74–5, 78–9, 341, 344–5
empiricism/empiricist 59, 141, 327–9
  constructive 55–6, 341, 343–5
enumerative induction see induction, enumerative
explanation 4, 6, 7, 34, 38, 82, 101, 120, 130, 240–42, 282, 331–3, 341–6, 349–50
  as an aim 34, 37–8, 51–2, 56, 68
explanatory power as virtue 39, 43–5, 54, 56, 61, 301, 332
expressivism 88–91

facts
  designer 277–8
  non-designer 277–8
  novel 47, 171, 234, 276–82, 349
falsifiability 44–5, 51–2, 137–8, 245–6, 253, 255–69
Feyerabend, P. 5, 39, 59, 78, 81, 96, 97, 264–5, 298–309, 350, 364–5
  on rationality 298–300, 304, 306–7
Feynman, R. 2, 3, 8
Field, H. 88, 89, 90, 357
Forster, M. 137, 139, 141, 358
Foucault, L. 76, 199
foundation/foundational/foundationalism 67, 68, 156
Franklin. A. 177
Freud, S. 50, 82
fruitfulness (as a value) 46, 47–8, 128, 238, 289, 296, 301

Galileo, G. 23, 53, 54, 110, 127, 172–3, 264–5, 305
Gauch, H. 7, 356, 358
generality as a virtue 43–4, 54, 76, 79, 93–4, 270, 301
Gibbard, A. 88–9, 357
Gillies, D. 24, 355, 356, 360
Goodall, J. 13
Goodman, N. 91, 131–4, 136, 153, 357, 358
Grünbaum, A. 245, 265, 269, 363
grue 130–4, 153, 358

Haack, S. 146–7
Hacking, I. 206, 213, 361
hard core (of SRP), 26–7, 274–6
Harman, G. 121
Harper, W. 356, 359
Hempel, C. 22, 24, 25, 35–6, 52, 112, 113, 124–5, 173–4, 179–83, 199, 356, 357, 360, 364
  and ravens paradox 182, 255, 267, 270, 325, 363
heuristic
  and methodology 26–8
  negative 26, 274–5
  positive 27–8, 274–6, 280–81
  rules of 24–5
holism 86, 96, 100, 293–6, 315–16
Howson, C. 244, 355, 359, 361, 362, 363, 366
Hume, D. 64, 85, 106, 131, 143, 148, 151

Huygens, C. 70, 170–71, 175
Husserl, E. 65
hypothetical imperative see imperative, hypothetical
hypothetico-deductive (H-D) method 170–83, 201, 270, 302, 317, 325–6, 360, 365
  and Bayesianism 202–4, 249
  and problem of irrelevant conjunction 178, 203, 360
  and solar neutrino experiment 177–8

imperative
  categorical 59, 62, 65
  hypothetical 60, 318–19, 321
incommensurability 286, 297, 364
induction 106–142, 143–69, 242–5
  and Bayesianism 242–5
  consilience of 126–7
  counter- 156–8
  enumerative 85, 113–18, 121, 130–32, 142, 152, 153–5, 157, 163, 243–5, 324
  and externalism 144, 163
  indifference rule of enumerative 116
  inductive justification of 152–8
  pragmatic vindication of 158–3
  and principle of uniformity of nature (PUN) 148–52, 159–60
  and reliabilism 163–8
  rules of enumerative (EI) 85, 115–18, 130–32, 142, 152–8, 163, 243, 245, 324
  sceptical argument against justification of 148–52, 154, 158, 161, 163, 167
  statistical 117–18
  straight rule of 118
  warrant for 163–8
inference to the best explanation (IBE) 118–30, 327–8, 331–2, 334
  and Bayesianism 240–42
inference to the best systematization (IBS) 333–4, 336
instrumentalism/instrumentalist 82–3, 320, 321, 330, 340–43, 344, 345
intuition 67–8, 79, 91–2, 135–8, 201–2, 269–72, 284, 308, 327
intuitionist 81, 291, 341, 357

Jaynes, E. 226
Jeffrey, R. 113, 218, 356, 361, 363
Jeffreys, H. 134–7, 186, 222, 225, 227, 358
justification

context of 19–21, 26, 121
  instrumental 143–69
  of methodology 80–103

Kant, I. 102, 301, 331
Kepler, J. 20, 23–5, 271
Keynes, J. M. 87, 204, 205, 223, 242, 277, 339
Koertge, N. 6
Kuhn, T. 5–6, 45–9, 61–2, 78, 81, 98, 99–100,
    236–9, 285–98, 309, 351–3
  Bayesianism and 234–7
  on strong programme 297–8
  on values 45–9

Lakatos, I. 26, 29, 39, 81, 85, 88, 98, 99,
    100–102, 272, 274–84, 287, 308, 322,
    326, 352
Lamarckian 341
Langley, P. 23, 25, 354
Laplace, P. 162–3, 226, 246, 248, 279
Laudan, L. 61, 63, 66, 81, 87, 88, 98, 103, 129,
    268, 284, 293, 314, 320–29, 330, 336,
    347–8, 350, 357, 364, 365, 366
legitimization 335
  problem of 331
Lehrer, K. 333
Levels 1, 2 & 3 (hierarchy of scientific
    theories, methods and metamethods)
    81–5, 88, 90, 92–4, 96, 99, 102, 152,
    153–8, 160–61, 167–8, 209, 215–16, 261,
    269–70, 282–3, 324–5, 329, 331, 332, 335
Lipton, P. 127–8, 240, 242
likelihood 40, 41, 123–9, 139–40, 187, 192,
    193, 196, 197, 198, 200, 201, 202, 217,
    222, 223, 231, 232, 233, 238, 240, 241,
    242, 243, 246, 247
local holism 293–6
Lycan W. 39, 121
Lyotard, J-F. 85, 260, 364

Mach, E. 53
Marx, K 50, 253, 271, 274
Maskelyne, N. 13–14
means–ends hypotheses 88, 263, 304, 320,
    321, 323–5, 327
Medawar, P. 1–2, 7, 271
Mellor, D. H. 164, 361
Merton, R. K. 50
metamethodology 80–103
  of Bayesianism 210–6

Feyerabend's 300, 306–9
Kuhn's 285, 291, 292, 293–7
Lakatos's 252, 281–4
Laudan's 321–7
Popper's 252, 269–74
Quine's 313–14, 315–16
of reflective equilibrium 91–8
Rescher's 329, 330, 335–6
metamethodological inductive rule (MIR)
    323–7, 330, 365
methods/methodology/methodological
  a priori test of 86–91, 312
  empiricial test of 86–91
  expressivism about 86–91
  naturalized 314–16, 321–9
  and pragmatism 312
  quasi-empirical test of 88, 271, 272, 282,
    283, 284
  rules of 311
  of science 347
methodology
  anti- 5–8, 84–5
  and clinical trials 15–19
  and historical turn 98–103
  and logic 28–31
  and material practices 14
  and mathematical practices 15
  and observational practices 13
methodological principle see principles of
    method
minimum mutilation, maxim of 39, 76, 94,
    316
models 27–8, 38, 55, 75, 77, 97, 102–3,
    124–5, 225, 321, 338
  idealized 26–8, 75, 172–3
modesty (as a virtue) 37, 40–41, 43, 44, 48
Mill, J. S. 170, 277
Millikan, R. 14, 115
Molina, M. 33
M-rules 84, 320
M-principles 59, 60, 62, 64–5, 67, 86, 290
Musgrave, A. 122, 130, 344–6, 364, 367

naturalism 312–336
  metaphysical 312–14, 328
  methodological 312–14, 328
naturalized
  epistemology 316–19
  methodology 314–16, 321–9
Neurath's boat 315–16

Newcomb, S. 323
Newton, I. 8, 15, 42, 58, 66, 68–74, 321, 324
  rules of method 68–74
Niiniluoto, I. 341
no miracles argument 343–5
normative naturalism (NN) 321–9, 330
normativity 20, 48, 63, 87–91, 98–9, 208,
    218–19, 284, 291, 293, 295, 312–14,
    317–21
novel
  facts 47, 171, 234, 276–82, 349
  predictions 60, 171, 234, 276, 329, 342–4,
    346, 351–2

observational categorical 314
Ockham's razor 42

paradigm (Kuhnian) 99–100, 286–90, 292,
    296
  and disciplinary matrix 289
parsimony 41–3, 68–9, 71
Passmore, J. 4, 6
Peirce, C.S. 120–22, 122, 130, 334
Platonic 102, 311
Popper, K. 21, 29, 34, 38, 44, 49–52, 81, 85,
    88, 99, 101, 312, 320–21, 324
  and conventions 88, 259–63, 267, 269
  and decisionism 258, 261, 267–8, 272–3,
    364
  and methodological rules 259–69
  and metamethodology 269–74
  Quine on negative methodology of 255–6
postmodern/postmodernism 6, 7, 54, 85,
    260, 298, 301
pragmatism 312, 321, 329–36
  methodological 329–36
  thesis 329
predictions, novel 60, 171, 234, 276, 329,
    342–4, 346, 351–2
premise circularity 145–6
principal principle 228–9
principle, correspondence 59, 326
principle 321, 323–4
principle of uniformity of nature (PUN)
    148–52, 155, 159–61, 164–7
principles of method 57–79
  a priori test of 86–91, 312
  empiricial test of 86–91
  expressivism about 86–91
  power of 64

reliability of 63–4
robustness of 63–4
speed of 65
probability
  and new evidence 111–12, 196, 216–17,
    219, 231–6, 238, 241, 276
  axioms of 189–91, 211–14, 228, 360
  inductive 109–10, 152, 203, 360, 361
  logical 110, 227
  principles of 186–219
  principle of total 193–4, 197, 222, 247,
    360
  and problem of old evidence 111, 196,
    220, 231–6, 239, 249
  and problem of priors 221–6
  subjective 204–10, 361
  tempered 222, 227–8, 234–5
  theorems of 186–219
problem of the criterion 330
progress 280–84, 338, 348–9, 352–3
  empirical 280–81, 285
  theoretical 280–81
proliferation, principle of 39, 301–3, 306,
    308, 364
Prout, W. 101, 274–5
provisos 125–6, 173
Psillos, S. 350, 366
Putnam, H. 214–15, 340, 341–3
puzzle-solving (as a value) 293–6

Quine, W. V. 37–45, 81, 88, 93, 94, 128, 255,
    256, 313, 314–21, 322, 330
Quine–Duhem thesis 75, 99, 176–7, 263,
    358–9
  and Bayesianism 245–9, 363
  and H-D method 204

rational tradition 306–7
rational reconstruction 101, 275–6, 283
rationality
  of science 27, 34–5, 85, 90, 98, 237, 284,
    297–8, 300, 304–9
  instrumental 60
  theory of 29, 90, 102, 103, 215, 282,
    290–93, 296
Ramsey, F. 165, 168, 205–10
Ravens paradox see Hempel, ravens paradox
Redhead, M. 363
realism/realist(s) 9, 47, 52–6, 77, 322,
    328–9, 335–50

axiological   3, 79, 321–2, 338, 340–41,
   347–50
 commonsense   338
 entity   339, 343
 epistemic   328, 338, 340–41
 ontological   338, 340–41
 scientific   337–50
 semantic   338, 340–41
reflection, principle of   229–30
reflective equilibrium   91–8, 102, 103, 228,
   271, 284, 300, 308–9, 316, 327
refutability   see falsifiability
Reichenbach, H.   100, 118, 149, 158–63, 165,
   359
relativism   44, 49, 84, 90, 91, 288, 292, 307–8
reliability   57, 63, 87, 146–7, 300, 324, 326,
   327, 349–50, 352
Rescher, N.   88, 123, 329–36, 358, 367
revolutions, scientific   99
Rosenkrantz, R.   215, 361
rules   57–79
   ad hoc   59, 60, 103, 306, 322, 323
   defeasible   61–2, 69, 95, 300, 301, 304–7,
   309
   of method   57–79
   supreme meta-rule   263, 269

Salmon, W.   4, 87, 147, 198, 215, 224–5, 232,
   237, 238, 239, 351, 362
scepticism, Pyrrhonian   330
science, internal and external   101
scientific research programme (SRP)   26–8,
   85, 99, 100, 102, 252–3, 274–6, 280–83,
   352
scientific realism   see realism, scientific
scope (as a value)   45–6, 47–8, 56, 128, 239,
   241, 288, 289, 296
severity of test   232–3, 357
Shimony , A.   86, 87, 222–3, 225, 227–9, 361
Siegel H.   97
Simon, H.   24–5
Skyrms, B.   358–9, 361
simplicity   41–3, 47–8, 95, 128, 163, 225, 238,
   270, 301, 328, 356, 358
   and curve fitting   138–42
   of equations   134–7
   Hempel on   137
   Popper on   137
   and trade-off with accuracy   48, 141
Sober, E.   114, 139, 140, 141, 258

Sokal, A.   6
Stich, S.   357
strong programme   6, 313, 316, 351
   Kuhn on   297–8
success
   instrumental   83–3, 350
   practical   330–31
   of science   341–7
success argument   341–7
   meta-level   347–50
systematization (as a value)   127, 271, 332–6

Talbott, W.   215, 216
Thagard, P.   358
theory choice   35, 37, 44, 47–9, 62, 64–5, 71,
   80, 82, 92, 94, 119, 128, 236–9, 289–93,
   295–8, 339
traditions   261, 306–9
truth   36, 46, 52, 54, 55–6, 119, 289, 337–50
   correspondence theory of   36, 329
   partial   341–4
   theoretical   328–9
truth-conduciveness   337, 347, 349
truth-indicativeness   330, 331, 334, 336, 350

Ullian, J.   37–45, 93, 94
unity as a value   53–4, 76–9, 127, 129, 328,
   332
unification, theoretical   53–4, 56, 71
Urbach, P.   355

values   32–56
   aggregation of   48–9, 332–4
   alethic   36–7, 38, 46, 52, 54, 55–6, 119,
   289, 301, 338
   cognitive   35, 215, 321
   epistemic   36–7, 55–6, 208, 319–20
   extrinsic   32
   intellectual   34, 35
   intrinsic   32
   non-evidential   315
   and pluralism   320
   pragmatic   36–7, 38, 54, 55–6, 74, 76, 79,
   119
   theoretical   32–56
   truth   36, 46, 52, 54, 55–6, 119, 289, 338
   weighting of   44, 48–9, 139, 140, 141,
   237–8, 289–92, 300–301, 333
verisimilitude   36, 46–7, 52, 55, 67, 119,
   123, 329, 338, 366